Microcomputing Today

MICROCOMPUTING TODAY

STEVEN L. MANDELL

WEST PUBLISHING COMPANY
MINNEAPOLIS/ST. PAUL
NEW YORK
LOS ANGELES
SAN FRANCISCO

Composition: Parkwood Composition
Index: Terry Casey
Cover Image: Bruce Peterson Photography

WEST'S COMMITMENT TO THE ENVIRONMENT

In 1906, West Publishing Company began recycling materials left over from the production of books. This began a tradition of efficient and responsible use of resources. Today, 100% of our legal bound volumes are printed acid free, recycled paper consisting of 50% new fibers. West recycles nearly 27,700,000 pounds of scrap paper annually—the equivalent of 229,300 trees. Since the 1960s, West has devised ways to capture and recycle waste inks, solvents, oils, and vapors created in the printing process. We also recycle plastics of all kinds, wood, glass, corrugated cardboard, and batteries, and have eliminated the use of polystyrene book packaging. We at West are proud of the longevity and the scope of our commitment to the environment.

West pocket parts and advance sheets are printed on recyclable paper and can be collected and recycled with newspapers. Staples do not have to be removed. Bound volumes can be recycled after removing the cover.

Production, Prepress, Printing and Binding by West Publishing Company.

British Library Cataloguing-in-Publication Data. A catalogue record for this book is available from the British Library.

COPYRIGHT © 1997 By WEST PUBLISHING COMPANY
610 Opperman Drive
P.O. Box 64526
St. Paul, MN 55164-0526
All rights reserved
Printed in the United States of America
03 02 01 00 99 98 97 96   8 7 6 5 4 3 2 1 0

Library of Congress Cataloging-in-Publication Data

Mandell, Steven L.
    Microcomputers today / Steven L. Mandell.
        p. cm.
    Includes index.
    ISBN 0-314-04624-0 (soft : acid-free paper)
    1. Microcomputers.   I. Title
QA76.5.M1996   1997
004.16--dc20
                                                                95-31207
                                                                    CIP

CONTENTS

CHAPTER 1
THE WORLD OF MICROCOMPUTERS 1

INTRODUCTION 1

A MICRO LOOK AT MICROCOMPUTERS 2
   Information Systems 2
   Computers in an Information System 6

Window on Computing: The Future is Here Living in a Programmable World 11

THE TECHNOLOGY RACE 13
   Early Developments 13

Profile: The Countess of Lovelace 17

   First Computers 18
   Computer Generations 20

USING COMPUTERS 27
   Personal Computers in the Home 27
   Education and Personal Computers 28
   Personal Computers Invade Business and Industry 29
   Computers in Science and Medicine 30
   Arts and Entertainment Embrace Micros

Window on Computing: Morphing 33

SUMMARY POINTS 34
REVIEW QUESTIONS 35
ACTIVITIES AND RESEARCH 36

CHAPTER 2
COMPUTER FUNDAMENTALS: THE INSIDE STORY 38

INTRODUCTION

DATA REPRESENTATION 40
   Binary Representation 40
   Computer Codes 42

THE SYSTEM UNIT 43
　　The CPU: The Microprocessor 43
　　Memory 45

Window on Computing: The Future Is Here: It's in the Cards!

Window on Computing: Risc-y Business 51

　　Connecting Up 52

INPUT HARDWARE 53

Profile: Grace Murray Hopper: A Lifetime of Computer Achievement 54

　　Interactive Input 54
　　Direct Input 58

OUTPUT METHODS 60
　　Display Outputs 60
　　Printers for Document Outputs 62
　　Voice Output 64

STORAGE 65
　　Magnetic Disks 65
　　CD ROMs and Other Optical Storage 66
　　Magnetic Tape 68

SUMMARY POINTS 68
REVIEW QUESTIONS 70
ACTIVITIES AND RESEARCH 70

CHAPTER 3
APPLICATION SOFTWARE: PRODUCTIVITY TOOLS 72

INTRODUCTION 73

GENERAL FEATURES OF APPLICATION SOFTWARE 74
　　Files 75
　　Menus 76
　　Windows 77
　　WYSIWYG 78
　　Macro Capability 78
　　Documentation and Help 79

WORD PROCESSING 81

Entering and Editing Text 82
Writing Aids: Thesauruses, Spelling Checkers, and Grammar Checkers 84
Print Formatting 85
Other Features 88

SPREADSHEETS 89
Spreadsheets Explained 89
General Features of Spreadsheets 92

Profile: Mitch Kapor: The Spreadsheet Blossoms 93

DATA MANAGEMENT SOFTWARE 94
Data Organization 94
Querying and Reporting 97

GRAPHICS SOFTWARE 97

Windows On Computing: Resumes that Make a Database Weep 98

Presentation Graphics Programs 99
Paint and Draw Programs 100

Window on Computing: The Future is Here: Real or Contrived 102

SUMMARY POINTS 104
REVIEW QUESTIONS 105
ACTIVITIES AND RESEARCH 106

CHAPTER 4
COMPUTER FUNDAMENTALS: SYSTEM SOFTWARE 108

INTRODUCTION 109

OPERATING SYSTEMS 110
Types of System Programs 110
Capabilities of Operating Systems 111
User Interfaces 114

Window on Computing: The Future is Here: massively Parallel Processing 115

Microcomputer Operating Systems and Shells 119
Window on Computing: Windows 95 - Hyperspace or Hype? 121

Profile: Jobs' Next Job 123

SOFTWARE DEVELOPMENT 125
   System Software and Language Translation 125
   Computer Programming Languages 126
   Stages of Program Development 136
   Structured Programming Techniques 139

Window on Computing: Chopping Off the Branches 143

SUMMARY POINTS 146
REVIEW QUESTIONS 148
ACTIVITIES AND RESEARCH 148

CHAPTER 5
COMMUNICATIONS: CONNECTIVITY FOR PERSONAL COMPUTERS 150

INTRODUCTION 151

TELECOMMUNICATIONS 152

COMMUNICATIONS CHANNELS 153
   Types of Channels 154
   Connectivity: Microcomputers and Modems 157

NETWORKS 161
   Wide-Area Networks (WANs) 164
   Local-Area Networks (LANs) 165

Window on Computing: The Future is Here: Wireless Networks 167

TELECOMMUNICATION APPLICATIONS 169
   Electronic Transactions 16
   Facsimile 170
   Electronic Mail 171
   Voice Mail 171
   Telecommuting 172
   Teleconferencing 173
   Information Utilities 174
   Electronic Bulletin Boards 175
   The Internet 176

Profile: Bill Gates and Microsoft 177

Summary Points 177

Review Questions 179

Activities and Research 180

Chapter 6
Power Applications: Tools for Special Jobs 182

Introduction   183

Desktop Publishing 184
   Desktop Publishing Explained 184
   Typefaces and Fonts 186
   Style Sheets and Templates 188
   Functions of DTP Packages 188
   Print Reproduction 192

Integrated Software and Suites 194
   Types of Integrated Packages 195
   Characteristics of Integrated Software 197

Multimedia Presentations 199
   Understanding Multimedia 199

Window on Computing: The Future is Here: Moving Pictures and Computers 201

   Multimedia Standards 202
   Software for Multimedia Management 204

The Sky's the Limit 205
   CAD/CAM 205
   Expert Systems 206
   Virtual Reality 208

Profile: Edward r. McCracken : Silicon Graphics' Chairman and CEO 210

Window on Computing: The Future is Here: This Vehicle Hasn't Passed Driver's Ed 211

Summary Points 212
Review Questions 213
Activities and Research 214

Chapter 7
Contemporary Concerns 216

Introduction 217

Criminal Conduct and Ethics: Responsibility for Computer Actions 21
      Computer Crime 219

Hacking 222
Piracy 224
Security Measures and Organizations 226

PRIVACY 229
Privacy Issues 229

Profile: Protector of Civil Rights on the Final Frontier: The Electronic Frontier Foundations 231

Legislation 232

WINDOW ON COMPUTING: THE DATA VENDORS 234

ERGONOMICS 235
Computer Related Health Problems 236
Ergonomic Design 238
Safety Issues 241

Window on Computing: The Future is Here: You Bet Your Life 242

SUMMARY POINTS 243
REVIEW QUESTIONS 244
ACTIVITIES AND RESEARCH 245

APPENDIX A
CONSUMERS' GUIDE TO COMPUTING 246

Introduction 247

Purchasing Computers: The big Picture 248
Software First 249
Which Computer? 249

BUYING YOUR COMPUTER AND SOFTWARE 252
Where to Buy 252
Buying by Mail 252
Getting Help: Customer Support 254

CHOOSING THE HARDWARE 254
The Microprocessor 255
Memory 255
Buses 256
Add-Ons and Add-Ins 257
Monitors 257

Keyboards 258
Alternate Input Devices and Other Equipment 259
Storage 260
Portable Computers 260
Printers 261

COMPUTER EQUIPMENT FOR PEOPLE WITH DISABILITIES 262

CARING FOR YOUR COMPUTER SYSTEM 263
Computer Care 263
Surge Protectors 266
Viruses 266
Disk Care 269

APPENDIX B
GOING ONLINE: THE INTERNET AND SOME INFORMATION UTILITIES 272

THE INTERNET 274
Why Use the Internet? 274
Finding Information on the Internet 275
Gaining Access to the Internet 276
Internet Etiquette 277

INFORMATION UTILITIES 277
CompuServe 278
GEnie 279
eWorld 279
Delphi 280
America Online 280

Prodigy 281
Dialog 281
BRS/After Dark 281
Down Jones News/Retrieval 282
The Microsoft Network (MSN) 282

APPENDIX C
BOMBS AND DISASTERS: WHAT TO DO WHEN YOUR COMPUTER DOESN'T COOPERATE 284

INTRODUCTION 285

SOFTWARE PROBLEMS 286

PROBLEMS WITH FILES 289

DISKS 290

MOUSE OR KEYBOARD 291

MONITOR 291

PRINTERS 291

CALLING TECH SUPPORT 292

PREFACE

MicroComputers have forever changed the landscape of information processing and revolutionized the manner in which individuals and businesses approach problem solving and decision making. The challenge I face in all my introductory computer courses is to present the fundamental concepts of computing within the context of personal computer power while not relegating the material to merely a user manual for applications software packages.

An understanding of basic computing concepts coupled with the current state of micro computing technology will allow students to cope with the very significant changes that will occur in the very near future. The virtual organization and internet web sites are only two of many new exciting concepts that have already altered the vision of the information society that was presented to graduating seniors when they were freshmen.

MicroComputing Today is my attempt at preventing students from believing that their academic computer course will be either obsolete or irrelevant before they graduate. In particular this material was designed to provide the basic support for any introductory computer course. It is my goal to provide a text that can provide either the basis for an entire short course on personal computers or serve as the conceptual backbone for a course focusing on any of the available software application packages or programming languages.

The seven chapters and two appendices provide an encapsulated but broad introduction to computer concepts and micro computing technology. Every effort has been made to maintain the currency of the information but in this field new generations are measured in months rather than years.

Chapter I	The World of Computers
Chapter II	Computer Fundamentals: The Inside Story
Chapter III	Application Software: Productivity Tools
Chapter IV	System Software
Chapter V	Communications: Connectivity for Personal Computers
Chapter VI	Power Applications: Tools for Special Jobs
Chapter VII	Contemporary Concerns
Appendix A	Consumers' Guide to Computing
Appendix B	Going Online: The Internet and Some Information Utilities
Appendix C	Bombs and Disasters: What to Do When Your Computer Doesn't Cooperate

CHAPTER STRUCTURE

The structure of the text was designed with a focus on student learning and an eye on faculty flexibility. The material in the chapters build on each other, yet can be used independently. Learning objectives are presented at the outset of each chapter so that students can recognize their responsibility in mastering the material. High interest material is presented throughout the chapters in two special features: Windows on Computing and Profiles. To further assist the students in mastering difficult material, Concept Summaries have been utilized to enhance the learning process.

SUPPORT MATERIALS FOR THE INSTRUCTOR

A complete Instructor's Manual includes Learning Objectives, Chapter Outlines, Answers to Review Questions, and Activities and Research Problems. In addition a test bank is available through Westest.

ACKNOWLEDGMENTS

It is appropriate at this point to thank the following people who reviewed the book and provided invaluable comments.

Ronald Dale Williams
Central Piedmont Community College

Jack W. Thornton
East Carolina University

Michael P. Harris
Del Mar College

Robert H. Seidman
New Hampshire College

Judith Mazzeo
Lakeland Community College

Jorge Gaytan
University of Texas at El Paso

Lowell Stultz
Kalamazoo Valley Community College

Alan R. Belcher
University of Charlston

Most prefaces for new books would conclude at this point; however, the tremendous efforts on the part of my assistants in creating Micro-Computing Today requires special recognition. Although I have been writing computer textbooks for nearly twenty years, I have been specially blessed on this project with the professional support of two outstanding individuals: Sarah Basinger and Sally Oates. Sarah Basinger is primarily responsible for the context of the text material while Sally Oates has established quality control and production coordination. This book would not have been published without the efforts of Sarah and Sally.

CHAPTER 1

THE WORLD OF MICROCOMPUTERS

OUTLINE

Learning Objectives
Introduction
A Micro Look at Microcomputers
    Information Systems
    Computers in an Information System
    Window on Computing: The Future Is Here: Living in a Programmable World
    Concept Summary: Data in an Information System
The Technology Race
    Early Developments
    The First Computers
    Computer Generations
    Concept Summary: Computer Generations

Using Computers
    Personal Computers in the Home
    Education and Personal Computers
    Personal Computers Invade Business and Industry
    Computers in Science and Medicine
    Arts and Entertainment Embrace Micros
    Window on Computing: Morphing
Summary Points
Review Questions
Activities and Research

LEARNING OBJECTIVES

After reading this chapter, you should be able to:

- Use and understand very basic computer terms.
- Define the terms data, information, and information system.
- Identify the components of an information system.
- Explain how input, processing, output, and feedback relate to an information system.
- Explain both early and more recent advances in technology in terms of specific needs for faster, more reliable methods of calculating and record keeping.
- Describe major improvements in computer technology as grouped into generations.
- State common computer applications in the home, school, government, and business.

Figure 1–1 Computerized Automobile Diagnosis
This mechanic uses a computer that pinpoints problems in a car's performance.

computer An electronic device used to accept, process, store, access, and display information without human intervention.

microcomputer A small computer (desk-size or less) that uses a single microchip as its processor; also called *personal computer* or *home computer*.

INTRODUCTION

Computers are fast becoming as prevalent as microwave ovens and VCRs. We may be surprised when we learn that a friend does not own one. Of course, computer manufacturers would like to put a computer in every house, and they may get their wish soon. Computers are getting smaller, easier to use, and less expensive as technology advances; besides, they have many new capabilities that make them ideal for entertainment and education—common uses that are apt to attract first-time buyers.

Even if you don't have a **microcomputer,** or personal computer, at home, it is very likely that you will use a computer at work. Computers at automobile dealerships help mechanics find out what is wrong with a car and enable sales personnel to complete a deal (see Figure 1–1). Government agencies use computers to store vast amounts of information about constituents. Hospitals have computers that help nurses, doctors, technicians, and clerks keep track of a patient's progress, tests, and—yes—bills. The computers at corporations help clerks to monitor transactions and secretaries write important documents. If you have ever worked in a fast-food restaurant, grocery store, or other shop, chances are you used special computerized cash registers and scanners that not only figure a customer's bill but also keep track of inventory. It seems there is no escaping learning how to use a computer. In fact, it makes sense to know just what a computer is and what it does.

▶ A Micro Look at Microcomputers

A computer is a machine that can help you to do a variety of jobs: write reports, figure budgets, file data, create pie charts, use a network, or play a game. These jobs require information; thus when you use your computer, you are actually part of an **information system.**

Information Systems

People and organizations cannot function without information. Decision makers use information to increase knowledge and reduce uncertainty. An information system, therefore, is designed to transform data into information and make it available to decision makers. It manipulates data in various ways to reveal verifiable, relevant, timely, accurate, complete, and easy-to-understand information.

The Components of an Information System

An information system has five major components: people, data, hardware, software, and procedures.

- The people in an information system can be categorized by their roles: providers, users, or clients. Providers are the people, such as programmers, who design and operate the system. **Users,** or end users, interact directly with the system to complete their jobs (see Figure 1–2). Clients, on the other hand, may not interact directly with the system although they do benefit from it. A customer ordering a product through a computer-based information system benefits when the product is received though does not enjoy direct use of the system's computer.

- **Data** refers to unprocessed facts, or raw material not useful for making meaningful decisions. For example, an admissions office has little use for each quiz or homework score. Once all of the scores are organized into a student's transcript of courses and final grades, however, the summary can provide useful **information** that helps the office evaluate the student's chances for success in college. Information, then, is processed data that increases understanding and helps people make intelligent decisions.

- **Hardware** is the physical equipment in an information system. A common **configuration,** or assortment of components, in a personal computer system consists of the computer itself, two storage devices (a hard disk drive and a floppy disk drive), memory (circuitry that temporarily holds data and information for processing), two input devices (a keyboard and a mouse), and two output devices (a monitor and a printer) (see Figure 1—3). The external devices, such as printers, monitors, keyboards, and mice, are referred to as **peripherals.**

---

information system A system in which data is the input and information is the output.

user A person who uses computer software or has contact with computer systems.

data Facts; the raw material of information.

information Data that has been organized and processed so it is meaningful.

hardware The physical components of a computer system (for example, keyboards, printers, monitors).

configuration The specifications for, or items needed to use, a piece of software or hardware.

peripherals External devices such as keyboards and printers that are attached to the computer.

Figure 1–2 People as Part of an Information System
Many people in an information system are end users, whether at work (a), at school (b), or at home (c).

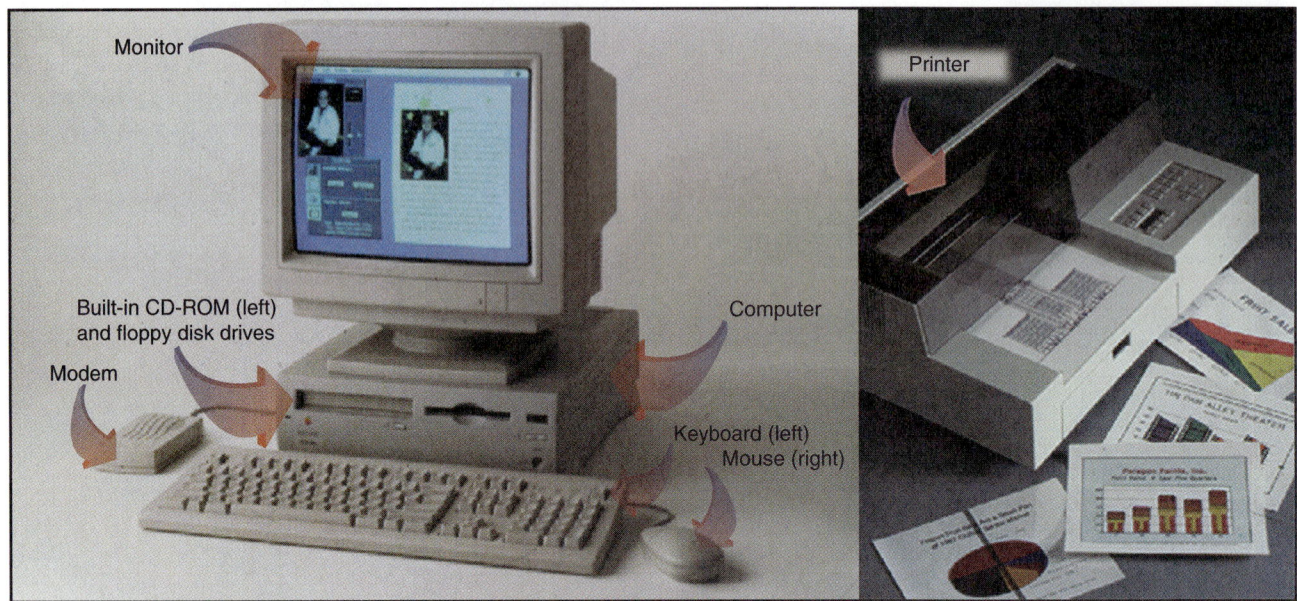

Figure 1–3 Microcomputer
This Macintosh system represents the components in a typical personal computer system.

program A set of instructions that, when executed, causes a computer to do particular tasks; also called software.

system software Programs that manage the computer circuitry at a low level and control the execution of user application programs.

application software A set of instructions that controls the execution of a user job.

- **Programs,** or *software,* are sequences of instructions that run computers. Software not only processes data into information required by users, but also provides the instructions needed just to get the computer running. Thus, a system configuration includes two types of software. The first—**system software**—manages the circuits of a computer so that the computer can activate a program or put a letter or number on the screen. PC-DOS and Macintosh System are system programs for IBM and Macintosh computers, respectively. The second type, **application software** (or, simply, an application), helps the user do a job. For example, the game *Flight Simulator* is application software for entertainment, and *Word* is application software for writing letters, reports, or fiction.
- Procedures are guidelines and instructions about using a particular system. They are compiled into printed documentation, such as manuals, that list the steps required to collect data, use hardware or software, and distribute the output. As tasks change, the procedures must be updated, too.

A computer system is far more than hardware. Its five components must work together efficiently for an information system to perform properly.

THE PATH OF DATA THROUGH AN INFORMATION SYSTEM

system A group of related elements that work toward a common goal.

A **system** is a group of related elements acting as a single entity toward a common goal. You may have already used the term in other contexts, such as the physical and the social sciences. For example, physiologists see the human body as a system made up of smaller subsystems, such as the respiratory system and the circulatory system. Any system is made up

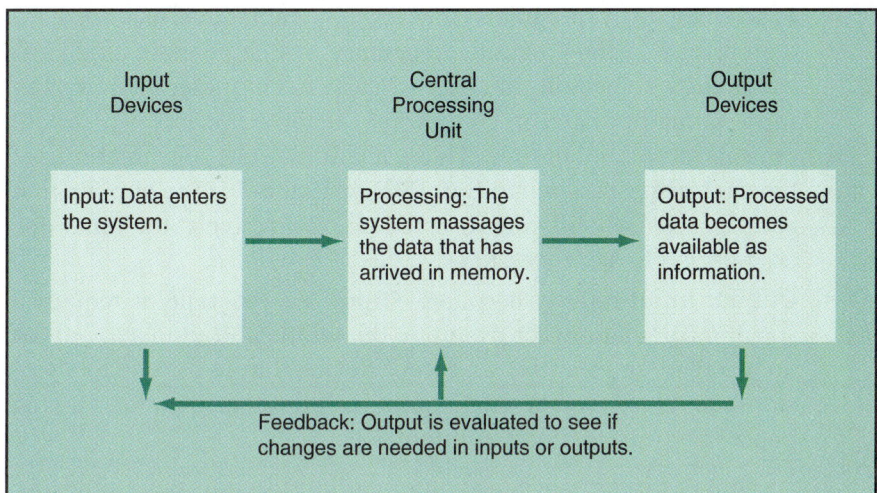

Figure 1–4 Data in a System
All data processing follows the same basic sequence steps.

Input typically involves three steps in order to prevent "garbage in, garbage out." The following procedures are the three steps in the input stage of information processing:
- **Collecting** the raw data and assembling it at one location.
- **Verifying,** or checking, the accuracy and completeness of data.
- **Coding** the data into a machine-readable form for processing.

Figure 1–5 The Input Stage of Information Processing
Input occurs when someone enters data via a keyboard or uses a device to scan an item for data.

of input, processes, and output. In an information system, data is what travels through these three stages (see Figure 1–4).

- **Input:** Input enters the system from the surrounding environment. You use an input device, such as a keyboard, a mouse, or a scanner wand, to enter data and commands into the computer (see Figure 1–5).

input Whatever goes into the computer, such as instructions, commands, or data.

process To transform data into useful information by classifying, sorting, calculating, or summarizing.

memory Internal physical storage that consists of chips.

central processing unit (CPU) The portion of the computer system that controls execution of program instructions and the processing of data items.

output Anything that comes out of a computer in a form that is useful to people.

feedback A check within a system that helps determine whether goals are being met; the return of information about the effectiveness of a system.

- **Processing:** Any programs and data in immediate use are held temporarily in the computer's **memory,** which consists of electrical circuits etched on tiny chips. While in computer memory, the input is manipulated in some way: calculated, classified, sorted, moved, stored, or output. These manipulations are functions of the **central processing unit,** or **CPU,** which holds the circuits that actually execute software instructions. Collectively, the functions are referred to as *processing*.
- **Output:** Input rapidly becomes output. As you type or request a specific calculation, for example, the words and numbers appear on a screen, or monitor, an output device that looks like a television set. Your system might also include a printer for making paper copy, also called a *printout*.

The output or performance of an information system is monitored and evaluated in a step called **feedback** (refer to Figure 1–4 again). In system theory, a system's primary goal is survival. Feedback helps the system survive by pinpointing the system's strengths and weaknesses. Based on the feedback information, a decision maker can modify the inputs or processes or both in order to get the most effective, accurate information.

Information systems are found in businesses, home-computing environments, and anywhere data is processed into information. The boundaries between such systems are not always clear, however. Assume, for instance, that your family uses a personal computer to calculate a monthly budget. Inputs might include bills and paycheck amounts. This data is processed, resulting in a list of bills to be paid, due dates, and excess amounts for savings. The feedback may determine whether you need to allocate more money to meet your debts. The bills that you pay are, in turn, inputs for larger information systems—the credit departments of different companies. Thus, your home system is actually a subsystem of a larger system. Note that a computer is not necessary for this budget system; the same process could be done manually. The larger the organization, the more information, however, and computers help organizations handle the tremendous load of data that comes in.

COMPUTERS IN AN INFORMATION SYSTEM

Modern computers can perform millions of instructions per second, sometimes abbreviated MIPS. Their speed—fast reaching the physical limit of the speed of light at 186,000 miles per second—is measured in terms of nanoseconds and other small units (see Figure 1–6).

Computers also do tedious, repetitive work with guaranteed accuracy. The notion that a computer is accurate may sound ludicrous to the person trying to persuade the gas company that he did pay his bill, but computer accuracy refers not to the degree of human error but to the inherent reliability of the computer's electronic components. That is, the same type of current passing through the same circuits yields the same results

Figure 1-6 Processing Speeds

Unit	Symbol	Fractions of a Second	
Millisecond	ms	one-thousand	(1/1,000)
Microsecond	µs	one-millionth	(1/1,000,000)
Nanosecond	ns	one-billionth	(1/1,000,000,000)
Picosecond	ps	one-trillionth	(1/1,000,000,000,000)

each time. We take advantage of this aspect of circuitry every time we flip a switch. When we turn on the hall light switch, we expect the hall light to come on, not the doorbell or attic fan. The computer is reliable for the same reason—its circuitry is reliable. Of course, the quality of input will affect the results of processing: garbage in, garbage out (GIGO). A simple analogy would be accidentally flipping the attic fan switch, which is located right next to the hall light switch: The circuits are still accurate, but the input—flipping the wrong switch—is faulty.

In a computerized information system, external **storage** media make storage capacity almost limitless. Similar vast quantities of data could be stored in paper files, which would become bulky and require an enormous amount of storage space. Retrieving specific data from paper files is a slow process. Computers, on the other hand, can retrieve the requested data at superfast speeds.

storage Retention of programs or data on media such as floppy disks or hard disks that are external to the computer's processor or memory.

Thus, people use computers in an information system because they are very fast, their circuits are reliable, and they can manage huge amounts of information with ease. In fact, hardware and software have been so successfully combined with people, data, and procedures in information systems that the term **synergism** is used to describe the relationship. A synergistic relationship is one in which the combined effort of all the parts is greater than the sum of the efforts of each part operating independently. A person working manually is slower and more prone to errors than a computer. A computer can deal with data faster and more accurately than a human, but requires human evaluation in order to remain effective. Together, however, the two can handle huge amounts of data with a high degree of speed and accuracy.

synergism A situation in which the combined efforts of all parts of an information system achieve a greater effect than the sum of the individual components.

COMPUTER CLASSIFICATIONS

The word *computer* may make you think of a machine small enough to put on your desk or even in your backpack or briefcase. There are many types of computers designed to fit many different information needs, however, and they are normally categorized according to size, capability, price range, and speed of operation. The traditional categories are supercomputer, mainframe, minicomputer, and microcomputer. Because the capabilities of the categories overlap considerably, some experts now

Figure 1–7 Supercomputer
This is the CRAY T90 Supercomputer System by Cray Research

supercomputer The most expensive, largest computer; can process over 1 billion instructions per second.

mainframe A large computer, so named because in the past the main processing unit of this computer consisted of a series of circuit boards mounted within a frame structure.

minicomputer A computer that is smaller in capacity and price than a mainframe but that delivers full-system capabilities. The minicomputer got its name by comparison with the large-scale computers that dominated the market when it was introduced in the mid-1960s.

lump all computers into just two categories: large computers and small computers.

The most powerful and most expensive computers are called **supercomputers,** which are acquired for the amount of complex processing they can do rather than for the number of users or equipment they can handle. Supercomputers are the largest, fastest computers made. Typically, they have productive capacities that are at least double those of mainframes and from 1000 to 1 million times faster than microcomputers. Supercomputers carry price tags to match their capacities, costing from $5 million to over $35 million (see Figure 1–7). Therefore, only the largest organizations tend to use these systems. Among them are large research and science facilities and giant corporations or federal agencies that study weather forecasting, oil exploration, energy conservation, seismology, nuclear reactor safety, and cryptography. In addition, supercomputers are used for simulations in nuclear energy research, stress tests in aircraft design, and special effects in films.

Organizations such as large corporations, banks, and airlines need large computers for storing and maintaining great quantities of data, but they will use less expensive and less powerful machines called **mainframes.** Mainframe computers can support thousands of users and peripherals, and often occupy entire floors of large office buildings. They require special installation and maintenance procedures, including heavy-duty electrical wiring, air conditioning, platforms, and security features. The computer alone can cost from $50,000 to over $5 million, but companies may lease rather than buy mainframes.

Because of the great cost of mainframes, many organizations buy smaller versions of mainframes called **minicomputers.** The size of a refrigerator or closet, a minicomputer has the same capabilities but operates more slowly and handles fewer users and data than a mainframe (see

Figure 1–8 Minicomputer
This is the VAX by DEC.

Figure 1–8). Their cost—anywhere from a few thousand dollars to over $100,000—became their primary selling point. Many colleges became early and continuing users of minicomputers. Minicomputers are also widely used to support the operations of some retail chain stores and hospitals. Even smaller computers have won the hearts—and pocketbooks—of some businesses and organizations, however. These are the microcomputers.

Types of Microcomputers

Technically, the microcomputer got its name from the fact that its processing unit is a **microprocessor** on a single chip (see Figure 1–9). Operationally, microcomputers are usually single-user systems that fit on a desk or even in a briefcase. For this reason, they are often called *personal computers* (or PCs) rather than microcomputers. Although they are small, they are so powerful that many organizations are using them exclusively.

The most powerful microcomputers are the **workstations,** or supermicrocomputers. Like all microcomputers, workstations depend upon microprocessors for processing, but most units include additional processors that expand mathematical and graphics capabilities. They have sophisticated monitors, extensive memories, and large storage capacities that in the past have well exceeded the configurations common for normal home and office applications.

At the other extreme, microcomputers are being shrunk into small, portable packages that qualify them as laptop, notebook, and palmtop computers. A **laptop,** in general, weighs less than 12 pounds; a **notebook,** less than 8 pounds, and a **palmtop** less than 1 pound. In fact, full-power portable microcomputers of more than 8 pounds are the exception rather

microprocessor A programmable processing unit on a single microchip.

workstation A term for a powerful microcomputer used primarily for engineering and design purposes.

laptop A portable microcomputer that weighs less than 12 pounds and can be fit into a briefcase. Laptop computers operate on batteries, making them usable in travel and remote situations.

notebook A portable microcomputer that weighs less than 8 pounds and can be fit into a briefcase.

palmtop A pocket microcomputer that weighs less than 1 pound and has limited functions.

Figure 1–9 Microprocessor and Microcomputers
Powerful microprocessor chips are enclosed in several sizes of personal computers.

than the rule. These computers can be operated on battery power, making it possible to use them in locations that range from airplanes to the park. Although the notebook computer is now powerful enough and convenient enough to be an owner's sole computer, the palmtop (or pocket personal computer) contains tiny keys and small amounts of memory, both of which preclude its use for serious computing. Pocket PCs are generally used for on-site collection of data that will be transferred to a larger microcomputer for more convenient display and manipulation.

RIGHT-SIZING

As the processing speeds and memory capacities of microcomputers increased, applications moved from mainframes and minicomputers to microcomputers. In fact, microcomputers have become so pervasive in small businesses and corporations that they have edged out the purchase

Window on Computing

The Future Is Here: Living in a Programmable World

Your great-grandparents probably kept little black books in which they noted every penny they spent: 3¢ for flour, 10¢ for bread, or 5¢ for an egg. They faithfully recorded every penny spent so as to avoid frivolous purchases and save for the future. Now you can do the same type of careful recording as you shop, in one of two ways: Using the pocket PC, or pocket personal computer (a computer barely larger than the palm of your hand), you can press the tiny keys and watch the numbers and words appear on a tiny display. With a notepad computer, you can actually write on the liquid-crystal screen pad with a special electronic stylus. Once you get home, you connect the small computer to your desktop model and dump the figures into software such as *Quicken*, which is a program for keeping track of financial affairs.

Eventually, you won't need the little black book or the palm-sized computer. In your pocket you'll carry a Neuron Chip that will record automatically every place you visit, every person you talk to, and every cent you spend. The chip could do other jobs, too: monitor sensors, manage light switches, tell time, and even beep when your 2-year-old wanders too far. It would receive and send signals through such channels as power lines, radio waves, cables, telephone wires, and infrared beams.

The Neuron Chip is a microprocessor-based technology designed by Echelon Corporation in Palo Alto, Calif. Businesses would, predictably, be the first users of systems developed around the chips. Echelon systems could be used to manage lighting in parking lots and monitor heating, air conditioning, and factory processes.

CONCEPT SUMMARY
DATA IN AN INFORMATION SYSTEM

Input Devices
Enter raw material called data.

CPU (Microprocessor)
A **program** tells the computer what to do.

Output Devices
Get meaningful **information** as a result of processing.

Enter input by typing on a **keyboard,** by **scanning** paper documents, or by **loading** a program from a disk.

Calculate a history grade.
Classify equipment according to use.
Sort student names alphabetically.
Summarize performance on standardized tests.

Watch a **monitor** for output.
Run the **printer** to get a paper copy.

Feed back: Check each aspect of information processing to be sure the output is effective. It must be timely, accurate, complete, concise, relevant, and clear.

---

network A communication system linking two or more computers and their peripherals.

right-sizing A term that describes using the correct equipment for a purpose and often includes moving applications to microcomputers from larger computers.

connectivity The capability of a computer system to use information gained by linking computers and information resources.

of new mainframes and minicomputers. The increased use of reliable **networks** of microcomputers has, in fact, expedited this **right-sizing,** or downsizing, trend. A network is a system connecting two or more computers and their peripherals. Through a variety of networks, people using microcomputers have **connectivity**—that is, easier access to large amounts of data from many sources, including their own companies and commercial data-distributing services. Thus, the role of existing minicomputers and mainframes is changing—from providing processing power to providing information.

Not only have microcomputers become powerful enough to support mainframe-type applications, it also is easy to acquire the computers and

Figure 1–10 The Abacus
On the abacus, each bead in the groups of five stands for one unit, and each bead in the groups of two stands for five units. You count or add numbers by pushing the beads toward the middle bar.

networking equipment through computer stores, office supply stores, and mail-order houses. You'll find microcomputers by such manufacturers as Apple, IBM, Compaq, Dell, Gateway 2000, Toshiba, and Zenith, among others. Packaged (or prewritten) software is readily available for microcomputers, too, usually in the same locations as you buy the computers and also in stores that specialize in software and electronic games. This off-the-shelf software includes **packages** such as WordPerfect, Word, Excel, dBASE, Quicken, and many programs offering functions that once were exclusive to the large, old dinosaurs of computers.

package A software program for retail sale that has been prewritten by professional programmers.

▶ THE TECHNOLOGY RACE

Computers have been around for quite a few years, but it has been only since the late 1970s that individuals could buy their own computers. Today it seems as if everyone is using computers. Lawyers, clerks, bank tellers, doctors, movie makers, athletes, writers, musicians, students, and even toddlers use computers. We do not see that as unusual. In fact, it is hard to imagine what life was like without computers.

EARLY DEVELOPMENTS

Since ancient times, people have had ways to deal with facts and figures. Early people counted on their fingers, tied knots in rope, and carved masks on clay tablets to keep track of livestock and trade. Some added and subtracted with an abacus, a picture-frame device containing beads strung on wires (see Figure 1–10). Much later, in the 1600s, John Napier designed a portable multiplication tool named Napier's Bones or Napier's Rods. The user slid the ivory rods along side each other to figure multi-

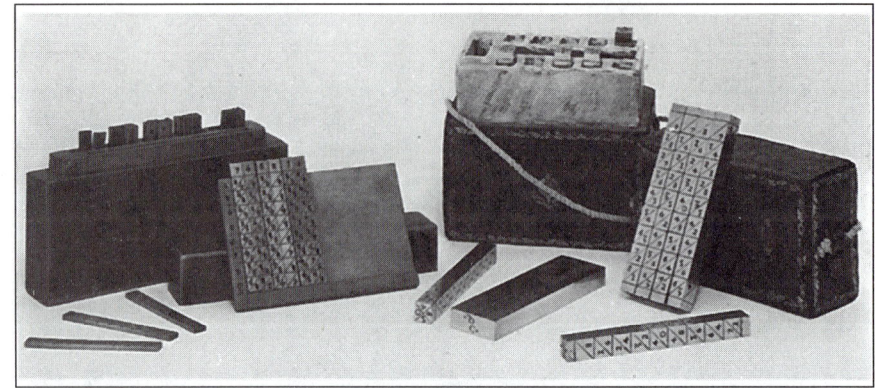

Figure 1–11 Napier's Bones
Napier's Bones were one of the forerunners of the slide rule, which was used by engineers for calculations well into the 1960s.

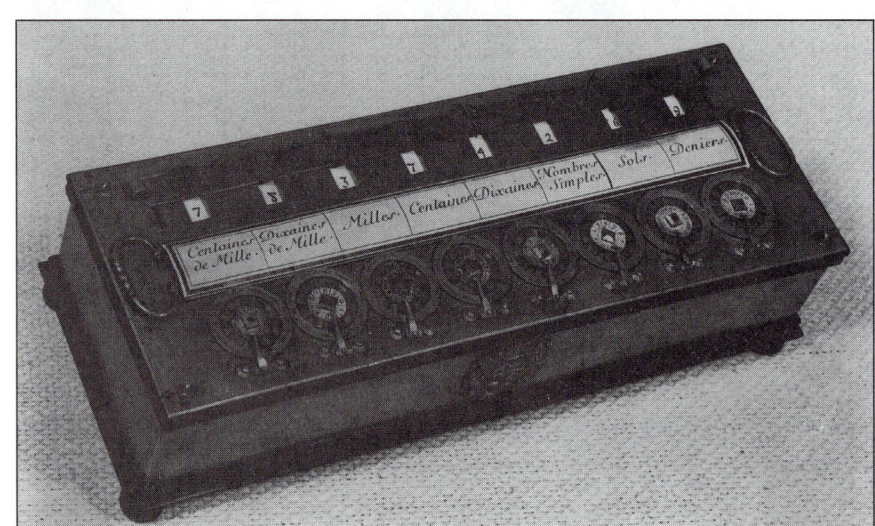

Figure 1–12 Blaise Pascal and the Pascaline
Each gear on the Pascaline stood for one place—ones, tens, hundreds, and so on. As the first wheel counted one complete turn from 0 to 9, a pin on its edge would turn the next wheel, the tens wheel, and so on. The machine worked very well for addition, but subtraction was accomplished by a roundabout adding method.

plication and division problems (see Figure 1–11). Napier's idea led to the invention of the slide rule in the mid-1600s. As trade grew and more people paid taxes, however, faster and more accurate methods were needed for doing math and keeping records.

The idea for the first mechanical calculating machine grew out of the many tedious hours a father and his son spent preparing tax reports. In the mid-1600s, Blaise Pascal and his father, a tax official, were rushing to complete tax reports by the French government's deadline. As the two agonized over long columns of figures, the 19-year-old Blaise decided to build a machine that would do the job much faster and more accurately. His machine, the Pascaline, had a set of eight gears that worked together to add and subtract numbers (see Figure 1–12). A market for the machine never grew. In fact, clerks refused to use it; they were afraid it might replace them on their jobs and thought it could be rigged, like a scale or roulette wheel, to give predetermined results.

Despite the initial reluctance to accept mechanical calculators, other inventors continued to experiment; and soon, machines were introduced for doing addition, subtraction, multiplication, division, and square roots.

Over a century and a half passed, however, before a calculator even remotely resembling a computer was designed.

THE ANALYTICAL ENGINE

Charles Babbage was an Englishman and professor at Cambridge University. In his work in mathematics and astronomy, Babbage often used tables of prefigured numbers, such as squares, square roots, and trigonometric functions. Existing tables were full of errors—errors made by the clerks who had figured the numbers and errors made by the printers. As a result, Babbage decided to build a machine that could compute and print the tables automatically and exactly. His first attempt in 1822 failed because the manufacturing technology was too primitive for the exact machining needed to build parts for it (see Figure 1–13). Besides, the machine could do only one type of calculation, and thus a separate machine would be needed for each different table. Babbage really needed an all-purpose machine.

His inspiration was the Jacquard loom, in which sets of heavy cardboard punched cards determined the weaving design (see Figure 1–14). All of the cards for one design were linked in a series like a belt. As the cards passed over a set of rods on the loom, the pattern of holes in the cards determined which rods were engaged, thereby adjusting the pattern of the product. When a weaver wanted to weave a new design, he put a different belt of cards on the loom. Thus, the loom could make exact copies of different rugs and cloth automatically.

Figure 1–13 Charles Babbage and the Difference Engine
The word engine in Babbage's day actually denoted any type of invention, for no real engine had yet been invented. This working version of the Difference Engine 2 was finished in 1991.

Figure 1–14 Jacquard's Loom
One "program" for this loom wove a portrait of the inventor himself.

Figure 1–15 Herman Hollerith and the Tabulating Machine
Hollerith's code fit a grid of 12 rows and 80 columns on punched cards. Once data was punched onto the cards, a tabulator read the cards as they passed over tiny brushes. Each time a brush found a hole, it completed an electrical circuit and caused special counting dials to increment the data. The cards were then sorted into 24 compartments by the sorting machine.

The concept contributed two ideas significant to Babbage's machine and consequently to the development of computers. The first was that information could be punched on cards, and the second was that the cards could be linked to provide a set of instructions that was machine readable. That is, the set of instructions was essentially a program, allowing a machine to do its work without human interference. Having observed the loom, Babbage began planning a new machine, the steam-powered analytical engine, which was amazingly like a computer. The machine would read a program from punched cards, carry out instructions in its "operator," and calculate results in its "mill." Its "store" would hold instructions and intermediate and final results, and it could print out the results automatically. Babbage died before he could build the machine, but his son made a model from his notes and drawings. To Babbage's credit, the model worked. (Recently, two scientists, Barrie Holloway and Reg Crick, built a full-sized working version from one of Babbage's plans, the Difference Engine 2. The machine was displayed publicly in London in 1991.) Because of his ideas, Babbage is called the father of computers.

THE TABULATING MACHINE

Charles Babbage was truly a man before his time. A few short years after he died, several things occurred that would have helped him build a successful analytical engine. Electricity was harnessed, and factories were able to fine-tune parts for machines. The adding machine and cash register were invented. With these advances well in place, Herman Hollerith was able to build a tabulating machine that helped calculate the 1890 census, a census being required by the U.S. government every 10 years (see Figure 1–15).

PROFILE

THE COUNTESS OF LOVELACE

Much of what we know about Charles Babbage and his "engines" comes from the papers of Augusta Ada Byron, Countess of Lovelace and daughter of the poet Lord Byron. Lady Lovelace did not lead a life typical of most aristocratic English women during the early 1800s. She was a genius in mathematics and contributed significantly to modern-day programming concepts.

Curious about Babbage's work, Lady Lovelace translated an article about the analytical engine from French to English. (The analytical engine was a device designed to perform mathematical calculations automatically from instructions coded by punched holes in cards.) She added some important notes of her own about how the machine would work. In 1842, at the age of 27, she began working with Babbage, helping him design programs for the analytical engine. During the first year of this association, several of her ideas were incorporated into the design of the analytical engine. The most significant idea was what is now called the *loop concept*. In her studies, Lady Lovelace noticed that the same sequence of instructions often had to be repeated for different data when a single calculation was being performed. She concluded that one set of instruction cards could be used if there were a way to loop back to those instructions. Using loops would decrease the number of cards, or instructions, that would have to be prepared. Lady Lovelace also suggested that Babbage use the binary system of ones and zeros in his machine rather than the more commonly used decimal system.

Sadly, like Babbage, Lady Lovelace never lived to see her ideas used. She died at age 36 while Babbage was still working on the analytical engine. Her work has long outlived her, and she is now referred to as the first programmer. A programming language used primarily by the U.S. government was named Ada in her honor.

U.S. population had grown so fast that the Census Bureau needed seven and a half years to compile and tabulate the 1880 census. By then the information was so outdated that it had little meaning. Anticipating even worse problems in 1890, the Census Bureau began looking for ways to speed up the work. Using Hollerith's machine, it tabulated the entire census in two and a half years, despite an increase of 13 million people in the previous decade. The machine read and sorted data from cards in which the pattern of punched holes represented particular data. The cards could be used repeatedly for different calculations without endless, manual copying and checking of data.

The machine was so successful that Hollerith formed his own company to market it. He eventually sold the company, and later it was combined with 12 others to form the Computing-Tabulating-Recording Company (CTR). In 1924, Thomas J. Watson, Sr., became president of CTR and changed the company's name to International Business Machines Corporation (IBM).

Figure 1–16 The ABC
The Atanasoff-Berry Computer was the first to use vacuum tubes as components.

THE FIRST COMPUTERS

Many kinds of adding machines and punched-card equipment were used to handle data in the United States well into the 1950s, but scientists were already dreaming of computers. They foresaw machines that could not only calculate numbers, but also handle a variety of logic statements. By 1938, in fact, Claude Shannon, an American mathematician, saw how mathematical rules developed by George Boole (Boolean logic) could be represented in the behavior of electric circuits.

World War II accelerated research into computing machines as Allied forces begged for machines that could decipher German codes and rapidly compute artillery trajectories. Mechanical computers such as the Mark I built by Howard Aiken at Harvard University provided some measure of relief; but, hoping for even faster results, the U.S. Army asked two other men, John Mauchly and J. Presper Eckert, Jr., to build an electronic computer. Not only would a computer have calculated trajectory tables; it also would have facilitated the Manhattan Project, which led to the development of the atomic bomb. This computer was not finished until after the war was over, however.

THE ENIAC

Even without the impetus of war, Mauchly and Eckert had already discussed building an electronic computer for large-scale, general use.

Figure 1–17 The ENIAC
The ENIAC's first job was calculating the feasibility of a proposed design for the hydrogen bomb. The computer was also used for studying weather and cosmic rays.

Mauchly heard about a prototype electronic computer called the ABC (Atanasoff-Berry Computer in Figure 1–16) and traveled to Iowa to talk with the computer's makers, John Atanasoff and Clifford Berry. Soon thereafter, Mauchly and Eckert began designing their own computer at the University of Pennsylvania Moore School of Engineering. This was the point at which the U.S. Army became interested. The machine, called ENIAC (for Electronic Numerical Integrator And Calculator), was finished after the war ended, however, and was used for studying weather, cosmic rays, and nuclear energy rather than for figuring trajectories.

The ENIAC was huge (see Figure 1–17). It weighed 30 tons and was some 8 feet high and 80 feet long. Its 18,000 **vacuum tubes** did its work. In 20 seconds, the ENIAC could do a math problem normally requiring 40 hours of one person's time. It seemed so fast that scientists believed seven computers like it could handle all of the calculations the world would ever need.

The ENIAC is traditionally considered the first electronic computer built in the United States. In a 1973 lawsuit, however, a Federal District Court justice ruled in a patent infringement suit brought by Sperry, holder of the patent on the ENIAC, that Mauchly and Eckert did not themselves first invent the automatic electronic digital computer, but instead derived that subject matter from John Atanasoff.

vacuum tube A glass bulb (resembling a light bulb) from which almost all air has been removed and through which electricity can pass.

Figure 1–18 John von Neumann and the EDVAC
As it turned out, two groups of people were working simultaneously on a stored-program computer. An English machine, the EDSAC (Electronic Delay Storage Automatic Computer) was actually the first stored-program computer in the world, having been completed only a few months before EDVAC.

stored-program concept The idea that programs can be stored in a computer's memory and can be switched electronically rather than by resetting switches and rewiring the computer.

THE EDVAC

A major problem with the ENIAC was that operating instructions had to be administered manually by setting switches and connecting wires on control panels called *plugboards.* This job was tedious, time-consuming, and error-prone. The solution involved the **stored-program concept,** the idea of storing both instructions and data in a computer's memory. In this type of architecture, a single, central processor ensures the sequential execution of all commands under the control of stored programs. This architecture is often referred to as *von Neumann architecture,* after John von Neumann, to whom the ideas for both the architecture and the stored-program concepts are traditionally attributed (see Figure 1–18). The computer would read the holes in a new set of paper tapes or cards to change what was held in memory. Thus, no rewiring or resetting of switches was necessary.

These ideas spurred the construction in 1950 of the first stored-program computer in the United States, the EDVAC (Electronic Discrete Variable Automatic Computer). Subsequent refinements of the computer have focused on speed, size, and cost.

COMPUTER GENERATIONS

True computers began when vacuum tubes, rather than mechanical parts, were used for counting and storing data in calculating machines. Since then, each major change in computer circuitry triggered a new **generation** of computers. As the circuitry became smaller, the speed and memory of computers increased. So far, there have been four generations of computers.

generation A stage; in computer technology, a stage usually much improved over an earlier stage.

Figure 1–19   The UNIVAC I
The most popular uses for the UNIVACs were payroll and billing.

THE FIRST GENERATION: VACUUM TUBES FOR NUMBER CRUNCHERS

The first generation of computers began in 1951, when the first commercial computer was sold to the U.S. Census Bureau. Another like it was installed at General Electric's Appliance Park in Louisville, Ky. The machines were UNIVAC I computers, short for UNIVersal Automatic Computer (see Figure 1–19). They were developed by Mauchly and Eckert, the ENIAC team. Before the UNIVAC I, computers had been one-of-a-kind machines made for calculating scientific and military mathematics. For this reason, computers were nicknamed "number crunchers." The UNIVAC I, however, was built with business number crunching in mind—payroll and billing, for example. And business acceptance of computers grew quickly: In 1953, Remington Rand and IBM had placed a grand total of nine installations, but by the late 1950s, IBM alone had leased 1000 of its first-generation computers.

First-generation computers were huge, slow, and expensive. They used thousands of vacuum tubes, which took up a lot of space and generated a great deal of heat, just as light bulbs do. To prevent overheating, the computers were housed in rooms with special air conditioning. Even so, there were many breakdowns. Already, however, scientists were developing substitutes for the vacuum tubes as well as replacements for the mountains of punched cards and paper tape used to enter data and instructions into the computers. In addition, programmers were developing more efficient, less tedious and error-prone codes with which to write the next generation of software.

Figure 1–20 Magnetic Core Memory
This type of memory was made of tiny donut-shaped rings placed on fine wires. It enabled real-time processing.

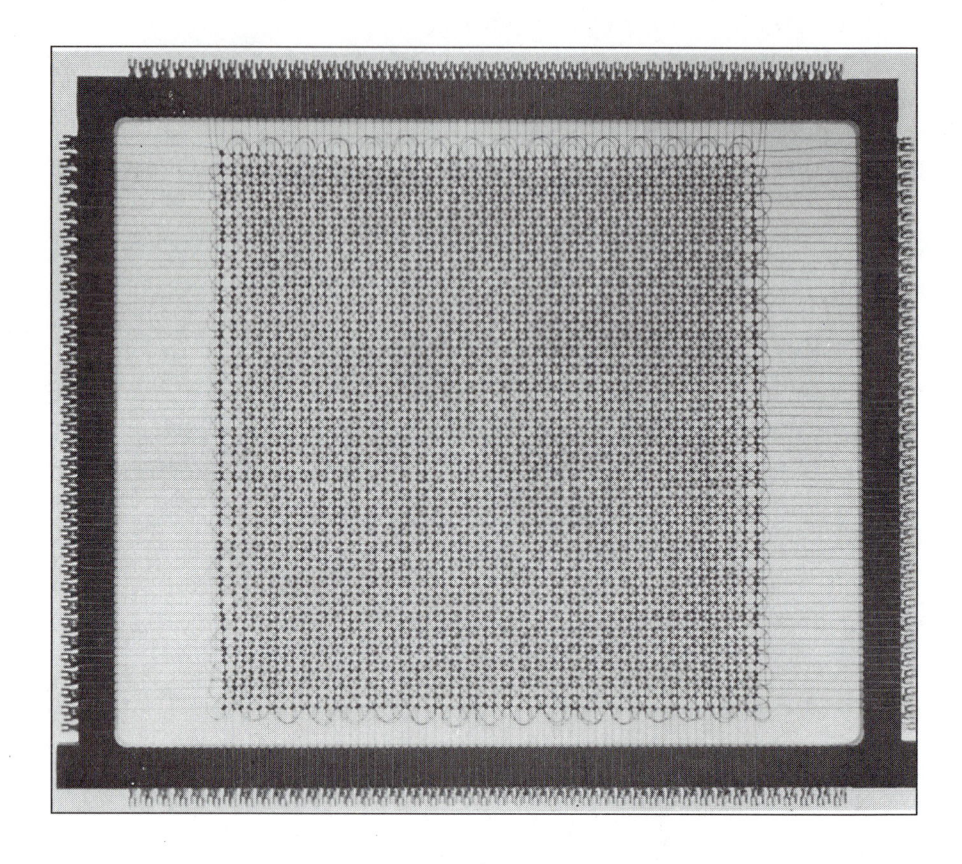

transistor A device that controls electric current flow without using a vacuum tube.

real-time Describes the ability of a computer to respond immediately and provide output fast enough to control the outcome of an event.

THE SECOND GENERATION: TRANSISTORS AND REAL TIME

The transistor was the primary component of second-generation computers in the early 1960s. A **transistor** is a small component made of solid material that acts like a vacuum tube in controlling the flow of electric current. Use of transistors rather than vacuum tubes resulted in smaller, faster, and more reliable machines that consumed less electricity and generated much less heat than the first-generation computers.

At the same time, the U.S. Navy was looking for a more advanced, reliable high-speed flight trainer. Known as Whirlwind I, the navy project was one of the most innovative and influential projects in the history of computers. Because of the high speed with which instructions and data could be located and retrieved using a new type of memory, the Whirlwind allowed the **real-time** processing necessary in flight simulation (see Figure 1–20). In real time, the processing occurs rapidly enough to produce output to control or affect the outcome of an activity. The development, along with magnetic-disk storage, led to other real-time functions, such as airline reservation systems, air traffic control, factory management, and battle simulations.

During this generation, sophisticated languages such as COBOL and FORTRAN enabled programmers to focus on solving problems rather than on writing tedious code. In more advanced languages such as these, several instructions are assigned to one command, thus shortening the amount of time spent on writing a program and increasing the accuracy of programming.

THE THIRD GENERATION: INTEGRATED CIRCUITS TAKE OVER

Transistors did not dominate computer architecture for long. Even as the second computer generation began in 1959, scientists at both Texas Instruments and Fairchild Semiconductor had announced successful **integrated circuits (ICs)**. Using different methods, they placed, or integrated, complete electronic circuits together onto small **chips** made of **silicon**. Soon a single silicon chip less than one-eighth inch square could hold 64 complete circuits, a small number compared with today's chips.

Common usage of the chips in computers marked the beginning of the third generation of computers in 1965. Third-generation computers used less power, cost less, and were smaller and much more reliable than previous machines. Although computers became smaller, their internal memories greatly increased due to the placement of memory on chips.

The 1960s also saw the development of minicomputers, which eventually enabled small businesses and organizations to have computer power without paying mainframe prices. In addition, the software industry began to emerge. Programs for payroll, billing, and other business tasks became available at fairly low cost. Yet the software often did not work correctly. Hardware improved so quickly that even skilled programmers had trouble keeping up with the changes—and skilled programmers were scarce. These problems led to a glut of computer-error horror stories: $200,000 monthly water bills for families of four, or $80,000 worth of duplicate welfare checks. Software surely had growing pains during the third generation.

> **integrated circuit (IC)** A complete electronic circuit on a tiny silicon chip.
>
> **chip** Solid-state circuitry on a tiny piece of silicon or gallium material; may contain millions of electronic components.
>
> **silicon** A material found in quartz and sand that conducts or does not conduct electricity, depending upon the material or chemical added to it.

THE FOURTH GENERATION AND THE MICROCOMPUTER REVOLUTION

Although the dividing lines among the first three generations of computers are clearly marked by major technological advances, historians are not so specific about when the fourth generation began. They do agree that the major switch to silicon chips for memory occurred in the fourth generation.

Engineers continued to cram more circuits onto a single silicon chip in large-scale integration (LSI), thus making computers even faster. LSI put thousands of integrated circuits on each chip. Each third-generation chip had its own special functions, but engineers quickly developed the microprocessor, or computer on a chip, that could be programmed to do many jobs. The arithmetic and logic circuitry needed for processing was packed onto a single chip that could be made to act like any kind of calculator or computer desired.

The microprocessor was made to be used in calculators, not computers. At the time, calculators used circuit chips that could perform only one function each, but a Japanese company wanted programmable chips

Figure 1-21 The Altair 8800
The Altair 8800 sold for $395 as a kit or for $498 fully assembled, but up to $2,000 worth of peripherals were needed to make it work.

for its line of calculators. An Intel chip, the Intel 4004, filled the requirements but also led to the invention of microcomputers.

The first microcomputer was a do-it-yourself mail-order kit, and it created a lot of interest. Kits were popular for a few years—that is, popular with people who knew how to use soldering irons and read the many complex diagrams and instructions that came in the kits (see Figure 1–21). Although a few kits were sold as assembled computers, a move by Tandy Corporation's Radio Shack made the kits obsolete. In 1977, the company introduced the TRS-80, and, for the first time, a person could walk into a store and buy a low-priced, preassembled personal computer off the shelf (see Figure 1–22).

Figure 1-22 John Roach and the TRS-80
The TRS-80 was available preassembled, off the shelf.

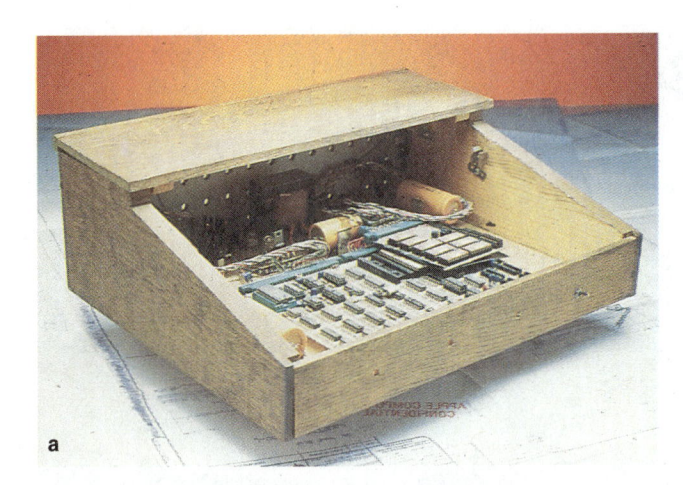

Figure 1–23 Early Apple and Commodore Machines
Photos of early microcomputers include (a) the original Apple I, (b) the Apple II, and (c) the Commodore PET.

Commodore Business Machines and Apple Computer followed Radio Shack's lead with the Commodore PET (Personal Electric Transactor) and the Apple II (see Figure 1–23). Better models soon followed: Apple IIe and IIc, Macintosh, Commodore 64, Amiga, and Tandy 3000. IBM entered the microcomputer foray in 1981 with the IBM Personal Computer, which quickly became the standard in small business computers (see Figure 1–24). The Intel 8086 microprocessor inside the IBM PC could process 16 bits of data at a time, a revolution in microcomputer speed. The success of the IBM PC prompted other microcomputer manufacturers to develop 16-bit microcomputers. Since then, IBM has introduced a number of microcomputers, including the IBM PCjr, IBM PC-XT, IBM PC-AT, PS/1, PS/2, and ValuePoint computers.

Engineers continue to research ways of packing ever more circuits onto chips. The increased miniaturization is called *very-large-scale integration,* or VLSI. Imagine a map showing every street in Los Angeles on the head of a pin, and you have an idea of how many circuits can be put on a single silicon chip. A single microprocessor based on VLSI is vastly more powerful than a room full of 1950s computer circuitry.

26 • THE WORLD OF MICROCOMPUTERS

Figure 1–24 The IBM PC
IBM introduced the PC in 1981.

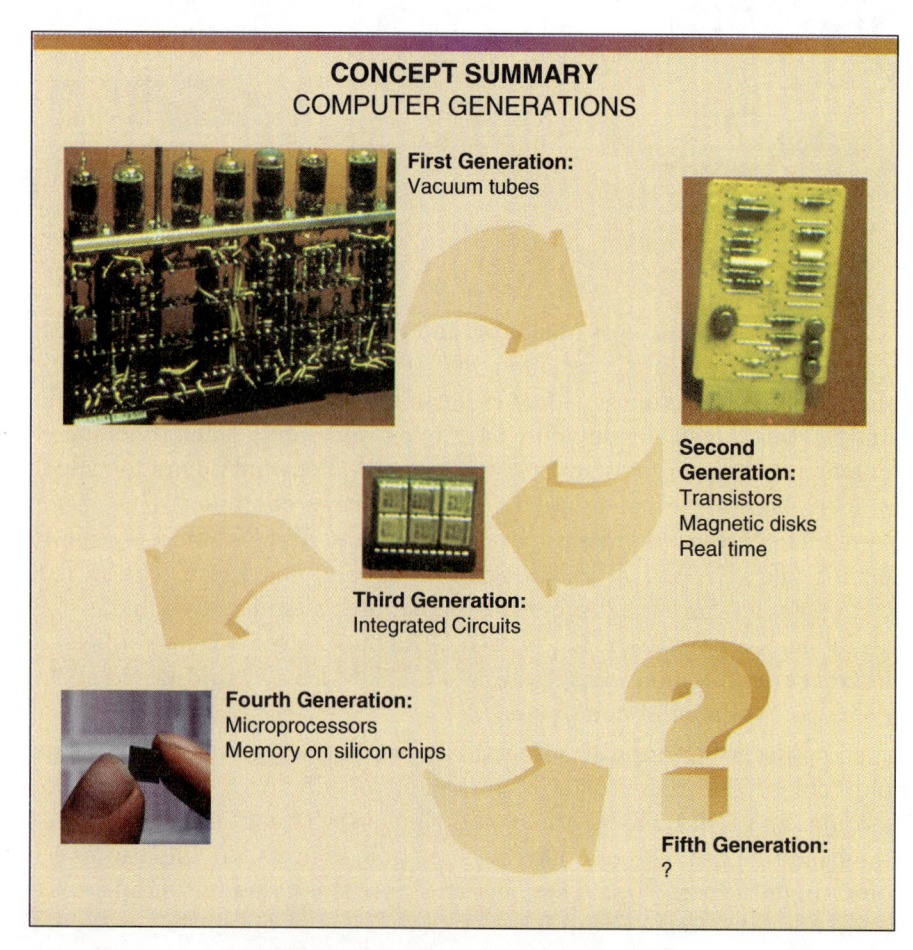

CONCEPT SUMMARY
COMPUTER GENERATIONS

First Generation:
Vacuum tubes

Second Generation:
Transistors
Magnetic disks
Real time

Third Generation:
Integrated Circuits

Fourth Generation:
Microprocessors
Memory on silicon chips

Fifth Generation:
?

The success of microcomputers led to a flood of software designed for use on the small machines. The early programs were games, but educational programs—generally designed for rote learning—soon began to appear. In 1979, the first spreadsheet program for microcomputers, *VisiCalc,* was introduced, and it revolutionized the way microcomputers were used. The spreadsheet program enabled people to see quickly how changes in some numbers could affect business performance. Thus for the first time, business and professional people saw the potential for microcomputers in planning their company's strategy. Today, a wide variety of software exists for microcomputer applications in business, school, and personal use.

When will the fifth generation of computers begin? For many years now, computers have been outfitted with VLSI chips. Future machines may depend on the simultaneous processing of several microprocessor chips. Other prototypes include optical computers, which are based on the behavior of light, and neural networks, which are patterned after the architecture of a human brain. Research into voice and handwriting recognition is already resulting in computers that can be used simply by speaking or writing rather than by typing in arcane coded commands. It will most likely be up to the historians of the future, however, to look back and identify one or two significant technological advances that propelled us into the fifth computer generation.

▶ Using Computers

Because of their costs and sizes, early computers were feasible for only very large corporations. Today's computers are quite different: Microcomputers are affordable for nearly every member of our society, and we relish the progression to ever more powerful machines and intriguing software.

Personal Computers in the Home

Organizing recipes, a widely touted use for home computers, provided grist for the joke mill for many years; but, in retrospect, the recipes won. For example, cookbook collectors and caterers may have so many shelves full of books that finding a favorite recipe can take an entire afternoon. The answer is to create a computer file containing the names of the best recipes along with the books and page numbers where they can be located. A good program designed especially for cooks can also adjust the amounts of ingredients to feed various sizes of crowds and spew out the amounts of calories and fat and other facts about a recipe.

Microcomputers can also be hooked up to various home systems to manage temperatures and energy use, answer telephone calls, and help safeguard a home during vacations. Using the computer with telephone

Figure 1–25 Voice Recognition System
Despite her muscular dystrophy, this woman is able to work on a masters degree using the DragonDicate system from Dragon Systems, Inc. The system enables the user to input data simply by speaking.

lines enables people to conduct banking transactions, shop from home, and communicate with a variety of people on a myriad of topics. People who wish to work at home can easily link their computers to their companies and to services that provide information essential to doing a good job. Computer use can be a boon to people with disabilities, who might use the computer to control their environment and communicate with others (see Figure 1–25).

EDUCATION AND PERSONAL COMPUTERS

Over the years, computers have gained wide acceptance as educational tools. The beginnings were marred by questions about the legitimacy of rote learning, the type of teaching technique computers did so well. Currently, computers provide many other teaching tools, including tutorials, games, and simulations of chemistry, physics, and history events (see Figure 1–26). Many programs combine text, sound, graphics, and animation in a concept called *multimedia,* giving students multisensory experiences for studying topics such as animals and labor unions. Many classrooms are also communicating with students around the world through computers in order to gain firsthand information about different countries and cultures. The various ways that computers are used in education are often lumped under the general term *computer-assisted instruction,* or CAI, a term once confined to describing rote programmed learning.

Seeing how effective a teaching tool a computer can be, businesses and industries are increasingly using computers to train employees to do specific jobs and to learn traditional school subjects. Training of this

Figure 1-26 Where in the World is Carmen SanDiego? Well-known and highly rated, this program requires students to uncover clues that lead them around the world while attempting to successfully identify and arrest Carmen and her gang for stealing national treasures.

nature is usually referred to as *computer-based training,* or CBT. Like many of the school applications, CBT also is designed for multisensory and interactive learning.

PERSONAL COMPUTERS INVADE BUSINESS AND INDUSTRY

In any business or office, large or small, computers can help reduce work done by hand and thus reduce the cost of routine jobs. Such jobs include billing customers, making out payroll checks and taxes, paying for supplies and products, and making reports for managers. In fact, the prevalence of computers, and especially microcomputers and their peripherals, has led business people to refer to their workplace as the electronic office. Every office function—typing, bookkeeping, billing, payroll, budgeting, filing, and communications—can be done with computers. Probably the most popular computer job in offices is word processing. With word processing, a clerk can prepare memos, letters, and reports easily by bypassing the problems of manual typing.

Computer users in businesses are often clerks and data-entry personnel; but with the right-sizing of applications to microcomputers, managers are increasingly becoming hands-on computer users. They rely on computers not only for manipulating data but also for receiving company messages and getting up-to-date information almost instantly from any computer with which they can link. With so much data available, managers can use microcomputers to help them analyze the data and make decisions about sales, marketing, new products, clients, and other aspects of their businesses.

Figure 1–27 Source-Data Automation in the Supermarket
Products marked with bar codes are passed over laser readers built into supermarket checkout counters. The computer decodes the bar label for each item and responds by retrieving product description and pricing information.

source-data automation Techniques for automating and speeding the input process by gathering data directly from documents or special instruments when and where an event takes place.

Much of this data is collected in a method called **source-data automation.** In source-data automation, information is entered directly into a computer without the middle step of typing information from documents such as sales slips and time cards. You see source-data automation in action at the supermarket where your purchases are slid over a scanner that reads the bar codes printed on the packages (see Figure 1–27). Source-data automation gets data about an event, in computer-ready form, when and where the event takes place. By eliminating the manual steps, it improves speed and accuracy. In many cases, the information is manipulated and stored so that records are updated and managers can get current reports about the status of the business. The information becomes part of the information system that managers rely on to make decisions. You'll find source-data automation in many business functions, including financial transactions, production management, retail sales, and office operations.

Computer graphics play a big role in businesses today, as they provide a visual picture of the information summarized in graphs and charts. Computer graphics also aid in the design of products, buildings, television and print advertisements, and company brochures.

COMPUTERS IN SCIENCE AND MEDICINE

Scientists use large computers to handle the huge amounts of data needed for monitoring the environment. Many science laboratories use microcomputers as receptacles for the monitoring and data collection during experiments and simulations (see Figure 1–28). In fact, some types of computer programs can reduce the number of monkeys and mice needed in drug testing and disease analysis. Computerized monitoring equipment is also used for studying the weather, earthquakes, and volcanoes. Often, different types of small sensing instruments, such as tiltmeters, strain meters, and seismometers, collect the data near known earthquake and volcano zones. Weather information is collected in a similar manner from instruments placed on ships, buoys, weather balloons, and airplanes. The data is often recorded with microcomputers and then sent on to a mainframe or supercomputer for analysis. The resulting computer models can help estimate when an earthquake is apt to occur, a volcano will erupt, or a thunderstorm will spawn a tornado, but computerized predictions of this nature are still in their infancy (see Figure 1–29). New devices and algorithms will be needed if predictions are to become more accurate.

Although most hospitals use mainframes or minicomputers, microcomputers are gaining in popularity in the medical field (see Figure 1–30). For example, many physicians' offices depend upon microcomputers for recording patient records, billing, and dealing with insurance forms. In addition, some doctors consult computer software especially designed as diagnostic aids. In fact, the software can sometimes be more accurate than physicians in correctly diagnosing heart attacks and other serious problems in which the importance of a symptom could easily be overlooked. Pharmacy databases help pharmacists warn customers of potential problems of mixing certain drugs with other drugs or particular foods. Computers are also used for health maintenance, keeping track of everything from weight loss to blood pressure and heart rates.

Figure 1–28 Using a Laptop in the Field
This scientist is able to enter data while doing research in the rainforest on his laptop computer.

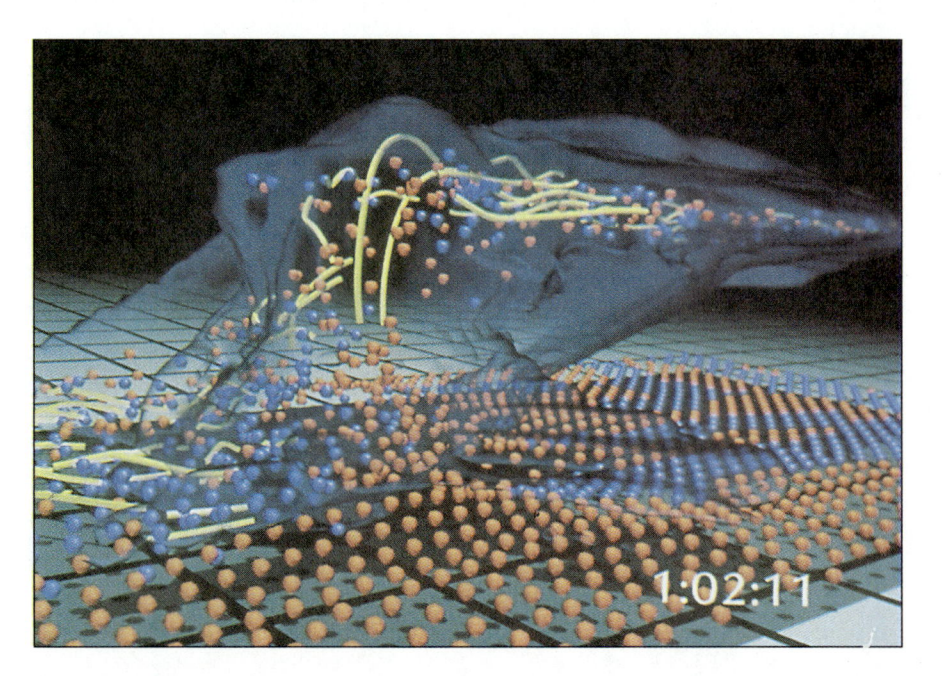

Figure 1–29 Numerically Modeled Storm
Numerical models of thunderstorms can help scientists understand the development of severe weather. These models condense data into graphic forms that are easy to read and monitor for changes.

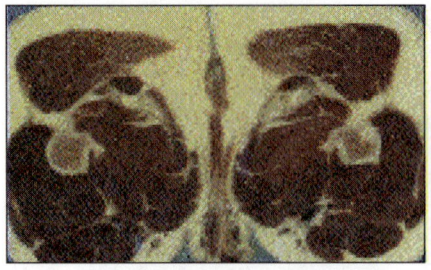

Figure 1–30 Medicine on the Internet
Students can study anatomy via the Internet. The Visible Human Project home page, created by the National Library of Medicine, features these images of a cadaver. The focus of this project is to build a digital library to advance the progress of medicine and public health.

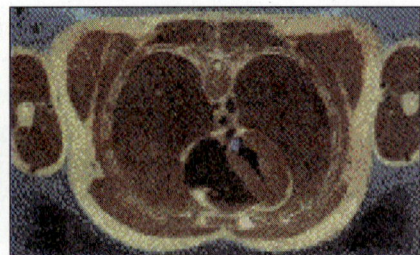

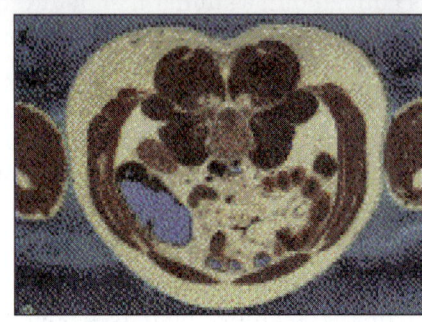

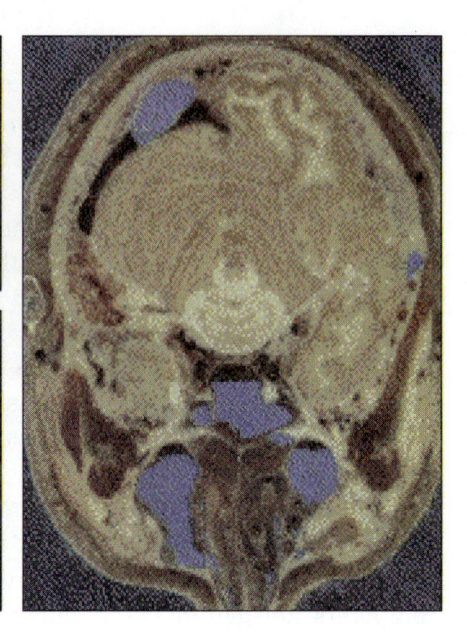

ARTS AND ENTERTAINMENT EMBRACE MICROS

Computer technology has been used in all areas of arts and entertainment. In music, the technology has allowed single instruments to synthesize (or simulate) any number of other instruments and sounds, including trumpets, bass drums, guitars, and even telephones ringing. Computers have been used for a number of years to produce extremely realistic special effects in films, with the first major success being the *Star Wars* trilogy (see Figure 1–31). Although many special effects are achieved only with the capabilities of supercomputers, microcomputers may soon be powerful enough for most jobs, as seen by the work on Disney's *The Lion King*.

Figure 1–31 Special F-X Stretch
The startling special effects in the film *The Mask* achieved frame by frame with a computer in a process called *morphing*.

Window on Computing

Morphing

As you watch heads transform from black to white to Indian to Oriental in Michael Jackson's video *Black or White,* you smile, shake your head, and wonder, "How did they do that?" One image smoothly dissolves into another, becoming the other, and Jackson himself turns into a panther.

The illusion is done through a visual trick called *morphing,* from the word *metamorphosis.* It began with the movie *Willow,* directed by Ron Howard. The filmmaker called Doug Smythe at Industrial Light and Magic, a special effects studio in San Raphael, Calif., for a method that would change the sorceress into different animals. Although the basic technique used in this film was developed by Tom Brigham of the New York Institute of Technology, Smythe laid out grids that simplified the decomposition of an image. Each mosaic piece of one image was matched with a piece in the same location of the other image. Then sample pieces would be transferred from one to the other gradually until the transformation was complete. It took up to two weeks to do one transformation on computer, but on the screen the change occurred in two seconds. The technique used in Jackson's video depended on a computer program to warp one image into the other automatically.

Maybe morphing can be expressed in a few words: What is, is not. An Exxon ad changes an automobile into a tiger, using a set of sequences filmed separately and then morphed and superimposed over each other. In the film *Terminator 2,* morphing techniques were used to change a chrome blob into a metal creature, and then into the actor Robert Patrick, emerging from a fiery blaze. In this particular sequence, the metal man needed to move like the actor and also display the effects of smoke, shadows, and reflections. In the movie *The Mask,* a real person was morphed with cartoon effects to create an entirely new character. Even a kid can morph at home, for there is a moderately inexpensive morphing software package available for Macintosh computers. These examples are legitimate entertainment uses of morphing; but as the technique becomes less expensive and accessible to more people, its applications have greater potential for misuse. We know it is not really possible for an automobile to turn into a tiger or for Michael Jackson to turn into a panther, but could a piece of footage from a news broadcast be changed to alter the event as it really happened? What is, is not.

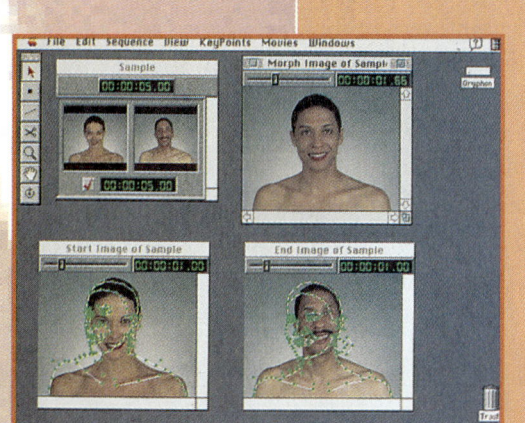

In addition, microcomputers are used widely for controlling lighting systems and stage sets in theaters for musical, opera, and ballet performances.

In sports, computers help keep track of ticket sales and scores. Athletes and trainers use computer graphics systems to predict the most likely moves of opposing teams, plan strategy, and analyze performance. In baseball, computers determine batting averages, runs batted in, and earned-run averages for pitchers. They also examine hitting probabilities between combinations of batters and pitchers. Golfers can use computers to analyze their swings and help them buy clubs. Players in football, tennis, and golf are ranked by computers. In football, computer use by coaches generated enough controversy that the National Football League finally established rules that forbid the use of computers either in coaching booths or on the sidelines during games.

It may seem unlikely that more powerful microcomputers are possible and further uses will be found for them. But if we look back at the skepticism with which the first microcomputers were greeted and realize that people in the 1970s were probably thinking the same thing, can there be any doubt that more will come?

►Summary Points

- A computer is a machine that can help people do many jobs. It is part of an information system that provides users with current information that increases knowledge and reduces uncertainty.
- The components of an information system are people, procedures, data, hardware, and software. The people that use the system are called users, and the procedures they follow are often outlined in manuals. Data refers to raw facts that, when organized and processed, become information that can be used in making intelligent decisions. Data follows a fairly well-defined path through the information system that consists of inputs (data), processes (manipulations), outputs (information), and feedback. The physical equipment that handles the input, processing, and output is called hardware. Software is the programs, or sets of instructions, that enable the hardware to do its work.
- The five components of information form a synergistic relationship in which the combined effort of all the parts is greater than the sum of the efforts of each part operating independently. Computers facilitate synergism because they are fast, their circuits are reliable, and they can manage huge amounts of information with ease.
- The types of computers, from smallest to largest, are microcomputers, minicomputers, mainframes, and supercomputers. The increasing power of microcomputers, combined with networks,

- has led many businesses and organizations to move applications from mainframes and minicomputers to microcomputers, a switch that is termed right-sizing, or downsizing.
- People have always looked for efficient ways to handle data. Among the early pioneers of mechanical computing machines are Charles Babbage, who developed an analytical engine amazingly like a computer, and Herman Hollerith, who designed a tabulating machine that handled census data.
- World War II increased pressure to develop better calculating machines for figuring artillery trajectories and code-breaking. Among the machines in development during the war was the ENIAC, the first all-purpose digital electronic computer.
- ENIAC needed to be programmed manually, which involved setting switches and connecting wires. A proposal to store both instructions and data in a computer's memory (the stored-program concept) was embodied in a machine called EDVAC.
- The advances in computer technology are grouped into four generations. First-generation computers used vacuum tubes for their circuits. Second-generation computers were characterized by transistors and by new memory and storage methods that led to real-time applications such as simulations, air traffic control, and computerized reservation systems. The development of the integrated circuit led to the third computer generation.
- Fourth-generation computers are based on large-scale integration and very-large-scale integration to cram more circuits on chips. They rely on silicon chips for memory. The development of the microprocessor led to the invention of microcomputers, also called personal computers.
- The success of microcomputers resulted in a flood of software. Business users first realized the importance of microcomputers when the first spreadsheet program, *VisiCalc,* was released.
- Microcomputers can be used for a variety of functions in schools, businesses, science laboratories, medical offices, and hospitals: filing, communication, instruction, simulation, training, graphics, monitoring, evaluations, and decision making.

►Review Questions

1. What is an information system? What are six qualities of good information? Describe each quality in terms of a real or hypothetical situation.
2. What are the components of a computerized information system? Define each. How does the term *synergism* describe the action of these components?

3. What is a system? Of what does it consist? Explain the importance of the adage *garbage in, garbage out* to the data traveling through an information system.
4. Why do people and organizations use computers in an information system? What four basic types of computers are available for use? How do they differ?
5. Explain the meaning of the term *right-sizing* in relation to information systems.
6. Many developments in technology occurred when people needed to solve a problem. Show how this was true for each of these people: Pascal, Babbage, and Hollerith.
7. Why is the Jacquard loom mentioned in a history of computer development?
8. State the significance of each of the following: the ENIAC, the EDVAC, and the UNIVAC.
9. Name two major characteristics of each computer generation.
10. What one development led to the invention of microcomputers? Of what significance was the first TRS-80? What impact did the program *VisiCalc* have when it was introduced in 1979?
11. How can a computer be used as a monitor in the home environment, science, medicine, and other areas?
12. How are computer graphics used in various workplaces?

▶Activities and Research

1. Look in the *Readers' Guide to Periodical Literature* from the 1940s, 1950s, and 1960s for articles about computers. Find and make copies of one or two articles to discuss in class.
2. Find out about Allan Turing and his contribution to computers.
3. Investigate computerization in business, preferably in an office or store in your town, but possibly through magazine articles. Find out whether manual methods exist along with computerization and how recently computerization was implemented. Think about first-generation computers. Why might people in business have liked the idea of computers? Why might they have delayed buying one?
4. Find out how computers in general and personal computers specifically are used in a field of work in which you are interested.

CHAPTER 2

COMPUTER FUNDAMENTALS: THE INSIDE STORY

OUTLINE

Learning Objectives
Introduction
Data Representation
    Binary Representation
    Computer Codes
The System Unit
    The CPU: The Microprocessor
    Memory
    Highlight: The Future Is Here: It's in the Cards!
    How the Computer Works
    Window on Computing: "RISC-y" Business
    Connecting Up
    Concept Summary: Components of the System Unit
    Profile: Grace Murray Hopper: A Lifetime of Computer Achievement
Input Hardware
    Interactive Input
    Direct Input
Output Methods
    Display Outputs
    Printers for Document Outputs
    Voice Output
Storage
    Magnetic Disks
    CD-ROMs and Other Optical Storage
    Magnetic Tape
Summary Points
Review Questions
Activities and Research

LEARNING OBJECTIVES

After reading this chapter, you should be able to:

- Explain the basic relationship between the binary number system and digital computers
- List the parts of the central processing unit and their functions.
- Describe the kinds of memory.
- Describe the various types of input and output equipment.
- Identify the types of storage and the characteristics of each.

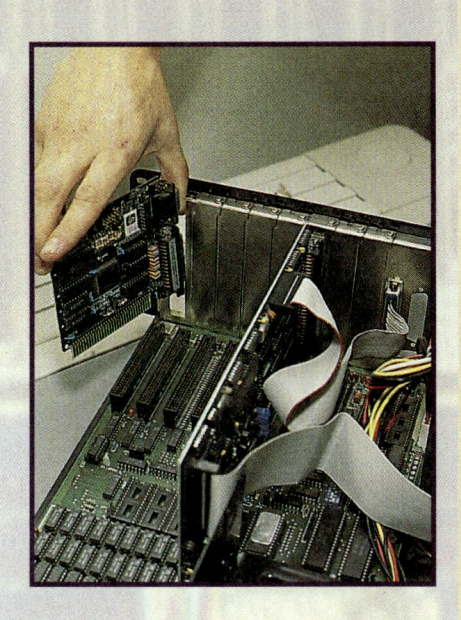

user friendly A descriptive term for hardware and software features that promote ease of use and lessen frustration for computer users.

INTRODUCTION

Many people flinch at the sight of a computer keyboard, resist programming their VCRs, and buy point-and-shoot cameras, just to avoid dealing with what they perceive as unfriendly technology. Fortunately, computer technology is becoming more **user friendly;** thus, families are buying more microcomputers, and one-time computerphobes end up parading phrases like *hard disk drive* and *8MB of RAM*. Indeed, knowing computer vocabulary and understanding how computers work helps a person to use a computer more effectively and to make more informed choices when buying a personal computer system. This chapter explains some of the terminology and concepts that should be helpful for evaluating computer hardware.

►Data Representation

Many times a day, you take advantage of the on and off states of electricity: You turn a light switch on or off, turn the alarm on or off, or turn the television on or off. The object reacts to changes in its circuit: It does its job when current is flowing and rests when current is not flowing. Similarly, a computer can pull data from storage, accept it from a keyboard, act on it, show it on a screen, and store it again—simply through changes in its circuits' on/off (conducting/nonconducting, yes/no) states. The instructions that direct the computer to do these jobs, or any other job, must be translated into a code that represents these two states. The **binary number system** is ideal for this purpose because it consists of only two digits, 0 (zero) for off and 1 (one) for on. Because computers count and keep track of these digits (or states), they are technically called **digital computers,** and the data they can interpret is said to be in "digital form."

Binary Representation

It is easy to understand how digits can be used for calculations (see Figure 2–1). If the computer can interpret items only in digital form, however, how does it handle alphabetic input? As you already know, codes are commonly used for representing data. For example, you can write two-letter codes for the states—FL for Florida and ME for Maine—and the post office uses zip codes for sorting mail. Similarly, combinations of the two digits 0 and 1, called **bits** (short for BInary digiTs), can represent data in a form the computer can use. Thus, it is possible to encode 26 lowercase letters, 26 capital letters, 10 digits (0 through 9), and all of the characters, such as *, #, and @—plus the codes for *Delete, Enter, Tab, Shift, Space,* and the other special keys on the computer keyboard. Here's how, in a simplistic description:

binary number system The number systme that uses the digits 0 and 1; often called base 2 as opposed to base 10, which is the decimal system with which we are familiar.

digital computer A computer that operates on discrete, or individually distinct, data.

bit Short for "binary digit"; an individual 1 or 0 value used in computer coding.

Figure 2–1 Binary Numbers
Each position in a binary number has a twos value, just as each place in a decimal number has a tens value.

Decimal System (base 10)

Digits: 0, 1, 2, 3, 4, 5, 6, 7, 8, 9
Place values: ones, tens, hundreds, thousands, ten thousands, and so on
        14 means 1 ten and 4 ones
        181 means 1 hundred, 8 tens, and 1 one
        Thus 2 + 2 = 4 means 2 ones plus 2 ones equal 4 ones.

Binary System (base 2)

Digits: 0, 1
Place values: ones, twos, fours, eights, sixteens, thirty-twos, and so on

        1110 means 0 ones, 1 two, 1 four, and 1 eight
        10101 means 1 one, 0 twos, 1 four, 0 eights, and 1 sixteen
        Thus 0010 + 0010 = 0100 means 1 two plus 1 two equal four.

In a one-bit (or one-place) code, there are only two possible choices—0 and 1; thus, only two items can be encoded (see Figure 2–2). In the two-bit code, there are four choices: two in the left position and two in the right, or $2 \times 2 = 4$ (or 2 to the second power—2^2). The codes would be 00, 01, 10, and 11. A three-bit code has two choices in each position and thus a total of eight choices: $2 \times 2 \times 2 = 8$ (or 2 to the third power—2^3). The codes would be 000, 001, 010, 011, 100, 101, 110, and 111. With four positions, there are 16 possible codes: $2 \times 2 \times 2 \times 2 = 16$ (or 2 to the fourth power—2^4). The more positions, the more possible items can be coded: Five bits provide 32 codes, the number of codes needed to encode the 26 letters of the alphabet, with six codes left over. And so on. (The general expression for these progressions of 2 is 2^n.)

In computer coding, data are often coded in blocks of eight bits. Each block is called a **byte.** An eight-bit byte allows for 256 codes, more than enough to write the uppercase and lowercase letters, 10 digits, special characters, and commands such as *Space Bar* and *Enter*. Each time a key is struck on the keyboard, the code for that key is generated and convert-

byte A series of bits, usually eight, used to encode a letter, number, or special character and operated on as a unit.

One-Bit Code (Two Possible Codes)

In many communities, you can signal with your porch light whether it is okay for trick-or-treaters to stop at your house for Halloween goodies: If current is not flowing in the lamp (0), then you are signaling that you will not answer the bell. If current is flowing in the lamp (1), then trick-or-treaters know they are welcome:

off
0
(Do not ring the bell.)

on
1
(Do ring the bell.)

Two-Bit code (Four Possible Codes)

A friend drives by your house every evening on the way home from work. The two of you work out a code that lets her know when it's okay for her to stop. The system codes four options, thus, in order to have enough codes, you can use two bits instead of one. With four possible choices, you would need two lights (the garage light and the front door light, for example):

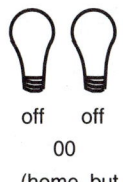

off off
00
(home, but gone to bed)

off on
01
(home, but busy)

on off
10
(gone away)

on on
11
(home and free to visit)

Figure 2–2 One- and Two-Bit Codes
The one-bit code offers two choices, 0 and 1. With two bits, there are four choices.

ed to a binary number, which is input to the computer. For example, one coding system encodes an uppercase letter *B* this way:

0100   0010

When you enter a *B* via a computer keyboard, the computer knows that you have struck the *B* key along with the *Shift* key instead of, say, a *g* key. The computer then sends the code on to the monitor, where you see the *B* as output on the screen. The computer does not understand the symbol *B*, but it can interpret the digital code. On a particular system, the same code always stands for the *B*.

The sizes of computer memory and storage are described in large groupings of bytes. A kilobyte, abbreviated K or KB, is equal to 1,024 bytes (or 2^{10} bytes). It is generally rounded to mean 1,000 bytes; thus, a 640KB memory can hold over 640,000 characters of information. Three other units are the megabyte, the gigabyte, and the terabyte (see Figure 2–3).

Today's microcomputers handle more than one byte at a time. The term **word** describes the common unit a computer can handle. A word may be 16, 32, or 64 bits in length. A general rule is: The more bits a computer can handle at once, the faster the speed of the computer.

COMPUTER CODES

The majority of computers use one of two common coding systems, ASCII or EBCDIC, for internal processing and for exchange of information with other computers. Within these codes, each character of data is assigned a specific code number.

ASCII (*Ask-ee*) stands for American Standard Code for Information Interchange, which is the most widely used binary code for microcomputers. The current version is an 8-bit form called ASCII-8 or extended ASCII (see Figure 2–4). EBCDIC (*EB-see-dik*) stands for Extended Binary Coded Decimal Interchange Code. It was developed by IBM for large computers and is in widespread use, partly because it is the standard for IBM computers.

word A group of bits, considered as a unit, that a computer can handle at once.

Figure 2–3 Units of Bytes
These terms typically describe the memory capacity of a computer and the storage capacity of a storage medium.

Unit	Abbreviation	Meaning
kilobyte	K or KB	1,024 bytes (2^{10}) (approximately 1,000 bytes)
megabyte	MB	1,048,576 bytes (2^{20}) (roughly 1 million bytes)
gigabyte	GB	1,073,741,824 bytes (2^{30}) (roughly 1 billion bytes)
terabyte	TB	1,009,511,627,776 bytes (2^{40}) (roughly 1 trillion bytes)

Character	ASCII	Character	ASCII	Character	ASCII
0	0011 0000	A	0100 0001	N	0100 1110
1	0011 0001	B	0100 0010	O	0100 1111
2	0011 0010	C	0100 0011	P	0101 0000
3	0011 0011	D	0100 0100	Q	0101 0001
4	0011 0100	E	0100 0101	R	0101 0010
5	0011 0101	F	0100 0110	S	0101 0011
6	0011 0110	G	0100 0111	T	0101 0100
7	0011 0111	H	0100 1000	U	0101 0101
8	0011 1000	I	0100 1001	V	0101 0110
9	0011 1001	J	0100 1010	W	0101 0111
		K	0100 1011	X	0101 1000
		L	0100 1100	Y	0101 1001
		M	0100 1101	Z	0101 1010

Figure 2–4 The ASCII Code
ASCII is the code commonly used with microcomputers.

Both coding systems provide options for computer error-checking during data transmission and storage. These checking operations detect and correct all errors immediately, or reject computation results and abort processing. Such safeguards are necessary because just as static can mar radio transmission, electronic interference can impair data transmission in computers, causing bits to be changed or lost.

Enough on data representation. Let's look inside the computer, where the work is done.

▶ THE SYSTEM UNIT

The portion of a computer in which processing takes place is called the **system unit.** It is housed in a plastic or metal casing that, in most cases, can easily be opened so that parts can be added or replaced. The system unit contains the **motherboard,** which is a flat board that holds the microprocessor, memory, and other electronic components. (The motherboard is sometimes called the *system board* or the *planar board*.)

The main components on the system board are chips (or microchips) made of semiconductor material, a material that is neither a good conductor of electricity (like copper) nor a good insulator (like rubber). The most common semiconductor material is silicon. A typical chip is less than a fourth of an inch square and holds millions of electronic components. It is housed in a dirt-free plastic or ceramic carrier package with a set of tiny legs or pins that plug into the board (see Figure 2–5).

THE CPU: THE MICROPROCESSOR

The most important chip on the motherboard is the **microprocessor,** the CPU of a microcomputer (see Figure 2–6). It is a complex collection of

system unit The part of a microcomputer that contains the CPU and memory.

motherboard The main circuit board of a microcomputer.

microprocessor The CPU of a microcomputer; contained on a single silicon chip.

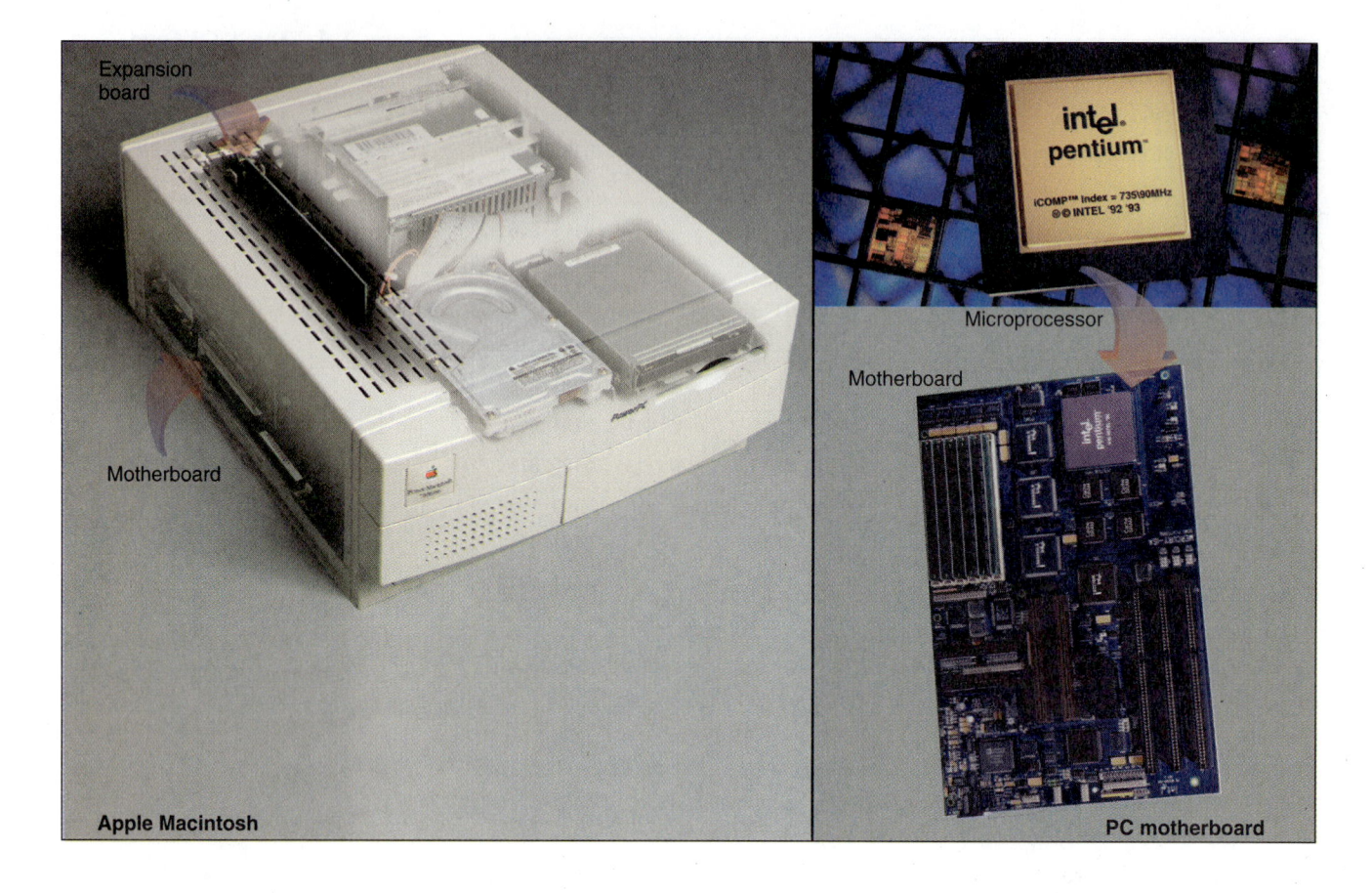

Figure 2–5 The Motherboard
The motherboard holds the microprocessor (such as this Intel Pentium chip), as well as memory chips, other circuit boards, the power supply, and a cooling unit for the computer. It is housed in a plastic case, and the whole unit is often called the *system unit.*

control unit The part of the microprocessor that controls operations of the CPU and coordinates the functions of other devices within a computer system.

electronic circuits that directs operation of and communication between all devices that make up a computer system. Its two major parts are the control unit and the arithmetic/logic unit (ALU). Each part does its own jobs, but the parts must work together to process data.

THE CONTROL UNIT

The **control unit,** as its name implies, maintains order and controls the activity that occurs in the CPU. It directs communication and coordinates operations between the microprocessor and other devices in a computer system. Specific examples of its tasks include the following:

- Directing the sequence of computer operations
- Interpreting instructions contained within programs
- Producing signals that act as commands to carry out the instructions
- Communicating with and directing operations of input equipment
- Finding data items to be processed
- Keeping track of instructions already executed
- Directing the results of processing to storage or output devices

Model or Name	Clock Speed	Use
Intel 80486	33, 50, 66 MHz and higher	IBM computers and compatibles
Intel Pentium	60 MHz and higher	IBM computers and compatibles
Motorola 68040	33, 40 MHz and higher	Macintosh computers
PowerPC 601	60, 66, 80 MHz and higher	Macintosh computers

Figure 2–6 Microprocessor Chip The microprocessor can be identified in a number of ways, including model number, clock speed, and bit architecture. Here are a number of common microprocessors.

Items being processed immediately typically are held in high-speed temporary "loading zones" called **registers,** which are located on the microprocessor. Registers can receive data, hold it, and transfer it rapidly, as directed by the control unit. Some registers accumulate the results of calculations, some keep track of where a particular piece of data or instruction is located, and some hold data temporarily on the way to and from memory.

register The special high-speed storage area on the microprocessor that receives data, holds it, and transfers it immediately during processing.

THE ARITHMETIC/LOGIC UNIT

The **arithmetic/logic unit (ALU)** performs calculations through arithmetic operations, and determines if a number is negative, positive, or zero. It also conducts logic operations that compare values for equality—for example, equal to, greater than, and less than (see Figure 2–7). The computer often uses the results of these comparisons to determine which program segments will be executed.

arithmetic/logic unit (ALU) The portion of a computer processor that carries out computations and the comparison functions that make up logical operations of a computer.

MEMORY

Memory holds the program instructions and data needed for processing or waiting to be output or stored. In microcomputers, it is located on chips plugged into the motherboard. Memory chips are designed to store data in locations called *bit cells,* which are capable of being either "on"

memory Internal physical storage that consists of chips and holds instructions and data needed for processing; sometimes referred to as *main memory, primary storage,* or *internal storage.*

Figure 2–7 Logical Comparisons
These operations compare two values, with results that often determine the next action taken.

> A = A (A is equal to A.)
>
> 236 > 214 (236 is greater than 214.)
>
> R < W (R is less than W.)

or "off." (Because of the way data is coded, a bit cell holds information whether it is "on" or "off." An "on" state is represented by a 1, and an "off" state by a 0.)

A vital characteristic of memory is high-speed operation, but different types of memory have different speeds. The two general types of memory are random-access and read-only.

RANDOM-ACCESS MEMORY

random-access memory (RAM) The array of microchips used to build the storage area within a computer's CPU. Data items and program segments can be recorded and retrieved on RAM devices.

Random-access memory, or **RAM** (rhymes with *clam)*, is the kind of memory we usually refer to when we speak of computer memory. It is the most widely used type, and consists of rows of chips with locations established in tables maintained by the control unit (see Figure 2–8). Instructions and data used during processing must be held in RAM before they can be used.

As the name suggests, items stored in RAM can be gotten (accessed) both easily and in any order (randomly) rather than in some sequence. To get data or use instructions, the CPU must be able to find them in memory. Each item in memory is put in a special place, and each place has an address, a built-in and unique number that identifies its location. This address helps the computer find the data just as a street address helps a taxi driver find someone's house or as a number on a post office box marks the proper place for mail. (Memory addresses are also given in terms of binary values; thus, they are a third way that computers interpret binary values—the first and second being numeric data and alphanumeric data, as described previously.)

Once an item is stored at a certain location, it can be read over and over again without being destroyed. That is, the same instructions can be read repeatedly to process many different pieces of data, and the same data can be read over and over in a single program. New data can be written into RAM, however, while any old data in the same locations is erased. This capability makes RAM the working area of the computer. For example, parts of the word-processing program you are using to write a report are stored in RAM, where they can be accessed by the computer as needed. The words you type and the changes you make are sent to RAM.

Figure 2–8 RAM Chip
The RAM chip is put into a carrier, which is then mounted onto a printed circuit board with other chips.

RAM relies on electric current for all its operations; however: If the power is turned off or interrupted, RAM quickly empties itself of all your hard work. Thus, we say RAM is volatile, or nonpermanent.

A special high-speed memory called **cache** (pronounced *cash*) **memory** holds the most frequently used instructions and data. A program looks ahead and tries to anticipate what instructions and data must be accessed often, and places these in cache memory for faster access by the CPU (see Figure 2–9).

Memory is measured in kilobytes and megabytes. Common amounts in today's microcomputers are 4, 8, and 16MB as well as a 256KB memory cache. Microprocessor chips include a small amount of cache memory, too, typically 8K. Knowing the amount of RAM in a computer is important because some software might require more memory than a particular microcomputer offers.

cache memory A type of high-speed RAM usually built onto the microprocessor, used to help speed the execution of a program. Also known as a *high-speed buffer* or *RAM cache*.

Read-Only Memory

Read-only memory, or **ROM** (rhymes with *mom)*, typically holds programs. These programs are manufactured, or "hard-wired," in place on the ROM chips. For example, a microcomputer has a built-in ROM chip (sometimes called *ROM BIOS,* for ROM basic input/output system) that stores critical programs such as the one that starts up, or "boots," the com-

read-only memory (ROM) The form of memory that holds items that can be read but that cannot be erased or altered by normal input methods.

Data Storage Area in a Computer	Floppy disk or magnetic tape	Hard disk	RAM memory	Cache memory	Register
Storage Area for Pocket Change to Be Used to Purchase a Vending Machine Snack	Your Piggy Bank: The coins are not readily available; you must load them into your wallet or purse. Access is slow.	Your wallet or coin purse: The coins are available, but you must open your coin purse to count them out, even though you have the coins with you.	Your pocket: The exact change is loose and readily available, but you must still take the time to reach in and remove the coins. Access is fast.	Your hand: The coins are ready for immediate processing—that is, for putting in the slot, but you must still move the coins up to the slot. Access is rapid.	Your hand poised at the slot: The coins are being sent directly to processing, that is they are falling into the machine. Access is immediate.

Figure 2–9 A Trip down Memory Lane
The varying speeds and uses of memory can be compared with how you store and use loose change for purchasing a vending machine snack.

Figure 2–10 Types of ROM
To meet the needs of clients, vendors have developed versions of ROM chips that can be customized.

Type of ROM	Abbreviation	Capability
Read-only memory	ROM	Can be read but not written to
Programmable read-only memory	PROM	Can be programmed by the manufacturer or a third party especially for the client; but once programmed, cannot be changed.
Electrically erasable programmable ROM	EEPROM	Can be erased by exposing it to an electrical charge. (A special type of EEPROM called flash memory can be rewritten while inside the computer. This is commonly in the form of a PC card that conforms to the PCMCIA standard.)

puter. ROM is "slower" than RAM memory, and as a result, items in ROM are transferred to RAM when needed for fast processing.

Items held in ROM can be read, but they cannot be changed or erased by normal input methods. New items cannot be written into ROM. The only way to change items in most forms of ROM is to change the actual circuits (see Figure 2–10). Thus, ROM is nonvolatile in comparison with RAM. By their very nature, ROM chips protect valuable programs and data, for they cannot be copied easily. Thus, software is sometimes built into ROM, and is called *firmware.* Building instructions into ROM makes the distinction between hardware and software somewhat fuzzy.

instruction set Rudimentary instructions built into the microprocessor for performing arithmetic, comparison, and storage and retrieval operations.

HOW THE COMPUTER WORKS

Once the data has been input, it is processed. Processing occurs in the CPU according to a predetermined **instruction set,** a basic set of instruc-

Window on Computing

The Future Is Here: It's in the Cards!

We don't recommend sticking a credit card into your disk-drive slot, but you may be using a similar "card" as memory, a modem, a disk drive, or other device on your notebook computer. This card is the *personal computer memory card,* or PC card. It is similar to a credit card, with pins in one end for plugging into a computer.

The card was originally conceived as a flash-memory device, in which the storage consists of special semiconductor memory that retains data even when the computer's power is turned off. A computer system treats a flash-memory card as if it were RAM memory. That is, programs on PC cards are not transferred to the computer's RAM but instead are executed directly from the card. The cards can also be configured with software, disk drives, modems, or other devices.

Although they are available for any style of personal computer, PC cards are especially suited to notebook computers, for several reasons. Excepting the miniature hard disk drives, they have no moving parts to fail. They are lightweight and rugged enough to withstand being dropped.

Standards, of course, help ensure that any card can be used in any slot. The standard for PC cards is PCMCIA, set by the Personal Computer Memory Card International Association. This organization sets the specifications for both the cards and the bus, or slot. There are three types of PCMCIA cards. All three are the length and width of a credit card and have a 68-pin interface. Type I cards are the thinnest at 3.3 millimeters and usually are reserved for use as RAM and various forms of ROM. The thicker Type II cards (5.0 mm) are used for input/output devices such as modems, fax modems, combination modems, and local area network (LAN) adapter cards. Type III cards, the thickest at 10.5 mm, can hold miniature hard disk drives or radio communication hardware. Type II cards and slots are the most commonly used. Type III slots can accept Type II and Type I cards, and Type II slots can accept Type I cards, but larger cards cannot be used in smaller slots. Although the current cost of a memory card will flatten your wallet considerably, the standards should help to bring down the costs, and so increasing numbers of computers will probably be equipped with the cards.

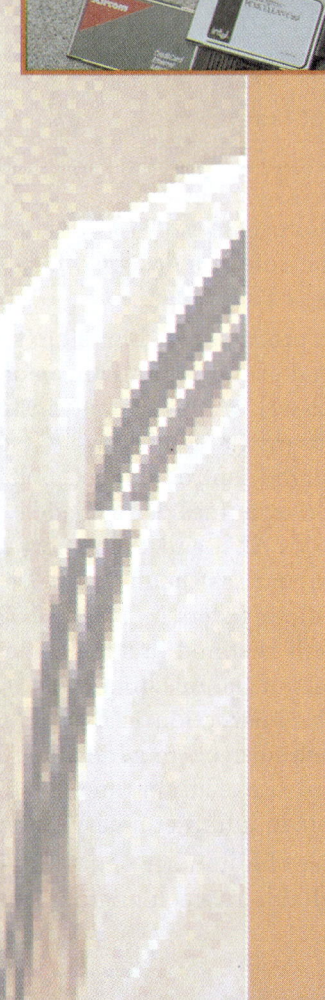

Figure 2–11 The Machine Cycle
The machine cycle works in two parts, instruction time and execution time.

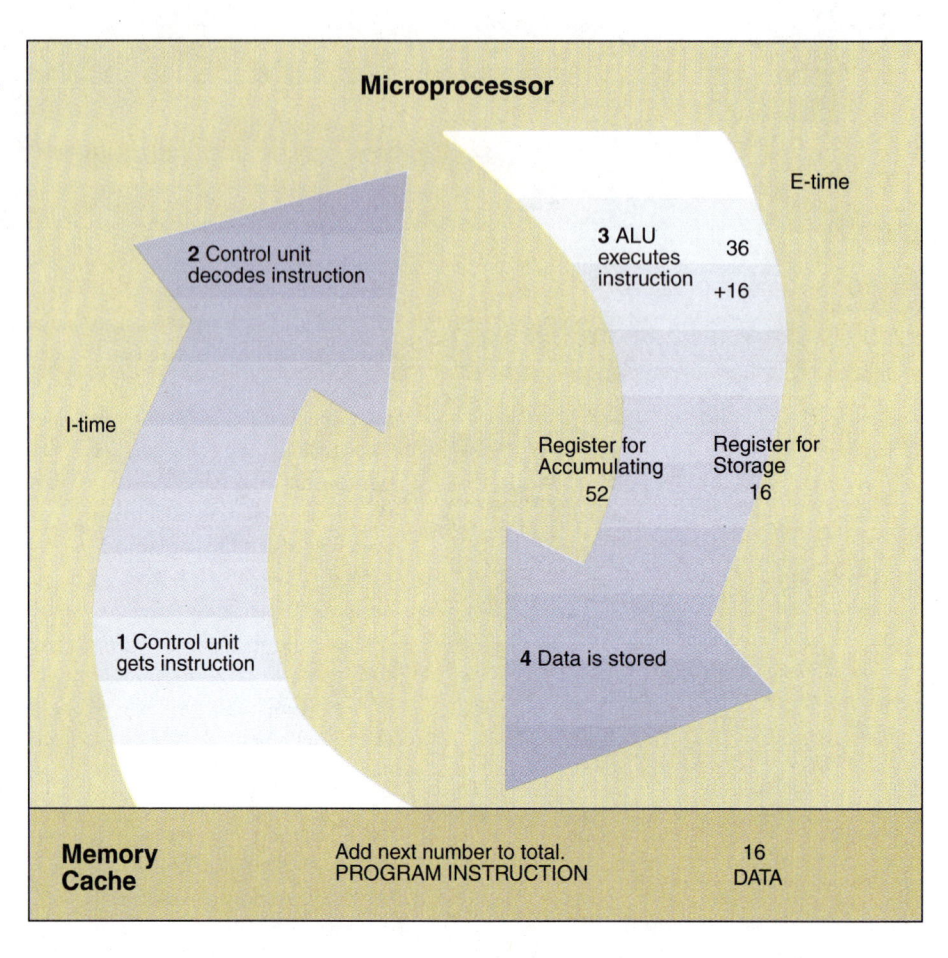

Microprocessor

- I-time
  - **2** Control unit decodes instruction
  - **1** Control unit gets instruction
- E-time
  - **3** ALU executes instruction 36 +16
  - Register for Accumulating 52
  - Register for Storage 16
  - **4** Data is stored

Memory Cache Add next number to total. PROGRAM INSTRUCTION 16 DATA

machine cycle The time period in which the CPU gets, interprets, and executes one computer instruction.

tions that varies among different microprocessors. (This variation is one reason Macintosh computers cannot run software designed for IBM-type computers without special additional software.)

As described earlier in this chapter, processing is limited to two basic functions, addition and comparisons, and occurs digitally in an operation called the **machine cycle** (see Figure 2–11). After data and instructions are moved to memory, the CPU waits for instructions on what to do next. Upon the command to begin processing, the control unit gets one instruction from memory and decodes it (or examines it to decide what it means). It sends electronic signals to the ALU and to memory that the instruction should be carried out. Data and instructions may be moved into a memory cache and, from there, into registers in the ALU. The ALU then manipulates the data, and the result is stored in a register and may be transferred back to memory. The part of the machine cycle in which the control unit gets and interprets the instruction is called *I-time,* or instruction time, and the part of the machine cycle in which the ALU acts and the result is stored is called *E-time,* or execution time. (Instructions are the fourth way in which computers can interpret binary values.)

A single machine cycle may consist of a number of smaller instructions that must be synchronized with all others. Each microprocessor has

Window on Computing

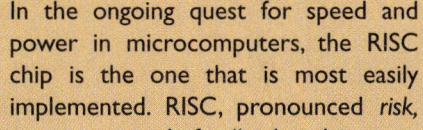

"RISC-y" Business

In the ongoing quest for speed and power in microcomputers, the RISC chip is the one that is most easily implemented. RISC, pronounced *risk*, stands for "reduced instruction set computer." It came about because the instruction set (set of basic instructions that a computer uses for doing any job) kept getting larger and larger. Instruction sets approaching 300 instructions can take up quite a lot of space, leaving less room for other components and slowing down processing speeds. In addition, many instructions are rarely used and can be implemented through a combination of other instructions.

The RISC set of instructions uses a very simple and small instruction set. It's like the stripped-down simplicity of a racing bicycle as compared with a 12-speed mountain bike: The stripped-down instruction set makes it possible for the microprocessor to zip through processing. Of course, two other technological features help speed up RISC computers: There are more registers, and RISC computers can move more than one instruction from memory into special registers where they can be accessed quickly. The Power PC chip by Motorola is an example of a RISC chip.

Experts disagree about the value of RISC vs. conventional architecture, noting that conventional microprocessors are becoming fast and cheap enough to match the RISC machines. In addition, the designers of RISC architecture are increasing the number of instructions present on the microprocessor, thus decreasing the margin of difference between the two.

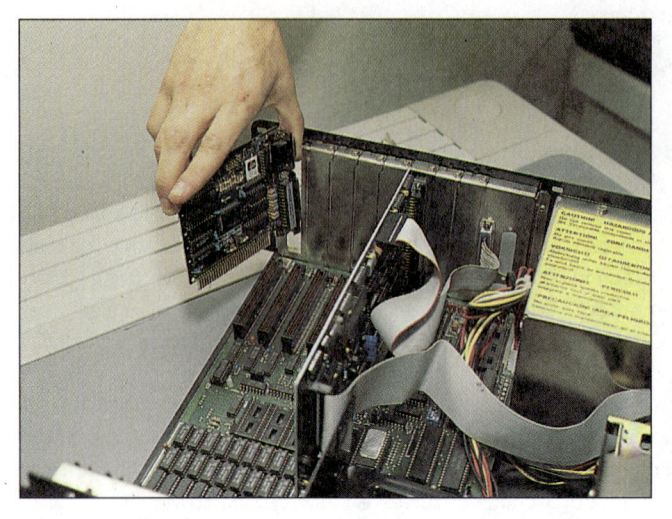

Figure 2-12
Inserting an Expansion Board
An expansion board with additional memory is inserted into a slot on the motherboard.

clock A timing device that generates the basic fixed-rate pulses by which the operations of a computer are synchronized.

megahertz (MHz) A unit of electrical frequency equal to 1 million cycles per second; measures a CPU's clock speed.

expansion board A board that holds chips and circuit paths and that can be inserted into a slot on the motherboard of a computer for the purpose of adding some feature to the computer, such as more memory or greater graphics capability. Also called *circuit board* and *interface board*.

slot An opening and connector inside a computer that allows for the installation of a circuit board for additional memory or some other capability that enhances the performance of the computer.

bus A set of wires, real or "printed," through which data is sent from one part of the computer to another.

an internal **clock** that regulates this synchronization with fixed-rate pulses. The fewer clock cycles per instruction, the better. Clock speed is expressed in **megahertz** (MHz). One megahertz is equal to 1 million ticks per second. Clock speed for microcomputers ranges from 8 MHz on early, very slow machines to over 100 MHz on today's speedy microprocessors (refer back to Figure 2–6).

CONNECTING UP

As we mentioned earlier, most system units can be opened up for the placement of additional components. Components commonly added to the motherboard are memory chips and coprocessors that help speed up computer operations by taking over special operations, such as calculating equations and generating graphics. These chips often are plugged directly into the motherboard. Some chips reside on separate **expansion boards** (also called *circuit boards* or *interface boards)* that are placed into special **slots** on the motherboard. There are circuit boards for additional memory; boards for governing peripherals such as disk drives, monitors, and mice; boards for sound; and boards for just about any other capability you might wish to add to your system—limited, of course, by the number of available slots (see Figure 2–12).

All of these components in the system unit must be linked to the other components and to other parts of the computer system. One type of connection is the **bus,** which is simply a channel or path for transferring data and electrical signals. If you think of a highway with multiple lanes on which cars travel in parallel, all either coming or going, you will have a picture of how a bus handles data. The number of lanes in a bus is the word size. For example, a microprocessor with an internal bus handling 16 or 32 bits at a time is called a 16-bit or a 32-bit microprocessor. The bus linking the microprocessor with memory is the data bus, and it may handle 32 or 64 bits at a time. Expansion boards, as described earlier, plug

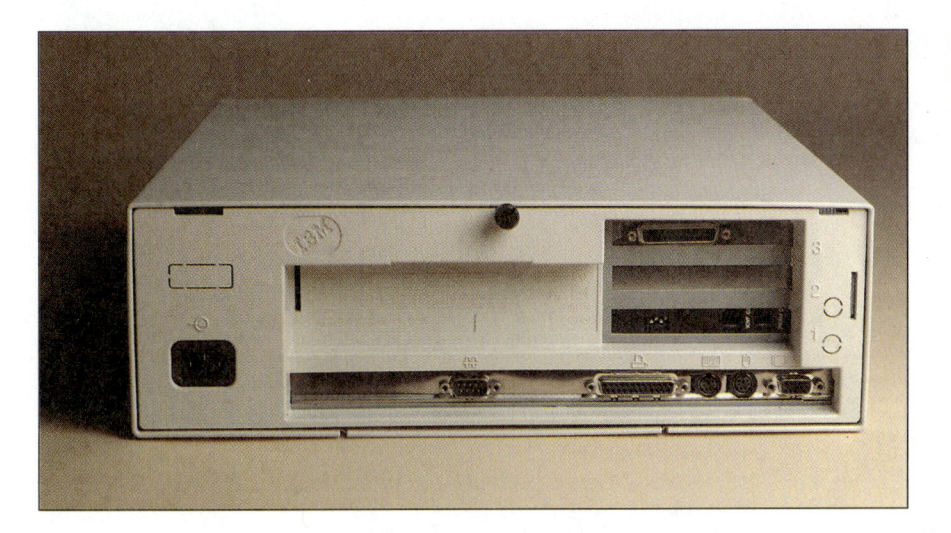

Figure 2–13 Ports
Printers and other devices can be attached to the computer through ports.

into slots that are connected to the CPU via the expansion bus. If you look at the motherboard or an expansion board, you will see that bus lines are usually fused onto the boards through printing or electroplating, which is why these boards are often called *printed-circuit boards*.

Another type of connection is the **port**. A port is a socket on the outside of the computer or on a circuit board into which other devices such as monitors and printers are plugged (see Figure 2–13). Parallel ports transfer several bits simultaneously and are commonly used to connect printers to the computer. Serial ports handle bits one by one in single file and commonly connect mice and communication equipment to the computer.

Each piece of equipment—keyboard, mouse, printer, or monitor—must not only be linked to the computer by a connection or combination of connections, but also have its own **controller.** A controller is usually a chip that is plugged into the motherboard or comes on its own printed-circuit board. It governs the transfer of data from the computer to the device, and vice versa. Each device, in addition, has its own **driver,** which is actually software that acts as a go-between for the device and the program. A driver is needed because each device has its own special commands whereas each program uses generic commands. The driver receives the generic commands from the program and translates them into the specialized commands for the device, and vice versa. Many drivers—for example, the keyboard driver—come with the system software that is already installed in a computer. Drivers for equipment that you add may need to be activated through a set of software commands.

port An interface on a computer where a printer or some other device can be plugged in.

controller The component that regulates the operation of a peripheral device; controls the transfer of data from the computer to a peripheral device.

driver The program that controls a device.

▶ INPUT HARDWARE

In order to use the information and applications of a computer system, you need some way to input commands and text to the system. (*Commands* are

Profile

Grace Murray Hopper: A Lifetime of Computer Achievement

Even at age 84, Rear Adm. Grace Murray Hopper served as a senior consultant at Digital Equipment Corp., a worldwide leader in computer systems and services. She spent over a half century on the leading edge of technology, primarily in the area of computer programming and language development.

In 1928, Hopper graduated from Vassar College, as a member of Phi Beta Kappa. She earned her master's and doctorate degrees at Yale University. In 1943, she was sworn into the Navy and later joined the United States Naval Reserve and attended the USNR Midshipman School. After graduation, she was commissioned a lieutenant. She began her service at the Bureau of Ordinance Computation Project at Harvard University, where she learned to program computers.

During her computer career, she taught at several colleges and universities, including Vassar, Barnard, Harvard, the University of Pennsylvania, and George Washington University.

She work-ed as a senior mathematician at Eckert-Mauchly Computer Corp. in Philadelphia, and helped program the UNIVAC I, the first commercial all-purpose computer. She was instrumental in the development of language translator programs and also worked on COBOL language projects.

Throughout her career, she continued to serve in the Naval Reserve, becoming a rear admiral in 1985. In 1991, she—along with 17 others—received America's highest technology award, the National Medal of Technology, which is sponsored by the U.S. Department of Commerce's Technology Administration. More than 40 colleges and universities awarded Hopper honorary degrees, and she became the first Computer Sciences Man of the Year. Hopper died in 1992 at the age of 85.

instructions that direct a device to perform a certain job. They can be words, keystrokes, or choices from a list.) A disk drive can be thought of as an input device, because you use it to put programs and data from a disk into the computer. You actually use it to get data from storage, not to enter new data, however. To interact with a computer or capture new data, you'll need an input device such as a keyboard or scanner.

Interactive Input

The idea of interactive input is to capture information directly into computers and get responses from computers as the input occurs. This happens when you type on a keyboard and immediately see the results of your work on a screen. It is easy to tell where you need to make changes, and all you have to do is press a few keys to make this happen. This implies that interactive input is "screen-dependent"; in other words, interactive input depends on the display screen as the means with which the computer responds to the user.

CONCEPT SUMMARY
COMPONENTS OF THE SYSTEM UNIT

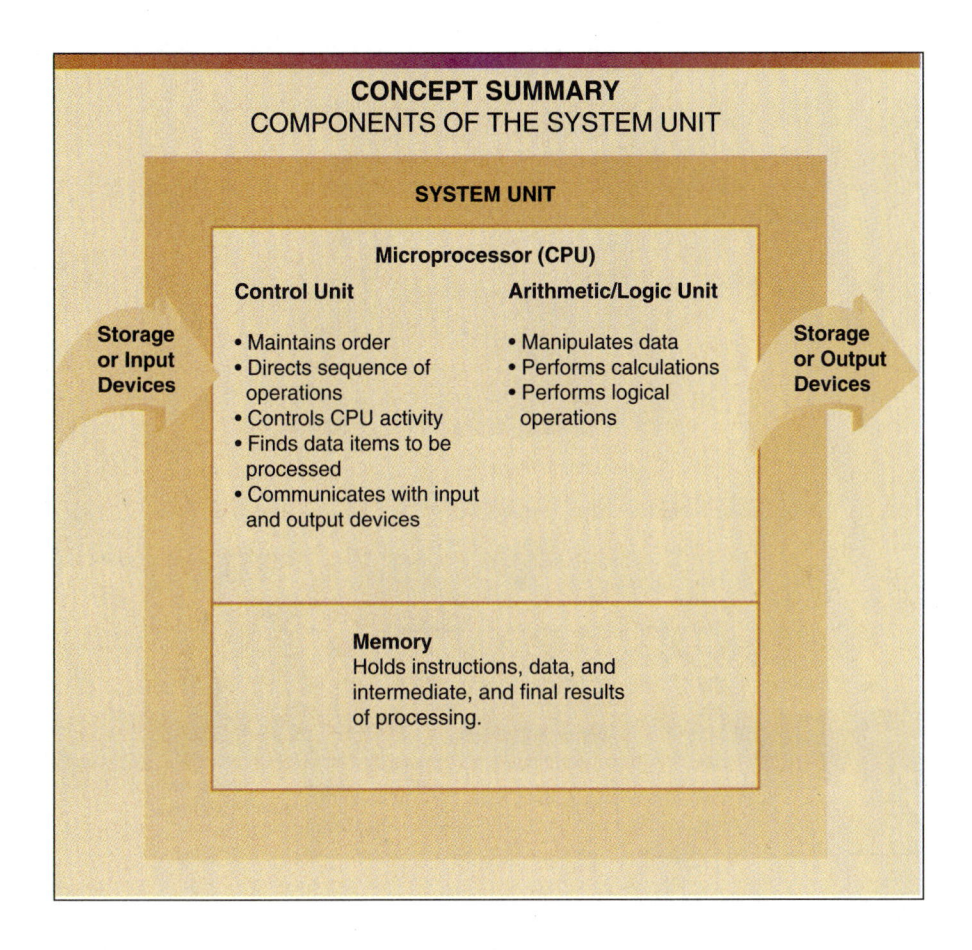

SYSTEM UNIT

Microprocessor (CPU)

Control Unit
- Maintains order
- Directs sequence of operations
- Controls CPU activity
- Finds data items to be processed
- Communicates with input and output devices

Arithmetic/Logic Unit
- Manipulates data
- Performs calculations
- Performs logical operations

Storage or Input Devices → **Storage or Output Devices**

Memory
Holds instructions, data, and intermediate, and final results of processing.

KEYBOARDS

The most common input device, the **keyboard,** lets you type input such as words and commands. It looks like the keyboard of a typewriter, with the addition of a numeric keypad, such as that of a calculator, and special function keys for deleting, tabbing, and other operations (see Figure 2–14). When you hold down a key on a computer keyboard, its character or function is repeated until you release the key.

The **cursor** is a vital part of keyboard input operations because it indicates your location on the screen. It is generally a solid, highlighted rectangle, a blinking underline character, or a vertical line that shows where the next character will be displayed on the screen. You move the cursor around the screen by using arrow keys or other special cursor-control keys such as *PgUp*.

keyboard An input device similar to a typewriter keyboard that permits the typing of alphanumeric characters as well as commands entered through special function keys.

cursor A symbol, such as a solid rectangle, an underline bar, or a vertical bar, that shows the current location on a computer screen and indicates the point at which the next input will appear.

MICE AND OTHER GESTURE-BASED INPUT DEVICES

Keyboard entry may be too slow or awkward for some jobs, but the keyboard can be bypassed by using one of a number of other interactive

Figure 2–14 Computer Keyboard
When you use a keyboard, we say you are *keyboarding*, rather than typing, and each press of a key is a *keystroke*. You can see what you are keyboarding by watching the cursor on a monitor.

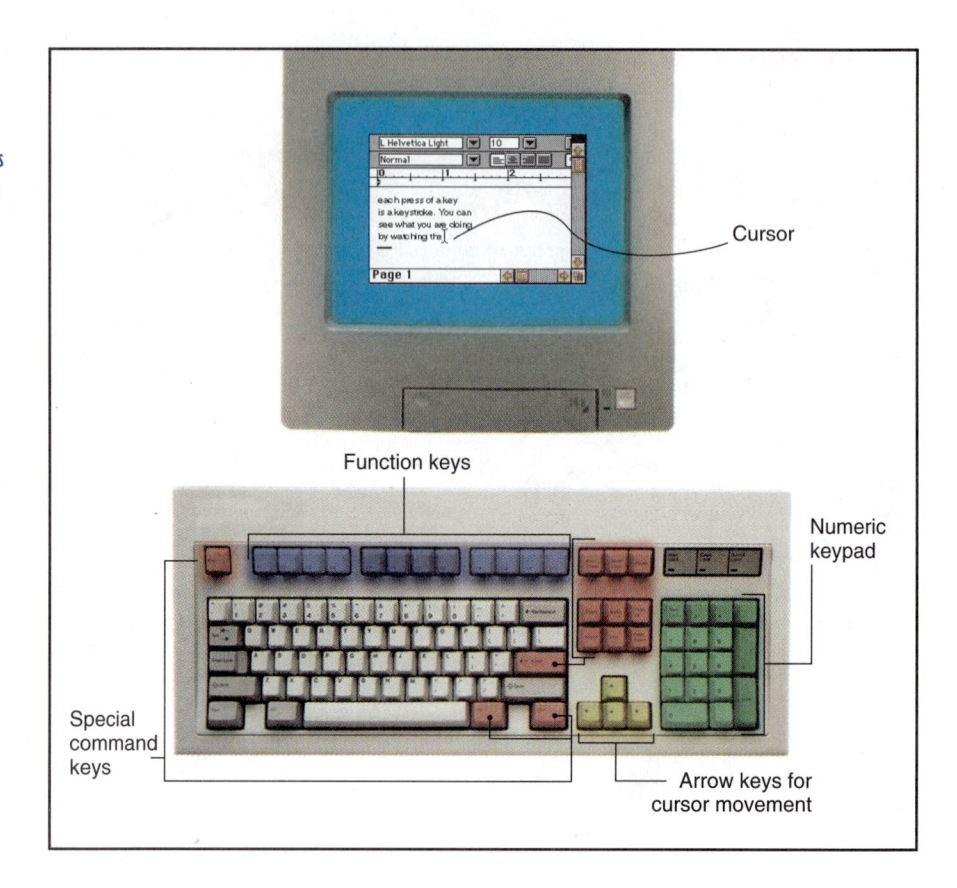

(Keyboard figure labels: Cursor; Function keys; Numeric keypad; Special command keys; Arrow keys for cursor movement)

mouse A gesture-based input device that can be rolled on a solid, flat surface to direct the movement of the cursor on a screen.

trackball A gesture-based input device in which a ball resting on top of a base is rolled to direct the cursor or other pointer on the screen.

touch screen A monitor screen that makes it possible for users to select programs and functions by touching designated places on the screen.

light pen A device that enables a user to enter images into a computer by moving a point of light across a display screen.

graphics tablet An electronic pad on which a user draws images with a puck or stylus. Sensors under the pad identify the locations and transmit image-creating data to the computer. Also called *digitizing tablet*.

devices (see Figure 2–15). Most of today's microcomputers, for example, include a **mouse** or a **trackball** that lets you use natural arm or hand motions to move the cursor. Either piece of equipment senses your motions and changes the signals into electrical pulses that are sent through cables to the computer.

Some screens themselves accept interactive input: The **touch screen** looks like a normal computer screen, but it can detect the point at which you touch it. Touch screens are especially handy when using menus, and often are found at kiosks that offer travel or consumer information.

Technical applications such as graphic arts, mapping, and engineering often require specialized input methods (see Figure 2–16). Perhaps the most natural tool is the **light pen.** It is a pen-shaped tool with a light-sensitive cell at its end used by touching it to the screen, making contact, and then drawing images for direct computer processing. Another input tool used in technical fields is the **graphics tablet,** or digitizer, which is a flat, boardlike surface with sensors located beneath its surface. You write or draw on it using a penlike tool called a *stylus* or a mouselike tool called a *puck*. The locations of touch points are communicated to the computer, which displays an image that can be controlled and altered.

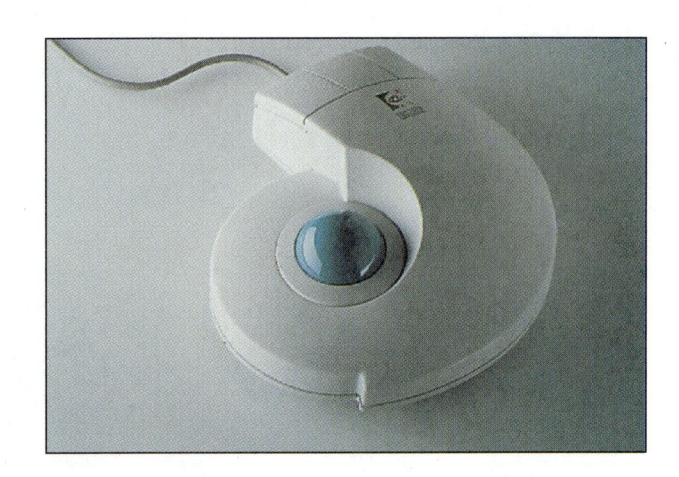

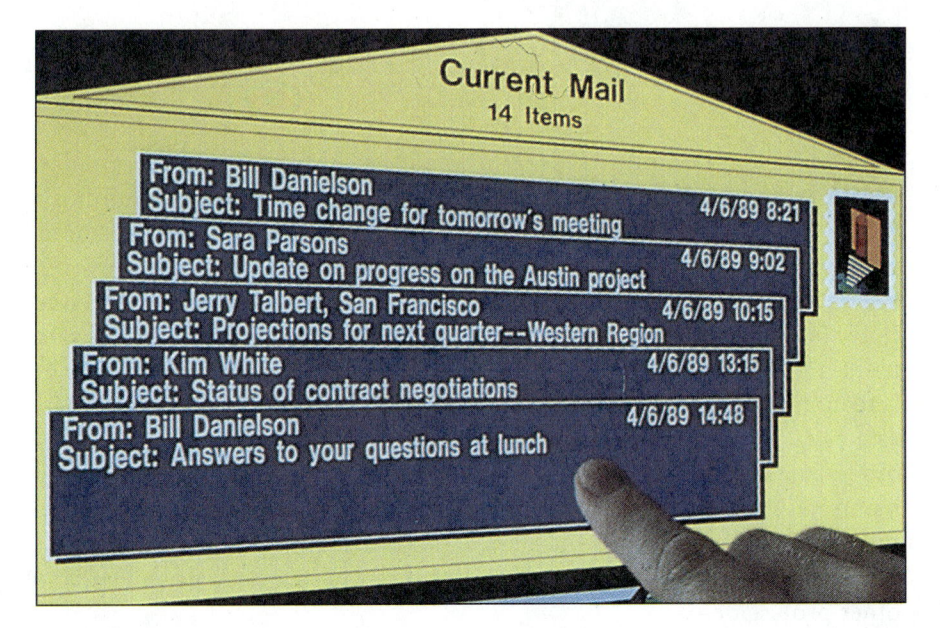

Figure 2–15 Input Devices
Many input devices enable you to use natural pointing action to move the cursor or pointer around the screen. These include the mouse *(top left)*, trackball *(top right)*, a touch screen *(left)*.

Figure 2–16 Methods for Graphics Input
Graphics input is possible with devices such as a light pen *(bottom left)* and a graphics tablet *(bottom right)*. With these devices, people and computers can communicate in images rather than being limited to characters and numbers.

Figure 2–17 Notepad Computer
Notepad computers enable you to use cursive handwriting for inputting data, but writing in printed characters produces the best results.

notepad computer A small, portable computer with a flat display screen that can detect and interpret the movements of a stylus with which you write on the screen.

Figure 2–18 Virtual Reality
Using data gloves, doctors can manipulate the anatomy of a virtual leg.

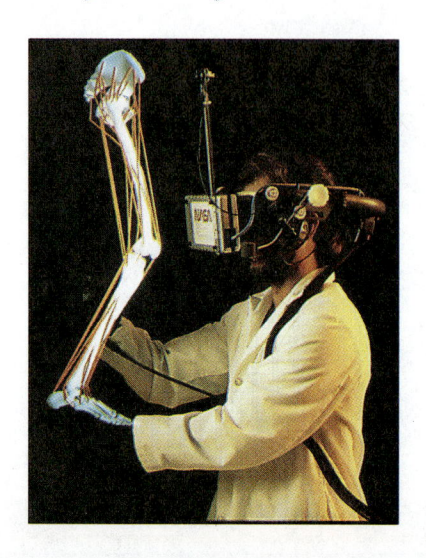

Pen-based computing is the most recent input development. Basically, it consists of a flat-screen computer somewhat resembling a child's Magic Slate. You write on it with a special stylus, and the characters you have written are redisplayed in printed text such as you would see on a standard computer screen. This system is called a **notepad computer** (see Figure 2–17). Many notepads are designed to accept input normally written on forms. An electronic version of the form appears on the screen, then you enter names, check off boxes, or circle answers to data requested on the form. Such systems are used by salespersons taking orders, clerks taking inventory, loading dock workers checking shipments, and police officers writing tickets. Although today's notepad computers are small, notepads the size of a drafting table or a blackboard may someday be used by teachers, students, executives, artists, designers, and other professionals.

The ultimate in gesture-based input is **virtual reality,** a technology that puts you in an artificial world. In virtual reality, devices such as styluses and gloves can be used as tools to study, design, or build virtual items (that is, items seen as a projected illusion). The hand devices have sensors that collect data about hand movements and allow you to "manipulate" what you see (see Figure 2–18). Motions used with these tools replicate those used in actually constructing a building or studying anatomy, except that the object of the study exists only as a projection. Most systems include special goggles that hold tiny three-dimensional stereoscopic screens by which you see full-sized, three-dimensional objects.

DIRECT INPUT

In an information system, the greatest majority of delays, errors, and problems occur during the input phase. To attack the problem, a number of methods have been developed to increase speed, accuracy, and reliability of input. Collectively, these techniques have been referred to as *source-data automation* (see Chapter 1). Scanning, voice input, and sensor input are three types of direct input.

Scanning

Scanners, also called optical scanners, are devices that read printed material so that it can be put in computer-readable form without your having to retype, redraw, reprint, or rephotograph the material. They work by illuminating the image and measuring the light being reflected from it. Thus, they are referred to as optical recognition devices. Two familiar uses of scanning are the processing of standardized multiple-choice tests and the reading of the ever-present bar code, or universal product code (UPC), at checkout counters. Scanners are also used widely in mail sorting and typesetting.

Microcomputer users have a number of scanning options. A handheld device typically scans a swath only 4 inches wide, but is handy for portable uses. The two common types of full-page scanners are sheet-feed and flatbed. Sheet-feed scanners work somewhat the opposite of printers: Rather than transferring the data in the computer to paper that slides out of a printer, the scanner reads the image on the paper copy fed into it and translates it into computer-usable form. The flatbed scanner, on the other hand, can accept almost any material, including books and periodicals (see Figure 2–19). It operates similarly to a photocopier: The page or book

virtual reality A computer arrangement, including hardware and software, that enables a person to experience and manipulate a three-dimensional world that exists only in projected images.

scanner A device for direct input that senses information by the reflection of light on a document and transmits the data in digital form to a computer.

Figure 2–19 Scanner
This flat-bed scanner can read images from a single sheet of paper or from an open book.

is laid upside down on a glass "table" and is read by a scanning device that moves under the glass. A number of software programs are available for interpreting and editing scanned material.

Speech Recognition

Speech-recognition, or voice-input, devices accept spoken words through a microphone and change the sounds into computer-ready signals. Current systems can detect and interpret either a small vocabulary of several dozen words or numbers spoken by many voices or a large vocabulary spoken by only one person. In the latter situation, you must train the system to recognize your voice. Under either system, you must speak clearly and distinctly. Voice-input devices are useful for people who need to use their hands for sorting products while entering data about laboratory experiments, packages, inventory, or quality control. They eventually could replace manual data entry in many situations and automate telephone tasks such as directory assistance and requests for mail order.

Sensor Input

Home computer users may link their systems to thermometers, light detectors, and motion detectors to help control energy use and deter vandalism. Input from these detectors is called *sensor input.* Sensor input is used widely with microcomputers in factories and in scientific and medical laboratories, too. Once the data is transmitted to the computer, the computer either simply records the data or takes an action based on changes in the data. For example, some homes use microcomputers attached to alarm systems. Sensors identify potential intrusions into a home. The computer reads these signals and, as appropriate, sounds an alarm or places a call to a police station. The computer output generated by changes in sensor input is referred to as a *control signal.*

➤Output Methods

Output devices are the delivery vehicles of a computer system—that is, output hardware either delivers information to users in human-readable form or stores the information for future use. The two common forms of human-readable output are displays (video output) and printed documents. Computers are also able to communicate in sounds that imitate the human voice.

Display Outputs

monitor A video display device or screen used for showing output; usually of cathode-ray technology.

The most common output device is the **monitor,** a cathode-ray tube (CRT) that is basically a television tube adapted to present text, data, or images generated by computers. Monitor output is fast: A monitor can display output almost as soon as you ask for it. The output can be edited directly—that is, data can be entered on the keyboard and checked on the

Term	Meaning	Example
Resolution	Clarity or sharpness of image; expressed in pixels	1,024 x 768
Dot Pitch	Distance between pixels; expressed in millimeters	.28 or less
Refresh Rate	The rate at which the image needs to be redrawn, or reactivated to prevent it from fading or decaying; expressed in hertz (Hz; cycles per second)	72 Hz or more
Interlacing	Technique by which every other line on the screen is refreshed, with the remaining lines being picked up on the next pass; used to increase resolution while saving costs.	non-interlaced (prevents screen flicker)

screen as it is keyed. Monitors show only a small portion of data at a time, however.

Most older monitors are monochrome units that display a single color, such as black, green, or amber, on a gray background. Today's popular monitors show color displays. High-quality color monitors receive three separate color signals (red, green, and blue) and thus are called RGB color monitors. The clarity or sharpness of the display is termed **resolution**. The resolution of a monitor indicates the number of image points, or **pixels** (picture elements), on its screen. The greater the number of pixels for a particular screen size, the better the resolution will be. Common numbers of pixels are 640 by 480 and 1,024 by 768. A monitor with 640 × 480 resolution has 480 lines of 640 pixels each. Resolution is only one indicator of a high-quality monitor (see Figure 2–20).

The **flat-panel displays** used on portable computers are less bulky and require less power than CRT monitors (see Figure 2–21). A common electronic imaging technique used in flat-panel displays is liquid-crystal display (LCD). LCD displays are formed when electric currents are applied to flat crystal materials, causing the crystals to align so that light cannot shine through. Many digital watches and calculators use LCD outputs. LCD displays, notoriously poor in strong light, have been improved by several technologies, described in advertisements as "backlit," "active matrix," or "supertwist." Two other flat panel displays are the gas plasma display, which uses electric current to cause gases to glow, and the electroluminescent display (ELD), which is similar to gas plasma but has layers of phosphor rather than gas.

The common denominator for all display devices is that they are temporary: Their output is **softcopy**. Computers create the displays on

Figure 2–20 Monitor
A number of factors other than resolution affect the quality of monitor output.

resolution The sharpness or clarity of displayed images or characters.

pixel Short for "picture element." An individual point of light on a display screen that can be lit or unlit; can be made of different shades of gray or different colors.

flat-panel display A flat screen that shows images much like the display on a digital watch; used on portable computers.

soft copy A temporary display, such as monitor output, of machine output.

Figure 2–21 Flat-Panel Display
The small size of notebook computers is made possible partly through technologies that provide screen displays only a fraction of an inch thick.

printer A machine that prints characters or other images on paper.

plotter A device that delivers outputs in the form of drawn images.

printout A document generated on a printer linked to a computer. Also known as *hard copy*.

hard copy Output that is printed on material such as paper.

impact printer A printer that forms impressions by striking a ribbon against a sheet of paper with a print mechanism.

dot-matrix printer A printer that forms character images as a series of points, using an impact mechanism that strikes an inked ribbon against the paper.

demand, and the displays can change on demand; thus, displays are valuable for the review and editing of information.

Printers for Document Outputs

Document outputs are produced on **printers** and **plotters,** devices that produce images or text on paper. These outputs are known as **printouts** or **hard copy.** Hard copy has the advantage of being relatively permanent. It can be used without the computer, can be written on, and can be passed around to other users.

Printers and plotters are classified by several criteria, including page quality and quantity printed at one time, but our focus is on impact and nonimpact printing methods.

Impact Printers

Printers that make images with a striking motion are called **impact printers.** They cause the plastic or metal parts that make a character to strike against an inked ribbon and paper. A common impact printer for microcomputers is the **dot-matrix printer,** which works by striking pins in a print element against the ribbon and paper. The pins are formed into a matrix, and different combinations of pins in the matrix shape the character or image.

Many dot-matrix printers supply *draft-quality* output, which means that the output is legible and good enough for informal purposes but not acceptable for important letters, documents, and brochures. Some dot-matrix printers have the ability to make multiple imprints that improve the appearance of the output. The results are known as near-letter-quality output.

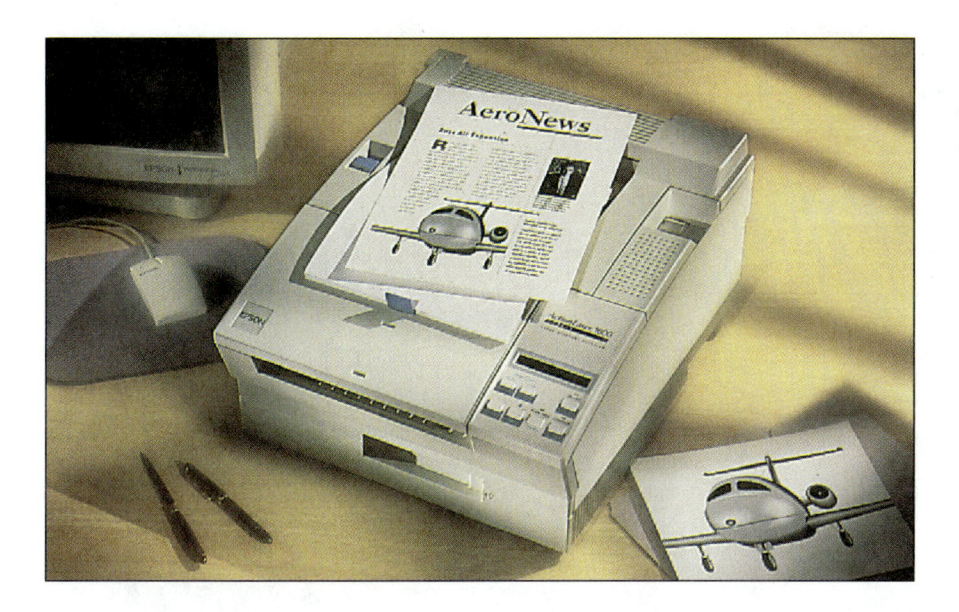

Figure 2–22 Laser Printer
Laser printers provide high-speed and high-quality output. Office units like this one output 8 to 12 pages per minute.

Although they are slow and noisy, dot-matrix printers are inexpensive and can reproduce graphics images as well as text. They also print through multiple copies such as invoices.

NONIMPACT PRINTERS

Nonimpact printers use heat, laser, or spraying techniques to print characters and images. Most of these printers are much faster than impact printers. They cost more than impact printers and need special cartridges of ink or other materials, which add to their cost. They cannot print carbon copies because they cannot strike through the several layers of paper and tissue constituting multiple forms.

Most nonimpact printers form characters made up of dots. The tiny dots are hard to detect, compared with those made by dot-matrix printers. The two major nonimpact technologies in use today are ink-jet and laser. **Ink-jet printers** shoot sprays of ink through nozzles toward the paper to form the images. The ink cartridges must be refilled or replaced, which can be a messy job, but the output of ink-jet printers is of fairly high quality. Even when special paper is used, the ink may smudge immediately after printing and when wet.

Laser printers use laser beams to make images on a drum (see Figure 2–22). The laser beam changes the electrical charge on the drum wherever it hits. The drum then spins through a reservoir holding a black powder called a *toner*, which is charged with a polarity opposite to the charged spots on the drum. The toner—basically tiny iron filings and minuscule beads of plastic—adheres to the charged spots on the drum, from which it is then fused to ordinary paper by heat and pressure. (This is also the way copy machines work.) An entire page is transferred to the drum at once, and thus laser printers are sometimes called *page printers*.

nonimpact printer A printer that forms impressions without requiring the physical striking of print characters against ribbon and paper by a print mechanism.

ink-jet printer A printer that forms impressions with fine sprays of ink onto paper.

laser printer A printer that generates images through use of a laser beam that passes over the surface of a xerographic drum.

Figure 2–23
Plotter Plotters use multicolor drawing instruments to produce full-color outputs such as charts and graphs.

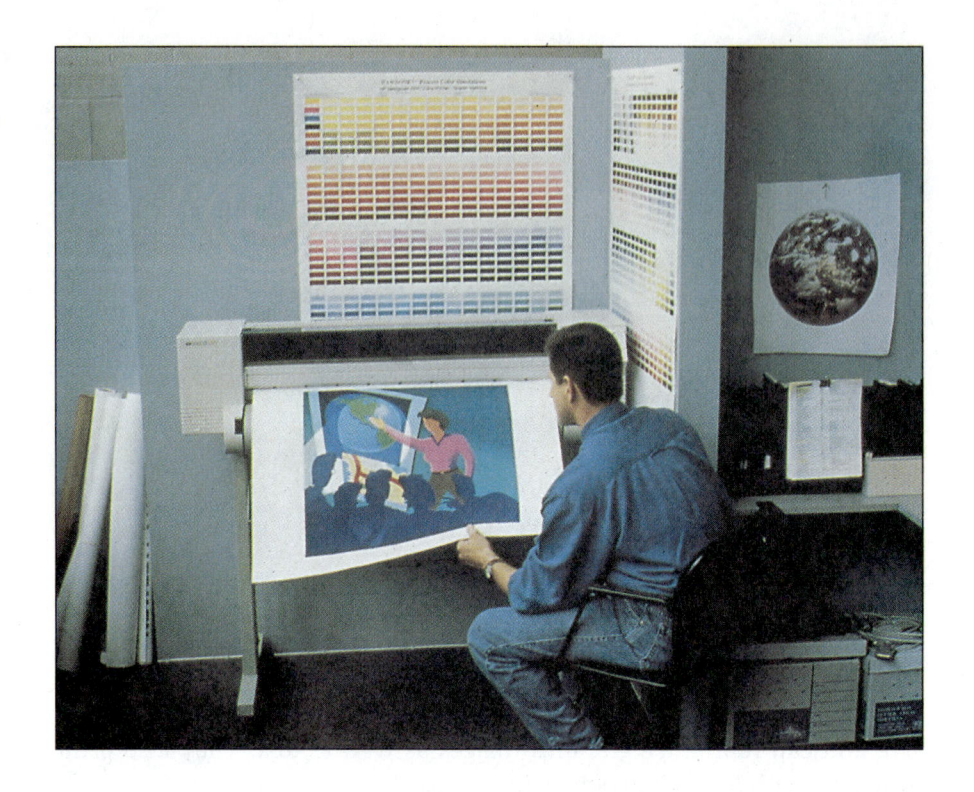

Laser printers operate at speeds of 4 to 20 text pages per minute. Although laser printers can be prohibitively expensive, some models cost less than $1,000—an attractive price for home buyers who want high-quality production of graphics images and text.

PLOTTERS

Although nonimpact printers do not use striking methods to print, they do form characters and images as sets of dots, just as dot-matrix impact printers do. Plotters, on the other hand, produce solid lines, just as you do when you write with a pen. A plotter uses pens to make precise hard copies of images such as bar charts, graphs, engineering drawings, maps, and other graphics (see Figure 2–23). It generates outputs by converting data items from the CPU into related positions on a grid, or mathematical division, of a flat surface. The two types of plotters are the flatbed plotter and the drum plotter. A *flatbed plotter* looks like a table with pens mounted on a track: On some, the pens move; on others, the table holding the paper moves. *Drum plotters* draw on paper that is rolled on a cylinder. Many plotters use a variety of pens—felt-tip, ballpoint, liquid roller, nylon-tip, and fine drafting pens in four, six, or even eight colors. Most home computer owners have no need for plotters.

VOICE OUTPUT

If you have ever ridden in a car in which an electronic voice tells you to buckle up or to close the door, you have experienced voice output. The "speaker" in a voice-output device may be a voice-response unit or a voice synthesizer. Voice-response units talk in half-second recordings of voice sounds or in short words. This approach is used in banks for reporting customer account balances and in supermarkets for telling customers the amount of each purchase. The units are well suited for short messages, such as "Door ajar!"

A **voice synthesizer** uses phonemes to create spoken words. *Phonemes* are the distinct sounds, or the smallest components, of speech. The voice synthesizer analyzes the letters in a word and determines which phonemes are created by the letters. The phonemes are then combined into "spoken" words. The program also uses rules for tone and accents (stress) to make the speech seem more realistic. Many voice synthesizers have poor sound quality, but research is improving this shortcoming.

Voice synthesizers can help people with special needs to lead meaningful and productive lives. For example, the Kurzweil Reading Machine, designed by Ray Kurzweil to aid the blind, scans a printed page and reads aloud. Other systems, called *screen readers,* are connected to microcomputers and direct all keyboard input and screen text to the voice synthesizer. This enables blind people to use popular software packages without any special preparation by the manufacturer.

voice synthesizer An output device that uses stored patterns of sound to assemble words for output that imitates the human voice.

➤ STORAGE

Storage, as opposed to memory, resides outside the motherboard and is used to record and save large amounts of data at low cost. It is independent of the electrical power that is supplied to the computer, and thus retains its data even after the computer is turned off.

Most storage devices in current use record data magnetically and in binary format. The actual materials, such as disks and tapes, that hold the data are referred to as *storage media.* Storage devices such as tape drives and disk drives that read from and record onto the storage media are placed in areas called *bays* inside the computer, although some are external devices. To us, they seem to work fast, yet storage is much slower than memory.

storage Retention of programs or data for later use on media such as floppy disks or hard disks that are external to the computer's processor or memory.

MAGNETIC DISKS

The **magnetic disk** is a circular platter with a smooth surface and a coating that can be magnetized. Data is stored on it as magnetized spots. Each pattern of spots matches the byte code for the character being stored. The reading and recording device, the **disk drive,** spins the disk past read/write heads that detect or write the magnetized spots on the disk. The spots are recorded in a set of invisible tracks that form concentric rings around the hub, or center, of the disk.

Both disks and the drives that read and write data on them come in a variety of sizes and capacities. **Hard disks** are made of metallic material

magnetic disk A circular storage medium on which data items are recorded magnetically for direct- (random-) access reading and writing.

disk drive A storage device that holds and processes magnetic or other disk media.

hard disk A rigid, disk-shaped storage medium, usually made of metal and coated with a magnetizable substance, encased in a hard disk drive; sometimes refers to the entire drive.

Figure 2–24 Hard Disk Drive
This Barracuda drive by Seagate has a number of platters and can hold 2.1GB of data.

hard disk drive The machine that rotates and reads the hard disk.

floppy disk The name given to the mylar, flexible, disk-shaped storage medium coated with a magnetizable substance; rotates within a plastic jacket.

floppy disk drive The mechanical device that rotates and reads the floppy disk.

direct-access storage Storage from which data can be obtained in any order.

optical disk A storage medium that relies on the use of laser beams for storing and retrieving data.

CD-ROM Pronounced see-dee-ROM; stands for "compact disc read-only memory." A form of optical disk from which data can be read but not altered or recorded.

WORM Stands for "write once, read many." An optical disk that can be recorded only once but read from many times.

and come singly or in disk packs of two or more. Their storage capacity is measured in megabytes. A common entry-level computer comes with a 170MB hard disk. Hard disks are read by **hard disk drives,** which normally are installed inside the computer, where you cannot see them (see Figure 2–24). Some are removable, however. Sizes range from the very small (1.3 inches in notebook and palmtop computers) to the standard 5.25-inch drives placed in desktop systems.

Flexible mylar plastic disks called **floppy disks,** or diskettes, are read by a **floppy disk drive** (see Figure 2–25). Floppies are used for backup and archival purposes, as well as for software transferal (most off-the-shelf software comes on floppy disks).

Magnetic disks are used for **direct-access storage.** "Direct access" has the same general meaning as random access. The idea is that the computer can find, process, and re-store items as needed, thus supporting direct inquiries for stored information.

CD-ROMs and Other Optical Storage

Optical disks need thin beams of concentrated light (laser beams) to store and read data (see Figure 2–26). To record data, the laser burns a series of points, or pits, into the surface of the disks, which are coated with special plastic. For reading, the positions of these pits are decoded to produce text and graphic images. This is the same process that is used for some videodisk recordings and for audio recordings on compact discs, although it is much more precise. In fact, one form of laser storage, called **CD-ROM,** is used for applications such as multimedia encyclopedias, children's books, and school subjects. Items on a CD-ROM cannot be written or erased by the user. A CD-ROM typically holds 640MB of data (see Figure 2–26).

There are two types of optical disks that can be user-recorded: WORM and erasable optical. **WORM** stands for "write once, read many": Data can

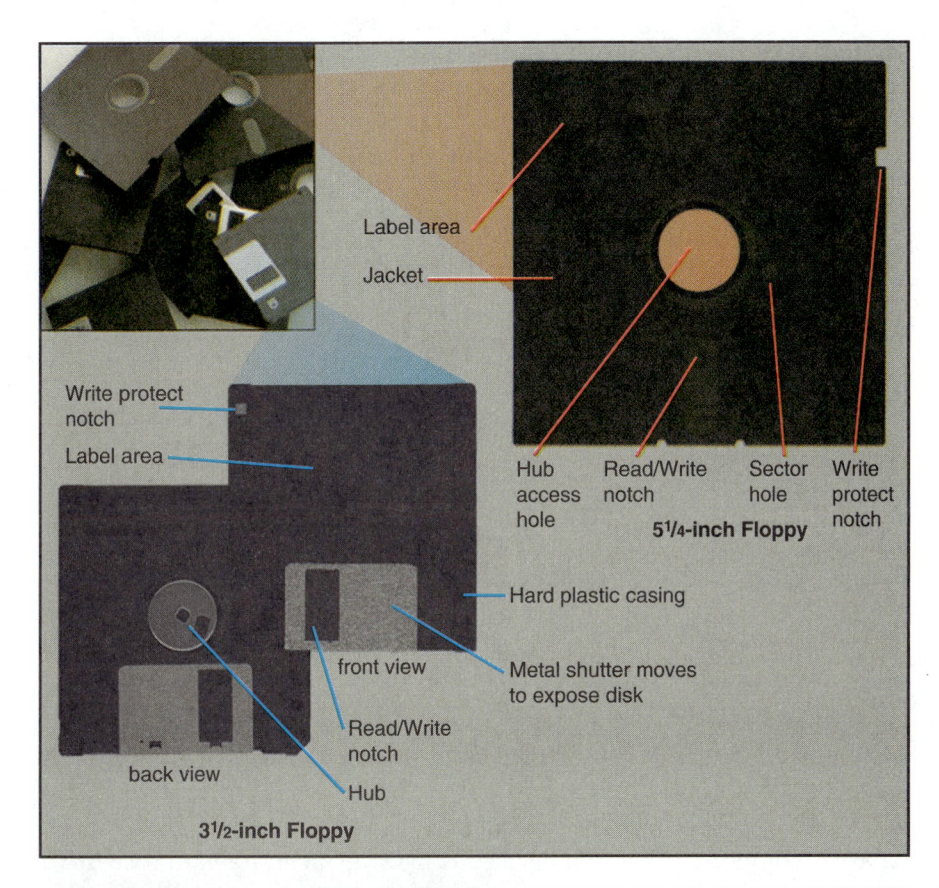

Figure 2–25 Magnetic Disks
The 3.5-inch disks have a storage capacity of 1.44MB, and the 5.25-inch disks hold 1.2MB.

Figure 2–26 Optical Disk
A laser beam burns tiny pits into the smooth surface of an optical disk. Optical, or laser, disks provide large capacities for storage.

erasable optical disk An optical disk technology that can be written to, read from, and erased.

magnetic tape A storage medium on which information is represented by magnetic spots on continuous ribbons of oxide-coated acetate.

tape drive A storage device that holds and processes magnetic tape media.

back up To make a copy to prevent data loss in case the original material is lost or damaged.

sequential-access storage Storage from which data items must be read one after another, in a fixed sequence from the beginning to the end.

be written to this disk just one time, but the data can be read many times. **Erasable optical disks** can be written to, read, and erased. The most common are magneto-optical disks, which make use of both laser and magnetic technology. Their drives write using magnetic technology and read using laser technology.

The various types of optical disks require their own special drives for use. At this point, only the CD-ROM drives are fairly standardized to read any CD-ROM disk.

MAGNETIC TAPE

A **magnetic tape** is a narrow plastic strip similar to the tape used in tape recorders. The tapes are read by **tape drives.** The drive moves the tape past a read/write head, which detects or writes magnetized spots on the iron-oxide coating of the tape. Each pattern of spots matches the byte code for the character being stored.

Magnetic tapes come in cartridges for use with microcomputers and are normally used to **back up,** or copy for safekeeping, the contents of hard disks. They are sometimes called "streaming tapes" or "streaming tape backup systems," because the tape moves in a continuous stream rather than starting or stopping, as is common on the big tape-reel machines found in mainframe systems. An advanced form is the digital audiotape (DAT) system, which operates so rapidly and holds so much data (2GB or more) that it can be used to back up an entire hard disk drive in 5 to 20 minutes.

Magnetic tapes hold large volumes of information in very small amounts of space and at very low costs. They can be erased and reused, and data can be transferred to and from the tape at very high speeds. Tape provides **sequential-access storage;** that is, the tape must be read from the beginning until the desired item is found. This makes tape unsuitable for interactive computer use.

▶SUMMARY POINTS

- In a computer, data is represented by the binary digits (bits)—0 and 1. This system suits the computer, which is based on the states of electricity, on and off. Bits are often grouped in eights, and each group is called a byte. Two common coding schemes are ASCII and EBCDIC.
- The microprocessor is the CPU of a microcomputer. It is the part of a computer in which processing takes place, and it consists of the control unit and the arithmetic logic unit (ALU).
- The control unit maintains order and controls activity in the CPU. It directs communication and coordinates operations between the

CPU and other devices. The ALU manipulates data through arithmetic and logic operations.
- Memory holds the program instructions and data needed for processing. Random-access memory (RAM) is a form of memory into which items can be read repeatedly, written, or erased. When the computer is turned off, items in RAM vanish.
- Read-only memory (ROM) is a form of memory that is built into chips at the factory. Items in ROM chips can be read over and over again, but cannot be changed by end-user input methods.
- Interactive input devices provide a way to manipulate data and get responses from the computer as the input occurs. The most common device is the keyboard, although there are other options, including mice, trackballs, touch screens, light pens, and graphics tablets. The most recent option is a notepad computer that includes a stylus for writing on the computer screen.
- Direct methods of input include optical recognition, voice input, and sensor input. Microcomputer users have a number of optical scanning options for inputting both characters and images.
- The most common output device is the monitor. Monitors for terminals and desktop models of computers use cathode-ray technology. Flat-panel displays such as liquid-crystal displays (LCDs) are used on portable computers. Display devices provide soft copy.
- Hard copy, or a printout, is produced by a printer. Impact printers form characters via a striking mechanism, and nonimpact printers use heat, laser, or photographic methods to create the images. A common impact printer used with microcomputers is the dot-matrix printer. Types of nonimpact printers are ink-jet and laser printers.
- Output devices for special uses include plotters and voice synthesizers. Plotters, which use pens to make hard copies in graphic form, are generally used for detailed and technical output. Voice synthesizers are instrumental in enabling people with certain disabilities to use computers.
- Storage devices permit the permanent recording of information. Magnetic tapes are used for sequential-access storage, in which a tape is read from beginning to end. Disks are used for direct-access storage, in which data can be found in any order.
- Magnetic tapes are read by tape drives, and magnetic disks are read by disk drives. Either type of drive includes a read/write head that detects the magnetized spots representing data and converts them into electrical signals that are sent to the CPU.
- Optical storage devices rely on laser beams to burn pits representing data into the surface of the optical disks or to detect the presence of the pits for reading.

▶Review Questions

1. Why is the binary number system suited for coding the data and instructions that a computer uses?
2. How is it possible that only two digits can be used to represent 26 letters (both uppercase and lowercase), nine digits, and all of the special characters?
3. What are the parts of the CPU? Briefly, what does each do?
4. Why could RAM be called read/write memory rather than random-access memory?
5. Describe the machine cycle.
6. Both ports and buses have to do with the way data travels through a computer system. What is the difference between the two?
7. What input device is used to enter the majority of data into information systems? How do you think this might change in the future?
8. How are scanners used for input? Name two or three situations in which you think the use of scanners would be beneficial. Under what circumstances could scanning be misused?
9. What type of output does a display screen provide? What is the most common use of flat-panel displays?
10. What are the most common types of nonimpact printers?
11. When would a tape be better for storage than a disk?
12. Describe uses for optical disks.

▶Activities and Research

1. What is an analog computer, and for what is it used?
2. This chapter explains that a computer is a two-state device. What other two-state devices can you identify? How do the capabilities of these devices differ from the capabilities of a computer?
3. Find a microcomputer that you can open. Look at the parts inside, and try to identify each part or group of parts.
4. Find descriptions of input and output devices. List some of the features, and find out how these devices should be connected to the computer.

CHAPTER 3

APPLICATION SOFTWARE: PRODUCTIVITY TOOLS

OUTLINE

Learning Objectives
Introduction
General Features of Application Software
    Files
    Menus
    Windows
    WYSIWYG
    Macro Capability
    Undo
    Documentation and Help
    Concept Summary: Software Features
Word Processing
    Entering and Editing Text
    Writing Aids: Thesauruses, Spelling Checkers, and Grammar Checkers
    Print Formatting
    Other Features
Spreadsheets
Spreadsheets Explained
General Features of Spreadsheets
Profile: Mitch Kapor: The Spreadsheet Blossoms
Data-Management Software
    Data Organization
    Querying and Reporting
    Window on Computing: Resumes That Make a Database Weep
Graphics Software
    Presentation Graphics Programs
    Paint and Draw Programs
    Window on Computing: The Future Is Here: Real or Contrived?
    Concept Summary: The Basic Computer Applications
Summary Points
Review Questions
Activities and Research

LEARNING OBJECTIVES

After reading this chapter, you should be able to:

- Describe some features common to many computer programs.
- Explain the primary function of each of the four major types of application programs: word processing, spreadsheets, data managers, and graphics software.
- Give specific uses for each of the four major applications.
- List features that distinguish among the four major applications.

Introduction

Before 1978, the business community looked upon the microcomputer as a mere toy—the province of visionaries and a playground for nerds. Most programs for microcomputers were games, characterized by jerky motion and little people made of squares. Then in 1978, along came the first spreadsheet program for microcomputers. Its name was VisiCalc and it ran on two computers, the Apple II and the Radio Shack TRS-80. It enabled business users to set up numbers and equations just as they would using a paper ledger sheet, except VisiCalc calculated the equations automatically.

What a revolution this program ignited! Users would no longer need to depend on mainframes for their work. They could go to a computer store and buy microcomputers and shrink-wrapped software packages. Then IBM introduced the PC for business use, and microcomputers quickly became more powerful, capable of handling more complex software. Soon, software manufacturers were loading their products with dozens of features in an effort to make their software the most popular, the most user friendly, or the most powerful.

With the widespread availability of high-quality programs for microcomputers, companies began to question the need to maintain staffs of highly talented, skilled—and expensive—programmers to develop applications in-house. They saw that commercial software could be implemented quickly, that it often contained more features than could realistically be included in a program developed in-house, and that it was reliable. Therefore, for many companies, buying and using software packages for microcomputers has become a common practice.

Today, you can buy software for just about any kind of job you wish to do with your microcomputer. The software reportedly used most frequently is word processing, but close behind—especially for business users—are electronic spreadsheets, data-management software, and graphics programs. This chapter introduces these four types of programs, presenting the features in common and the distinguishing characteristics of each.

▶ GENERAL FEATURES OF APPLICATION SOFTWARE

Commercial software comes on floppy disks packaged in shrink-wrapped boxes along with instruction books or leaflets called *user's manuals;* thus, a particular program is often called a **software package** (see Figure 3–1). Software is written for different brands of computers, such as Macintosh, IBM, or Sun. The computer, the system software, and the application software must be **compatible** with one another. Otherwise, when you try to use a program, it will not work.

Today's programs often come on CD-ROM disks or on three, four, or even more floppy disks. They must be **installed** on a hard disk before they can be used. Each package contains directions on how to begin the installation process and set up the software for use on your system—noting the type of printer you are using, for example. When you are ready to use a program, you must put it into the computer's memory. This operation is called **loading.** Loading can be as complex as typing a special code along with the program's name or as simple as "pointing and clicking" with a mouse.

Although the various types of software do very different jobs, they are often similar in the way they handle files, use windows and menus, are displayed on the screen, and offer help. These characteristics are described in the following sections.

---

software package A prewritten program that can be purchased for use with a particular computer to do a specific job; usually includes the program, on disks, and a user's manual.

compatible Descriptive of software and hardware that can be used together without any bad effects, even though they have been produced by different manufacturers.

install To put a program onto a hard disk.

load To read information such as a program or data into computer memory.

Figure 3–1 A Software Package
A software package should tell you everything you need to know to use the program.

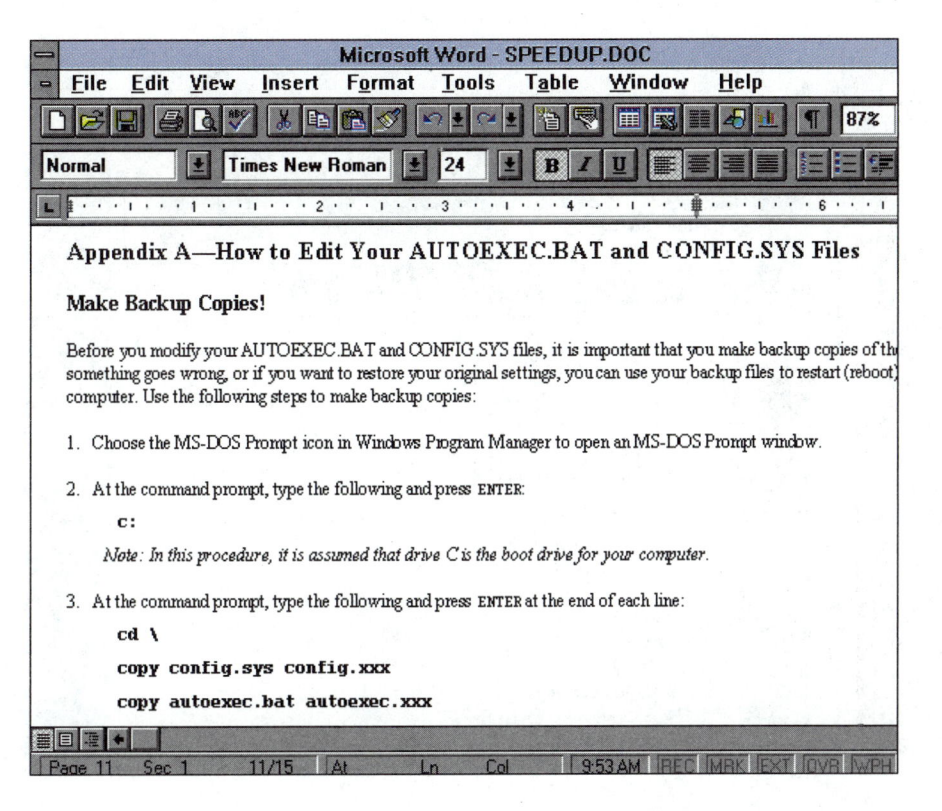

Figure 3–2   File Information
A file created with Microsoft Word for Windows shows a variety of information that lets the user know the status of the file.

FILES

An application such as word processing, a report or a drawing that you create, and a spelling dictionary are all kept in files. A **file** is a set of data grouped under the same name called the **file name,** which is given to the file when it is created. There are specific limits for naming files, including the number and kind of characters allowed.

Files are listed in directories. Any time you want to use a file, you must type its name exactly. In some systems, files are shown as **icons** with the file names beneath. The icon is easily dealt with using a mouse. For example, pressing the mouse button twice quickly in succession (called double-clicking) after you have selected an icon **opens,** or activates, that file. Once opened, the file usually displays information such as the file name and your location in the file. A status line may show which page, line, or column you are in. It may also show how parts of the file have been formatted (see Figure 3–2).

Files commonly are too large to be displayed in their entirety on the screen. In order to see all of the material, you move, or **scroll,** it out of the way to make room for more. Vertical scrolling moves material up or down, and horizontal scrolling moves material to the right or left. In many programs, scroll bars at the right side and the bottom of the window let you visualize your location in relation to the whole file. Within the scroll bar is a tiny square that shows your location in the file. If you are in the middle of the file, the square is about halfway down the bar. If you

file A specific unit of data stored on a disk or tape.

file name A name given to a file for purposes of storage and retrieval.

icon A picture or graphic symbol used to represent such things as an application, a software function, a document, a folder, or a disk.

open To activate a document or application.

scroll To move text or images on and off the screen in order to see all of the material in a file.

Figure 3–3 Pull-Down Menu
Clicking the mouse button on the Style option in *Quark* activates a menu that "hangs" from the Style label.

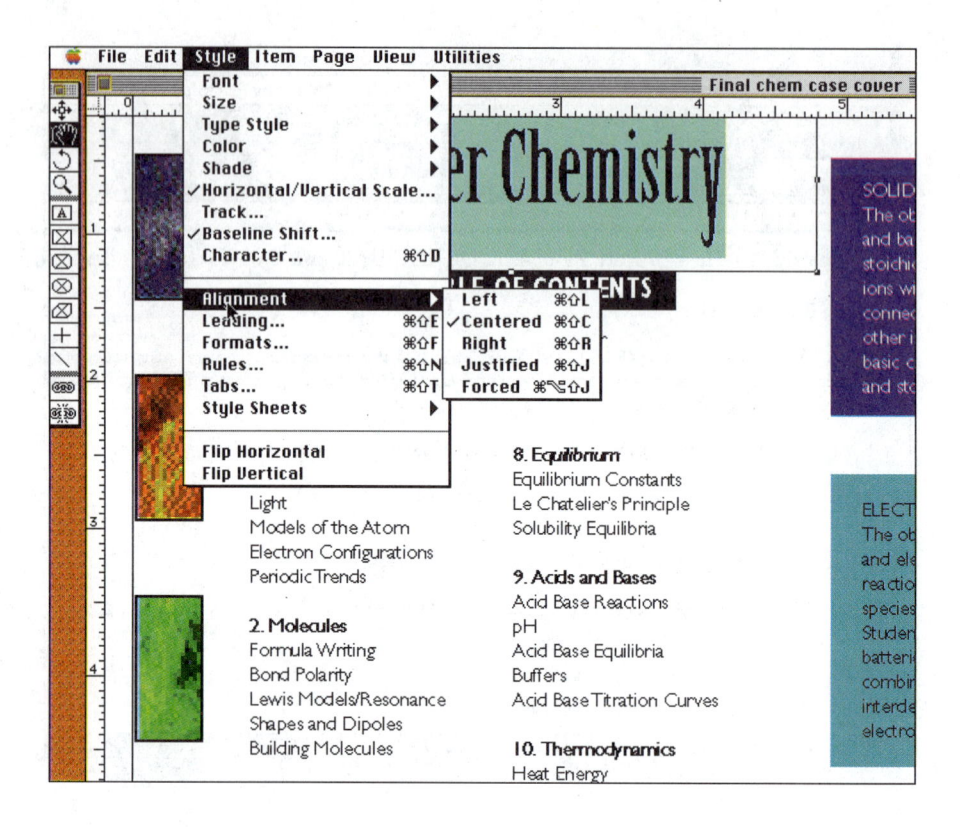

menu A list of available functions or information displayed on the screen.

are three-quarters of the way into the file, the square is about three-quarters of the way down the bar, and so on (refer to Figure 3–2).

There are a number of features for using multiple files. For example, most programs let you work with more than one file (or document) on the screen at a time, link several files for printing, or move items from one file to another. (Bringing material into one file from another is called *importing;* sending material out of one file to another is called *exporting.*) A popular feature that must be supported by the system software being used is the linking of information among files, so that when a piece of information is changed in one file, it is automatically changed in all affected files.

MENUS

A **menu** is a list of options displayed on the screen. You choose the option you want by typing the option's code or by highlighting the option and pressing the *Return* or *Enter* key. A menu-driven program has a primary menu that appears in a full-screen view or in a menu bar at the top of the screen. Choosing one option from a menu may lead to another menu that pulls down from a menu bar or pops up in the middle of the screen (see Figure 3–3). Many menus appear in boxes called *windows* (see next section). Special menus called *toolbars, ribbons,* or *toolkits* show options as icons.

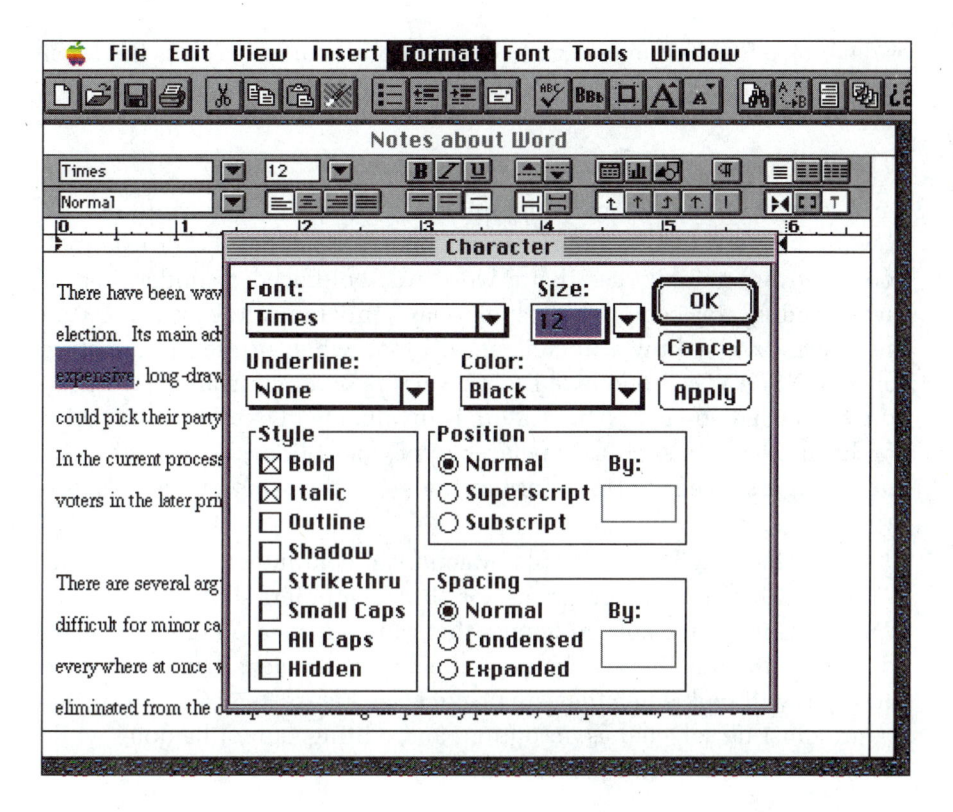

Figure 3–4 Character Dialog Box
By choosing from among the check boxes and radio buttons, you can specify the appearance of characters.

WINDOWS

Windows are outlined sections of the screen that contain files, menus, or messages. For example, each file or program displayed on the screen has its own window, and each window has its own title bar that identifies the file. The size of a file window can be changed so that more than one window can be seen at once. In addition, a file window can be split for dealing with long files: If you want to compare two different parts of a file, for example, you can divide the window into two sections and scroll the display in one section independent of the display in the other section.

Some windows are best called *boxes;* they contain information that guides you through a program. **Dialog boxes** require input from the user. For example, in *Microsoft Word for the Macintosh,* menu choices followed by an ellipsis (. . .) result in a dialog box. When you choose Character . . . from the Format menu, a dialog box appears in which you can specify the size and looks of characters—i.e., boldfaced, underlined, italicized, and so on. You make selections by clicking in a check box or a button beside the option (see Figure 3–4). Buttons may be either rectangular with rounded corners or radio buttons that are small circles in which dots indicate selection. Generally, in a set of radio buttons, only one can be chosen, but in a set of check boxes, several can be selected. **Alert boxes** give information about something that is about to happen, and may contain warnings about potentially damaging operations, such

window A frame that displays all of or a portion of a file, message, or menu on the screen.

dialog box An outlined area that appears on the screen to request user input.

alert box An outlined area that appears on the screen to give information or a warning or to report an error message during use of an application program.

as deleting a file. You may need to click a mouse button or press the *Enter* key to acknowledge an alert box and make it go away.

WYSIWYG

Early software provided many options for printing, but you could not see how a document would look until you actually printed it. For example, you could not actually see that a word was boldfaced or underlined or that a heading was centered. Most of today's programs, however, show on the screen exactly how a document will look when printed in a feature called **WYSIWYG**. Pronounced *wizzywig,* the acronym stands for "what you see is what you get." This feature is invaluable in experimenting with graphical elements such as typefaces, type sizes, lines, boxes, columns, and margins (see "Print Formatting" in the section on "Word Processing").

From the beginning, Apple Macintosh computers embodied the WYSIWYG concept. In programs for IBM computers and compatibles, WYSIWYG is often a special feature that can be turned on or off as needed. Some programs have a feature called *print preview* that shows how full pages will look when they are printed (see Figure 3–5). Generally, this feature must be selected as an option, and editing cannot be done while the screen is in the print preview mode.

> **WYSIWYG** Pronounced wizzywig, and stands for "what you see is what you get"; identifies a program's capability to display text on the screen as it will appear when printed on paper.

Macro Capability

A **macro** basically is a keystroke shortcut. It enables you to assign some text or commands to only one or two keystrokes. Essentially, you assign a short program for a specific task to a keystroke or two. The entire set is retrieved by pressing the assigned key or key combination. For example, if a hard-to-spell name is used throughout a report, you could type the name once as a macro command and then, whenever you use that name in the report, you would press the keystroke that retrieves the macro, causing the entire name to appear on the screen. Likewise, a set of multiple printing instructions can be stored as a macro.

> **macro** A keyboard command of only one or two keystrokes that, when translated, activates a series of machine-language statements—in this case, the assigned sequence of instructions or string of text.

Undo

An undo function cancels an action, returning your work to a previous state. For example, if you delete a sentence, begin writing another, and then change your mind, using the undo command returns the deleted sentence to the screen. If you accidentally delete a long paragraph instead of moving it, you can get it back. The undo function often acts as a toggle between the original state and the changed state; thus, in many programs, it works only for the last action taken. If you delete a page by mistake and then type even one new character or press the *Enter (Return)* key, you cannot get your work back. Some complex programs, however, allow multiple undo operations to retrieve five or more items.

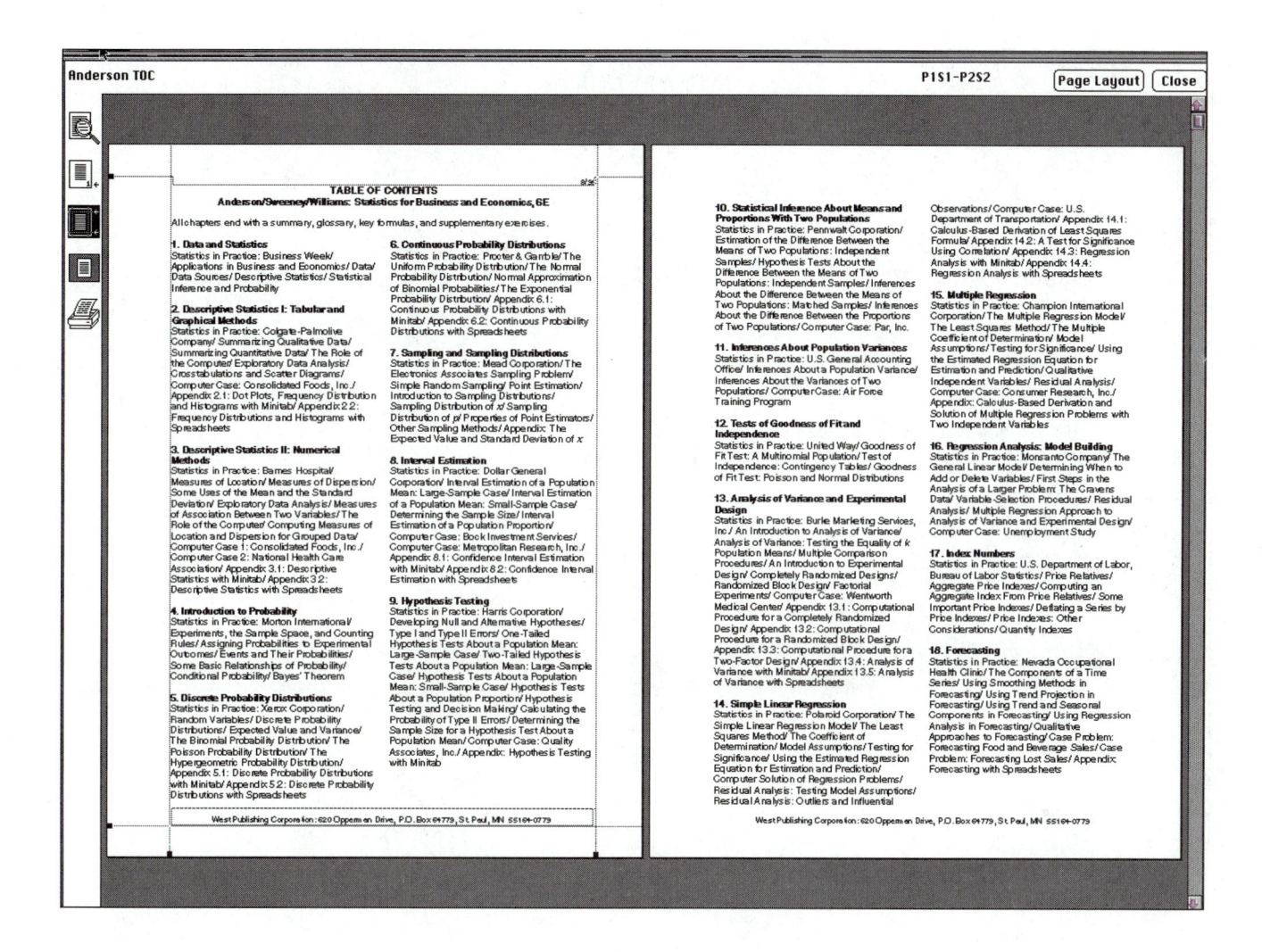

Documentation and Help

Software packages do include written documentation, usually in the form of the user's guide or a reference manual or both. The user's guide leads the new user step by step through the functions of the software. The reference book, which describes every option of the program, is arranged either by topic, from easy to complex, or in alphabetical order. Some packages also include a "getting started" manual, which explains the very basics of installing a program and beginning to use it.

In the effort to increase the user-friendliness of a program, manufacturers are putting instructions into the software itself so that users do not need to get out their paper manuals. Access to this help is initiated by selecting the Help option from a menu or by pressing a function key or a key combination such as *Control-?*. A reference to **context-sensitive help** means that the computer displays help only for the specific task at hand rather than for the entire menu of help topics.

Figure 3–5 WYSIWYG
Microsoft Word for Macintosh displays pages exactly as they will appear when printed.

context-sensitive help On-screen help that is relevant to the action currently being accessed or completed.

CONCEPT SUMMARY
SOFTWARE FEATURES

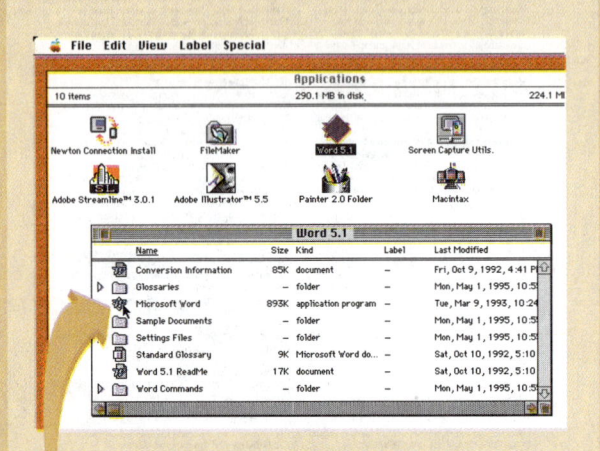

Load program by double-clicking on application icon.

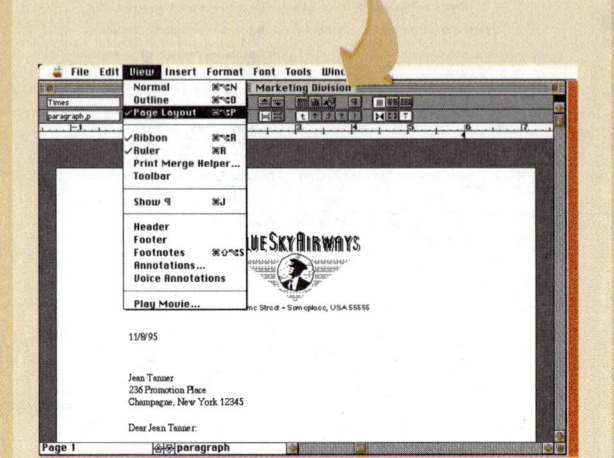

Use menu bar, pop-up menu, and WYSIWYG.

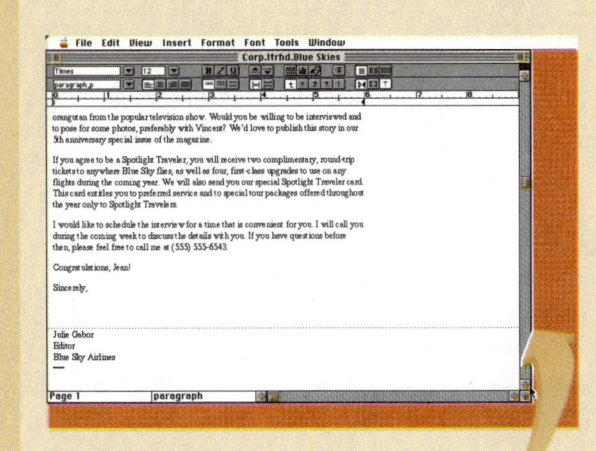

file name

Scroll to read more.

Scroll bar

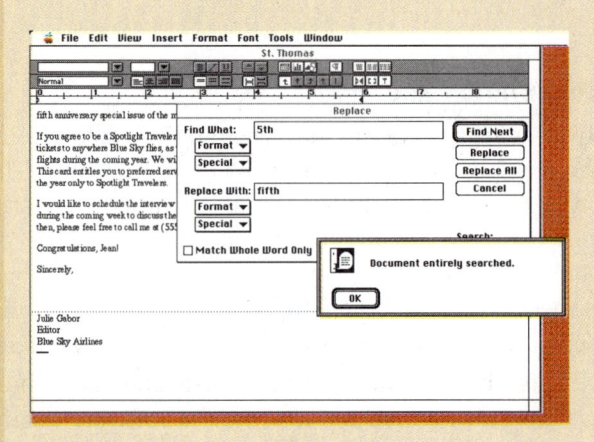

Use dialog boxes and alert boxes.

Figure 3–6 Word Processing
Microcomputers have replaced typewriters at millions of workstations in business today.

▶ WORD PROCESSING

Writing can be frustrating. Have you ever wadded up a fresh piece of paper after writing just a few words and making a mistake? You might have made five or six false starts before you actually got a paragraph on paper. Using a typewriter instead of handwriting a page is not much better. With **word processing,** however, you can start over many times without wasting paper. Essentially, you can add, erase, copy, scramble, and experiment with words without worrying about neatness.

A word processing program is a program that lets you write, edit, format, and print text. The purpose of all word processors is the same: to help the user create a good-looking and well-written document. Using a word processor makes it much easier to revise a document and print a clean paper copy with no strikeovers, dots of correction fluid, or erasures. If you find a misspelled word on page 2 of a finished report, you do not have to type a whole new page 2. You can correct the mistake at the computer and print out a new copy.

You might wonder what you would do with a word processor. If your writing consists mostly of personal letters, then you may not need one. If you are involved with a club, have school-aged children, do freelance writing, or keep a journal, then a word processor could help you create good-looking documents easily. The aggregate of features of an individual word processing package may make it suitable for personal, professional, corporate, legal, or publishing use. For example, teachers want features for formatting tests, worksheets, and newsletters. Business users want to create important letters, reports, brochures, memos, training manuals, newsletters, and catalogs (see Figure 3–6). They need the capability to merge names and addresses from a database file into "personalized" form letters. People in legal or scientific professions want characters, symbols,

word processing A computer application designed for the preparation of text; involves writing, editing, formatting, and printing.

Figure 3–7 Cursor Movements
Most systems offer many possibilities for cursor movements, activated by pressing a key or key combination.

Home	Moves the cursor to the top left corner of the screen
Top of page	Moves the cursor to the first character on the screen
End of page	Moves the cursor to the last character on the screen
Tab	Moves the cursor to the right a set number of spaces
Page up	Displays the previous screen of text
Page down	Displays the following screen of text
Next word	Moves the cursor to the first character of the next word
Previous word	Moves the cursor to the first character of the previous word
Beginning of line	Moves the cursor to the first character of the first word in a line
End of line	Moves the cursor to the first character of the last word in a line
Next Sentence	Moves the cursor to the first character of the next sentence
Previous Sentence	Moves the cursor to the first character of the previous sentence
Next page	Shows the following page of the document and places the cursor at the first character on that page
Previous page	Shows the previous page of the document and places the cursor at the first character of that page
Goto	Moves the cursor to a specified location entered in response to a prompt or dialog box

and functions specific to their fields. Popular general-purpose word processors for doing these jobs include *Microsoft Word, WordPerfect, Ami Pro,* and *MacWrite.*

Word processing consists of two basic operations: text editing and print formatting. In the text editing process, you type and revise text (that is, words). In the print formatting process, you adjust the appearance of the document in order to get it ready for printing.

ENTERING AND EDITING TEXT

As you type using a word processor, you see the words appear on the screen. The **cursor** moves along as you type, showing where you are on the screen. You can hit the *Delete* or *Backspace* key to erase a mistake, or you can position the cursor in another sentence or paragraph to delete, modify, or add some words. You then save your work onto a hard disk or floppy disk.

cursor The marker on the display screen that indicates the point at which the next input will appear on the display screen.

CURSOR POSITION AND AUTOMATIC WORD WRAP

Cursor positioning is an important part of word processing because it enables you to move the cursor to any location to edit text. The cursor is a symbol on the screen that shows the point where text can be entered. Most word-processing programs allow cursor movement anywhere on the screen (see Figure 3–7).

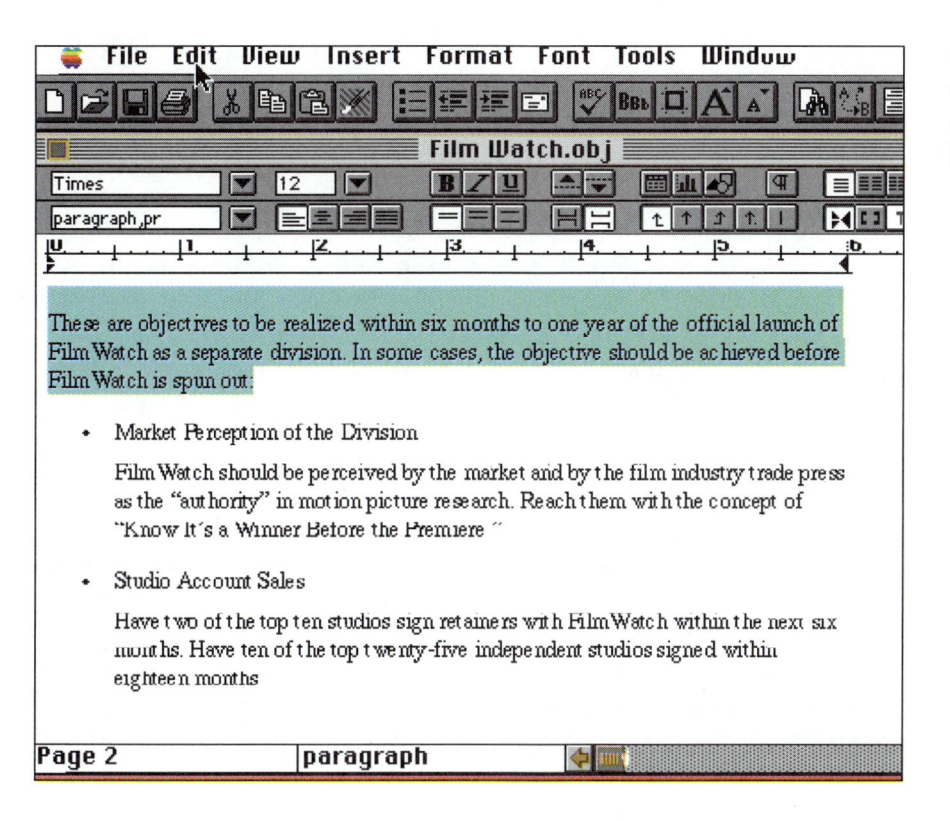

Figure 3–8 Block Operations
Once a block of text is selected, as shown, it can be deleted, copied, or moved to a new location.

If more characters are typed on a line than the margin allows, the program forces the cursor to the next line, carrying with it any incomplete word. This is called automatic **word wrap.** This feature lets you keep typing without using a carriage return at the end of the line, as you need to do on a typewriter. If you want to end the line before it reaches the right margin—at the end of a paragraph, for instance—simply press the *Enter* (*Return*) key.

word wrap A feature in word processing that starts a new line automatically when the current line is filled.

INSERTIONS AND DELETIONS

With a word processor, you can insert or delete characters, words, sentences, and paragraphs. If you want to add text, you position the cursor at the correct location and begin typing. To delete characters, you press the *Backspace* or *Delete* key. To delete a few sentences or paragraphs that do not fit or are incorrect, you can use key commands or the mouse to select a large portion of text before hitting the *Delete* key.

Any text selected for deletion is called a **block,** and it is marked or highlighted so that you can see what text you are operating on. Operations that involve blocks of text are called **block operations** (see Figure 3–8). Besides deletion, other block operations are moving and copying. Sometimes the move operation is called *cut-and-paste.* This feature enables you to change the order or flow of the material. During cutting, the text is transferred to a temporary holding area called a buffer, or clipboard. Pasting involves repositioning the cursor and pressing the

block A selected section of a document.

block operation A feature by which a section of a file can be selected for copying, moving, or deleting.

appropriate keys to insert the moved text in its new location. A new method of cutting and pasting is called "drag-and-drop," which requires the use of a mouse. In drag-and-drop, you hold down the mouse button, select the text to be moved, and drag (or slide) the text to its new location.

A block that has been copied can be pasted into new locations as many times as needed. For example, a survey about physical fitness may use the answers (a) always, (b) often, (c) sometimes, (d) occasionally, and (e) never. After writing and formatting these answers, you copy them as a block, and then paste them after each survey question that uses those answers. After any insert, delete, or move function, the program automatically adjusts the text to fit the margins.

SEARCH FUNCTIONS

search A function that finds a designated string of characters in a document.

The **search** function lets you look for a word or phrase (called a *string*) in a document. If you used the name of your guild's vice president several times in the minutes when you meant to use the president's name, you can engage a search that finds and changes all of the wrong names.

There are three types of searches: find, find and replace on a per-word basis, and find and replace all instances of the offending word (called a *global search and replace*). You can usually select options such as uppercase/lowercase match, in which, for instance, only the name *Leader* would be found even if there are occurrences of the word *leader*. An *attribute match* finds formatted words, such as italicized or boldfaced words. A *whole-word match* finds only a separate and entire word, not a string of characters in another word. For example, a whole-word match for the string *good* would bypass the string in the word *goodness*. Some word processors have a *wild-card match* that searches for words containing specific characters in a specific location in a word. For example, if * were a wild-card character, searching for *rep** would find *report, reprieve, repress,* and so on.

WRITING AIDS: THESAURUSES, SPELLING CHECKERS, AND GRAMMAR CHECKERS

Using a word processor may not make you a better writer, but it can make it easier to edit your writing. Depending upon the complexity and price of a package, a word processing program may offer a thesaurus, a spelling checker, and a grammar checker—options that can help you improve your writing:

- An *electronic thesaurus* lets you request synonyms for any word contained in the thesaurus, thus helping you choose the best word for a particular situation (see Figure 3–9).
- A *spelling checker* is an electronic dictionary that helps detect incorrectly spelled words. When you activate the spelling function, the program runs through the text to locate and highlight

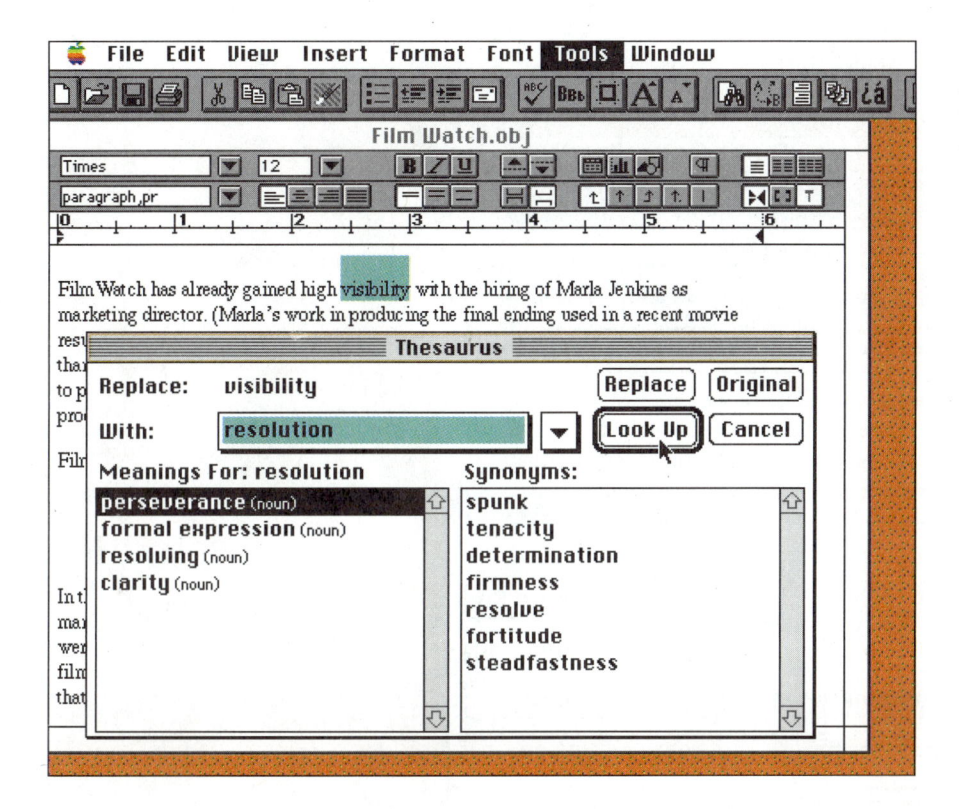

Figure 3–9 Electronic Thesaurus
Microsoft Word includes a thesaurus from which you can choose words, look up different words, replace words, and view previous queries.

words that do not appear in its dictionary (see Figure 3–10). Using a spelling checker does not eliminate the need for careful proofreading, however. If you type *there sales* instead of *their sales,* the checker will not highlight *there* as a misspelled word. For that type of correction, you need a grammar checker.

- *Grammar checkers* help you use the correct syntax of a language. They may flag a point where the noun and verb do not agree, highlight double words, or locate sentence fragments. They should note run-on sentences, missing verbs, incorrect capitalization, incorrect verb tenses, and errors in agreement between pronouns and antecedents. Here are some examples:

My boss ride the subway to work every day.

He found those mistake when he proofread the manuscript.

He had gave his friend a birthday gift.

PRINT FORMATTING

Print formatting features determine how a document will look when it is printed. Most programs have **default settings** for the format of a document—that is, values automatically used by the program unless otherwise instructed. The defaults usually include plain text, single spaced lines, and preset tab stops, for example. Most users change the defaults to increase the readability and appearance of documents.

print formatting The function of an application program in which the appearance of the text is set up for printing.

default setting A built-in value, such as a format setting for single-spaced lines, that a program applies unless instructed otherwise by the user.

86 • APPLICATION SOFTWARE: PRODUCTIVITY TOOLS

Figure 3–10   Spelling Checker
Microsoft Word's dictionary can quickly scan a document for spelling errors. Note how an incorrect word is highlighted and suggestions are offered.

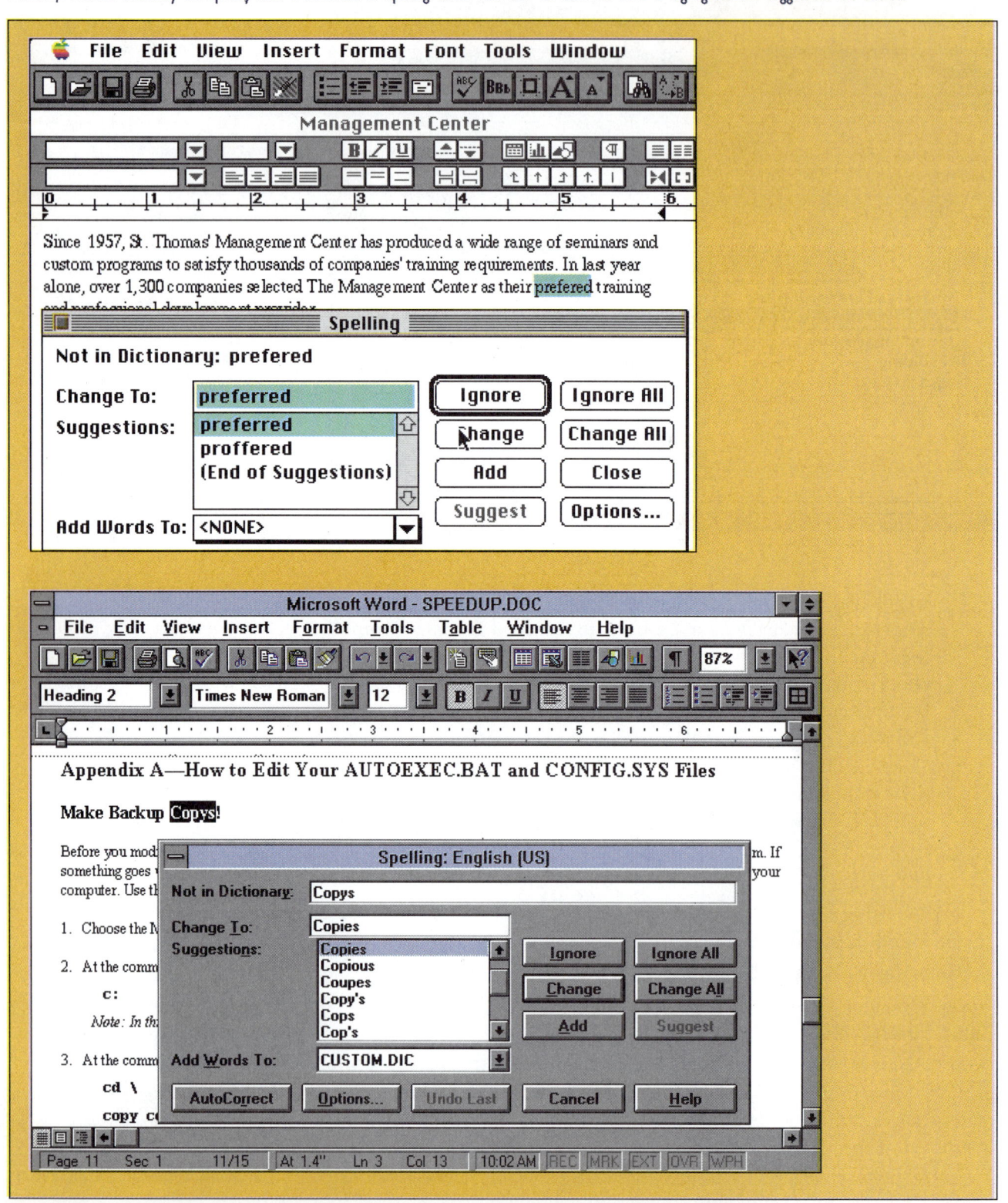

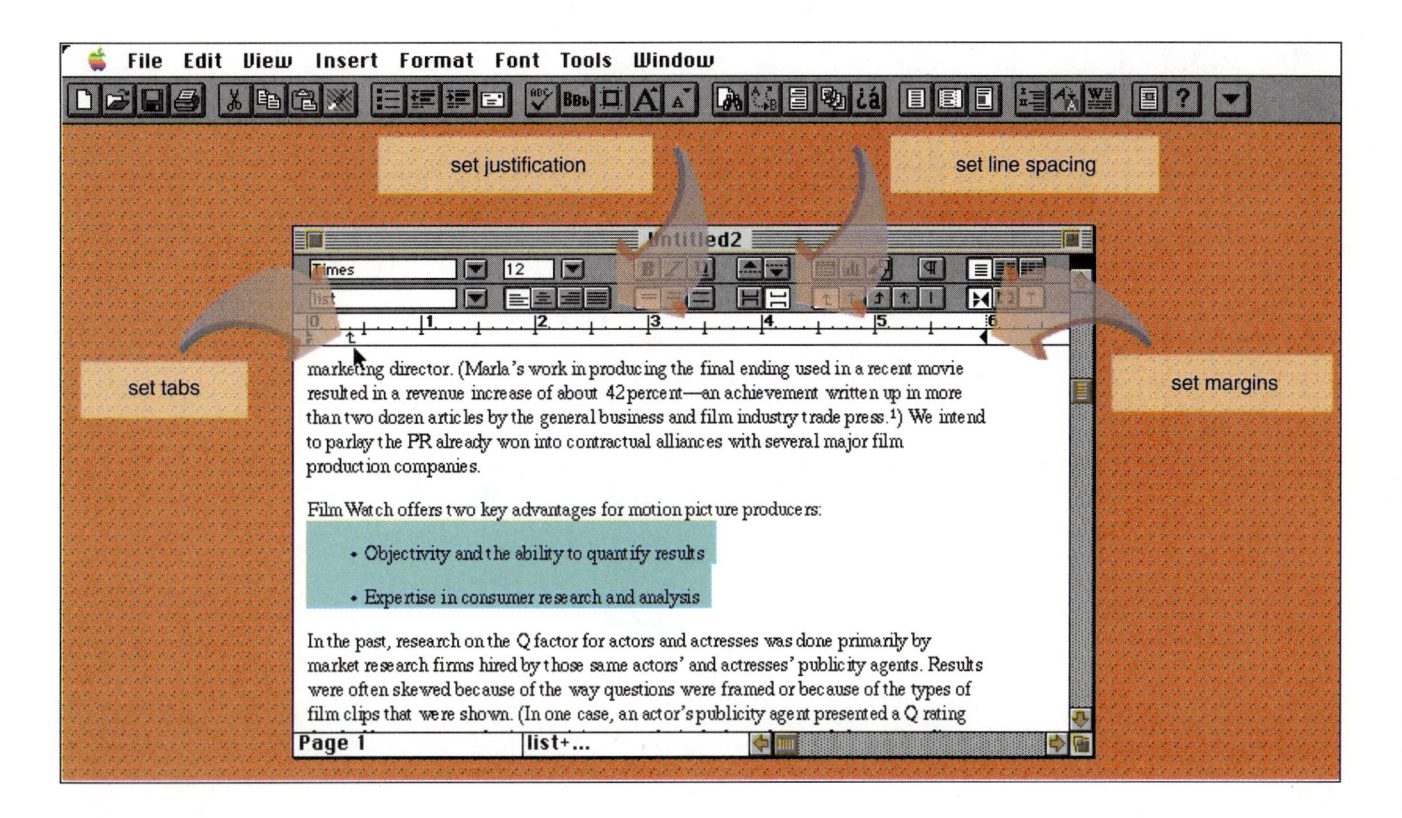

Many word processors let you adjust formats through menus or by using a ruler displayed at the top of the screen (see Figure 3–11). The options almost always include the following:

- Margin settings for the side, top, and bottom margins of a page
- Margin settings that control margins on a single paragraph, overriding page margins
- Character appearance (plain, **boldface,** *italics,* $_{subscript}$, ^{superscript}, and outline)
- Typefaces and sizes (10-point Times, **14-point Helvetica**)
- Line spacing (single, double, or triple)
- Underlining
- Justification (aligning text in relation to the side margins: centered, left, right, fully) (see Figure 3–12)
- Page length (standard 8.5 by 11 inches or optional 11 by 17 inches, for example)
- Pagination, which prints the page number and determines the page breaks
- Headers or footers (text at the top or bottom of the page that identifies a chapter title, a page number, a date, and so on)

Once you have set the format for one type of document, you can save it as a **style sheet** to use in the future. Most word processors come with some preset style sheets for standard documents such as business letters.

Figure 3–11 Formatting Ruler
Microsoft Word for the Macintosh displays a ruler that enables you to set margins, tabs, line spacing, and justification.

style sheet A file that contains formatting instructions for text but no text; may include margin settings, line spacing, paragraph indentation, and the like.

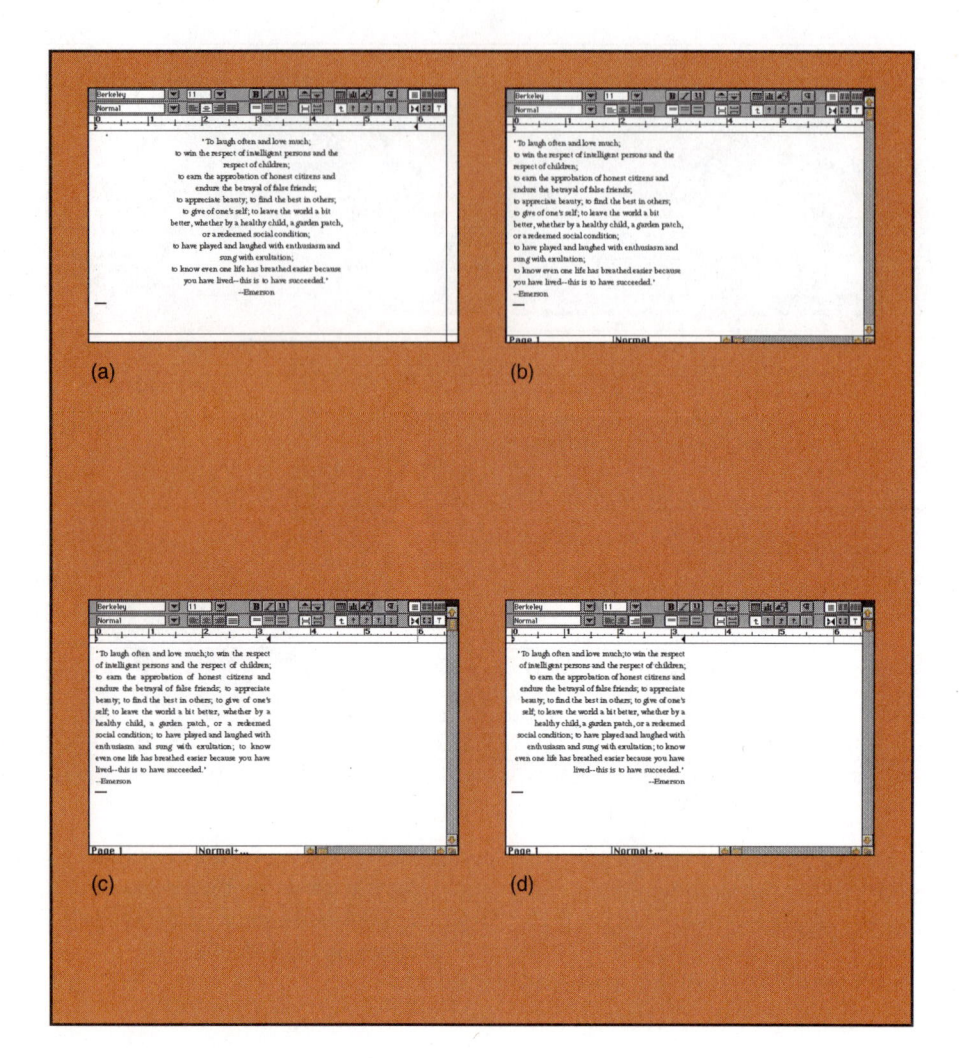

Figure 3–12 Examples of Text Justification with Microsoft Word
a. Centered text
b. Left-justified text
c. Right-justified text
d. Fully justified text

mail merge The process of printing form letters automatically, using, for example, both a word-processing file containing the letter and a database file containing the names and addresses.

A common formatting feature is the **mail merge** option for generating form letters, in which each letter is printed with its own recipient's name and address. Mail merge typically requires two different files: the text of the letter created by the word processing program, and the file of names and addresses created in a database program.

OTHER FEATURES

A word processor that offers more than the basic functions is described as full-featured. The following features are often found in a full-featured word processing package:

- Draft mode for fast data entry, and graphical mode for print formatting
- Footnoting options
- Generation of tables of contents
- Generation of indexes
- Outlining with different levels of headings and subheadings

- Redlining (that is, marking text that you have edited or changed so that the next reader knows what you have done)
- Simple math calculations
- Multiple columns of text
- Extensive character formatting and page-layout options
- Graphics tools for drawing pictures

Today's word processors are often so full-featured that they can be used for desktop publishing, which is the process of creating documents complete with text and graphics, fully ready for printing (see Chapter 6).

▶ SPREADSHEETS

An electronic **spreadsheet** program lets you record numbers and solve math problems. You can use a spreadsheet program to budget money, compare costs of computer equipment for your company, and keep track of scores for your softball league. If you do not have a data-management program, you can even use a spreadsheet program as a database to collect, store, and search for data.

spreadsheet An application program that takes the place of paper ledger sheets to store, manipulate, and analyze numeric data.

Spreadsheet programs are popular tools for businesses to keep track of money, goods, and employees. Business data such as sales figures, expenses, payroll amounts, and prices, among other numbers, are stored in the spreadsheet. Formulas can be entered for computing profits, losses, taxes, increases in expenses, and so on. Then businesses can predict what would happen to profits and losses when some numbers on a spreadsheet are changed. This **"what-if?" analysis** consists basically of designing numerical scenarios that reflect the results of changes in prices, raw materials, taxes, and other important business figures.

"what-if?" analysis A planning activity during which numerous values are changed in a spreadsheet in order to project consequences of possible future conditions; sometimes referred to as a *scenario*.

Complex spreadsheets can be used in science and engineering. Scientists use spreadsheets to calculate the outcomes of experiments under different conditions. Engineers use them to calculate the strengths of materials or to estimate the cost of a job when preparing bids on a contract. Popular spreadsheet programs are *Lotus 1-2-3*, *Excel*, *Quattro Pro*, and *WingZ*.

SPREADSHEETS EXPLAINED

Before computers and software existed, people used paper spreadsheets to record financial data. These usually green "ledger sheets" have printed grids of columns and rows into which numbers and descriptions are written (see Figure 3–13). The columns and rows keep the numbers and words in line for easy viewing. With an electronic spreadsheet program, you see the spreadsheet on the computer screen rather than on paper, and you use the keyboard rather than a pencil to enter numbers and descriptions. Making changes is easy, and you do not need a calculator at all—the program does all of the figuring for you.

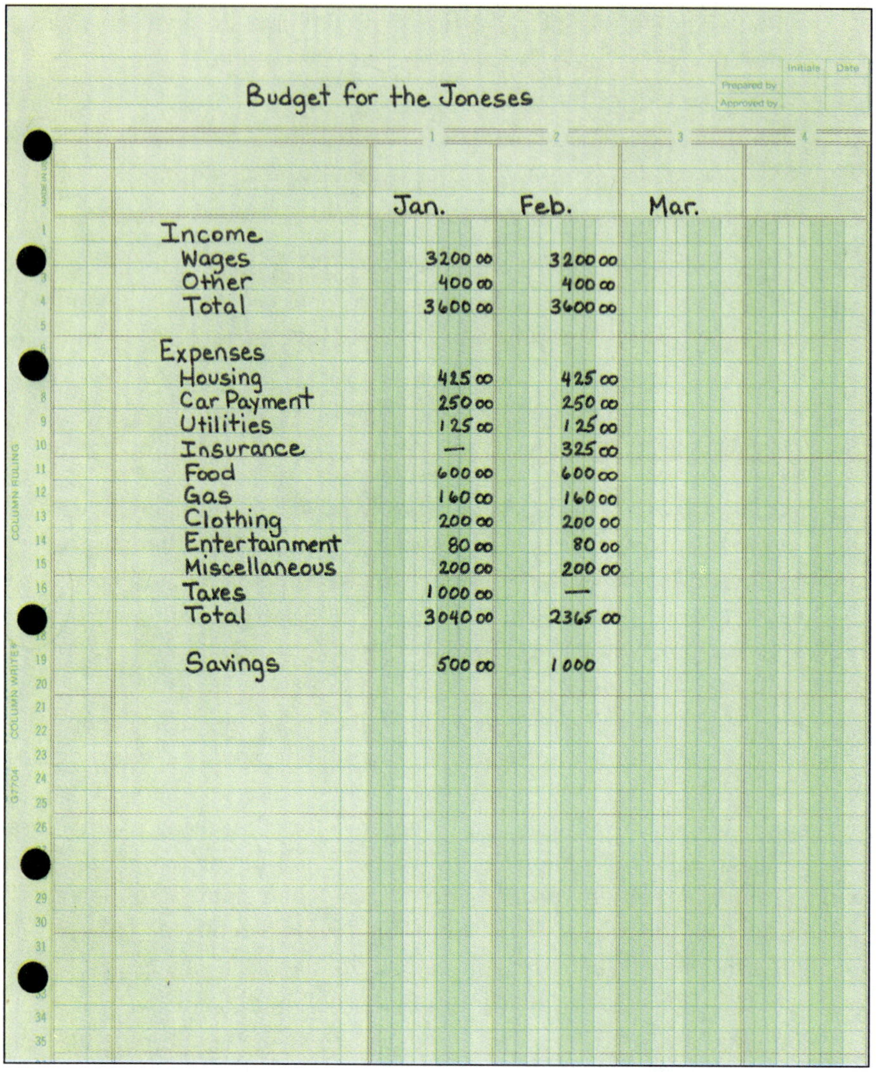

Figure 3–13 A Paper Spreadsheet
The rows and columns on a paper spreadsheet (or ledger sheet) are easy to see because lines are printed to show them clearly.

	Jan.	Feb.	Mar.
Income			
Wages	3200 00	3200 00	
Other	400 00	400 00	
Total	3600 00	3600 00	
Expenses			
Housing	425 00	425 00	
Car Payment	250 00	250 00	
Utilities	125 00	125 00	
Insurance	—	325 00	
Food	600 00	600 00	
Gas	160 00	160 00	
Clothing	200 00	200 00	
Entertainment	80 00	80 00	
Miscellaneous	200 00	200 00	
Taxes	1000 00	—	
Total	3040 00	2365 00	
Savings	500 00	1000	

Budget for the Joneses

cell The unique location in an electronic spreadsheet where a row and a column intersect; can hold a label, a value, or a formula.

value A number that is entered into a cell.

label A word or other information in a cell that describes the contents of another cell, a group of cells, or an entire spreadsheet. A label cannot be used in calculation.

formula A mathematical expression, or equation; in a spreadsheet, a formula uses the values of one or more other cells to derive new figures, such as totals.

The spreadsheet consists of a table of rows and columns used to store and manipulate any kind of numerical data. The point in a spreadsheet where a row and a column meet is called a **cell**. Each cell has a unique location identified by coordinates, which consist of a letter for its column and a number for its row. For example, the cell located in column C, row 15, would be identified as cell C15 (see Figure 3–14). The cell in current use is the *active* cell. A block of cells is called a *range*.

Cells can contain values, labels, and formulas (refer to Figure 3–14). A **value** is a number that can be used in calculations. A **label** is a word or number, such as COSTS or the year 1993, that identifies what a particular value means. **Formulas** are mathematical expressions, ranging from simple averages to complex statistical and trigonometric functions, that can use values from other cells. If a number used in a formula is changed, the program automatically recalculates, using the new number. Formulas

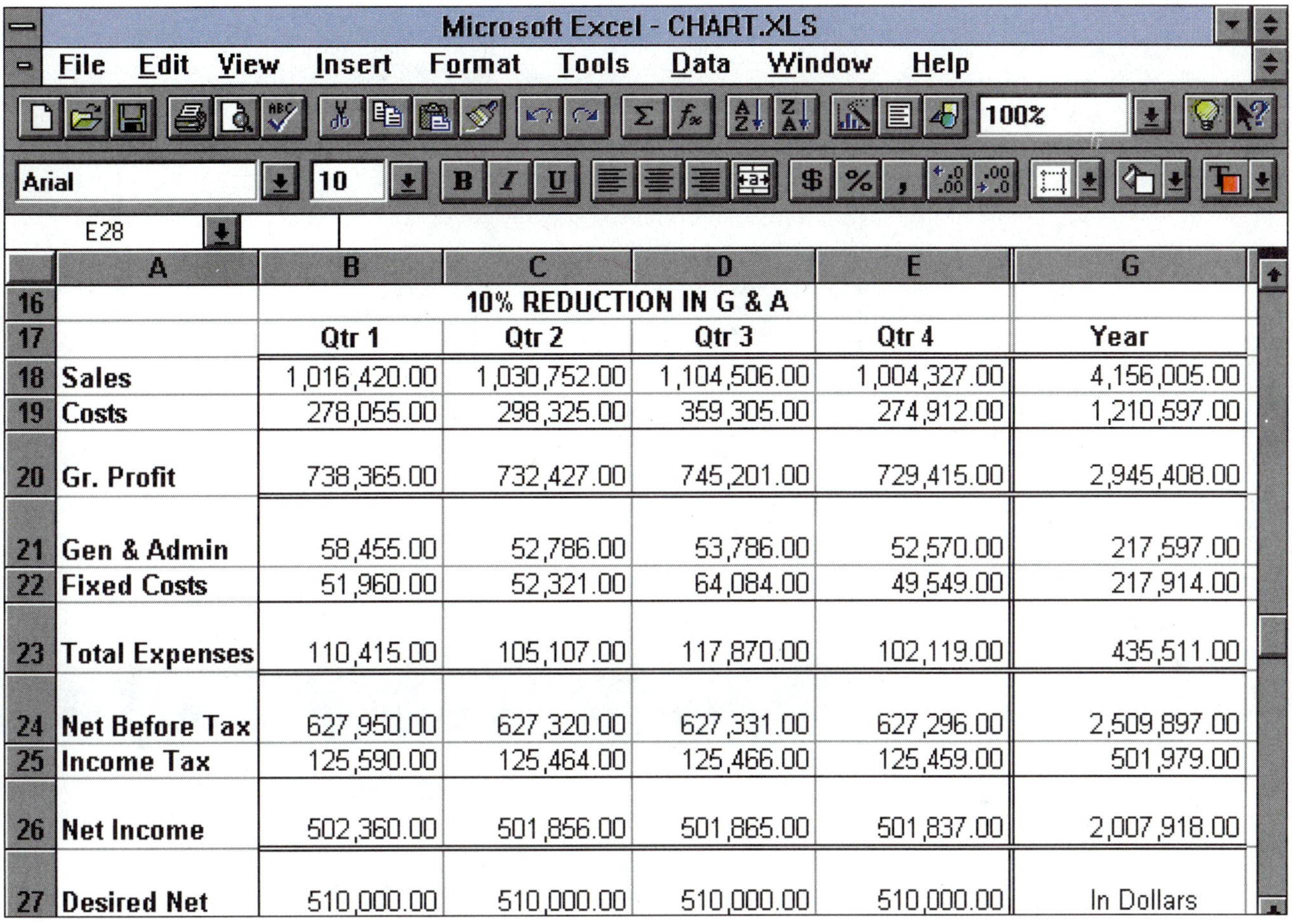

	A	B	C	D	E	G
16		10% REDUCTION IN G & A				
17		Qtr 1	Qtr 2	Qtr 3	Qtr 4	Year
18	Sales	1,016,420.00	1,030,752.00	1,104,506.00	1,004,327.00	4,156,005.00
19	Costs	278,055.00	298,325.00	359,305.00	274,912.00	1,210,597.00
20	Gr. Profit	738,365.00	732,427.00	745,201.00	729,415.00	2,945,408.00
21	Gen & Admin	58,455.00	52,786.00	53,786.00	52,570.00	217,597.00
22	Fixed Costs	51,960.00	52,321.00	64,084.00	49,549.00	217,914.00
23	Total Expenses	110,415.00	105,107.00	117,870.00	102,119.00	435,511.00
24	Net Before Tax	627,950.00	627,320.00	627,331.00	627,296.00	2,509,897.00
25	Income Tax	125,590.00	125,464.00	125,466.00	125,459.00	501,979.00
26	Net Income	502,360.00	501,856.00	501,865.00	501,837.00	2,007,918.00
27	Desired Net	510,000.00	510,000.00	510,000.00	510,000.00	In Dollars

Figure 3–14 Cell Locations
The item in cell A26 is Net Income.

can include special preset functions for sums, averages, minimums and maximums, and rounding. Values and results of formulas can be formatted as integers, dollar amounts, or floating-point numbers. (A *floating-point number* is a real number—that is, one that can contain a fractional part.)

The use of formulas is what makes spreadsheets powerful. A formula can be applied to the contents of specified cells to obtain a result. For example, you could calculate the amount of monthly payments on a loan, depending on the interest rate being charged. It would be a simple matter to determine monthly payments for different lengths of payment time— say, 36, 48, or 60 months. The ability to alter variables within the spreadsheet and easily see what happens to all of those values dependent upon the variables is what makes such analysis a useful tool. As mentioned earlier, this type of analysis is called "what if?" analysis, because you use the formulas to "ask" the spreadsheet *what* would happen to certain figures *if* certain other figures were changed. For example, what happens to your income tax rate if you take a part-time job or a job working on commission rather than on salary? How is your income affected if interest rates

Figure 3–15 Cell Formatting
The values in spreadsheet cells can be formatted to contain commas, dollar signs, percent signs, and a specified number of decimal places. All cells with values in this worksheet are aligned on the right.

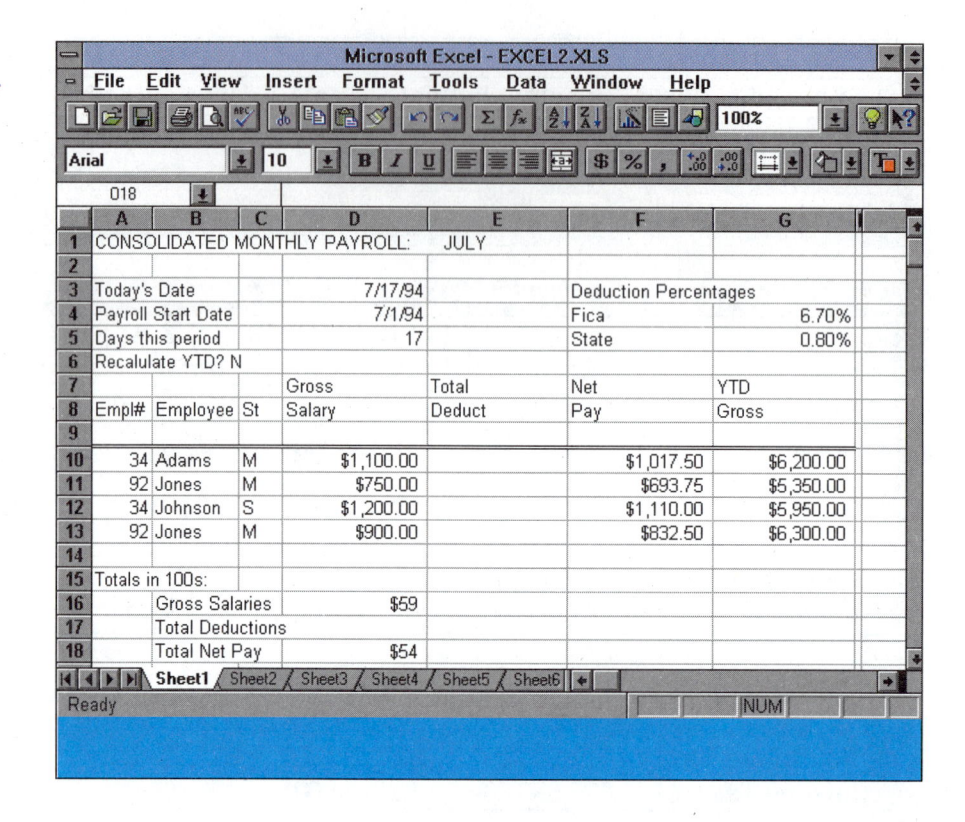

drop to 3.2 percent? Could the PTA earn more money if it sold candy rather than gift wrappings? Multiple "what if?" simulations can be performed to test a range of optional plans. A "what-if?" analysis is sometimes called a *forecast*.

GENERAL FEATURES OF SPREADSHEETS

Spreadsheet programs contain capabilities already described, such as cursor movements, scrolling, undo, insertion, deletion, search, copy, and move. Operations such as move and copy involve ranges of cells rather than blocks of text. Once you have created a spreadsheet file (also called a *worksheet*), you can do a variety of unique jobs, such as locking cells so values cannot be changed, inserting or deleting an entire row or column of cells, sorting data alphabetically or numerically, or changing the width of columns. An autofill function automatically completes a series of numbers or labels that you have begun—for example, the months of the year; a series of numbers counting by ones, tens, or hundreds; or a set of even numbers. Most programs offer predefined **templates** for doing common jobs such as amortizing loans or planning a budget, but you can also design and save your own templates.

Like word processors, spreadsheet programs offer a number of formatting options. The options, such as the following, control the appearance of a cell's contents (see Figure 3–15):

template In a spreadsheet program, a set of predefined formulas and formats ready for user entries.

Profile

Mitch Kapor: The Spreadsheet Blossoms

Comparatively few of the thousands of software packages for microcomputers have been commercial successes. Mitchell Kapor is one person who succeeded in introducing a best-selling and long-lived business application program, *Lotus 1-2-3*.

Kapor's early educational and career program would not predict that success. After graduation from Yale University in 1971, he became a deejay for a rock and roll station in Hartford. Later, in Boston, he taught transcendental meditation, earned an M.A. degree in psychology, and got a counseling job in a psychiatric ward. Simultaneously, however, he did teach himself computer programming, and he designed two statistical and graphics programs for personal computers, one of which was called Tiny Troll. Later, he revised the programs and sold the rights to VisiCorp.

In 1981, he started thinking about the usefulness of an integrated software package—one that would combine spreadsheet, graphics, and information-management capabilities. Kapor teamed up with Jonathan Sachs, a programmer who had already designed three spreadsheet packages, to de-velop the integrated spreadsheet program *Lotus 1-2-3*.

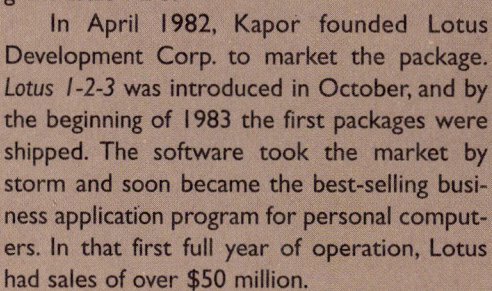

In April 1982, Kapor founded Lotus Development Corp. to market the package. *Lotus 1-2-3* was introduced in October, and by the beginning of 1983 the first packages were shipped. The software took the market by storm and soon became the best-selling business application program for personal computers. In that first full year of operation, Lotus had sales of over $50 million.

Some years later, Kapor left Lotus to pursue other interests, among them the issue of free speech and privacy rights on computer networks. He is currently the chairman of Electronic Frontier Foundation, which deals with this issue as well as others raised by the computer era. As a result of his outspokenness on the subject, he has provided input about the role of the so-called information superhighway. Watch for his opinions in newspaper and computer magazine columns.

- Embedded commas
- Dollar signs
- Percent signs
- Number of decimal places
- Position of data in a cell (centered, to the left, or to the right)
- Typeface and type size

The format rule is stored for each cell along with the cell's value. Most programs display the formatting rule for the active cell in a status line.

The package you are using may generate graphs using data from the spreadsheet. Common graphs are pie charts, bar graphs, and line graphs. Special-purpose graphs include scatter charts, exploding pie charts, and 3-D bar graphs. Many programs go far beyond simple graphs and include features for creating presentation graphics—that is, graphics that are dressed up using different typefaces, colors, lines, borders, clip art, and drawings (see the later section on Graphics Software).

►Data-Management Software

Schools, hospitals, restaurants, and almost every type of business need to store a lot of data. In fact, the ability to retrieve, sort, and analyze data quickly and efficiently could make the difference between a company's success and failure. No other business application has more strategic importance to a company than a **database.** The types of data collected include employee records, customer and supplier records, inventory, invoice information, and insurance information. In the past, the most common way to organize data was to store the records in folders in file cabinets. File cabinets use a lot of space, however, and sometimes several departments may keep the same data. This duplication of data is a waste of time, effort, and space, and can lead to confusion or errors when data has to be updated. By using **data-management software,** an organization can eliminate duplication and improve access to information.

Data-management software (also called a *data manager,* a *database management system,* or a *DBMS)* makes use of a computer rather than filing cabinet drawers and folders for entering, storing, and retrieving data. The data is stored on tapes or disks. With such a program, the boss's secretary can find the names of employees who have several things in common—for example, those who missed 20 or more days of work in the last three months and have a poor performance record. Imagine how long it would take to find these names from the filing cabinets of a large corporation.

A computer and a database program increase the ease of handling large amounts of data, as you might find in a large company, university, or research project. Pharmacies use databases to store drug and patient information that can be cross-referenced in order to avoid giving patients medicines that may be harmful when used together. Mail-order companies use databases to find consumers who would be most likely to use particular products. Data managers are popular software packages for home use, too. They can be used to create and organize addresses, to catalog collections such as stamps or baseball cards, or to keep track of favorite recipes from an extensive library of cookbooks. Popular database programs include *dBASE, Paradox,* and *Approach.*

Data Organization

Data is organized in a hierarchy, from the field to the database:

- A **field** is one data item, such as a student name, an insurance policy number, or an invoice number. A field can be numerical (such as a cost), character (such as a name), or logical (such as Y or N for yes or no) (see Figure 3–16). Items in numeric fields can be used in calculations. Items in logical fields keep track of true-or-false conditions. Some programs allow a date field, which is preset with the correct format for month, day, and year (for example, 10-24-95).

---

database A collection of facts that are stored in a well-organized way so that many people can access the same information for different purposes; a collection of integrated related files.

data-management software An application program used to organize, access, and control information arranged in fields, records, and files.

field An item consisting of one or more characters that are related logically.

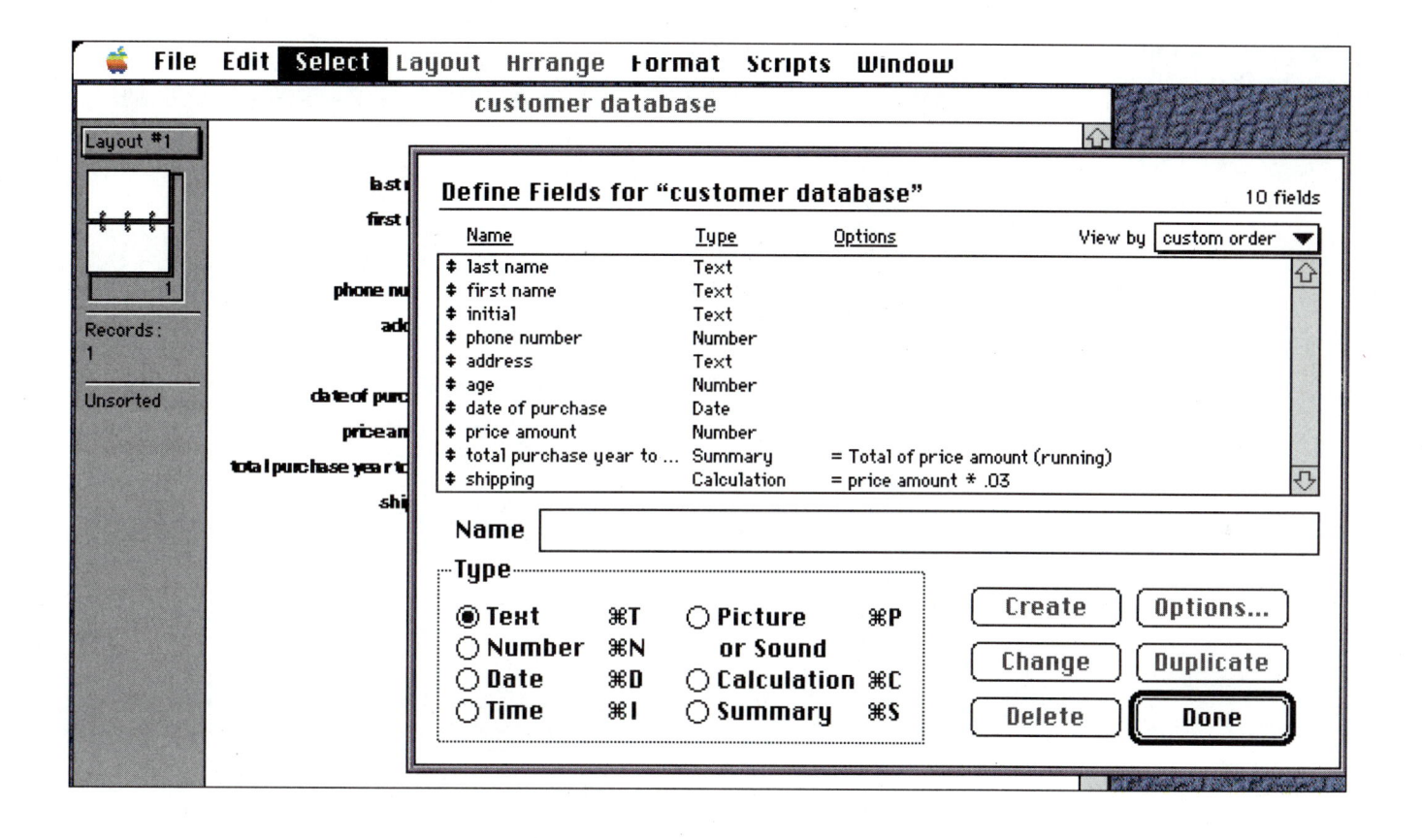

- A group of related fields form a **record**. One student's record might contain fields for name, address, social security number, major, courses taken, and grade-point average.
- A **file** is a group of related records. For example, student records would constitute the college's enrollment file, and alumni records might make up an endowment file.
- A database consolidates various files into one integrated unit that different people can access for different purposes.

With data-management software, you typically set up the structure of the file—that is, the type of information to be included in each record in a file. You enter meaningful names for the fields. For example, if you are creating a file for clients' addresses, the fields might include client name, street address, city, state, zip code, and telephone number. For each field, you designate the type of field (character, numeric, date, or logical) and the field width—that is, the number of characters or digits allowed in a field. For example, the width of a state field might be 2, for two characters. This setup operation may include designing the looks of a screen through which you enter the data for each record (see Figure 3–17). After designing the file, you enter detailed information for each subject in the file. Once the file is created, it can be used to select specific information

Figure 3–16 Setting up Fields Using Data-Management Software
When setting up a new database in Filemaker Pro, the user specifies field name, the type of character (character or numeric), calculations to be executed, and other options for data.

record A collection of related fields.

file A group of related records stored together.

Figure 3–17 A Form for Entering Data
Some programs allow you to enter data through a standard form designed to increase user friendliness.

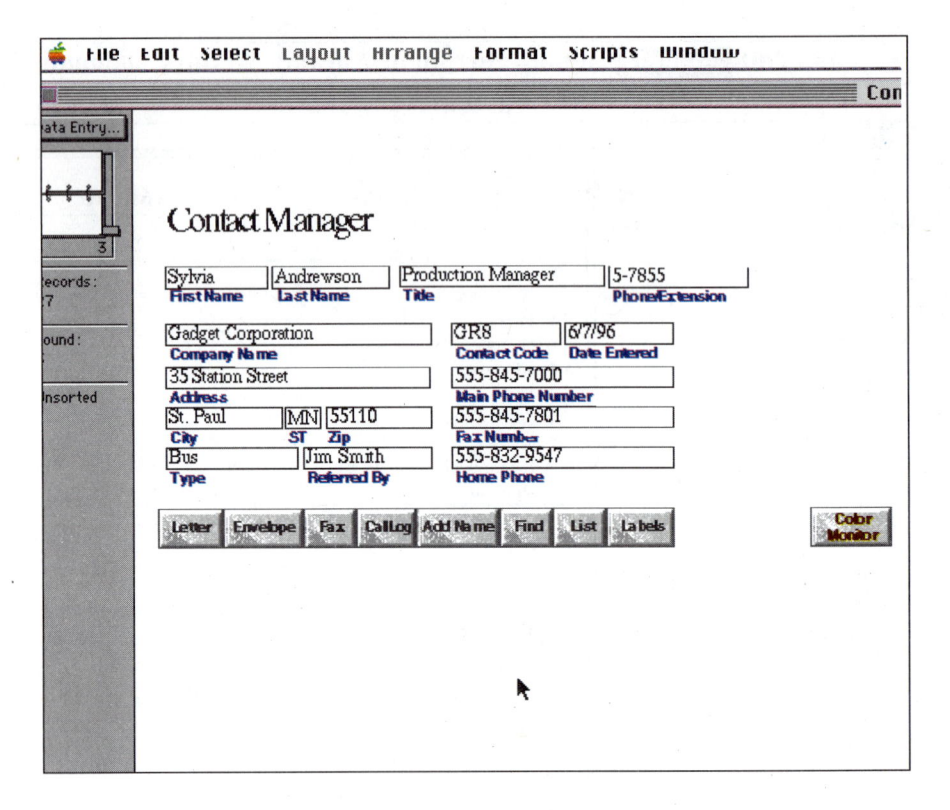

and generate displays or printed reports. The data can be manipulated in these ways:

- Add or delete data within a file.
- Search a file for certain data.
- Update or change data in a file.
- Sort data into some order, such as alphabetically or by zip code.
- Print all or part of the data in a file in some form of report.
- Perform simple mathematical calculations, such as totaling the data in a numeric field.

relational database A database, arranged in tables, that enables the user to open and use data from several files at one time for cross-referencing and linking information in the files.

Many current data managers are called **relational databases.** This means that the data is stored in tables of rows and columns and the software can manage a collection of interrelated files. In a relational database, several files can be opened and used at once. An item that is changed in one file is changed in all of the files in which it appears. This is because the files are linked through one or more shared relations. A shared relation involves data that is common to all the files—that is, a common field or fields. An employee name could be the common field, for example. Since the files are linked, an employee's salary file would not need to include an address and telephone number because that information would already be in the general employee file. (There is some controversy about the exact definition of a relational database, but this book does not go into detail about this problem.)

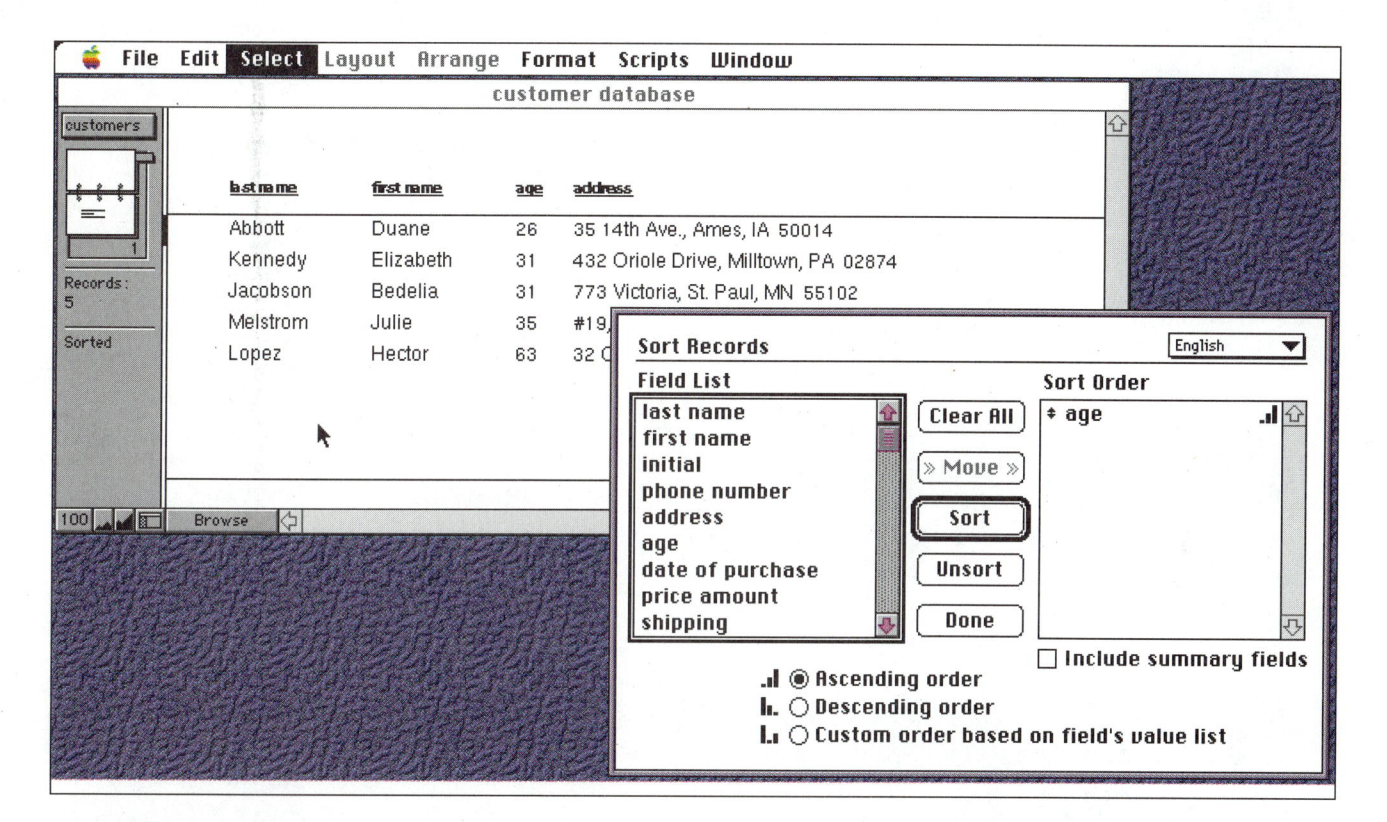

Querying and Reporting

Once a database is created, it can be **queried,** or questioned, to find particular information (see Figure 3–18). For example, a "suppliers" database could be queried to find all suppliers within 25 miles that offer consumables such as paper products. Querying is often called *browsing*. Queries can be stated in terms of relational operators (OR, AND, NOT, =, +, >, <, and so on) and commands (SELECT, DISPLAY, LIST, ADD, and so on). They also include a key that indicates the field in which items can be found.

Queries can be written so that a report is printed containing the answers to the query. The report function of data-management software is called a *report generator*. The power and flexibility of report writers vary greatly from program to program. Some simply print lists, while others print in column-and-row format and do calculations. Most report generators include features for titles, boxes, lines, and other formats that can make a report easy to understand. A widely used language for browsing and reporting is *SQL* (pronounced *sequel)*, which stands for Structured Query Language.

Figure 3–18 Query Facilities
Filemaker Pro by Claris uses the sort feature to browse particular information. This screen shows the results of a sort for all customers over 20 years old listed in ascending order.

query To ask for, or request, specific information from a database.

▶Graphics Software

Today's computer graphics are so advanced that it is hard to tell if a picture was made by computer or by trick photography. You see examples of

Window on Computing

Resumes That Make a Database Weep

Forget the elegant blue or gray paper. Forget the exotic typefaces and decorative graphics. Forget the double columns and small print. You might confuse the computer—that is, if you are counting on having your resume scanned into a commercial resume database. Instead, use white or beige paper and a standard font, and do not fold the paper, because the scanner might misread words in the crease. And please, beef up the technical jargon: Words that turn on the company recruiter—*streamlined* and *implemented*, for example—go totally unnoticed by a database search. Specific skills and attributes, such as Unix operating system experience, foreign languages spoken, previous jobs, and college degrees, make a database search stop in its tracks.

Companies are receiving such huge piles of resumes that many worthy applications are going unnoticed. To handle all of the material, some companies, such as Nike (the athletic-shoe maker) and Ortho Pharmaceutical, have been scanning the resumes into company databases. Employment specialists then conduct computer searches through the databases to come up with a short list of qualified candidates. Other companies, such as AT&T and Citicorp, are making use of independent resume databanks such as Job Bank USA, SkillSearch, and National Resume Bank. That's why job seekers need to gear their resumes to the database rather than to the company recruiter: Computers ignore all the fluffy words and sharp graphics, and hone in on the basic stuff that indicates a worthy candidate. In fact, when you subscribe to an independent resume database (which may run from $20 to $50 for a six-month or a year-long listing), you may need to fill out a special application rather than sending in your normal resume.

Using a resume database doesn't mean that you should neglect your normal resume activities: Four months or longer can pass before you get that phone call for an interview. It does mean, however, that you might want to consider preparing two types of resumes, one for the recruiter and one for the computer.

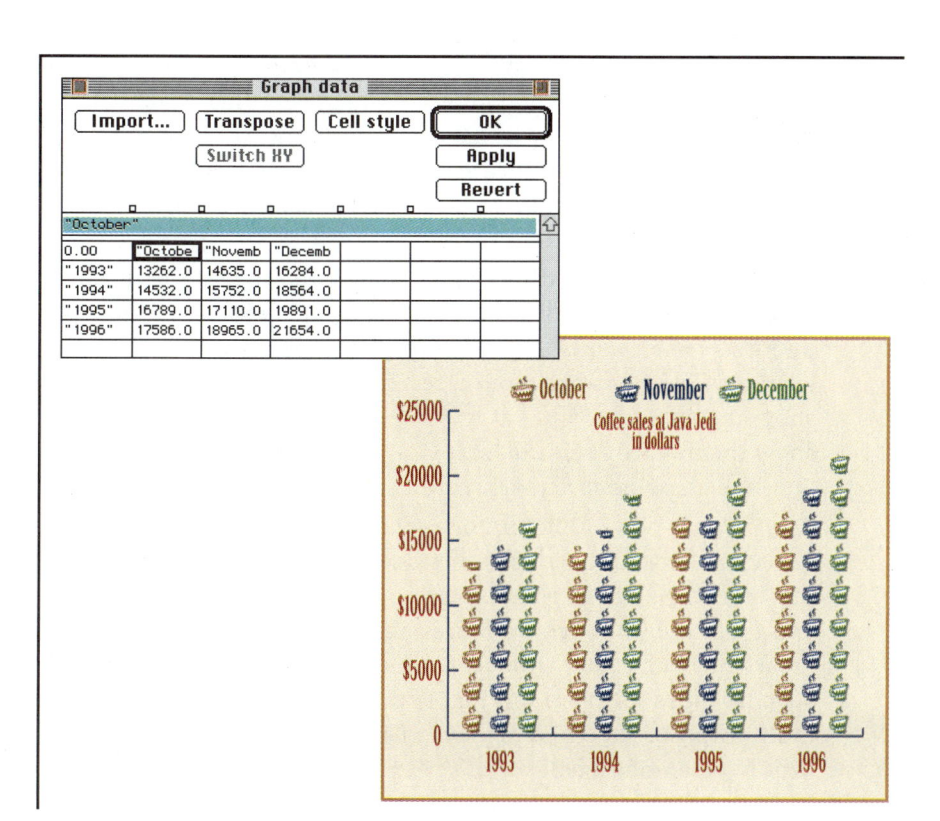

Figure 3–19 Numbers and Graphics
Presentation graphics can increase understanding by showing a visual relationship between numbers.

computer graphics in commercials and sports broadcasts on television. Videos and movies make use of computer graphics for special effects and cartoons. Businesses use programs that turn complex numbers into bar graphs and pie charts that are easy to understand. Special computer-aided design (CAD) packages can help engineers and architects design cars, machines, buildings, and sports shoes. Some programs offer animation options. And you can have fun simply drawing pictures and creating special effects with a paint program.

The two basic types of graphics software are **presentation graphics** and **paint programs** and **draw programs.** Presentation graphics programs (often included to some degree of complexity in spreadsheet programs) are used to create charts, graphs, and other images for business presentations. Paint and draw programs are used to create and edit pictures.

Presentation Graphics Programs

Presentation graphics are used to make an impression on an audience, such as a company's customers or its employees. A presentation may be designed to persuade customers to buy a new product, to justify a recent product price increase, or to introduce a new employee pension plan or a change of suppliers.

A presentation graphics program accepts imported or entered numerical data and translates it into a picture that shows the relationship among the various numbers. Several types of these "pictures" are bar graphs, line graphs, pie charts, and pictographs (see Figure 3–19).

presentation graphics High-quality, professional-looking graphics that present numerical information in an easy-to-understand format, such as a pie chart or bar graph.

paint program A program for creating and manipulating pixels in order to create images; appropriate for free-hand drawing.

draw program A program used for creating and manipulating objects such as lines, curves, ovals, circles, rectangles; appropriate for creating images to scale.

- *Bar graphs* are made up of vertical or horizontal bars that compare the performance of several subjects in a given time. Each bar represents the value of one subject. For example, a bar graph could represent a town's organizations' raising money for a new community recreation center, with each organization being represented by its own bar.
- *Line graphs* show the direction of change in the performance over time of a subject being studied. Several line graphs can be superimposed over each other to compare the performance of several subjects. The line representing each subject connects points that show the subject's value at a particular time. A line graph could show the monthly sales of, say, Pepper's Pizza Shop, with the second line showing last year's volume.
- A *pie chart* shows a picture of a whole subject divided into parts. The chart looks like a circle divided into wedges, like slices of a pie, and it shows the relationships among the sizes of the wedges and the whole pie, which represents the total. A pie chart could break down the total shoe sales of an athletic-shoe supplier into specific types of shoe: running, tennis, golf, bowling, aerobic, and multipurpose. An *exploding pie chart* bursts out any wedges that should be emphasized.
- A *pictograph* shows values in terms of pictures, with each individual picture representing a fixed number of the subject being studied. For example, a picture of an athletic shoe could represent 1,000 shoes sold. Thus, a pictograph could be used to show the number of athletic shoes sold by one supplier versus those sold by a competitor.

Full-featured presentation graphics software offers numerous functions that help dress up a chart, including a variety of typefaces, colors, drawings, arrows, boxes, and clip art. It provides a method of creating the legend, or explanation, of the elements in the graph. It may generate three-dimensional displays.

Some programs provide capabilities for creating "slide shows" using the images displayed on the computer screen. They may generate transitions from one image to the next by fading out the first or by peeling it down from one corner until the new picture is exposed. The slide shows can be presented via very large monitors, large-screen televisions, or adapters for overhead projectors.

Paint and Draw Programs

Paint and draw programs are used to create pictures. Usually, a paint program is simpler to use than a draw program. A paint program is ideal for freehand drawing because it treats an image as a group of individual pixels that can be manipulated at will. It offers a variety of tools for creating an image (see Figure 3–20). You select the tools from a set of icons (also

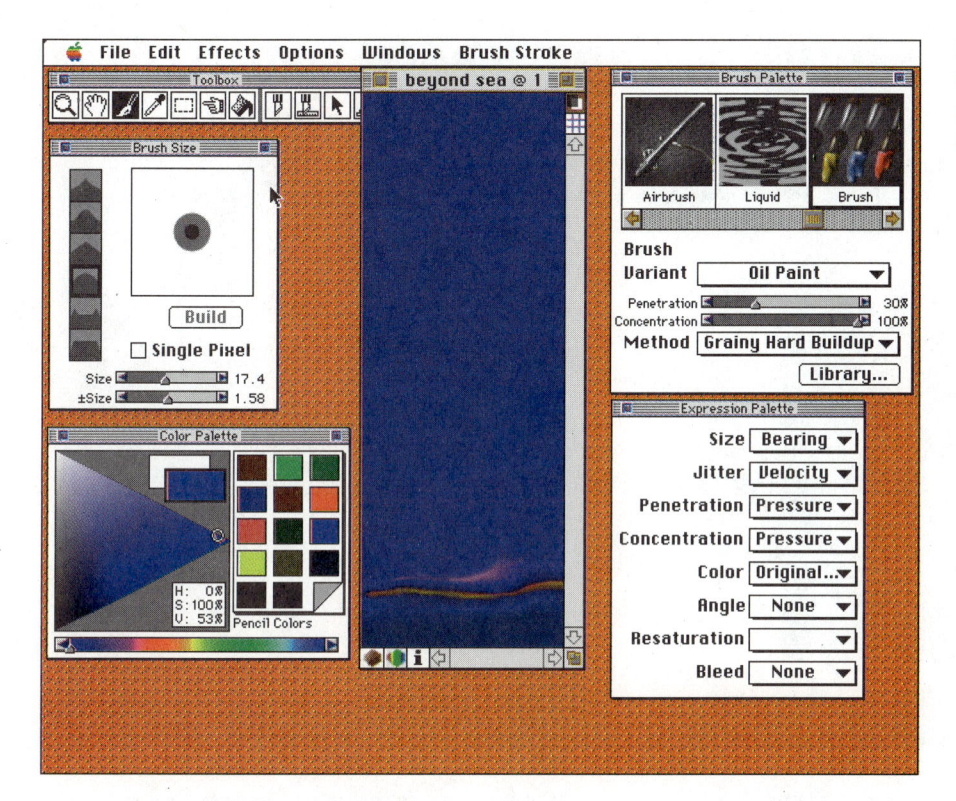

Figure 3–20 Paint Software
Painter 2.0 simulates natural media tools and textures to create original artwork as well as image editing capabilities.

called a *palette* or a *toolkit*). For freehand painting, you would select the brush icon and a brush shape and width. To draw lines, select the pencil icon and a pencil width. The spray-paint (or airbrush) function gives a line soft edges rather than the hard edge of a brush or pencil line. Other tools include the following:

- The paint bucket (or fill) icon, for dumping "paint" into an entire outlined area
- The eraser icon, for deleting some or all of a picture
- The marquee icon, for selecting a rectangular section of a picture to copy, move, or delete
- A lasso icon, for "tightening" around the shape of a selected image so that you move or copy only the image, but none of the background
- A "grabber," for moving a selection once it is chosen
- Tools for drawing circles, straight lines, ovals, and rectangles
- Tools for rotating, flipping, enlarging, or flattening an image
- A function for typing alphanumeric data
- A zoom function (from *zoom lens*), which enlarges a portion of a drawing for detailed work

Many features of paint programs, such as line and brush variables, shape options, zooming, and rotating, are available in draw programs. A

Window on Computing

The Future is Here: Real or Contrived

Remember the TV commercial that asked, "Is it live or is it Memorex?" With the widespread use of very powerful computer capabilities, you might be asking a similar question about a lot of events.

In the area of entertainment, you have already seen music videos, movies, and special effects in which a real event has been altered by superimposing photographs or video on top of others. In 1993, effects wizards of the popular movie *Jurassic Park* created "real" dinosaurs through complex and highly developed graphics modeling software. Some studios are colorizing old black-and-white movies. What is the truth and what is contrived?

A similar question could be asked of evidence used in a courtroom. A videotape taken by a passerby rallied much of the nation on the side of Rodney King in a Los Angeles incident involving the question of police brutality. The tape presented a live event, and although it did not depict the action from the beginning, its truthfulness was validated by witnesses.

But what about a 1991 case in Corte Madera, Calif., in which porn-movie king Jim Mitchell drove to the home of his younger brother and business partner, Artie, and shot him. The district attorney did not believe that the killer shot eight times in self-defense. Because there were no eyewitnesses, the prosecution persuaded the judge to let the jury watch a video of the shooting. Rather than actual footage, however, the video was a simulation of the event, based on bullet trajectories and created with the help of computer-aided design software after the evidence found at the scene was analyzed. The video did convince the jury that Jim was guilty, but an appeal is in process, in part because the defense attorney claims the contrived video had no place in a court of law. One problem with the tape is that the figure who was shot did not brandish his beer bottle in a threatening manner, which might have indicated that Jim needed to defend himself. This raises the following questions: Can such a graphics simulation be used fairly in a courtroom? Can it really illustrate exactly what happened?

CONCEPT SUMMARY
THE BASIC COMPUTER APPLICATIONS

Word Processing
A word-processing program lets you write, edit, format, and print text.

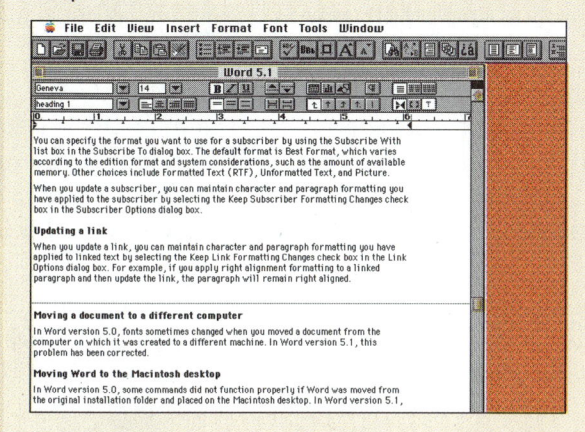

- word wrap
- insertions and deletions
- delete, copy, and move block operations
- search and replace
- spelling checkers and thesauruses
- print formatting and style sheets

Spreadsheets
A spreadsheet lets you record numbers and solve math problems

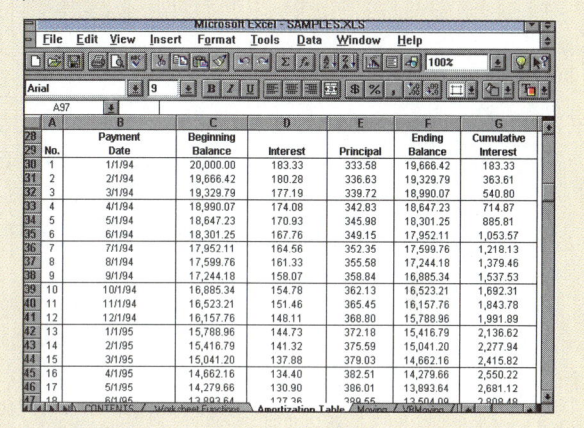

- what-if? analysis
- cells
- labels, values, and formats
- recalculation
- templates
- cell formatting

Data Management Software
Data management software lets you set up files and databases and enter, store, and retrieve data.

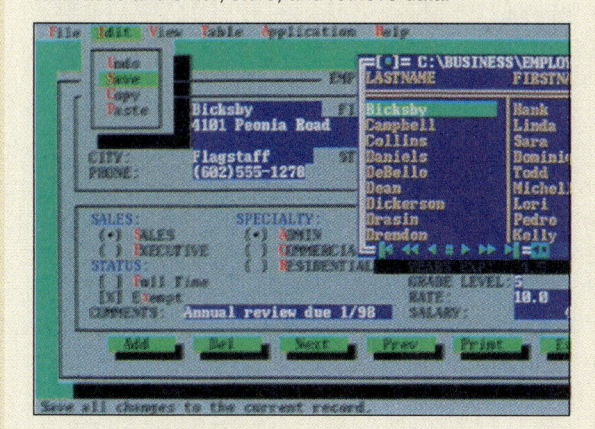

- relational databases
- fields, records, and files
- queries
- report generators
- query language

Graphics Software
Graphics Software lets you create graphics images.

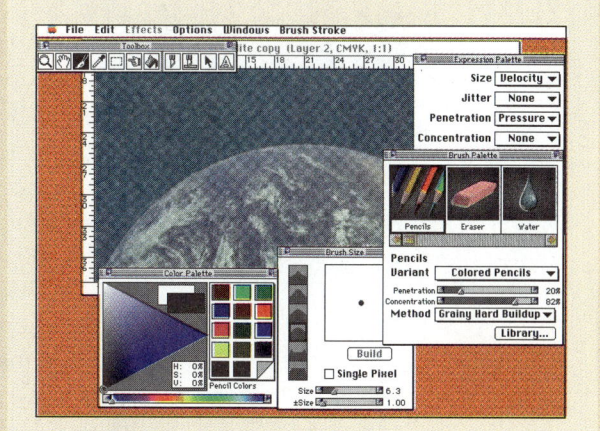

- presentation graphics for audiences
- paint programs for drawing images
- draw programs for creating images
- pixels
- resolution

draw program, however, treats the various parts of an image as objects (lines, circles, arcs, squares, and so on) that are handled mathematically. Thus, you manipulate the object, not the pixels. For this reason, a draw program scales images to different sizes without sacrificing the smoothness of curves in the image. The higher the resolution of the monitor, the better the image looks. Some programs include "filters," which simulate brightness, sharpness or blurriness, and contrast through a series of math calculations.

Draw programs are also called *illustration software* or *design software,* and advanced draw programs are called *computer-aided design (CAD)* software (described in detail in Chapter 6). Most draw software is used for drafting and engineering purposes, and requires high-quality graphics monitors, light pens or digitizers for drawing, and special printers or plotters.

The software described in this chapter brings the power of microcomputers to computer users at home as well as to employees of organizations. Many people can find uses for one or all of these packages, and each month billions of hours go into working with this software. Yet frustration mounts when a user cannot install a coveted package on her computer because the package is not compatible with the system software. The next chapter covers the system software options and the role system software plays in the compatibility problem.

▶Summary Points

- Commercial software comes on disks, from which it is installed on a hard disk and then loaded into computer memory for use.
- Data and programs are kept in files, each of which needs a file name. Files appear on the screen in boxes called windows. When a file is opened, you may need to scroll through a file to see all of the information it contains.
- Today's programs offer a variety of user-friendly features, including menus from which choices are made, dialog boxes that require user input, and alert boxes that give information about something that is about to happen. A feature called WYSIWYG ("what you see is what you get") displays a document on the screen as it will look when it is printed on paper. Other user-friendly features include macro capability, undo functions, and on-screen help.
- Word processing lets you write, edit, format, and print text. Common features are automatic word wrap, insertions, deletions, and search. Block operations involve the selection of a block of text for deleting, copying, or moving. Full-featured packages offer redlining, footnoting, outlining, calculations, multiple columns, and generation of indexes and tables of contents.

- Print formats in word processing include options for margins, tabs, character appearance, line spacing, justification, pagination, headers, and footers.
- An electronic spreadsheet program is used to set up columns of numbers and formulas in order to solve mathematically oriented problems. It is commonly used for "what-if?" analysis, in which scenarios are designed to reflect the results of changes to some numbers.
- A spreadsheet is set up in rows and columns. Values (numbers), formulas, and labels are entered into the cells formed by the rows and columns. Each cell is identified by its coordinates.
- Unique features of spreadsheet programs are autofill (for entering a series of numbers), templates (predefined worksheets), sorting, cell formatting, cell locking, and generation of graphs.
- Data-management software is used to create, store, and manipulate data. Each data item stored is called a field. A group of related fields form a record, and related records make up a file.
- Data managers perform these basic tasks: adding or deleting data within a file, searching a file, updating data, sorting data, printing data, and performing math calculations.
- Relational databases organize data into tables of rows and columns, and provide for the opening and use of several files at once. Files are linked through one or more shared relations. The database can be queried, or questioned, to find particular information.
- Presentation graphics software is used to create charts, graphs, and other images for business presentations. Common charts are bar charts, pie charts, and line graphs.
- Paint and draw programs enable the creation of pictures. With a paint program, each individual pixel on the screen can be controlled. In draw programs, entries (such as lines, arcs, circles, and squares) are translated into geometric formulas. Draw programs handle objects with curves well because the curves remain smooth whenever an object is sized larger or smaller.
- Most paint and draw programs offer a number of features for lines, brush widths, textures, and shapes. Objects can be copied, moved, rotated, flipped, enlarged, or flattened.

▶Review Questions

1. What is the function of files? How do you identify a file?
2. Of what benefit is WYSIWYG? What do the letters stand for?
3. Describe three jobs that can be done with word processing but not with a typewriter.

4. Describe three block operations in a word processor.
5. What is meant by *print formatting?* Describe some things you can do with this aspect of word processing.
6. How does the recalculation feature of spreadsheets facilitate business forecasting?
7. Where would cell G17 be located in a worksheet? Cell K1?
8. How is a style sheet in a word processor like a template in a spreadsheet?
9. What is the purpose of data-management software? What are some of its basic functions? What is a major advantage of a data manager versus a file cabinet?
10. How could a relational database help control data redundancy in an organization?
11. What is the purpose of presentation graphics? Give an example.
12. In what situation would it be better to use a paint program rather than a draw program? Why?

▶Activities and Research

1. Discuss some features you would like a word processor to have. Why would it be useful to work with multiple windows? Use a word processing program to try some of the word processing features described in this chapter, including moving text, formatting some text for printing, and searching for text.
2. Think of two ways that you personally could use a spreadsheet program. Explain these uses. Set up a simple spreadsheet that demonstrates the items in Figure 3–13.
3. Collect some examples of bar charts, pie charts, line graphs, and other graphic material. List the types of information most effectively displayed by each type of graphic. How do presentation graphics aid communication in a business setting?
4. Select a topic that would be suitable for use with data-management software. Describe how you would set up the fields for this topic. Would you require just one file or several files for the information? Why? Find out if there is a commercially prepared database available about the topic you chose.

CHAPTER 4

COMPUTER FUNDAMENTALS: SYSTEM SOFTWARE

OUTLINE

Learning Objectives
Introduction
Operating Systems
 Types of System Programs
 Capabilities of Operating Systems
 Window on Computing: The Future Is Here: Massively Parallel Processing
 User Interfaces
 Microcomputer Operating Systems and Shells
 Profile: Jobs' Next Job
 Concept Summary: The Operating System as a Link

Software Development
 System Software and Language Translation
 Computer Programming Languages
 Stages of Program Development
 Structured Programming Techniques
 Window on Computing: Chopping Off the Branches
 Concept Summary: Software Development
Summary Points
Review Questions
Activities and Research

LEARNING OBJECTIVES

After reading this chapter, you should be able to:

- Describe the functions of system programs.
- Explain how features such as task switching and multitasking increase a computer's power.
- Describe four types of user interfaces, and list advantages of each.
- List characteristics of several commercial microcomputer operating systems.
- Distinguish among several programming languages.
- Explain the four steps in software development, and show how structured programming techniques facilitate the production of software.

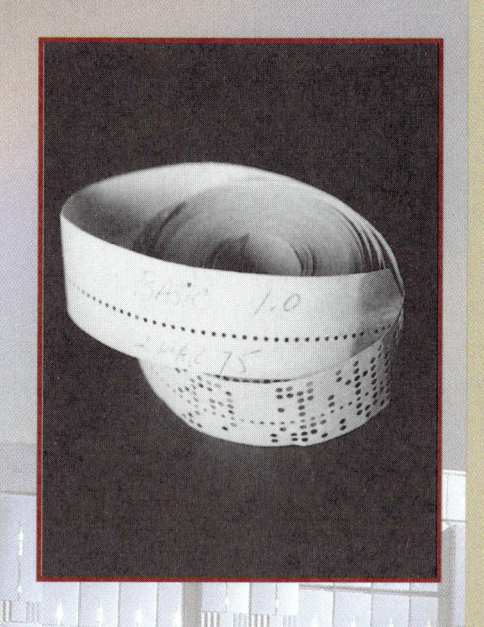

system program Software, such as the operating system and utility programs, that manages computer resources at the machine level rather than at the user level; programs that coordinate the operation of computer circuitry and assist in the development of application programs.

operating system The set of system programs that a computer uses to manage its own operations.

IBM-compatible All computers that are compatible with IBM PCs, meaning they can run the same software as an IBM PC.

INTRODUCTION

As you recall from Chapter 1, the two types of programs are system software and application programs. **System programs** control the operation of a computer *system*. Application programs are programs that users apply to get their everyday work done. As a computer user, you are apt to be concerned with applications that enable you to write a report, prepare charts to illustrate your point, and print out a copy. So why should you be concerned with system software?

First of all, application software cannot be used without system software; and as you enlarge your software library, you want to be sure the two are compatible. For example, IBM PC computers use programs that the Apple Macintosh cannot use, because the two have very different **operating systems.** Second, there are several operating systems even for the same machine, and each has its advantages and drawbacks. For example, IBM PCs and **IBM-compatible** PCs commonly use DOS (Disk Operating System). Because of the limitations of DOS, however, other more powerful operating systems, such as OS/2 and Unix, have been developed to make use of the powerful microprocessors now on the market. Third, system software determines the way to interact with the computer and supports some of the capabilities of applications. This chapter helps you understand what an operating system does, and describes commercial operating systems for microcomputers. It also explains briefly how any program—system or application—is defined, designed, coded, and tested.

▶ Operating Systems

System programs affect directly the operation of the computer, usually without your knowing it. They manage the components of a computer system, keeping data from "bumping" into each other and allocating storage. They provide a way to communicate with the computer, and support applications in such a way that programmers do not have to deal with the internal workings of the hardware each time they write a new program. System programs are included in your computer system when you buy it, but can also be bought separately (see Figure 4–1).

Types of System Programs

Some system programs are manufactured into ROM chips. They basically ensure that the hardware is working properly. Three common types are described here:

- The *bootstrap loader* starts up, or **boots,** the computer when you turn it on. (Yes, the name does come from the phrase "Pulling yourself up by your bootstraps.") The bootstrap loader also loads the operating system into memory from the hard disk.

- Immediately after you turn on the computer, other system programs, called *diagnostic routines,* begin their "rounds"—testing memory, the CPU, and other hardware to be sure they are operational. Some computers display a message telling you that the diagnostic tests are occurring.

boot To load the first piece of software (usually the operating system) that starts a computer.

Figure 4–1 Packaged System Software
Although operating systems include many utilities, collections of utility programs are often sold as separate packages—for example, Norton Utilities from Symantec Corp. for IBM-compatibles and Now Utilities from Now Software, Inc., for Macintosh computers.

- *Input/output instructions* enable the computer to interpret keyboard input, transfer data, and control instructions between the computer and its peripherals. For instance, they cause an *m* to appear on the screen when you press the *M* key, and they make sure output goes to the proper device—the screen instead of the printer, for example. These jobs are very often considered "traffic cop" jobs. In IBM PCs and compatibles, some of these instructions are located on the BIOS (basic input/output system) chip.

The operating system itself is usually stored on the hard disk, although in some computers, parts of the operating system are located in ROM. The operating system coordinates the resources of the computer, interprets your commands, and enables you to interact with application programs. It frequently determines the way you interact with programs, too.

Among the operating system programs that you actually interact with are **utility programs.** These programs do the "housekeeping" jobs related to managing computer system resources. They eliminate the need for inserting the routines in application programs and include the following:

- Disk preparation for formatting, or initializing, blank floppy disks. (This prepares a disk so that data and programs can be stored on it by a particular operating system and computer.)
- File handling for keeping track of, duplicating, erasing, and renaming files.
- File recovery, in case a file is accidentally erased, trashed, or lost.
- Disk optimizer for defragmenting the hard disk, in which all the pieces of a file are collected into one place on the hard disk to increase speed and efficiency. "Fragmenting" occurs because the operating system "writes," or records, data in the first available spot on a disk; thus, a document that is changed and saved many times has parts in several places on the disk.
- Screen savers—programs that blank the screen or cause objects to glide over the screen in order to prevent images from imprinting themselves permanently into the screen (see Figure 4–2).
- Virus-protection programs, which help prevent the entry of rogue instructions that could sabotage software or data.

utility program A program that performs a specific task, usually relating to managing system resources such as files and disks.

CAPABILITIES OF OPERATING SYSTEMS

Most operating systems for personal computers are single-user systems in which one user does one job at a time. Mainframes and minicomputers enable two or more users at a time to run programs; thus, they are called multiuser systems. Over the years, programmers have developed operating systems for microcomputers that bring such computers ever closer to the power of mainframes (see Figure 4–3). Some of these advances are described in the following sections.

Figure 4–2 Screen Saver
This screen saver from After Dark displays flying toasters, which seems frivolous and fun but actually prevents images from burning themselves into the screen elements while you are away from your computer.

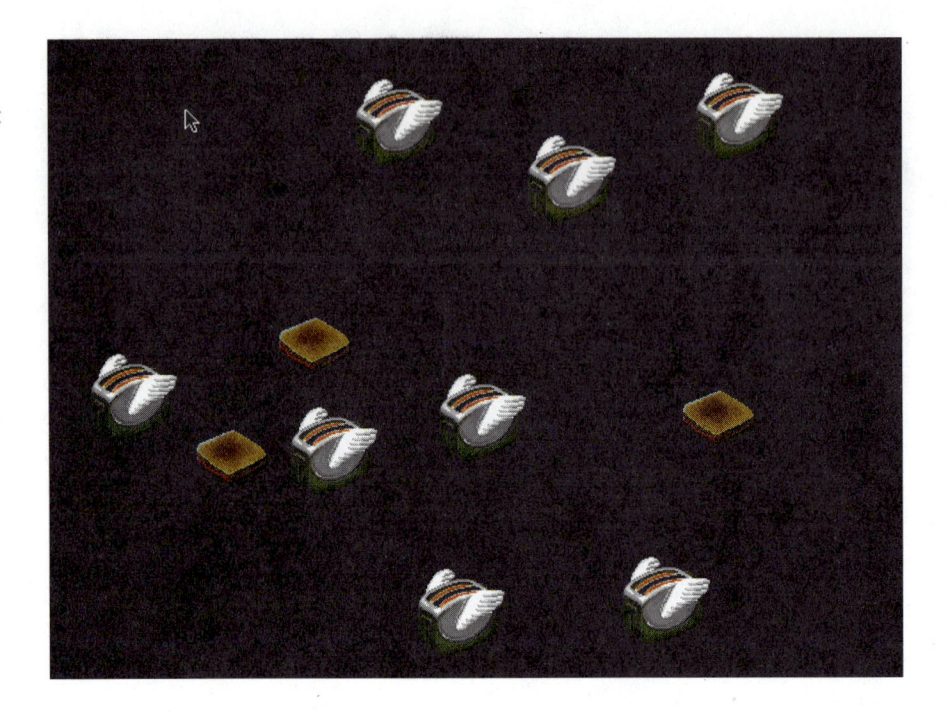

TASK SWITCHING

The earliest operating systems allowed microcomputers to handle only one program in memory at a time. The first step toward the use of multiple programs was **task switching.** Task switching lets you load multiple programs—word processing software and a database program, for example—into memory so that they will be available for use. Then you can stop working on a report in a word processing program in order to look

task switching The capability of an operating system that enables you to have two programs loaded at the same time so that you can work back and forth between them.

Figure 4–3 Recent Trends in Operating Systems
These trends in operating system development demonstrate the My-Fair-Lady principle: Why can't a microcomputer be more like a mainframe?

Today's operating systems for microcomputers are providing more and more of the following characteristics:

- Relatively bulletproof (that is, safe from user errors)
- Networking capabilities for linking microcomputers
- Multitasking
- Virtual memory
- Security controls designed to prevent sabotage and unauthorized access to files
- Efficient administration of operations
- Support for very large amounts of data and files
- Multiplatform support (that is, for PCs, Macs, and Unix-based workstations)
- Multimedia applications (that is, those that include text, graphics, sound, and motion)
- User friendliness, resulting in fewer user calls for technical support from manufacturers

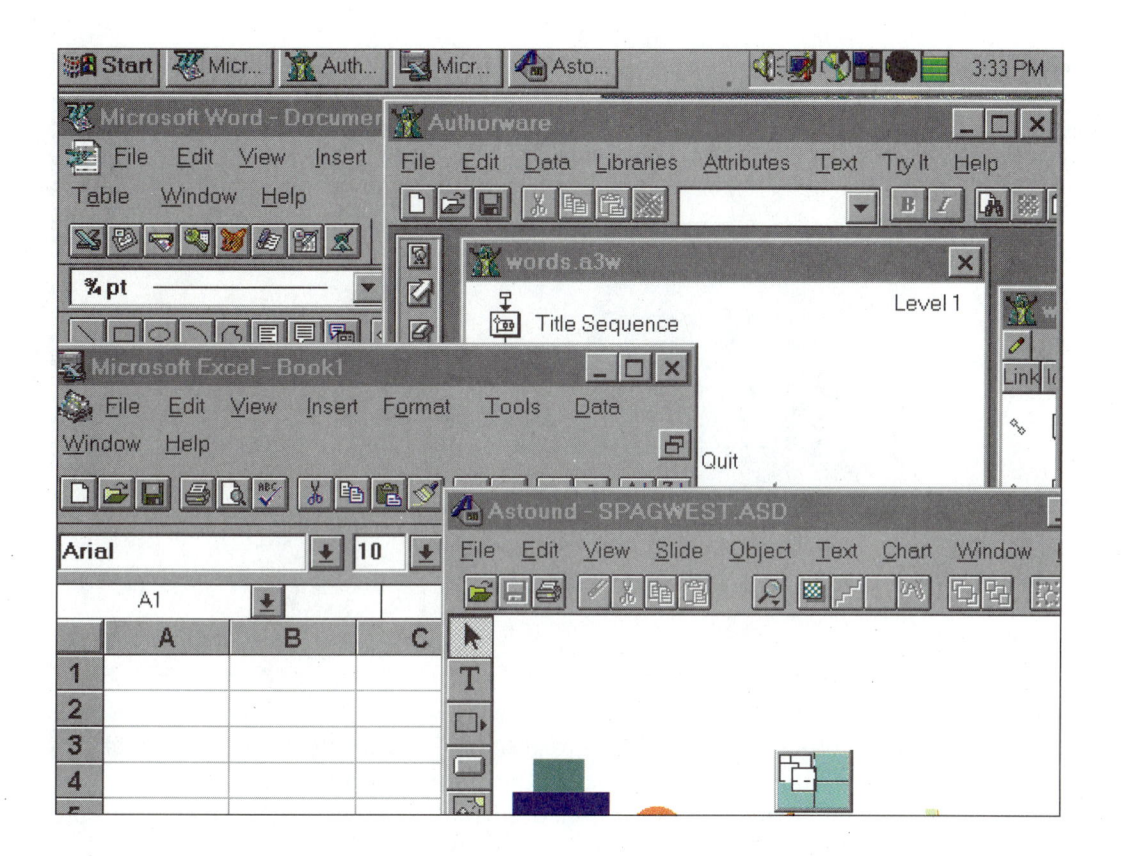

up some information in a database without quitting one program and starting another. Basically, the process *interrupts* one application and switches it for the other; however, it does *not* allow two or more programs to be run *concurrently*.

Multitasking

A **multitasking** operating system allows you to run two or more tasks at the same time. The task that is currently accepting input is the foreground task, and the task that is operating beside it is the background task. A background task, such as printing or searching a database, cannot accept input while you are working in the foreground task, such as word processing (see Figure 4–4).

You will frequently see the term *memory protection* in connection with multitasking. This process keeps each program and set of data being used in confined regions, or partitions, of memory so that the items do not "stray" into memory locations that are already taken.

One problem with multitasking is that memory is not large enough to hold all of the programs and data being used at once. This problem is alleviated by the use of **virtual memory** (see Figure 4–5). Virtual memory is based on the principle that only the immediately needed portion of a program or data must be in memory at any given time. The rest of the program or data can be kept in direct-access storage, such as the hard disk.

Figure 4–4 Using a Variety of Software
A user can work with several applications at a time when the computer's operating system is OS/2.

multitasking Running two or more programs on a computer at once.

virtual memory A technique in which portions of programs and data are swapped back an forth between storage and memory, giving the illusion that memory is unlimited.

Figure 4–5 Virtual Memory and Swapping
Virtual memory enables an operating system to treat storage as if it were memory.

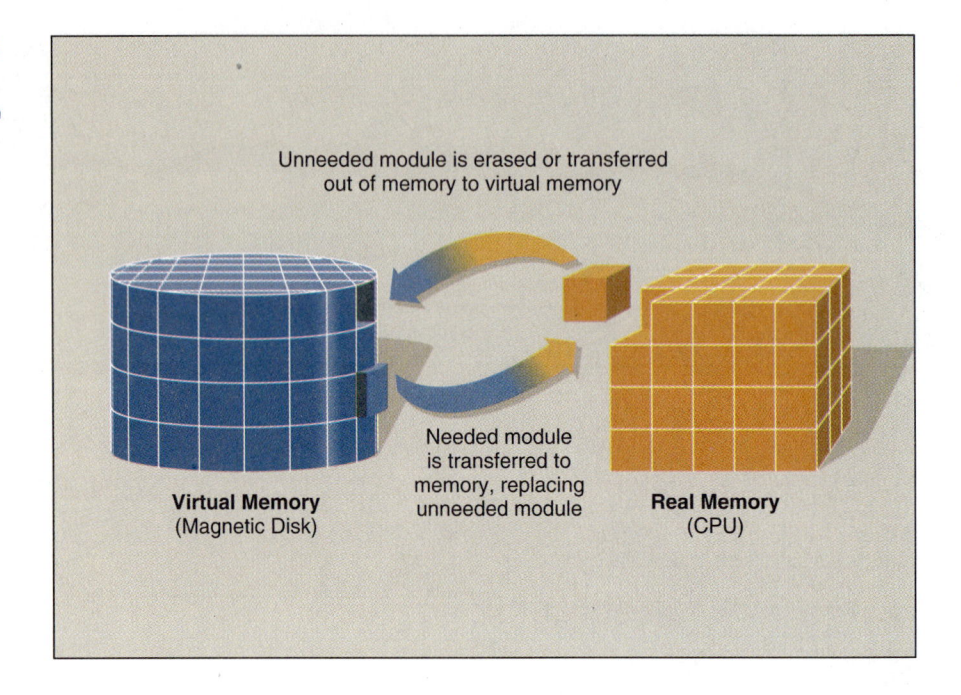

[Diagram: Unneeded module is erased or transferred out of memory to virtual memory. Needed module is transferred to memory, replacing unneeded module. Virtual Memory (Magnetic Disk) ↔ Real Memory (CPU)]

When other portions of the program or data are needed, virtual memory "swaps" unneeded portions for the needed portions. This gives the illusion that memory is unlimited, or virtual—that is, in effect practically but not actually. (When differentiating between memory and virtual memory, the term **real memory** is usually given to memory.)

real memory Actual RAM memory, as opposed to virtual memory.

DATA AND INSTRUCTION EXCHANGE

Many current operating systems not only permit two programs to run at once, but also enable the linking of data and instructions among programs. Such links are referred to as *dynamic*. For example, in files that are linked, data that is changed in one file is automatically changed in all affected files. In addition, one program can "broadcast" a request for information to other programs so that the first program will have the most recent data to use. This might occur when a spreadsheet program needs the most recent price increase, which it can get from a database program that is updating inventory and prices. The most advanced of these exchanges occurs in programs in which data has been "embedded," or imported, from another program. The link allows you to "click" on the embedded data and have access to the functions of the program with which you created the data. Different operating systems have different names for these capabilities—for example, dynamic data exchange (DDE), and object linking and embedding (OLE), both found in Microsoft products.

USER INTERFACES

The method by which you communicate with the computer is called the **user interface.** The most basic user interface—the command-line interface—can be frustrating: You must type codes that vary from program to

user interface The method by which a user communicates with a computer.

Window on Computing

The Future is Here: Massively Parallel Processing

While the term *massively parallel* may conjure up images of traffic flow on Los Angeles freeways, it really refers to the design of computers. Instead of routing operations one at a time through a single, central processor the way almost all computers now operate, massively parallel computers use hundreds, thousands, and even tens of thousands of processors, all working in concert but each doing its own chunk of an operation. If you imagine a dozen people on riding mowers cutting swaths through a two-acre property, you see that they can finish the job much faster than can one person on a lone mower. The principle is the same for massively parallel computers: Rows of microprocessors can do a job more quickly than the single, lone central processor.

This concept has worked successfully for scientific work on supercomputers, but it is being tried on microcomputers, too. Several makers, including Sequent Computer Systems Inc. and Pyramid Technology, are using multiprocessors consisting of 30 or so microprocessors working together. Hyatt Hotels is running its reservations system on a Pyramid Technology multiprocessor, and Tootsie Roll Industries Inc. is using a Sequent Computer for data processing. On these systems, the operating system parcels out various jobs among the processors, each of which is running a copy of the program. This way, the computers can use existing software rather than require specially written software. Entry-level microcomputers with tens of thousands of processors may be on the mass market soon.

Massively parallel architecture is being implemented as well on mainframes for business purposes. Here the idea is to use dozens or hundreds of low-cost microprocessor chips instead of expensive, specially built processors. Massively parallel mainframes may be-come so cheap that they could reverse the trend toward "downsizing." Yet, for business, parallel computers not only have to be much cheaper, they must also be able to do things that traditional mainframes cannot do as well. Some experts believe the future of multiprocessing computers is in database management, because multiple processors can plow through enormous databases much faster than a single processor can. For example, K-Mart uses parallel processing to help monitor store-by-store sales. American Express plans to employ a parallel machine to examine credit-card records, and Prudential Securities Inc. uses one to evaluate financial instruments. Multiprocessing should also be especially good at handling online transactions such as banking and airline reservations systems.

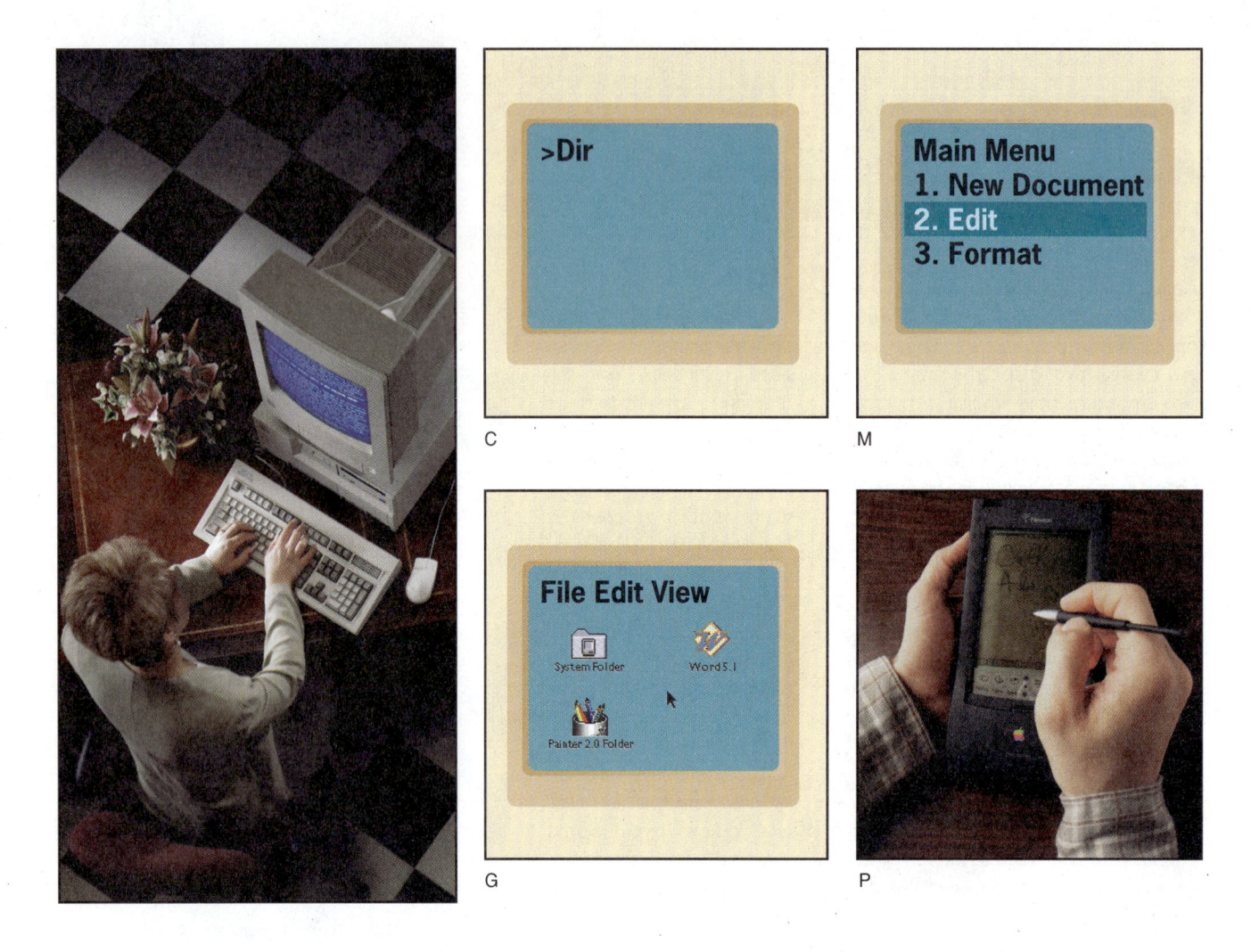

Figure 4–6 User Interfaces
There is a user interface for almost everyone's level of tolerance for technology.

shell An operating environment layer that separates the operating system from the user and that typically involves a menu-driven or a graphical user interface.

command-line user interface A user interface that requires the user to type commands in a special code in order to tell a computer what to do next.

prompt A symbol, message, or cue that indicates that the operating system or a program is ready for input.

program and seem to bear no relation to the job you want to do. For the sake of user friendliness, operating system manufacturers have developed **shells** that provide a layer between you and the operating system. Shells are often included in an operating system package, but they can be bought as separate packages to load on top of operating systems. Different types of shells provide different user interfaces: menu-driven, graphical, and pen-based. The four basic user interfaces are described next (see Figure 4–6).

COMMAND-LINE USER INTERFACES

A **command-line user interface** requires you to type commands in the form of codes that the operating system interprets and acts on. DOS, for example, provides a command-line user interface. DOS displays a **prompt** that indicates it is ready to accept a command. The prompt may be nothing more than >. Normally, you type the command and then press the *Enter* key to activate the command. The commands can run from the simple, such as DIR, to the cryptic, such as COPY %1*.* NUL > NUL. You must type the codes precisely for them to work.

Figure 4–7 Menu-Driven Programs
There are a number of different types of menus from which a user can type a code or highlight an option to initiate a new action.

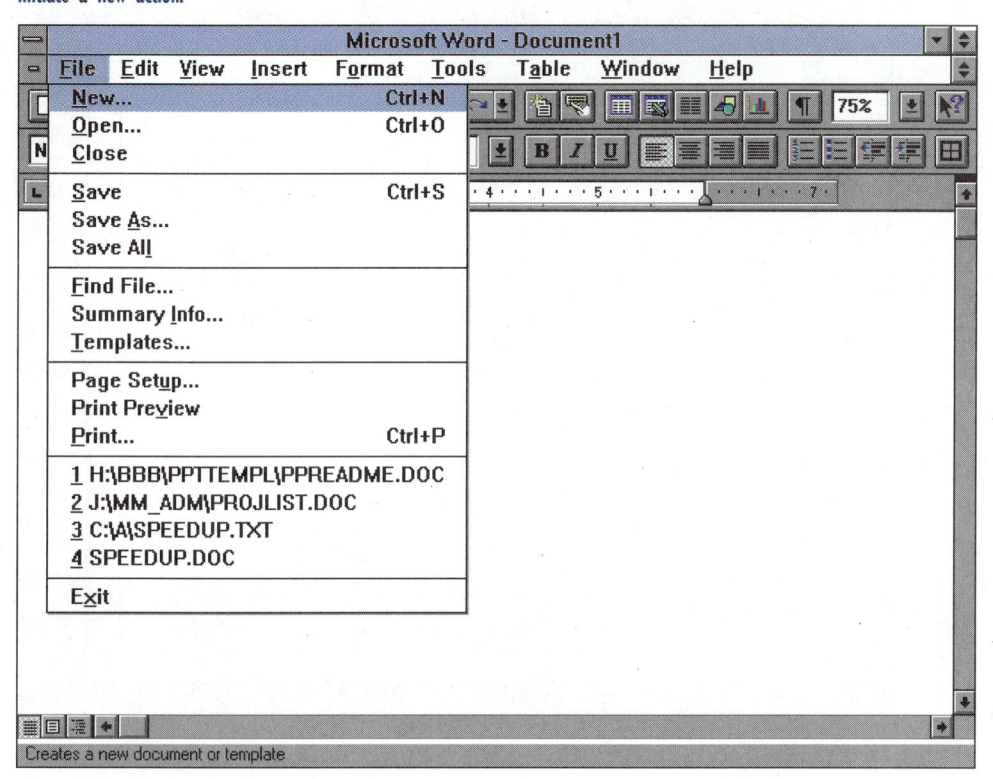

Once you learn most of the commands in an application program that uses this type of interface, you can speed through the tasks that you want to do. There is only one piece of equipment to manipulate—the keyboard—and you don't have to plow through several lists of tasks to find the one job you want to do. The commands often vary from program to program, however, so that the command that calculates a set of figures in one spreadsheet program may center text in another.

MENU-DRIVEN PROGRAMS
One type of shell designed to overcome the difficulty of command-line user interfaces employs menus (see Figure 4–7). A program used primarily by choosing from menus is called a **menu-driven program.** Menus, like the commands in a command-line user interface, vary from program to program. In addition, there may be several layers of menus to sift through until you arrive at the specific job you want to do.

GRAPHICAL USER INTERFACES
A **graphical user interface,** or **GUI** (pronounced *GOO-ee*), displays a computerized desktop as the interface between you and the operating system (see Figure 4–8). It incorporates four elements. These are sometimes

menu-driven program An interface design under which access to functions and services is controlled through lists from which options are selected.

graphical user interface (GUI) A user interface that employs graphics (icons, menus, pointers, buttons, and windows) to simplify the user's interaction with the computer; usually includes a mouse for input.

Figure 4–8 Graphical User Interface
The graphical user interface usually starts up with a display such as this "desktop" from the Macintosh computer.

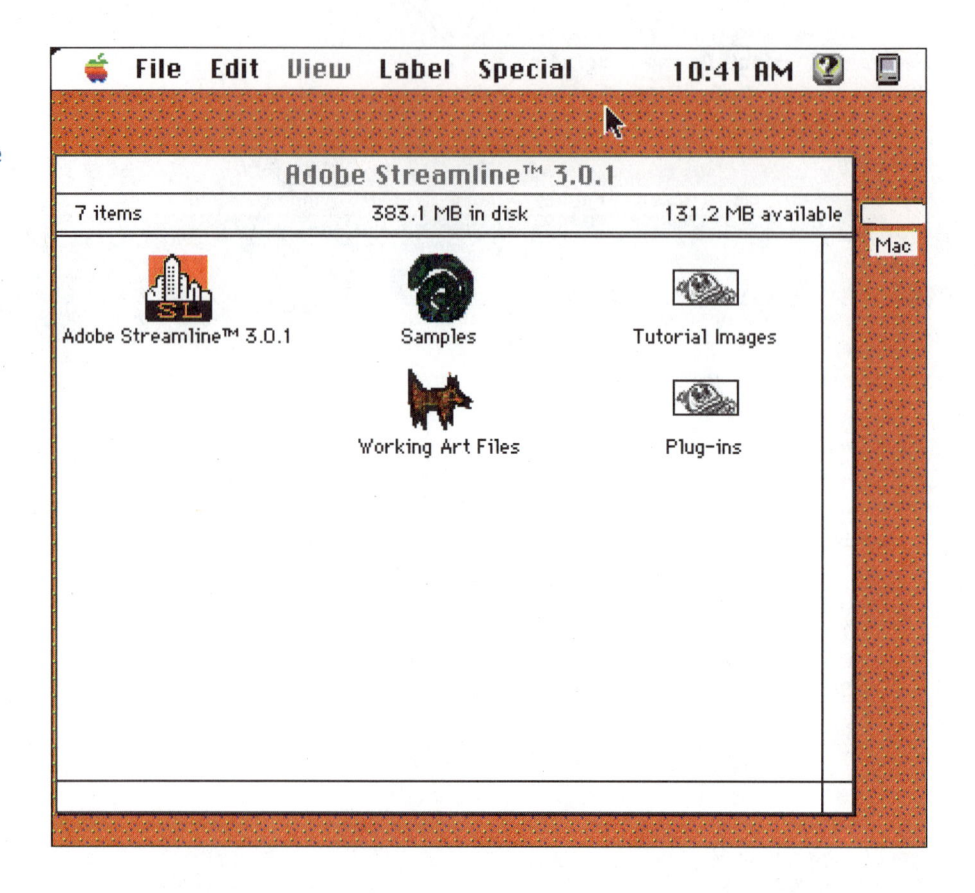

referred to by the rather disparaging acronym *WIMP*, which stands for "windows, icons, menus, and pointing devices":

- *Windows:* A GUI makes use of windows that hold documents or functions.
- *Icons:* Icons, or pictures, represent documents, programs, and functions.
- *Menus:* The commands are shown in pull-down or pop-up menus.
- *Pointing devices:* Normally, you use a pointing device—a mouse or a trackball—to point to and select the options you want. As you move the mouse, you will see a pointer symbol such as an arrow or an I-beam move across the screen.

A GUI is easy to use and provides a consistent means of using software: Once you have learned to use one application through the GUI, you can easily transfer your knowledge to all other applications written for that GUI. Many experienced computer users, however, say that using a command-line user interface is much faster and see no need to change. For people who use one primary application, such as word processing or a spreadsheet, the command-line user interface can be very efficient. People who plan on using many programs may find it easier to convert to a GUI.

Pen-Based Interfaces

Pen-based interfaces (also called *gesture-based interfaces*) are found on notepad computers (refer to Chapter 2). Pen-based interfaces allow direct interaction with programs and data, much as if you were writing with a pencil on a clipboard.

To input data, you use a special electronic stylus. The stylus emits a faint signal from its tip so that the notepad can detect its presence. As you write, the screen grows darker where the stylus touches it. The notepad may use built-in pattern recognition software to recognize, interpret, and change your writing (or printing) into a normal computer typeface. (Otherwise, it stores your work as graphical images.) The stylus can also act as a mouse: To make a selection or initiate an action, for example, you tap the stylus on the appropriate icon. Using a stylus as an input device eliminates the constant moving back and forth between the mouse and the keyboard in GUIs. Most people will still prefer the keyboard for long sessions of writing, however.

> **pen-based interface** A user interface in which the primary input is handwriting and the operating system contains pattern recognition software to interpret the input.

Microcomputer Operating Systems and Shells

Current operating systems for microcomputers usually come preinstalled, and this is fortunate, because some are packed on as many as two dozen diskettes and take a long time to load. The following sections describe the most popular operating systems.

PC DOS and MS-DOS

The acronym *DOS* can refer to any disk operating system, but it has become synonymous with PC DOS and MS-DOS, developed by Microsoft Corp. PC DOS (Personal Computer Disk Operating System) was designed for use on IBM PCs. As a result of its agreement with IBM, Microsoft was able to market its own version of the operating system called MS-DOS (Microsoft Disk Operating System). The two operating systems are nearly identical from a user's viewpoint. Today, more than 100 different computers use DOS, and a very large selection of application software—more than 20,000 packages—for business and education is based on DOS.

Earlier versions of DOS were notably arcane. Numerous shells for DOS—including one by its developer, Microsoft—relieve this problem somewhat. DOS does have a built-in memory limitation of 1MB, of which 640K is directly accessible, and special memory software is required to overcome the limit. PC DOS and MS-DOS are single-user, single-tasking operating systems.

Microsoft Windows

Windows, by Microsoft Corp., is a graphical user interface designed to operate with DOS. Like other GUIs, *Windows* enables you to employ a mouse to select icons and menus, use dialog boxes, and click buttons (see

Figure 4–9 The *Windows* Control Panel
By selecting options from this control panel, you can customize *Windows* to suit your personal tastes.

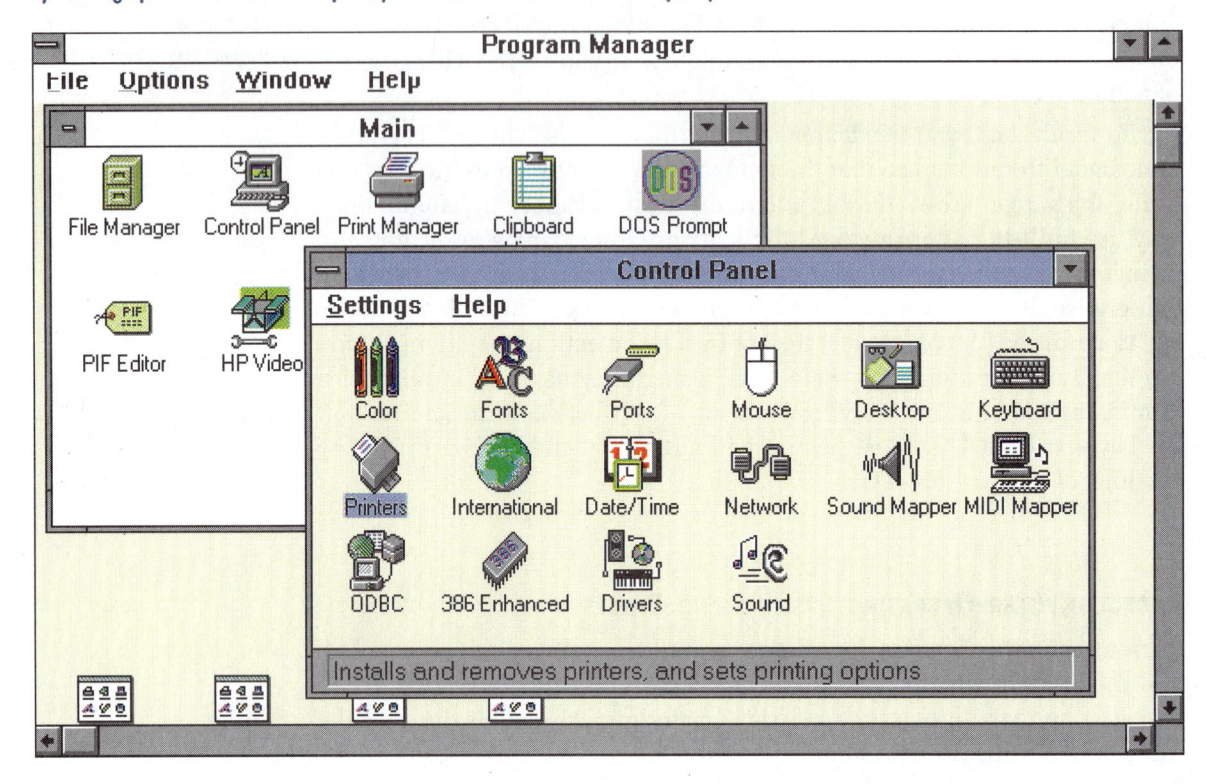

Figure 4–9). It provides limited multitasking capabilities and extends memory usage beyond the 1MB limitation of DOS via a program called a *memory manager*. It has an enhanced mode that uses the virtual memory capabilities found in today's advanced microprocessors. Any software that you plan to use with *Windows* must be compatible with it.

Windows comes with miniapplications for word processing, graphics, communication, and data management. It also includes a variety of accessories: a notepad, a clock, a calendar with a month-at-a-glance view and a daily appointment book, and a calculator. It requires considerable memory (8MB) and a 80386 microprocessor or better. Most new IBM computers and compatibles have DOS and *Microsoft Windows* already installed.

The latest edition of *Windows,* dubbed *Windows 95,* does not require DOS. *Windows 95* provides home users with many of the capabilities of the expensive, high-end *Windows NT* (for "new technology") operating system used primarily by businesses. It runs 32-bit applications, uses protected memory, is multitasking, and provides networking functions including Microsoft Network (MSN). It includes an improved OLE (Object Linking and Embedding) and a new-looking, easy-to-use interface. It handles files and folders much like the Macintosh system and OS/2. Its Plug-and-Play capabilities make it easy to add peripherals that support "PnP." It also runs current Windows- and DOS-based programs. Contrary to popular belief, DOS is still present, although well hidden.

Window on Computing

Windows 95—Hyperspace or Hype?

"Since its opening in 1931, when the first experimental transmission of television took place, the Empire State Building has always been involved with new technology."

This statement's proclaimer, Lydia Ruth, Director of Public Relations for the Empire State Building, went on to say "We are excited to be part of the world-wide launch celebrations of Windows 95."

Not only was the Empire State Building aglow with the colors of the Windows 95 logo, but launching events also took place in dozens of places world-wide including Paris, Toronto, London, Vienna, Singapore, and Hong Kong.

What a reception! All this for a system that some critics call "Windows for Workgroups on steroids" and others say is a step backward from OS/2 Warp.

Yes, Windows 95 is easy to use with its point-and-click Start button and Taskbar. It offers backward compatibility and has fast video playback. It treats files much as the Macintosh system does. It provides aids for people with limited dexterity, vision, or hearing. It handles e-mail and faxes with aplomb, and supports networking. But some new features have caveats attached:

- *Reliability.* Windows is notorious for crashing—according to one user, several times a week with Windows for Workgroups. Although more reliable, Windows 95 still crashes.
- *Speed.* Windows 95 is speedy—if you have at least 16MB of RAM. With 8MB, the applications are slower than when run under Win 3.1.
- *Easy installation.* Windows 95 installs easily and detects and maintains most current system settings. Problems involve getting existing device drivers and graphics boards to work.
- *Plug and Play.* "PnP" lets you easily install and configure hardware. The system does not always recognize non-PnP de-vices, however.
- *Long filenames.* File-names can contain up to 255 characters each, but old programs don't understand the longer filenames and the long file-names take up more directory space.
- *Shortcuts.* Short-cuts are icons you create to launch files easily. If you rename or move the file, however, the link breaks between shortcut and file—and you're left wondering where your file is.
- *Seamless online functions.* You can easily use operating system or application functions with online operations. If you close the function or application, you could assume that you also signed off the online service when in actuality, you hadn't.
- *Backward compatibility.* Back-ward compatibility often limits what a new operating system can do. Windows 95 supposedly no longer needs DOS, but DOS is still there, albeit well hidden.
- *New features.* Some of the best features of Windows 95, such as the, Internet Browser, advanced data compression, games, and items that require a 486 or higher microprocessor, are not in Windows 95 but are sold separately in Microsoft Plus!

Hyperspace, as defined by Webster's, is a fictional space held to support extraordinary events. Windows 95 is no longer fictional and it does support some extraordinary events. It can't hold a candle to Windows NT, however, and most of its purported innovations date back to the early Macintosh computers. So what's all the hype about? That first television transmission was considerably more monumental than the delivery of Windows 95.

Figure 4–10 A QuickTime Movie
A movie takes up a lot of memory space, so current technology provides only small windows for displaying full-motion video like the QuickTime movie shown. This is A Hard Day's Night by the Beatles. This CD ROM is published by The Voyager Company.

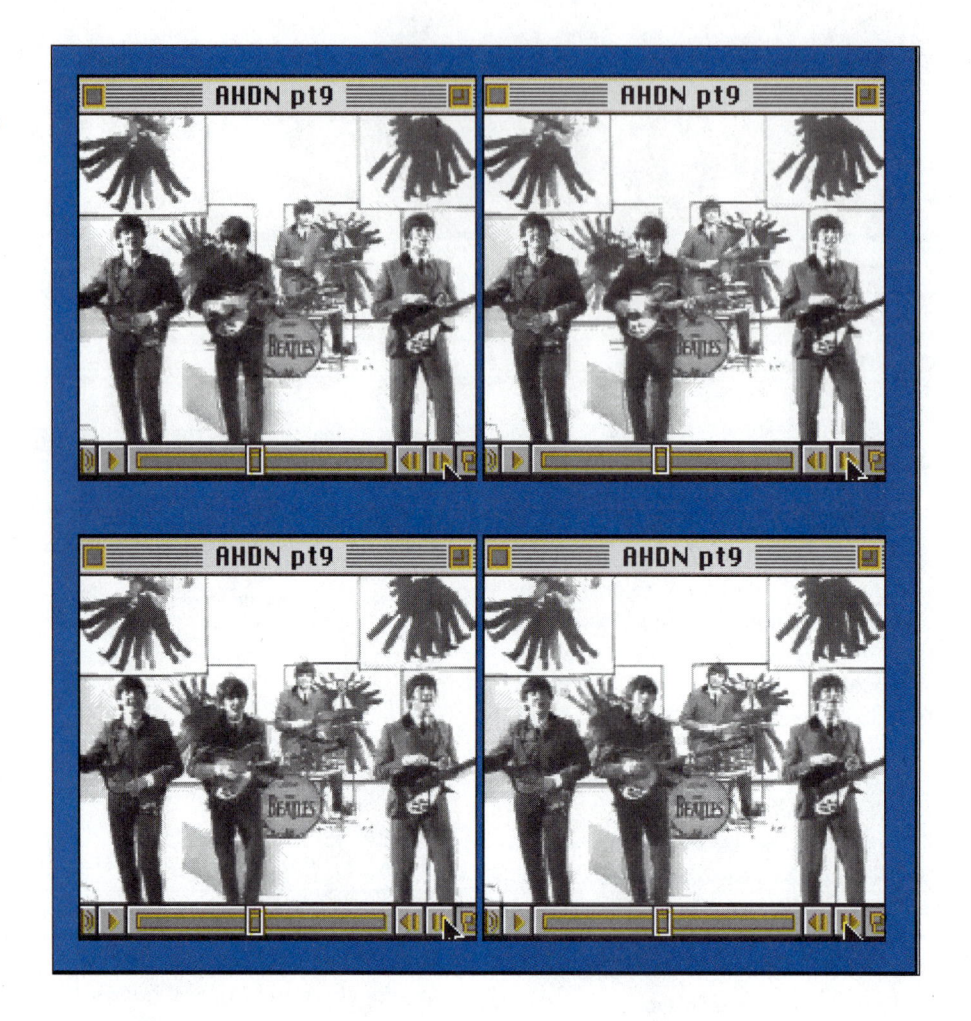

SYSTEM 7

Apple's Macintosh family of computers employs System 7, an operating system that is both easy and fun to use. The part of this operating system visible to the user is the Finder, which serves as the interface between the Macintosh user and the operating system. The Finder refers to the on-screen working environment as the Desktop, which includes icons and pull-down menus and requires the use of a mouse. It provides interactive on-screen help and "desk accessories" such as an alarm clock, a calculator, and a note pad for memos.

System 7 permits virtual memory and provides links among files that enable the sharing of data and instructions among programs. It offers a number of typefaces, provides advanced color capabilities, and lets you play full-motion video (or "movies") through a module called *QuickTime* (see Figure 4–10). It has high memory and microprocessor requirements.

The latest version of System 7 is designed for the new Power Macs, which use speedy Power PC microprocessors developed as a result of an alliance among Apple, Motorola, and IBM. The Power Mac system includes *SoftWindows,* a program from Insignia Solutions that lets you run *Windows* software on a Mac.

PROFILE

JOBS' NEXT JOB

Steven Jobs had been interested in computers since his high school days in Silicon Valley. His interest soon landed him a job at Atari and prompted him to attend meetings of the Homebrew Computer Club with some friends, including Stephen Wozniak. Wozniak had built a small computer using microprocessor technology. Jobs was impressed with the machine and wanted to market it. After persuading Wozniak to leave his job at Hewlett-Packard, Jobs sold his Volkswagen and Wozniak's scientific calculator for $1,300 so they could build their first computer. They named the machine the Apple after a memorable summer the two men had spent working in an apple orchard. The first Apple II, released in 1977, launched the company on the road to success. In the early 1980s, Apple introduced Jobs' brainchild, the Macintosh, a computer designed for its ease of use.

In 1985, Jobs was forced from his position as chairman of the board of Apple Computer, but not without much controversy. Within months, however, he started a new company called NeXT, Inc., to build computers for the higher-education market, particularly to support science and math programs at universities. Jobs is now realizing that what attracts people to his computer is not the beautiful machine but the operating system, Next-Step, which incorporates object-oriented programming, or OOP. As a result, Jobs closed down the hardware division in 1993, promising to continue to support hardware customers, and announced NeXT would focus on making its object-oriented software an industry standard.

This focus ultimately moved NeXT into the corporate environment, and OpenStep, the first volume object standard for developing cross-platform, object-oriented applications was created. In addition, in August of 1995, NeXT announced the development of WebObjects which provides for universal application development across clients, servers, and database servers (including the World Wide Web) regardless of underlying operating systems or hardware.

Jobs' next job is to lead the object revolution and become the leading supplier of object technology for desktop and server operating systems in the corporate marketplace.

OS/2

OS/2 (Operating System 2) is a single-user operating system developed by IBM and Microsoft for use on the IBM PS/2 computers (PS stands for "personal system"). A very powerful and fast system, OS/2 has multitasking capability. Its user-friendly features include WorkPlace Shell, a Macintosh-like GUI that supports the use of a mouse and icons and provides consistency in commands from program to program. OS/2 also offers dynamic data exchange and was designed for networking applications. It does not have the memory limits of DOS.

Most programs written for DOS, as well as many written for *Windows,* will run well under OS/2. It should be employed with, at minimum, an 80386 microprocessor. Of interest to corporate users is that OS/2 supports connectivity to all computers, including large ones. On the negative side, OS/2 requires a great deal of memory and hard disk space. Currently, it has fewer users than DOS and few applications have been developed especially for it.

**CONCEPT SUMMARY
THE OPERATING SYSTEM AS A LINK**

Unix

Unix, a multiuser operating system developed by Bell Laboratories, can be used on mainframes and minicomputers as well as microcomputers. It is what you might call an "industrial-strength" operating system. Like OS/2, Unix allows multitasking , supports virtual memory and networking.

Although it is quite powerful, Unix is not an easy system for a nonprogrammer. In fact, it was developed primarily for programmers, and remains arcane. The problems with Unix's cryptic commands can be overcome by installing a GUI such as *Open Look, OSF/MOTIF, X-Windows, NextStep,* or Amiga's *Workbench.*

Unix is used primarily with the most powerful microcomputers and is popular with engineers and other technical people. There is no standard version, which means that programs written for one version may not run on other versions. Versions for microcomputers include Xenix2 by Microsoft Corp. for IBM PCs and compatibles and A/UX for Macintosh computers.

48	00	23C0	
4C	00	23C2	
40	00	2310	
D2	01	2310	2310
48	00	2310	
4E	00	2028	
F3	17	3002	
9G	F0	3003	2028

Figure 4–11 Machine Language
These machine language instructions are expressed in the hexadecimal (base-16) number system, a shortcut to writing instructions entirely in 1's and 0's.

▶ SOFTWARE DEVELOPMENT

Today, software development is not just a matter of sitting down and starting to write **code** with some vague notion about what a program should do. In fact, software development is not always synonymous with "coding." Modern programming techniques involve a great deal of planning and testing, and even leave room for relying on shrink-wrapped application packages rather than "reinventing the wheel." They enable the programmer to concentrate more on the problem being solved and less on the actual coding.

code Short for the lines of instructions written in a programming language, which is a set of vocabulary and syntax, or grammatical rules, for writing a computer program.

SYSTEM SOFTWARE AND LANGUAGE TRANSLATION

Early computers were programmed through plug boards and extensive rows of electrical switches. Each time a new job was run, the entire setup had to be changed. In order to avoid this manual operation, John Mauchly and two of his colleagues implemented the concept of stored programs on the EDVAC and UNIVAC computers (refer to Chapter 1).

The first stored programs were written in **machine language,** the tedious first-generation language based on the 0 and 1 digits of the binary system (see Figure 4–11). Further, the programmer had to "map" memory and allocate all memory locations to be used. The time requirements and costs for program development were a major obstacle to utilization.

Improvements resulted with the first **language-translator programs.** The first of these programs was the assembler, which translated the second-generation **assembly languages** into machine language (see Figure 4–12). Assembly language used familiar letters and symbols, such as ST for STore and LD for LoaD, but like machine language, it still required extensive knowledge of the particular computer being used.

Eventually, third-generation languages, or **high-level languages,** were developed and that employed common symbols and English words (see later subsection "High-Level Languages"). These languages are translated by compilers or interpreters. A **compiler** translates the entire program (called the *source code*) into machine language at once, and the translated version (called the *object code*) is then run as a unit. By this method,

machine language The only language that a computer can run directly. It codes the computer's electrical states in combinations of 1's and 0's.

language-translator program A program (often classified as a system program) that changes into machine language a computer code made up of words and symbols.

assembly language A low-level—that is, machine-oriented—programming language that uses abbreviations to code instructions rather than 1's and 0's or complete words.

high-level language A language based on macro commands that cause a computer to execute a full sequence of instructions from a single entry.

compiler A language translator that accepts an entire program or module (the source code) written by a programmer and generates machine-language instructions (the object code).

Figure 4–12 Assembly Language
Assembly-language symbols consist of mnemonic codes.

| EXAMPLES OF ASSEMBLY-LANGUAGE MNEMONIC CODE ||
Operation	Typical Assembly Language Op Code
Add memory to register	A
Add (decimal) memory to register	AP
Multiply register by memory	M
Multiply (decimal) register by memory	MP
Subtract memory from register	S
Subtract (decimal) memory from register	SP
Move (numeric) from register to memory	MVN
Compare memory to register	C
Compare (decimal) memory to register	CP
Zero register and add (decimal) memory to register	ZAP

interpreter A high-level language translator that evaluates and translates a program one statement at a time, enabling the programmer to work interactively while programming.

mistakes are flagged, whereupon the entire program must be corrected, resubmitted to the compiler for translation, and run again before the programmer knows whether the program runs properly. An **interpreter** translates and then executes coding line by line. This feature enables a programmer to interact with the program, alternately writing and running code, correcting mistakes as they crop up.

Most software that you buy is already translated into machine language, but many operating systems include a language translator for one or more programming languages. For example, most include the language translator for some version of a language called BASIC. Additional language translators for other programming languages are sold as separate software packages.

Computer Programming Languages

Each programming language has different objectives. For instance, one language may be well suited for handling large amounts of data, another may harness the computer's ability to compute scientific formulas, and yet another may push the computer to the limits of its speed for games. Chances are you already know the names of some programming languages.

High-Level Languages

To reduce the costs and errors involved in using machine or assembly language, it was necessary to develop programming languages that would use macro instructions. A macro instruction causes the computer to execute an entire sequence of steps in response to a single command. Thus, a single high-level language instruction can stand for several machine-language instructions. While a number of machine instructions are required to spell out exactly where the data is located and what should happen to it, a high-level language would simply state PRINT X.

High-level languages are so called because they are geared more toward the user than toward the internal operations of the computer and they use common words to specify jobs. This reduces the time needed for writing a program and makes programs shorter and easier to read and change. The first high-level language was Fortran, but today literally hundreds are available. The following list describes just a sampling of the many available.

- *Fortran.* Fortran, or FORmula TRANslator, dating from 1957, is the oldest high-level programming language (see Figure 4–13). Fortran has extraordinary math capabilities and is best suited to situations involving complex calculations. Conversely, Fortran has traditionally been ill-suited to the file handling, data editing, and docu-

```
C         **********************************************
C         **              Payroll Program              **
C         **********************************************
          Character*20 fname
          Character*16 employee_name
          INTEGER*2 hours_worked, overtime_hours
          Real net_pay

C         ** Opening an input file **
C         * Prompt the user for the file name *
          write(*, '(A\)') 'ENTER EMPLOYEE MASTER FILE NAME --> '

C         * Read the file name *
          read (*, '(A)') fname

C         * Opening the file *
          open (5, file = fname)

C         **********************
C         **** MAIN PROGRAM ****
C         **********************

C         * Print heading *
          write(1,5) 'EMPLOYEE NAME' , 'NET PAY'
5         format(//,1x,A13,8x, A7)

10        read(5,12,END = 99,ERR = 90) employee_name,hours_worked
     1    wage_per_hour
12        format(a16,i2,f5.2)

          if (hours_worked .gt. 40) goto 20

          gross_pay = hours_worked * wage_per_hour
          goto 25
```

Figure 4–13 Payroll Program Written in Fortran
Fortran is being used in businesses primarily for complex business statistics and analysis.

```
C         * Overtime pay *
20        regular_pay = wage_per_hour * 40
          overtime_hours = hours_worked - 40
          overtime_rate = wage_per_hour * 1.5
          overtime_pay = overtime_rate * overtime_hours
          gross_pay = regular_pay + overtime_pay

C         * Tax calculation *
25        if (gross_pay .gt. 250.00) then
              tax = gross_pay * 0.20
          else
              tax = gross_pay * 0.14
          endif

          write(1,30) employee_name, net_pay
30        Format(/,1x,a16,5x,f7.2

          goto 10

90        write(*,*) 'Error Reading File'
          close(5)
99        stop
          end
```

EMPLOYEE NAME	NET PAY
LYNN MANGINO	224.00
THOMAS RITTER	212.42
MARIE OLSON	209.00
LORI DUNLEVY	172.00
WILLIAM LUOMA	308.00

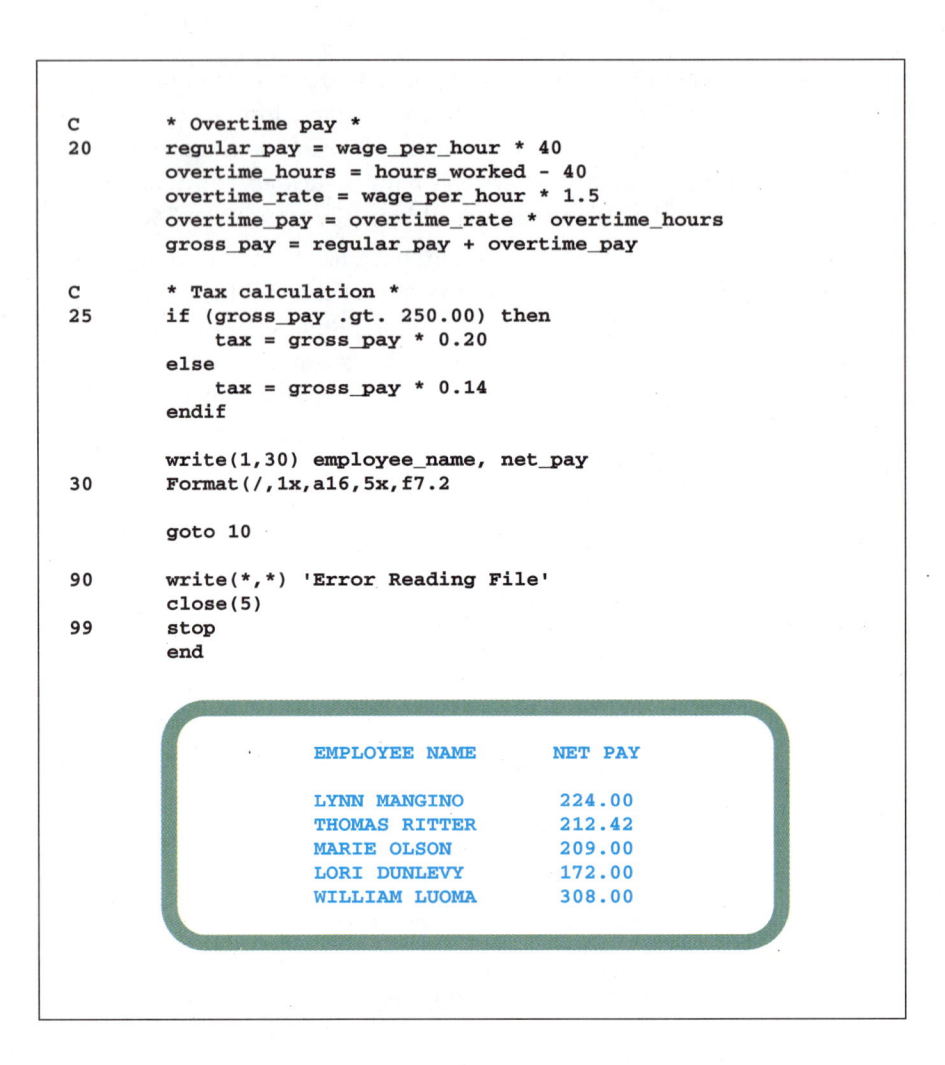

Figure 4–14 The First Microcomputer BASIC

BASIC was first developed for use by students on mainframe computers, but Bill Gates and Paul Allen wrote the first version of BASIC for microcomputers and founded Microsoft Corp.

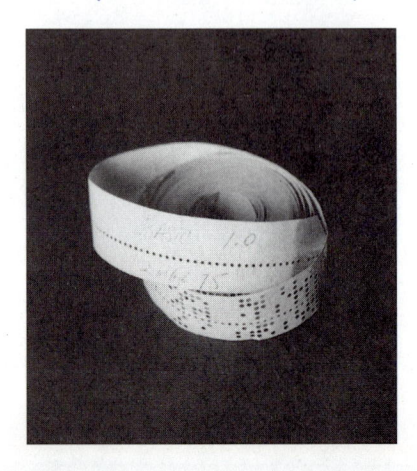

ment production required in a business setting. Its popularity is growing, however, for business applications such as feasibility studies, forecasting, and production scheduling. The latest Fortran standard supports high-volume character and file handling.

- *BASIC.* The first programming language that a student learns is often BASIC (Beginner's All-purpose Symbolic Instruction Code). It is so popular that most microcomputers have a BASIC language-translator stored in ROM. BASIC is easy to learn and can be used for solving a wide variety of problems (see Figure 4–14). The main criticism of BASIC is that many versions promote poor programming habits, although many new versions require a structured approach to programming (see Figure 4–15).
- *Pascal.* Named for Blaise Pascal, the inventor of the Pascaline, Pascal was the first major programming language to implement structured programming techniques (see Figure 4–16). Because it is so highly structured, Pascal is popular in scientific program-

Figure 4–15 Payroll Program in BASIC

BASIC programs are generally easy to understand

```
10 REM ********************************************
20 REM **              PAYROLL PROGRAM           **
30 REM ********************************************
40 REM
50 PRINT "EMPLOYEE NAME",," NET PAY"
60 PRINT
70 READ NME$,HOURS,WAGE
80 WHILE NME$ <> "END OF DATA"
90    IF HOURS <= 40 THEN GROSS = HOURS * WAGE ELSE GOSUB 1000
100   IF GROSS > 250 THEN LET TAX = .2 ELSE LET TAX = .14
110   LET TAX2 = TAX * GROSS
120   LET PAY = GROSS - TAX2
130   PRINT NME$,,
135   PRINT USING "$$###.##";PAY
140   READ NME$,HOURS,WAGE
150 WEND
999 END
1000 REM
1010 REM ********************************************
1020 REM **               OVERTIME PAY            **
1030 REM ********************************************
1040 REM
1050 LET REGULAR = 40 * WAGE
1060 LET OVERTIME = (HOURS - 40) * (1.5 * WAGE)
1070 LET GROSS = REGULAR + OVERTIME
1080 RETURN
1090 REM
2000 DATA "LYNN MANGINO",35,8.00
2010 DATA "THOMAS RITTER",48,4.75
2020 DATA "MARIE OLSON",45,5.50
2030 DATA "LORI DUNLEVY",40,5.00
2040 DATA "WILLIAM LUOMA",50,7.00
2050 DATA "END OF DATA",0,0
```

```
EMPLOYEE NAME       NET PAY

LYNN MANGINO        224
THOMAS RITTER       212.42
MARIE OLSON         209
LORI DUNLEVY        172
WILLIAM LUOMA       308
```

ming and in high schools and colleges where teachers want students to learn good programming habits (see later subsection "Structured Programming Techniques"). It is ideal for solving complex math problems and creating graphics.

- *Ada.* Ada is named after Lady Augusta Ada Byron, Countess of Lovelace, who, during the 1800s, devised the concept of looping operations. Developed under the sponsorship of the U.S. Department of Defense (DOD), Ada was designed for weapons systems. Today, it also has commercial uses. Like Pascal, it is highly structured.

Figure 4-16   Payroll Program Written in Pascal   The indented lines highlight the structured nature of this language.

```pascal
            (*         Payroll Program           *)
        program payroll (emplfile, output);

        type
            array20 = array[1..20] of char;

        var
            emplfile : text;
            name : array20;
            wage, hours, grosspay, tax, netpay : real;

        procedure readname (var name : array20);

        var
            i : integer;
            count : integer;

        begin    (* readname *)

            i := 1;
            while not eoln (emplfile) and (i <= 20) do
            begin (* while *)
                read (emplfile, name[i]);
                i := i + 1
            end; (* while *)

            for count := i to 20 do
                name[count] := ' '

        end;    (* readname *)

        begin    (* payroll program *)

            Assign (emplfile, 'PAYROLL.DAT');
            reset (emplfile);

        writeln;
            writeln ('EMPLOYEE NAME':13, 'NET PAY':27);
            writeln;

            while not eof (emplfile) do
            begin    (* while *)
                readname (name);
                readln (emplfile, hours, wage);

                (* Calculate gross pay *)
                if hours <= 40
                    then grosspay := hours * wage
                    else grosspay := hours * wage + (hours - 40) * wage * 0.5;

                (* Calculate net pay *)
                if grosspay > 250
                    then tax := 0.2 * grosspay
                    else tax := 0.14 * grosspay;
                netpay := grosspay - tax;
                writeln (name:20, '$':14, netpay:3:2)

            end (* while *)
        end.    (* payroll program *)
```

Figure 4–16 Payroll Program Written in Pascal—Continued

```
EMPLOYEE NAME          NET PAY
LYNN MANGINO           224.00
THOMAS RITTER          212.42
MARIE OLSON            209.00
LORI DUNLEVY           172.00
WILLIAM LUOMA          308.00
```

- *C.* C is quite popular with programmers who write system programs, database software, utility programs, and graphics applications. C is a highly structured language (see Figure 4–17). It is sometimes referred to as a mid-level language because it has some capabilities similar to those of assembly language, such as the capability to manipulate individual bits and bytes in memory

Figure 4–17 Payroll Program Written in C

Programs written in C generally are portable, meaning they are independent of machine architecture and can be implemented on different computers.

```c
/*      Payroll Program      */

#include <stdio.h>
#include <string.h>

/* Function prototypes */

int main(void);
static float calc_gross_pay(float hours, float wage);
static float calc_net_pay(float gross_pay);

int main(void)
{
   FILE *emplfile;
   char input_buf[133];
   char output_buf[81];
   char emp_name[21];
   float hours, wage, gross_pay, net_pay;

   /* Open payroll data file */
   if ((emplfile = fopen("PAYROLL.DAT", "r")) != NULL)
   {
      /* Print headers */
      sprintf(output_buf, "%-20.20s %s\n\n", "EMPLOYEE NAME",
         "NET PAY");
      printf(output_buf);
```

Figure 4-17 Payroll Program Written in C—Continued

```c
        while (fgets(input_buf, 132, emplfile) != NULL)
        {
            /* Separate input line from file into name, hours and wage */
            sscanf(input_buf, "\"%[^\"]\",%f,%f", emp_name, &hours, &wage);

            /* Calculate gross pay */
            gross_pay = calc_gross_pay(hours, wage);

            /* Calculate net pay */
            net_pay = calc_net_pay(gross_pay);

            /* Print results */
            sprintf(output_buf, "%-20.20s $%6.2f\n", emp_name, net_pay);
            printf(output_buf);
        }

        /* Close data file */
        fclose(emplfile);
    }
    else
        printf("\nError Opening File\n");

    return 0;
}

float calc_gross_pay(float hours, float wage)
{
    float gross;

    if (hours <= 40.0F)
        gross = hours * wage;
    else
        gross = hours * wage + (hours - 40.0F) * wage * 0.5F;

    return gross;
}

float calc_net_pay(float gross_pay)
{
    float tax, net;

    if (gross_pay > 250.0F)
        tax = 0.2F * gross_pay;
    else
        tax = 0.14F * gross_pay;
    net = gross_pay - tax;

    return net;
}
```

```
EMPLOYEE NAME        NET PAY
LYNN MANGINO         224.00
THOMAS RITTER        212.42
MARIE OLSON          209.00
LORI DUNLEVY         172.00
WILLIAM LUOMA        308.00
```

locations. Yet it also offers many high-level language features, such as a wide variety of built-in functions and other useful structures.

- *COBOL.* COBOL (COmmon Business-Oriented Language) was designed for business use. It is the main language employed by businesses and the federal government. Despite predictions of its death, COBOL prevails, being periodically updated to incorporate new programming methods. It is a standardized language; thus a firm can switch computer systems with little or no rewriting of existing COBOL programs. It is well suited for handling large amounts of data, a common business task. COBOL programs consist of sentences and paragraphs, very much like a report written in English (see Figure 4–18).

Figure 4–18 Payroll Program Written in COBOL
The Englishlike nature of COBOL can result in programs that are very wordy.

```
        IDENTIFICATION DIVISION.
        PROGRAM-ID. PAYROLL.
        INPUT-OUTPUT SECTION.
        FILE-CONTROL.
            SELECT CARD-FILE ASSIGN TO UR-S-SYSIN.
            SELECT PRINT-FILE ASSIGN TO UR-S-OUTPUT.

        DATA DIVISION.
        FILE SECTION.
        FD  CARD-FILE
            LABEL RECORDS ARE OMITTED
            RECORD CONTAINS 80 CHARACTERS
            DATA RECORD IS PAY-RECORD.
        01  PAY-RECORD.
            03  EMPLOYEE-NAME       PIC A(16).
            03  HOURS-WORKED        PIC 99.
            03  WAGE-PER-HOUR       PIC 99V99.
            03  FILLER              PIC X(58).

        FD  PRINT-FILE
            LABEL RECORDS ARE OMITTED
            RECORD CONTAINS 132 CHARACTERS
            DATA RECORD IS PRINT-RECORD.
        01  PRINT-RECORD            PIC X(132).

        WORKING-STORAGE SECTION.
        77  GROSS-PAY               PIC 9(3)V99.
        77  REGULAR-PAY             PIC 9(3)V99.
        77  OVERTIME-PAY            PIC 9(3)V99.
        77  NET-PAY                 PIC 9(3)V99.
        77  TAX                     PIC 9(3)V99.
        77  OVERTIME-HOURS          PIC 99.
        77  OVERTIME-RATE           PIC 9(3)V999.
        77  EOF-FLAG                PIC X(3)            VALUE 'NO'.
        01  HEADING-LINE.
            03  FILLER              PIC X               VALUE SPACES.
            03  FILLER              PIC X(21)           VALUE 'EMPLOYEE NAME'.
            03  FILLER              PIC X(7)            VALUE 'NET PAY'.

        01  OUTPUT-RECORD.
            03  FILLER              PIC X               VALUE SPACES.
            03  NAME                PIC A(16).
            03  FILLER              PIC X(5)            VALUE SPACES.
```

Figure 4–18 Payroll Program Written in COBOL—Continued

```
            03  AMOUNT              PIC $$$$.99.
            03  FILLER              PIC X(103)           VALUE SPACES.


       PROCEDURE DIVISION.
       MAIN-LOGIC.
           OPEN INPUT CARD-FILE
                OUTPUT PRINT-FILE.
           PERFORM HEADING-ROUTINE.
           READ CARD-FILE
                AT END MOVE 'YES' TO EOF-FLAG.
           PERFORM WORK-LOOP UNTIL EOF-FLAG = 'YES'.
           CLOSE CARD-FILE
                 PRINT-FILE.
           STOP RUN.

       HEADING-ROUTINE.
           WRITE PRINT-RECORD FROM HEADING-LINE
                BEFORE ADVANCING 2 LINES.
       WORK-LOOP.
           IF HOURS-WORKED IS GREATER THAN 40
                THEN
                    PERFORM OVERTIME-ROUTINE
                ELSE
                    MULTIPLY HOURS-WORKED BY WAGE-PER-HOUR
                        GIVING GROSS-PAY.
           PERFORM TAX-COMPUTATION.
           PERFORM OUTPUT-ROUTINE.
           READ CARD-FILE AT END MOVE 'YES' TO EOF-FLAG.

       OVERTIME-ROUTINE.
           MULTIPLY WAGE-PER-HOUR BY 40 GIVING REGULAR-PAY.
           SUBTRACT 40 FROM HOURS-WORKED GIVING OVERTIME-HOURS.
           MULTIPLY REGULAR-PAY BY 1.5 GIVING OVERTIME-RATE.
           MULTIPLY OVERTIME-HOURS BY OVERTIME-RATE
                GIVING OVERTIME-PAY.
           ADD REGULAR-PAY, OVERTIME-PAY GIVING GROSS-PAY.

       TAX-COMPUTATION.
           IF GROSS-PAY IS GREATER THAN 250
                THEN
                    MULTIPLY GROSS-PAY BY 0.20 GIVING TAX
                ELSE
                    MULTIPLY GROSS-PAY BY 0.14 GIVING TAX.
           SUBTRACT TAX FROM GROSS-PAY GIVING NET-PAY.

       OUTPUT-ROUTINE.
           MOVE EMPLOYEE-NAME TO NAME.
           MOVE NET-PAY TO AMOUNT.
           WRITE PRINT-RECORD FROM OUTPUT-RECORD
                BEFORE ADVANCING 1 LINES.
```

EMPLOYEE NAME	NET PAY
LYNN MANGINO	$224.00
THOMAS RITTER	$212.42
MARIE OLSON	$209.00
LORI DUNLEVY	$172.00
WILLIAM LUOMA	$308.00

- *RPG.* RPG (Report Program Generator) was designed to help people produce business reports quickly and easily. Essentially, a programmer using RPG describes the kind of report desired, but need not specify much of the logic involved in generating that report. Instead of coding statements, the programmer completes specification forms that ask for descriptions of files and processing operations. Thus, little skill is needed for programming in RPG.

Fourth-Generation Languages

A **fourth-generation language (4GL)** requires less training to use than other languages. Basically, its users focus on "what" needs to be done without having to specify "how" it can be accomplished. Once a problem has been defined, the 4GL determines what program instructions are required to solve the problem. 4GLs are usually associated with database systems. Typically, 4GLs contain three tools that are used in the development of an application. These are query languages, report generators, and application generators.

> **fourth-generation language (4GL)** A high-level technique that makes it possible to assemble a series of query commands as an operational program, enabling end-users to develop some programs directly.

- The *query language* enables inexperienced users to construct statements that extract and manipulate data in a database. The terms that initiate queries are based on everyday English usage. Examples include GET, DISPLAY, ADD, COMPUTE, MOVE, PRINT, and LIST.
- The *report generator* is used to format reports that display the extracted data.
- An *application generator* provides a simplified, short-cut method of developing a query. It consists of preprogrammed modules for manipulating the data associated with the query.

Fourth-generation languages are the closest of the computer languages to the language we speak and write every day. The standard is SQL (Structured Query Language, pronounced *See-kwel*). In practice, the most advanced languages today are fourth-generation languages, but fifth-generation languages should be making their way to the mass market by the late 1990s. These languages are termed *natural languages,* because the user can simply state a problem in everyday, commonly used language.

Object-Oriented Programming

Object-oriented programming, or OOP, is a type of programming technique that utilizes and manipulates objects. The object can be a graphics symbol, data, or a set of instructions, or some of each, that can be pasted into or used by any application. The properties that distinguish an object are as follows:

> **object-oriented programming (OOP)** A programming technique in which program modules are usable with different objects, or elements, rather than having to be recoded for each different use.

- *Encapsulation.* An object is a structure that is self-contained but that can also contain other data types and even the functions that act on those data types. For example, a document can have text

and images, and thus includes functions for changing both. You do not need to know how an object works to use it, and you will not see everything that an object includes when you use it.
- *Inheritance.* An object can transfer characteristics to other objects. For example, if you have a document template for preparing a resume, you can employ characteristics of that template to create another template—perhaps for preparing a questionnaire.
- *Polymorphism.* Objects can respond differently when given the same command. In a draw program, for example, one object may create circles and another object may create squares when given the same command to draw to the screen.

Thus, blocks of computer instructions or other items are treated as objects that can be pasted into, or used by, any application. Changes to a particular job can be made to the object rather than to a file, and any project that uses that object benefits from the change. For example, if you are working on a word processing document and click on a graph that has been included, the functions change from word processing to graphing operations. Objects can also be anything in a GUI interface. For example, the icons in the Macintosh Desktop are objects. The trash can opens, just as a file does, when you double-click on it. To delete a file, you drag a file icon to it. Its function changes, however, when you drag a floppy disk's icon to it: Upon this action, the trash can functions to eject the floppy disk from the floppy disk drive.

OOP is highly modular, so an object can be reused in a number of programs. For example, an object containing the code to sort items alphabetically can be written once and used repeatedly—perhaps in a billing program to sort invoices and in an employee program to sort names. Programs can be built quickly and reliably from objects because the objects have already been tested. Popular object-oriented languages are C++ and Smalltalk, as well as object-oriented versions of Pascal. "Hybrids," or versions that are not considered pure OOP languages, include Visual Basic and HyperCard. OOP is well suited for designing graphical user interfaces. For a program to support objects, the operating system must support objects.

STAGES OF PROGRAM DEVELOPMENT

No matter which programming language is involved, the creation of application programs is sufficiently complex and time-consuming that a systematic approach is essential. Although specific steps and checkpoints vary, the description that follows represents a general model for a software project. It includes four stages, each of which should be thoroughly documented:

- Define the problem.
- Design a solution.

- Write the program.
- Debug and test the program.

DEFINING THE PROBLEM

An important aspect of defining a problem is establishing communication between the program developers and the end users of the software. This ensures that each party knows exactly what the program should do. Because such analysis skills often differ from the skills required of a programmer, a **system analyst** may carry out the definition stage.

Typically, the analyst begins by creating sample output in the form of reports or displays. Work then proceeds to the type and source of input required to get these results. This information helps determine the equipment and processing steps needed to deliver the output.

> **system analyst** A computer professional responsible for analyzing an organization's objectives and operations for ways to improve operations that may include implementing computer technologies.

DESIGNING A SOLUTION

Once the outputs, inputs, and processing requirements have been determined, a programmer designs a solution to the problem. Programmers may use one or more of a number of design aids, such as flowcharts and pseudocode, to illustrate the solution (see Figure 4–19). Each shows the basic **algorithm,** or sequence of steps, used in the program. In this stage, the analyst may decide to purchase commercial software rather than prepare the software in-house.

> **algorithm** A sequence of steps needed to solve a problem.

WRITING THE PROGRAM

Note that the actual writing of the program is the third of four steps in the programming process. The point is that it is better to understand the need and to plan the program before coding begins. In fact, a programming language may not be selected until the coding stage. In coding, the pseudocode or the symbols in the flowchart are translated into program instructions. The programmer writes the program according to the **syntax,** or grammatical rules, of the chosen programming language.

> **syntax** The grammatical rules of a programming language.

DEBUGGING AND TESTING THE PROGRAM

Every program contains **bugs.** Some are obvious very early in the programming process. Some bugs do not surface until an uncommon job is initiated or some rather obscure data is entered. So what are bugs? They are errors, and the errors are found during a process called **debugging.**

> **bug** A program error.
>
> **debug** To find and correct errors in a program.

Programmers often do informal desk-checking of a program before they actually run the program, much as you would edit a research paper by reading through it. Many errors show up after a program is compiled or interpreted, however. Two common types of errors are syntax errors and logic errors. A syntax error involves the grammar and spelling rules of the programming language. For example, the word PRINT may be mis-

Figure 4–19 Flowchart with Pseudocode
The flowchart offers a picture of program logic, and the pseudocode gives a structured summary in English.

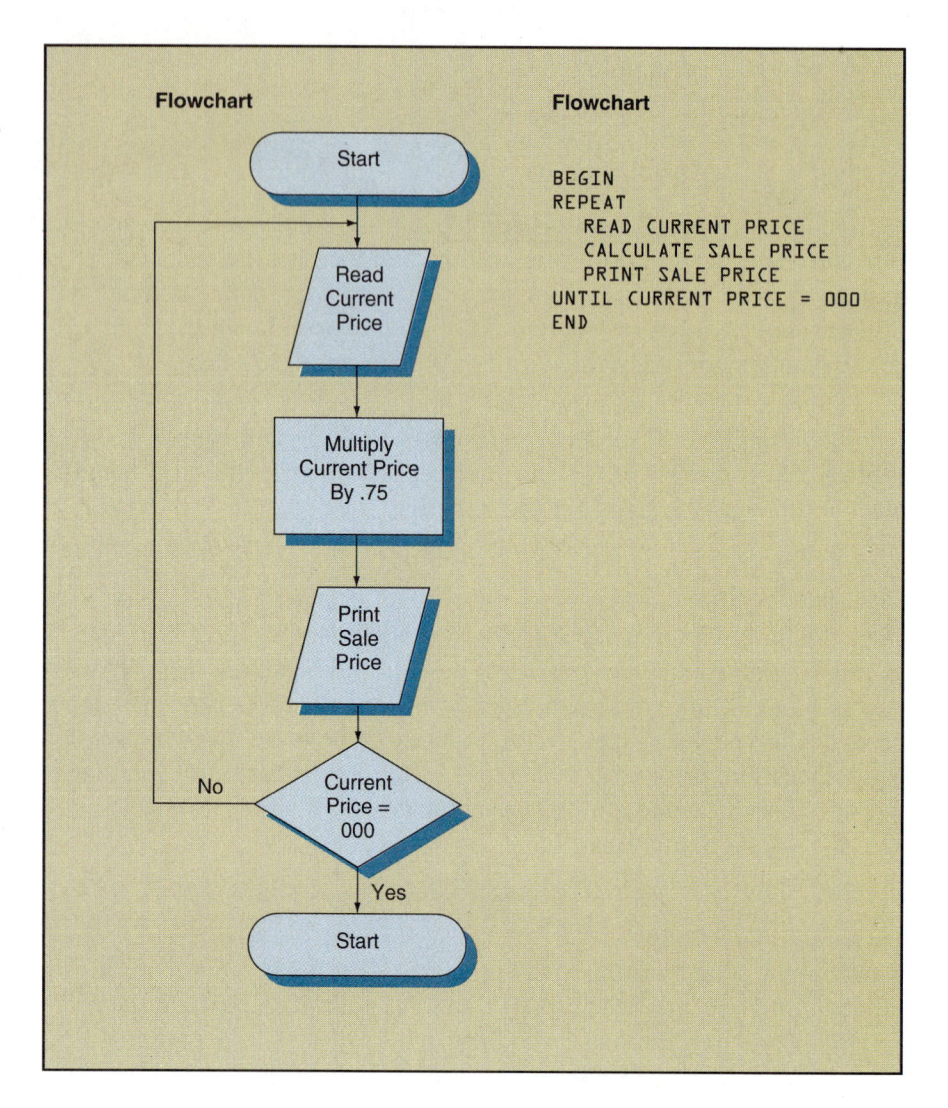

Flowchart

Start → Read Current Price → Multiply Current Price By .75 → Print Sale Price → Current Price = 000? → No (loop back) / Yes → Start

Flowchart

```
BEGIN
REPEAT
   READ CURRENT PRICE
   CALCULATE SALE PRICE
   PRINT SALE PRICE
UNTIL CURRENT PRICE = 000
END
```

spelled. A logic error is more difficult to detect than a syntax error because a program with a logic error may run as if everything were working fine. The program simply returns the wrong answer. In the case of Volume Equals Length Times Width, the formula Vol = Length + Width will return an incorrect answer, and close scrutiny is needed to see the erroneous plus sign among lines and lines of coding.

Logic errors are found through tests that involve running the program with trial input data. A programmer will have already determined the output manually for comparison with the computer output. He may even enter incorrect data in order to see how the program reacts.

After extensive testing and debugging, the program is ready for end-users. Continued evaluation, testing, and maintenance ensure that the program remains relevant. For example, minor adjustments may be needed to reflect a new company policy or a change in tax forms. When a program is deemed irrelevant and outdated, however, the programming process begins again with the first stage, defining the problem.

Structured Programming Techniques

A jazz musician "noodles" around on the keyboard or clarinet, playing sequences of melodies, harmonies, and variations and experimenting with sounds, chords, and embellishments. A computer programmer might noodle around with a programming language, testing the limits of the computer she is working on and trying to get it to do new tasks.

For both the musician and the programmer, noodling often results in insightful and creative directions in which to proceed. In programming, however, it doesn't expedite writing reliable, easy-to-update software that will be sold to businesses and the general public. In fact, in the early days of programming, such disorganized programs were likened to plates of intertwined spaghetti by experts who advocated a more structured approach to programming, an approach that reaches far beyond noodling. These experts introduced **structured programming** techniques for improving programmer productivity and program clarity and reliability. The techniques include top-down design, limited control structures, documentation, testing, and use of a chief programmer team.

> **structured programming** A top-down, modular approach to program design that emphasizes division of a program into logical sections to improve programmer productivity and program clarity.

Top-Down Design

The most difficult part of programming is learning to organize solutions in a clear, concise way. One method of overcoming this difficulty is to use a modular approach, which consists of setting up the major steps of a solution and then breaking each major step into smaller and smaller steps in a process referred to as **stepwise refinement.** The method—proceeding from the general to the specific—is called **top-down design.**

Each step of the solution has its own **module,** which performs a specific task. The most general level of organization is the main control module, which contains broad descriptions of the job to be done. The steps are detailed further in several layers of lower-level modules, with the lowest levels containing the greatest amount of detail. The modules can be written, tested, and documented independently. Top-down design is illustrated by the structure chart (see Figure 4–20).

> **stepwise refinement** The process of repeatedly refining steps in a top-down design.
>
> **top-down design** A programming design technique in which a solution is defined from the general to the specific in terms of functions and subfunctions to be performed.
>
> **module** A part of a whole; a program segment or subsystem, such as that found in an integrated software package.

Control Structures

Programmers generally confine program logic to three basic patterns of sequence. These patterns, also called **control structures,** enable programmers to write a program in an orderly fashion and avoid jumping around within the program (see Figure 4–21). The fundamental control structures, upon which all others are based, are as follows:

> **control structure** A method used to direct the flow of logic in a computer program.

Figure 4–20 Basic Structure Chart for Top-Down Design
At the top of this chart is a statement of the general problem. Level 1 contains three basic processing steps. Further refinements stem from each module in level 1.

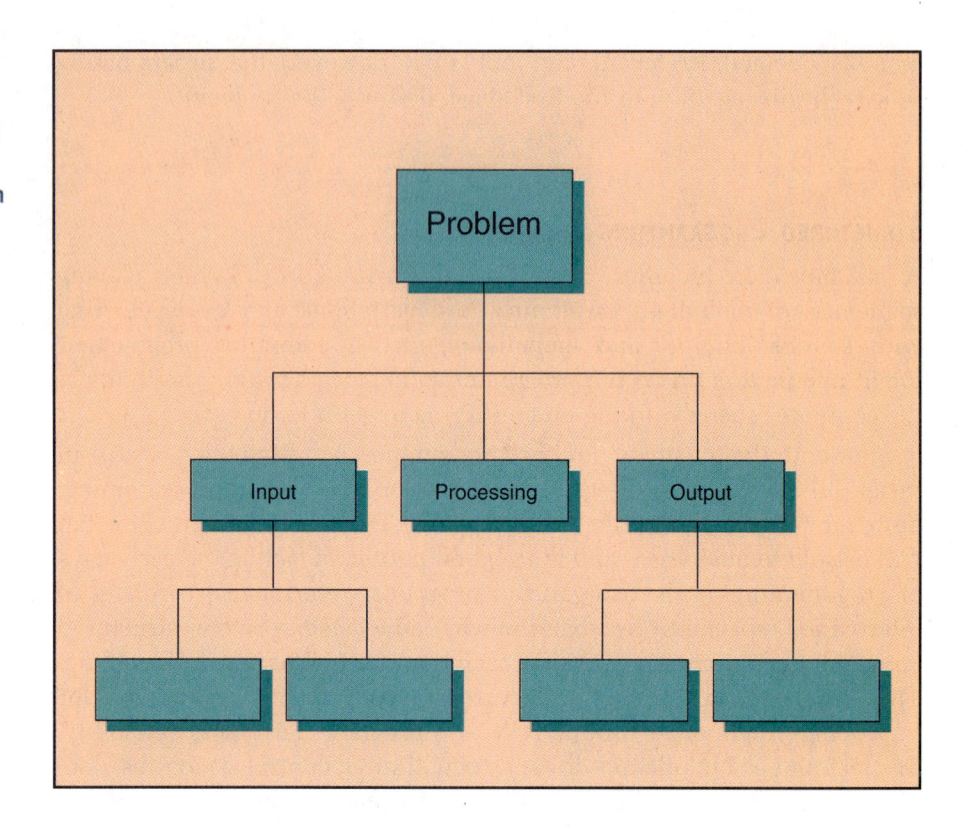

---

simple sequence A program logic pattern in which statements are executed one after another in the order in which they are stored.

decision step A program logic pattern in which the computer makes a choice based on an evaluation between two or more paths that can be taken; also called selection.

loop A program logic that causes a series of instructions to be executed repeatedly as long as specified conditions remain constant.

proper program A program in which each module has only one entry point and one exit point.

documentation Written material that tells about a program; includes definitions, explanations, charts, and changes to the program.

- The basic pattern is the **simple sequence**, in which steps occur one after another in order.
- A **decision step**, or selection structure, requires the program to make a comparison, the results of which determine which path of execution will occur next.
- The **loop**, or iteration, pattern allows a set of instructions to be repeated as needed.

Limiting a program to these control structures results in a **proper program**, in which the modules have only one entrance point and one exit point (see Figure 4–22). By following these patterns, programmers can avoid patching up their programs using the notorious GOTO statements, which send control of a program willy-nilly from point to point.

DOCUMENTATION

Documentation is a written description of a program. It includes all of the instructions and explanations that help people to understand, maintain, and use programs. Although you receive user manuals that document a software package that you buy, the documentation used by programmers is different. It explains what a program should do, what data is needed, how data items are defined in a program, and how output is formatted. It describes the modules and explains their individual functions and their relationships to the program as a whole. It should include the descriptions and results of tests completed before the program was put into use

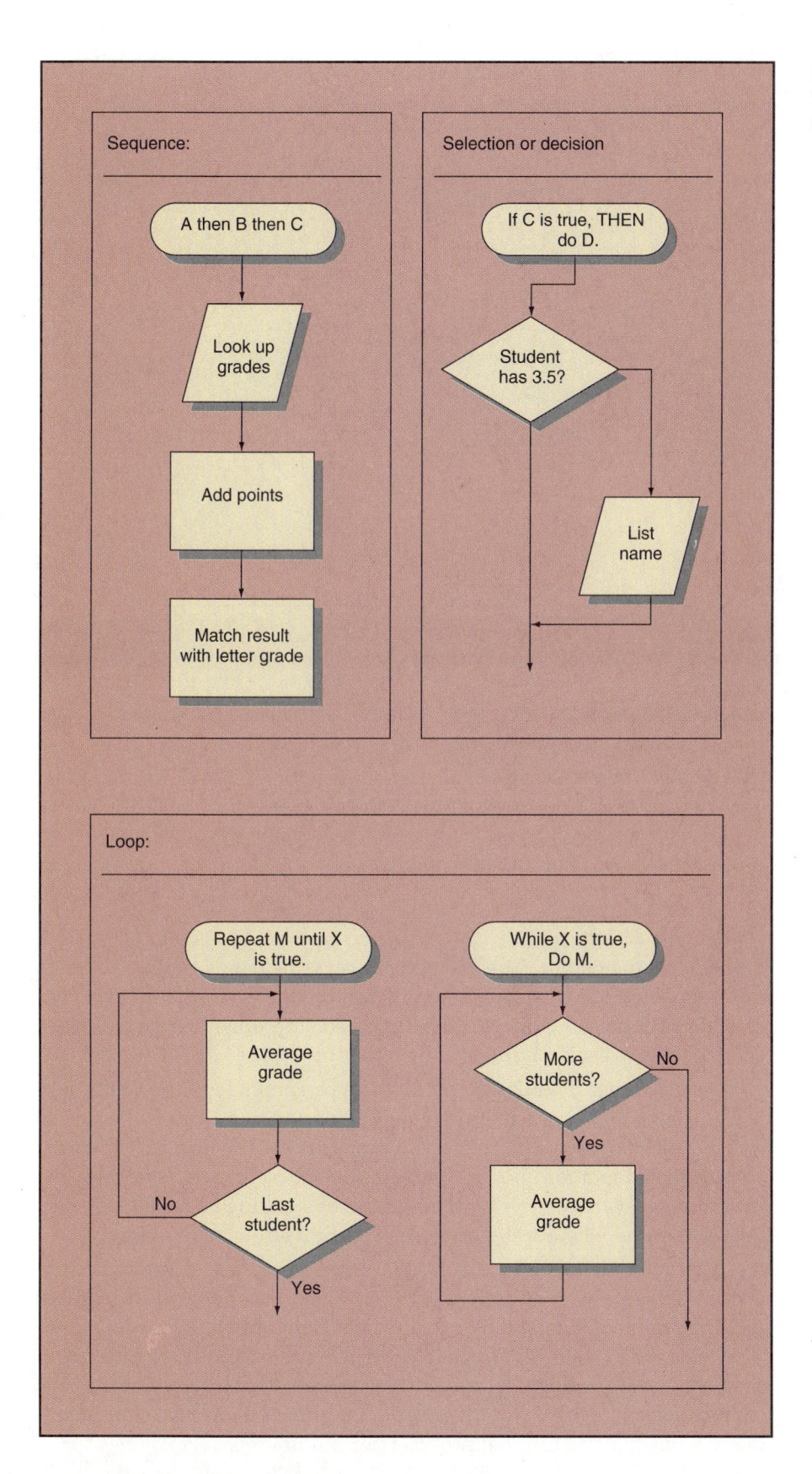

Figure 4–21 Control Structures
The control structures state the order of logic flow.

Sequence:

A then B then C → Look up grades → Add points → Match result with letter grade

Selection or decision

If C is true, THEN do D. → Student has 3.5? → List name

Loop:

Repeat M until X is true. → Average grade → Last student? (No → loop back; Yes → exit)

While X is true, Do M. → More students? (No → exit; Yes → Average grade → loop back)

Figure 4–22 A Proper Program
Using this rule helps prevent some of the jumping around to different routines that was common in spaghetti programming.

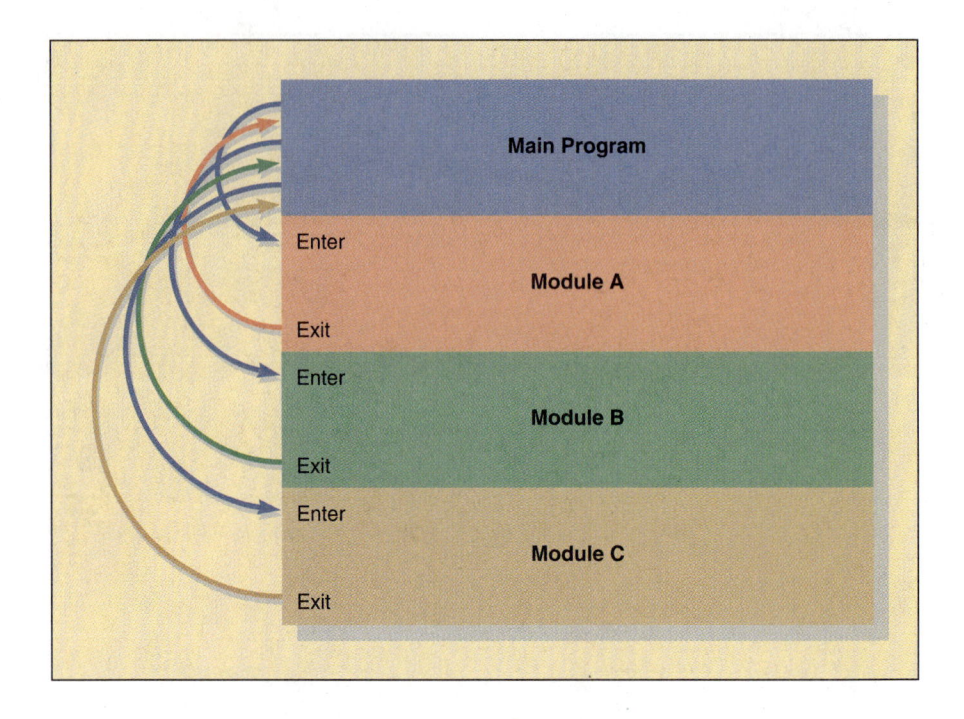

and any changes made after the program is activated. Documentation also should contain an actual listing of the program code and any charts that illustrate the program.

The process of documentation is ongoing. It begins with the initial request for a program and continues throughout the problem-solving process and into program maintenance.

Program Testing

Program testing could be neglected because of demands to get a program finished quickly. Yet programmers know that at each step of development, a program should be thoroughly tested. Top-down design facilitates testing because each module can be tested by itself.

Because other modules do not need to be completed for a test to take place, testing can occur as an ongoing process rather than at the end of program development. In fact, an informal design review, in which the design documentation is reviewed by selected managers, analysts, and programmers, can uncover errors before actual coding begins. It can even help determine whether the proposed solution will actually work.

After more detailed documentation and coding has occurred, the formal design review, or structured walk-through, is conducted. It involves distributing the documentation to a review team of two to four members. This team meets with the program designers to discuss the overall quality of the design and trace through the programs for errors. Because the team members have a fresh outlook on the project, they can often identify problems that the original programmer did not recognize.

Window on Computing

Chopping Off the Branches

A dramatic success for structured programming led to its widespread acceptance. This success involved the development of programs to support online access to the text of articles stored in the reference library of the *New York Times*. A program design, or algorithm, already had been developed for this application. The immediate problem was that the programming costs would exceed the original estimate by more than four times. The contractor on the project, IBM, asked one of its eminent computer scientists, Dr. Harlan Mills, to look into the problem. Mills, who had been an early advocate of structured programming, decided to try the new methods in this case.

When he started his review, Mills was handed an algorithm that contained 47 pages of processing steps. The program design was loaded with branching operations that called for jumping to different routines to implement an information search. After applying structured-programming methods, Mills returned a few days later with a 16-line algorithm. The programs were developed at about one-third of the estimated cost.

THE CHIEF PROGRAMMER TEAM

A **chief programmer team (CPT)** involves a group of workers supervised by one programmer. The number of team members varies with the complexity of the job. The purpose of forming a CPT is to facilitate the goals of structured programming and to utilize each member's talents effectively.

The chief programmer, often a system analyst, is responsible for overall coordination, development, and success of the programming project, and is the link between other team members, the project, and management and users (see Figure 4–23). Other members may include a backup programmer who assists the chief programmer in designing, testing, and evaluating the program and a librarian who maintains complete, up-to-date documentation. Depending on the size and complexity of the project, the team may also include other programmers, each working on different modules. Team members review the documentation and each other's work at each stage of development.

A CPT can tilt a project toward success in meeting the goals of structured programming and the goals of the organization for whom the project is intended:

- To increase the productivity of programmers
- To produce a software product that is reliable and easy to understand

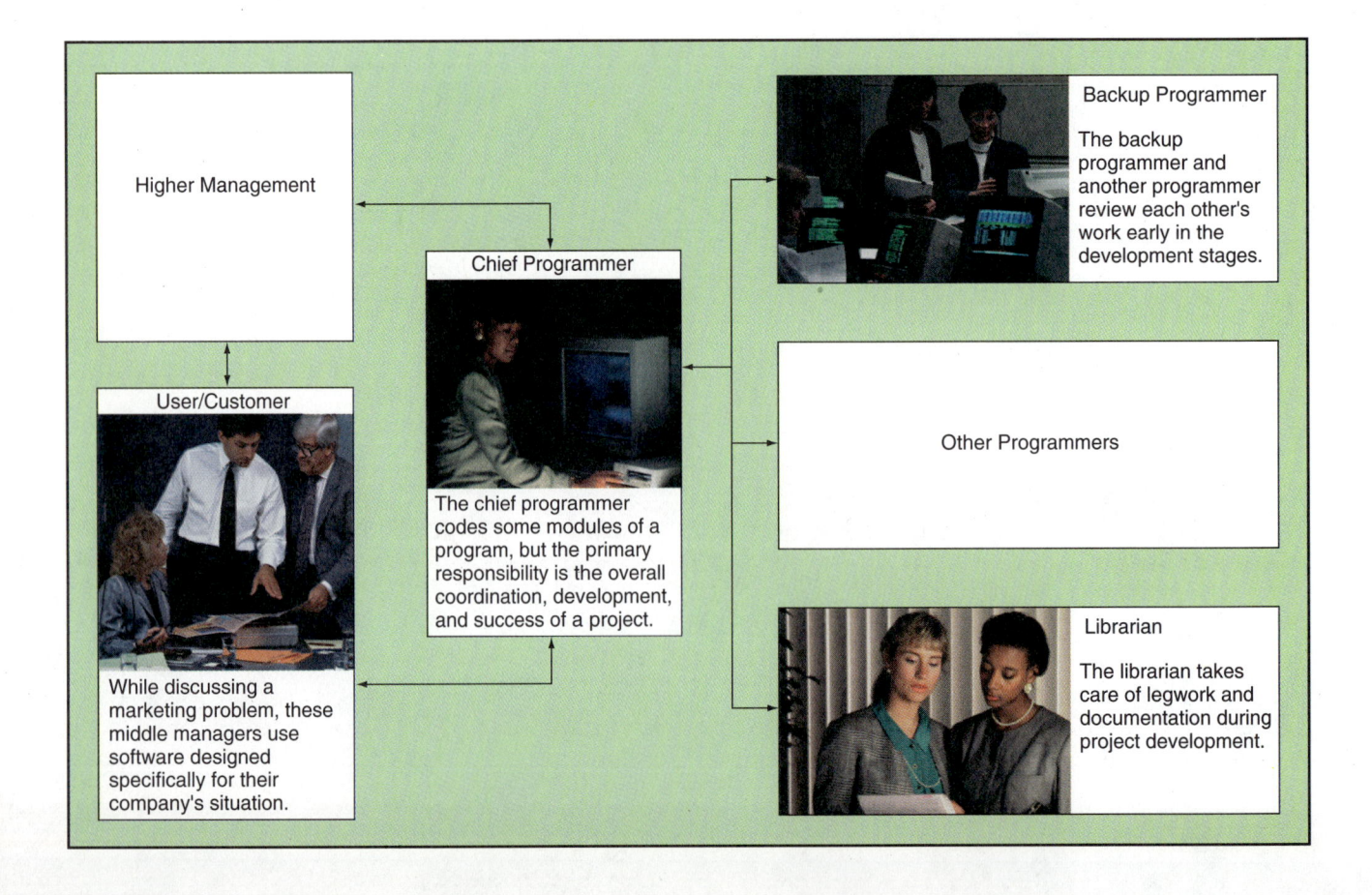

chief programmer team (CPT) A method of organization used in managing software development projects under which a chief programmer supervises programming and testing.

Figure 4–23 The Chief Programmer Team Method
The chief programmer coordinates a team effort toward reaching the goals of structured programming.

Higher Management

User/Customer
While discussing a marketing problem, these middle managers use software designed specifically for their company's situation.

Chief Programmer
The chief programmer codes some modules of a program, but the primary responsibility is the overall coordination, development, and success of a project.

Backup Programmer
The backup programmer and another programmer review each other's work early in the development stages.

Other Programmers

Librarian
The librarian takes care of legwork and documentation during project development.

- To reduce the costs and time associated with programming and testing
- To decrease the time and effort required to update a project once it is implemented

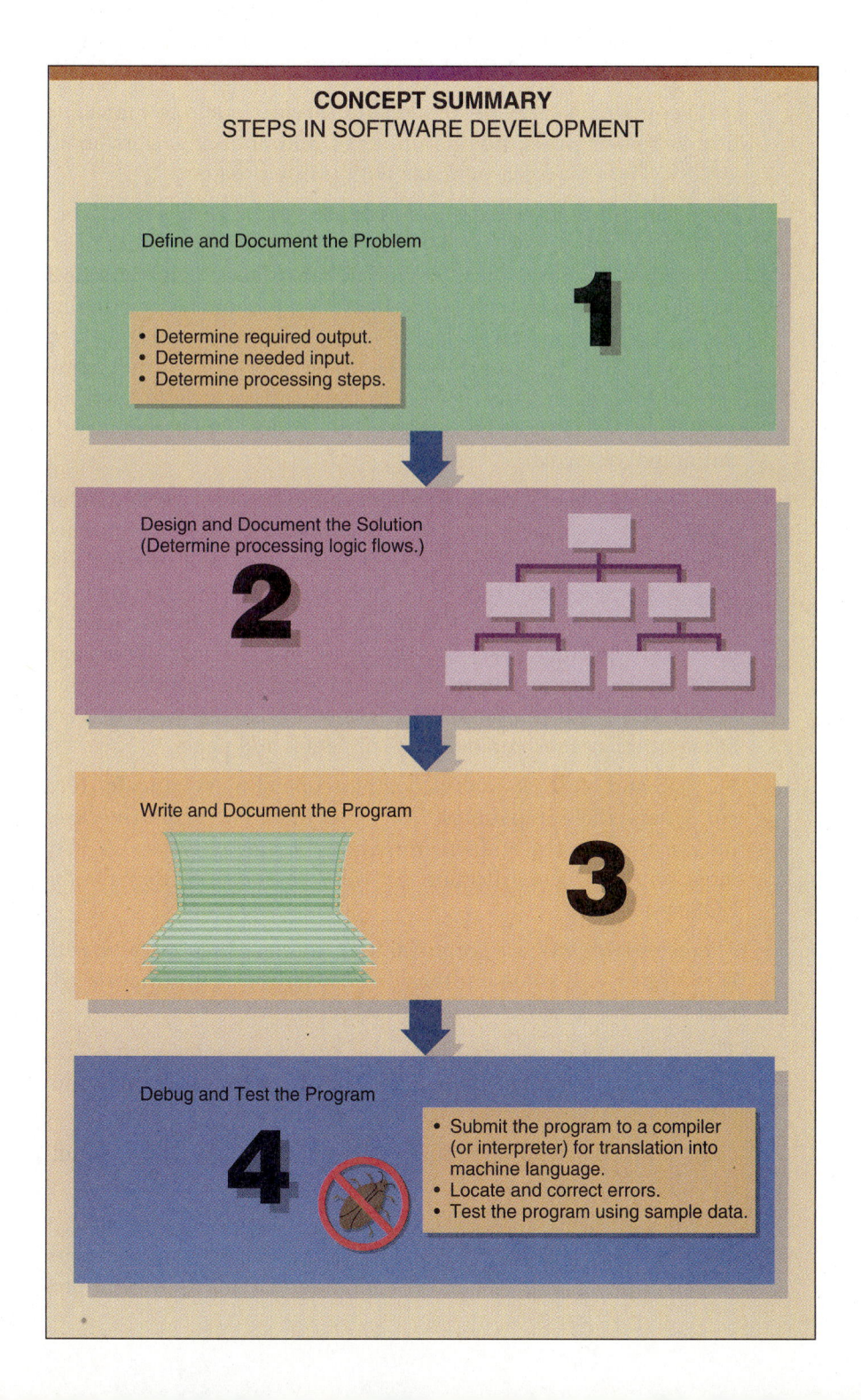

CONCEPT SUMMARY
STEPS IN SOFTWARE DEVELOPMENT

1. Define and Document the Problem
- Determine required output.
- Determine needed input.
- Determine processing steps.

2. Design and Document the Solution (Determine processing logic flows.)

3. Write and Document the Program

4. Debug and Test the Program
- Submit the program to a compiler (or interpreter) for translation into machine language.
- Locate and correct errors.
- Test the program using sample data.

➤Summary Points

- The computer uses system programs to manage its own operations. Operating systems are coordinated collections of system programs designed for specific computers that manage transfer of data, allocate storage, control execution of applications, and provide an interface for the user.

- Utility programs provide processing services such as managing files stored on disks, tidying up disks, and notifying users about viruses. The user often interacts with utility programs.

- Microcomputers are single-user systems; large computers are considered multiuser systems, because they enable two or more users at a time to run programs. Techniques that take microcomputers beyond the one-user, one-job configuration include task switching (which permits two programs to be loaded at once), multitasking (which permits two programs to be run at once), and virtual memory (which enables the system to treat storage as if it were an extension of memory, thus giving the illusion that memory is unlimited, or virtual).

- The user interface is the method by which a user interacts with an operating system or a program. A command-line user interface requires the user to type coded commands after a prompt displayed by the operating system. A menu-driven program enables the user to activate most jobs by making choices from menus. A graphical user interface makes use of windows, icons, menus, and pointing devices, providing an easy-to-learn interface that is consistent across all applications designed to be run with it. Pen-based interfaces resemble the use of pencil and paper.

- PC DOS and MS-DOS are the common operating systems for IBM computers and compatibles. They provide a command-line user interface, and have built-in limitations for memory use. A very large selection of application software has been written for the DOS systems.

- *Microsoft Windows* is a graphical user interface that operates with DOS. It provides some multitasking capabilities and supports virtual memory. It also includes miniapplications.

- The Apple Macintosh computer was the first to popularize a GUI. The current operating system is System 7.5, which supports virtual memory and a variety of file-linking functions.

- OS/2 is an advanced operating system designed for IBM computers and compatibles. It supports multitasking, but also runs most DOS and *Windows* programs.

- UNIX is a heavy-duty operating system that can be employed with large computers as well as microcomputers. It allows several programs to be run at the same time and supports multiple users, but there is no standard version.

- Machine language and assembly language, which are low-level languages, require extensive knowledge of the computer system being used. They are tedious to learn.
- High-level languages use macro instructions that cause a computer to execute an entire sequence of machine-level steps in response to a single high-level command, often a common English word or phrase. They are geared more toward the user than toward the internal operations of the computer.
- Examples of high-level languages are Fortran (the oldest), Basic (easy to learn), Pascal (highly structured), COBOL (commonly used by businesses), Ada (used by the Department of Defense), and C (very portable).
- Fourth-generation languages (4GLs) are suitable for nontechnical people to use because of their Englishlike qualities. They are frequently associated with database systems and include query languages, report generators, and application generators.
- Object-oriented programming (OOP) treats data and functions as objects that can be reused in a variety of projects without recoding. Once an object is tested, it can be reused without misgivings about its reliability.
- The software development process consists of four stages: defining the problem (the most important step); designing a solution (which involves setting up the algorithm, or sequence of steps in a program); writing (or coding) the program in a programming language; and debugging and testing the program. Each stage should be well documented.
- Structured programming techniques help improve programmer productivity and program clarity and reliability. They help decrease costs and time associated with programming and testing, as well as with maintaining and updating a program.
- A major structured programming technique is top-down design, in which program planning proceeds from the general to the specific. Each step is a module, and the modules occur in levels according to their generality.
- Structured programming also dictates the use of control structures (simple sequence, decision step, and loop) that result in a proper program—that is, one that has only one entrance point and one exit point so that program logic does not jump randomly from one routine to another.
- Every stage in program development should be documented, thus facilitating future changes, testing, and debugging. The top-down method increases the effectiveness of testing because each module can be tested by itself.

- A chief programmer team, consisting of the chief programmer, a backup programmer, a librarian, and other programmers (depending on the complexity of a project), helps reach the objectives of structured programming because work is divided according to talents and reviewed among the members for feasibility.

►Review Questions

1. In any computer system, which is first to be presented, or loaded, into memory—system software or application software? Why?
2. What do operating systems do? Describe some tasks performed by utility programs.
3. Compare task switching and multitasking. What other techniques take the microcomputer beyond single-user, single-job?
4. What is the advantage of using a command-line user interface? On the other hand, what are specific user-friendly characteristics of a graphical user interface? Name two other types of user interfaces.
5. Classify five popular operating systems or shells as to multitasking, multiple users, and user friendliness.
6. What do programming languages have to do with system programs?
7. Name three programming languages and their common uses.
8. What are the main advantages in application development that can be realized through use of a 4GL? through object-oriented programming?
9. What are the four stages of program development? At what stage is the algorithm set up?
10. Of what benefit is structured programming?
11. How does the term "big picture" relate to top-down design? How does top-down design contribute to program testing?

►Activities and Research

1. Why do you believe system and application programs are considered separate packages? In other words, why aren't system programs simply combined with application programs and sold together, as a unit?
2. Try at least one of the user interfaces mentioned in this chapter. Describe your response to the user interface. If you have never used a computer before, try to compare a command-line user

interface with a GUI. If you are used to one of the operating systems, describe your reaction to another.

3. Compare the methods of saving a file, seeing a list of files, and deleting a file via DOS and via System 7. List some other jobs you can do through each operating system.

CHAPTER 5

COMMUNICATIONS: CONNECTIVITY FOR PERSONAL COMPUTERS

OUTLINE

Learning Objectives
Introduction
Telecommunications
Communication Channels
    Types of Channels
    Connectivity: Microcomputers and Modems
    Concept Summary: Communication Channels
Networks
    Network Configurations
    Wide-Area Networks (WANs)
    Local-Area Networks (LANs)
    Window on Computing: The Future Is Here: Wireless Networks
    Concept Summary: A Client/Server LAN

Telecommunication Applications
    Electronic Transactions
    Facsimile
    Electronic Mail
    Voice Mail
    Telecommuting
    Teleconferencing
    Information Utilities
    Electronic Bulletin Boards
    The Internet
    Profile: Bill Gates and Microsoft
Summary Points
Review Questions
Activities and Research

LEARNING OBJECTIVES

After reading this chapter, you should be able to:

- Define *data communication* and *telecommunication*.
- Tell the purpose of communication channels, and differentiate between the types.
- Describe the use of a modem.
- Define *network*, and explain the various network configurations.
- Differentiate between wide-area networks and local-area networks.
- Describe the two models of local-area networks, and evaluate their characteristics.
- Describe common telecommunication applications.

Figure 5–1 Worldwide Networks
Telephone and data communication uses networks of computers to route and monitor the transmissions of signals all over the country and the world.

network A system in which various input and output facilities, which may include computers, are linked over communication channels.

INTRODUCTION

Businesses moving away from the cities are nothing new: When electric power lines and railroads were installed, industries moved from cities and sources of water power to locations where the new resources reached. Later, the interstate highway system enabled even more factories and corporate headquarters to move into suburban and rural areas.

As in the past, technology continues to help business operations move away from the major metropolitan areas. Citicorp has installed its credit-card operations in South Dakota. Clothing vendor Patagonia placed its customer service staff in Montana. Motorola sends its designs for electronics products directly into its suppliers' computers. People who transcribe television shows for Journal Graphics work at home all over the country and transmit their work to the company's computers. Using **networks,** businesses can send information all over the world (see Figure 5–1).

This chapter presents a brief history of modern telecommunication, discusses communication channels—from early types like telegraph lines to modern communication satellites—and then focuses on how microcomputers are connected to those channels via modems and communication software. The various kinds of networks for connecting computer equipment and databases are described and contrasted, along with the numerous telecommunication applications available through computers.

►TELECOMMUNICATIONS

The need to communicate over distances grew to national proportions long before computers were invented. At one time, the nation had networks of telegraph offices and teletypewriters for transmitting messages and news reports (see Figure 5–2). Investment companies handled hundreds of thousands of buy and sell orders at stock markets through telegraph and teletypewriter circuits. As the message traffic increased, bottlenecks were bound to happen. Computers simply made the problem worse by generating more information than existing networks could handle.

With the addition of disk drives to computer systems, business gained the ability to handle orders in real time. As a result, it made sense to link computers directly with sales locations to eliminate the duplication and errors of manual data entry. **Telecommunication** facilities—namely, the telephone lines—presented the most natural path for this transmission of data; however, two major problems needed to be resolved. First, computers of the day used one data coding system, EBCDIC, and telephone lines used an entirely different, incompatible coding format, ASCII (refer to Chapter 2). Second, computers and telephone systems sent entirely different kinds of signals. Computer systems process digital signals, a series of stop-start (0 and 1) pulses carried by direct current (DC), but telephone systems were designed originally to carry sounds—human voices—through **analog transmissions** (see Figure 5–3). Analog signals are tones, or electrical values that travel in a series of continuous alternating current (AC) waves that vary in volume with the sounds of voices. They are not compatible with digital signals.

telecommunication The transfer of data from one point to another over distances, using telephone lines, microwaves, and/or satellites.

analog transmission The sending of data in which the signal is in the form of a wave.

Figure 5–2 Teletypewriters
Teletypewriters used to be the primary means for transmitting news and other information.

The solution to these problems, which began to take shape in the 1960s, lay in devices that translated one type of signal into the other. These devices were placed between computers and telephone circuits, making it possible to send and receive digital codes over analog transmission links. Once compatibility was established, networks of computers and telecommunication channels could speed data from business headquarters to branches around the world. This electronic transmission of data from one location to another is called **data communication,** and it is safe to say that today's business, governmental, commercial, defense, transportation, and other systems could not exist without data-communication links. These links can exist between terminals that are in the same room or that are separated by an ocean. The difference between these two situations lies in the type of communication channels through which data flows.

data communication The process of enabling digital devices such as computers to communicate with each other.

▶ Communication Channels

A **communication channel** is the link that permits the transmission of electrical signals among the devices in a computer system. It provides a way for data to be transmitted within a single computer, between a computer and its peripherals, or among multiple computers over long distances. Computers can be linked via wires and cables in an organization's private network. They can also be hooked into a telephone line to transmit data through the same public networks used to make a phone call. The types of channels available for networks are described next.

communication channel A medium, or pathway, for carrying data or voice transmissions from one place to another.

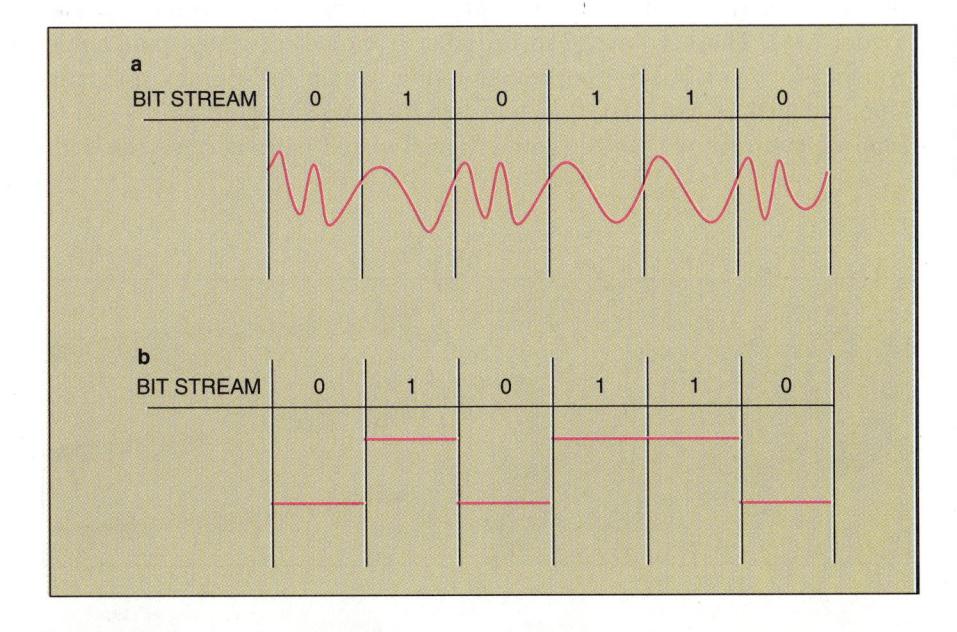

Figure 5–3 Signal Transmissions
Communication signals are transmitted in two different forms: Analog signals (top) are represented by continuous waves; digital signals (bottom) are represented by pulses.

Types of Channels

If your microcomputer is connected to some type of network, data you receive through the network may have gone through a variety of channels before it gets to your computer. The oldest type of channel is the single wire, or telegraph line. The other channels are twisted pairs, coaxial cable, fiber-optic cable, microwave links, and satellites.

Telegraph Lines

A telegraph line consists of a single strand of wire connecting two points. The name *telegraph* ties this kind of channel to the days when transmissions took place over wires that usually ran beside railroad tracks. Signals were initiated at telegraph keys that served as switches to make or break connections. Communication occurred when trained operators decoded the series of clicks that made up Morse code. The teletypewriter circuits used telegraph lines.

This kind of channel is simple and inexpensive but slow and limited in capacity. The services available are simplex and half-duplex transmissions. **Simplex transmission** permits transmission in only one direction. One station on a simplex line is designated as a sender; the other is a receiver. Under **half-duplex transmission,** the line can send signals in either direction, but in only one direction at a time. The station receiving a message cannot send a message until the connection is broken and switches are reset to reverse direction.

Twisted Pairs

Obviously, one-way-at-a-time transmission would not work for telephone calls. People want to be able to talk whenever they feel they have something to say. Therefore, telephone lines use two carriers, or a pair of copper wires, so that signals can be sent and received at the same time (see Figure 5–4). These wires make up what is called a **twisted-pair cable,** which allows for **full-duplex transmission.** Under full-duplex transmission, two people can talk at once or two data transmission points can be sending and receiving at the same time. Twisted pairs became the com-

---

simplex transmission Transmission in which data travels along a line in one direction only.

half-duplex transmission Transmission in which data can travel along a line in either direction, but in only one direction at a time.

twisted-pair cable A communication channel that consists of pairs of wires twisted together and bound into a cable; commonly used for telephone transmission.

full-duplex transmission Transmission in which data travels along a line in both directions at once.

Figure 5–4 Twisted Pairs
The speed at which voice or data is carried over twisted-pair wire depends upon the line quality and signal generation methods.

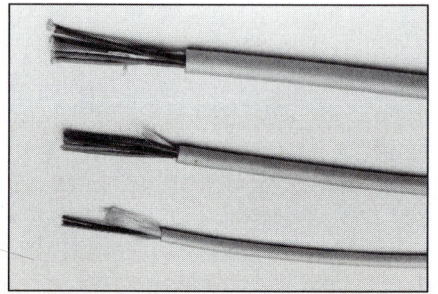

mon channel for computer communications because they had already been installed in buildings for other purposes.

Telephone lines have a far greater transmission capacity, or **bandwidth,** than telegraph lines. While a single telegraph line can carry about 60 words per minute, a single pair of wires that make up a telephone line can carry 1,200 or more words per minute. Line capacity is expressed in bits per second (bps), and by this measure ordinary telephone lines permit transmission between 300 and 9,000 bps. The quality of twisted-pair wire commonly used in telephone lines is referred to as "voice grade," but a higher quality, called "data grade," or 10BaseT, has a greater transmission capacity. Telephone lines are susceptible to noise (electrical and electromagnetic interference from high-voltage equipment and even the sun), which can distort the signals.

COAXIAL CABLES

A **coaxial cable** is a high-grade link that provides "broadband" services running into the millions of bits per second. Each individual cable consists of a single wire surrounded by insulation and a woven copper braid or foil (see Figure 5–5). The insulation reduces electrical interference, or noise, that is common on standard telephone lines. Coaxial cables are used for television transmission as well as in buildings for linking the parts of a computer system. Bundles of the cables can be further enclosed and shielded so that they can be laid underground or undersea.

FIBER-OPTIC CABLES

Fiber-optic cables carry pulses of light through thin glass strands about the thickness of human hair or sewing thread (see Figure 5–6). The tiny staccato pulses of light occur at 90 million times per second. Full cables of fiber-optic strands can handle thousands of times as much traffic as conventional telephone wires.

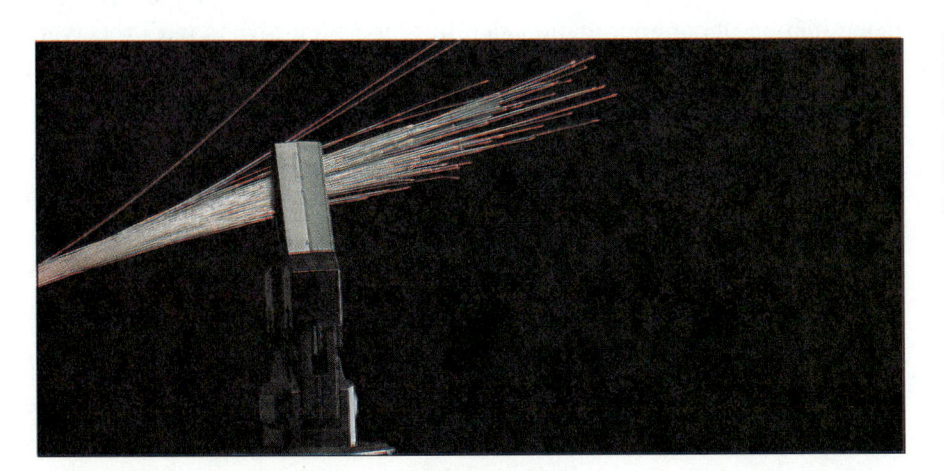

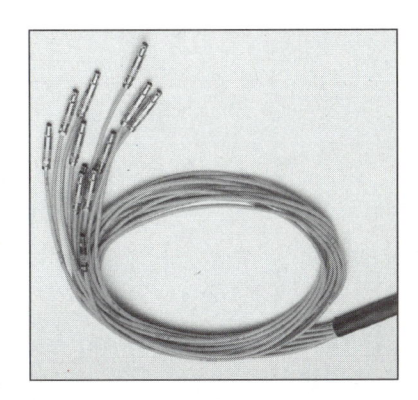

Figure 5–5 Coaxial Cable
A common use of coaxial cable is to transmit TV signals from cameras to broadcast transmitters or across the country for broadcast into different regions.

bandwidth A rating of communication channel capacity; expressed in bits per second and also known as *grade*.

coaxial cable A high-capacity transmission link that consists of a single wire, insulated and bound as protection from electromagnetic interference.

fiber-optic cable A communication carrier that consists of hair-thin strands of glass that carry data as pulses of light.

Figure 5–6 Fiber-Optic Cable
Fiber-optic filaments the width of a human hair or sewing thread are able to carry hundreds of voice or data transmissions. Eventually, fiber-optic systems are expected to be used within computer processors.

With fiber optics, transmission is fast, high quality, and reliable; yet the materials used are lightweight and less expensive than coaxial cables. Transmission is digital, and the broadband width of fiber optics makes it possible to send not only voice and data, but also pictures, video, and music. The cables are not affected by electrical interference and corrosive substances and are difficult to tap, increasing the security of transmissions. Because of these advantages, fiber-optic cables are becoming a mainstay of telecommunication networks. Currently, they are found in some local-area networks (described later in this chapter), but telephone companies are also using them as replacements for standard wires in certain localities.

Changing over to fiber optics from standard telephone lines will be expensive, however, and not all communities will change house-to-house wiring to fiber optics. Most likely, schools, hospitals, and businesses will have direct fiber-optic connections, whereas homes will be able to connect to fiber-optic trunk lines via standard telephone wires.

Because of the capabilities for tremendous speed and accuracy, the use of fiber-optic cable may bring many different types of information services to our homes, including high-definition television, interactive education, dial-up encyclopedias, and movie libraries, among other services. This scenario is often referred to as the "information superhighway."

Microwaves

microwave link A communication channel that transmits and receives signals through use of high-power, short-wavelength radio signals carried through the atmosphere in straight lines.

A **microwave link** involves the transmission of signals through the air, like ordinary radio broadcasts but at high frequencies that are shorter and closer together than ordinary analog signals. As communication channels, microwaves provide high-quality links because the powerful signals usually are not affected by weather or other types of interference common to radio transmission. One limitation is that microwave signals travel in straight lines (sometimes referred to as "line-of-sight"); thus, the curvature of the earth would cause the signals to travel into space and be lost. To be useful over long distances, microwave signals must be relayed, or received and retransmitted, every 90 to 100 miles (see Figure 5–7). A combination of communication satellites and high towers with receivers and transmitters enable cross-country signals to be carried from place to place. The signals are then delivered through telephone lines from the receiving towers to users.

Communication Satellites

communication satellite An earth-orbiting vehicle equipped and positioned to relay microwave signals from earth stations, or towers.

Communication satellites make it possible to send microwave signals over thousands of miles, providing worldwide microwave communication. A communication satellite typically is put into "stationary orbit" about 22,300 miles above the earth. At this altitude, a satellite moves at the same speed and in the same direction as the earth rotates. This gives the satellite a fixed location over the earth so that microwave signals can be aimed at a known target (see Figure 5–8). Satellite links make extremely wide bandwidths possible, as transmission rates can run into millions of bits per second. Stormy weather can interrupt the signals, however.

CONNECTIVITY: MICROCOMPUTERS AND MODEMS

As you know, the differences in signal handling must be overcome if a microcomputer is to send signals over telecommunication channels. These differences are bridged by devices that perform two separate functions: modulation and demodulation—terms that describe the signal processing that takes place when computer-generated messages are transferred to and from analog telephone circuits. The term *modulation* refers to a process for converting digital pulses from computers to analog wave patterns—actually, audio tones—that can be carried by conventional telephone lines. *Demodulation* is the reverse step: It converts analog signals back to digital (see Figure 5–9).

TYPES OF MODEMS

The device used for transmission of computer-generated data over telephone lines takes its name from the two functions modulate and demodulate. It is the **modem.** A modem can be internal or external (see Figure

Figure 5–7 Microwave Transmissions
Microwave communication can be employed to carry local message traffic (*left*) or to transmit data to and from communication satellites (*right*).

modem An acronym for modulator/demodulator; a device that prepares digital computer signals for analog transmission over telephone lines and then prepares the analog signals for reentry into a computer.

158 • Communications: Connectivity for Personal Computers

Figure 5–8 Satellite Communication
International communication between distant computers is made possible through microwave relays handled by satellites in stationary earth orbit. Satellite signals are relayed via ground transmission lines.

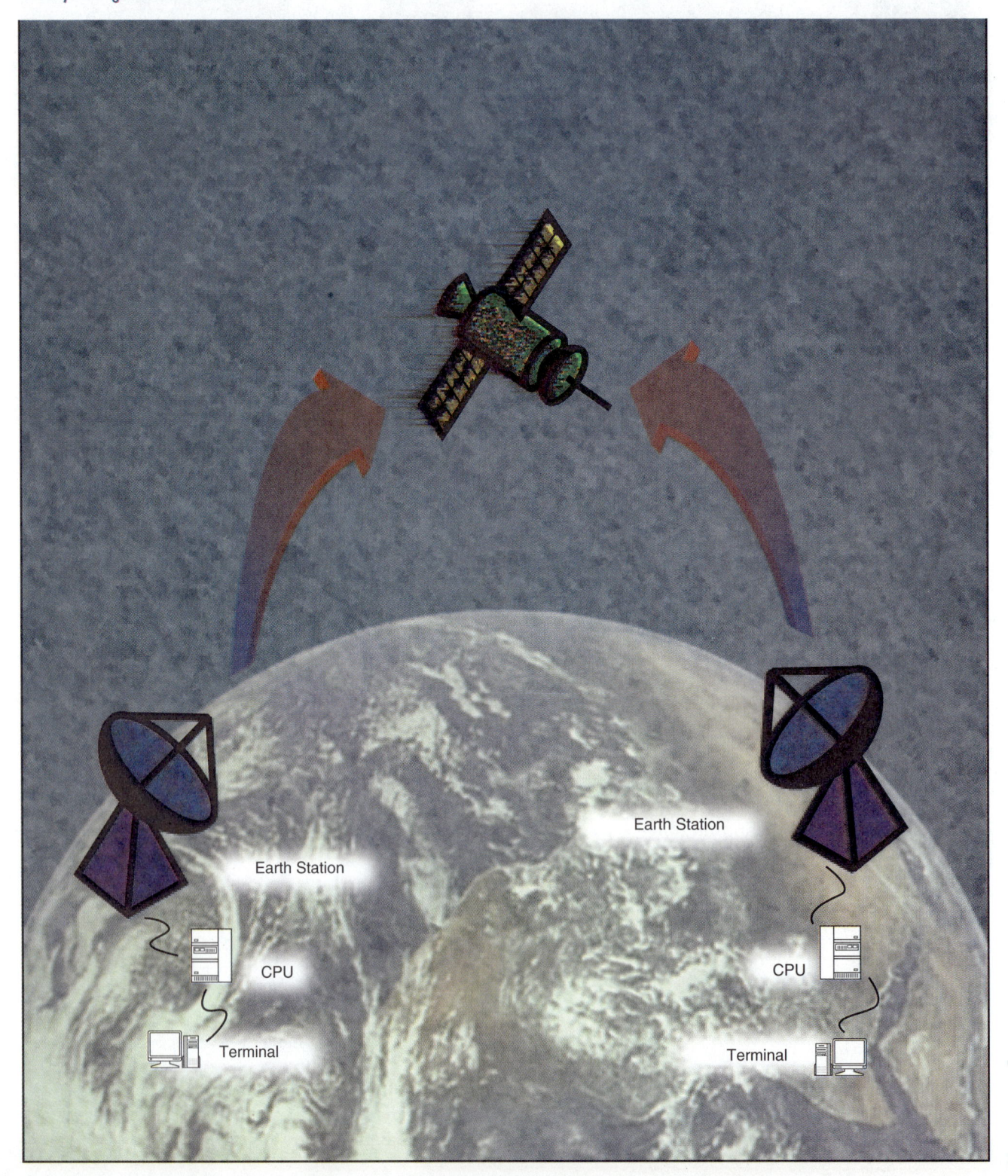

Figure 5–9 Transmission by Modem
The modem prepares signals for transmission over channels that carry a different form of signals than computers use.

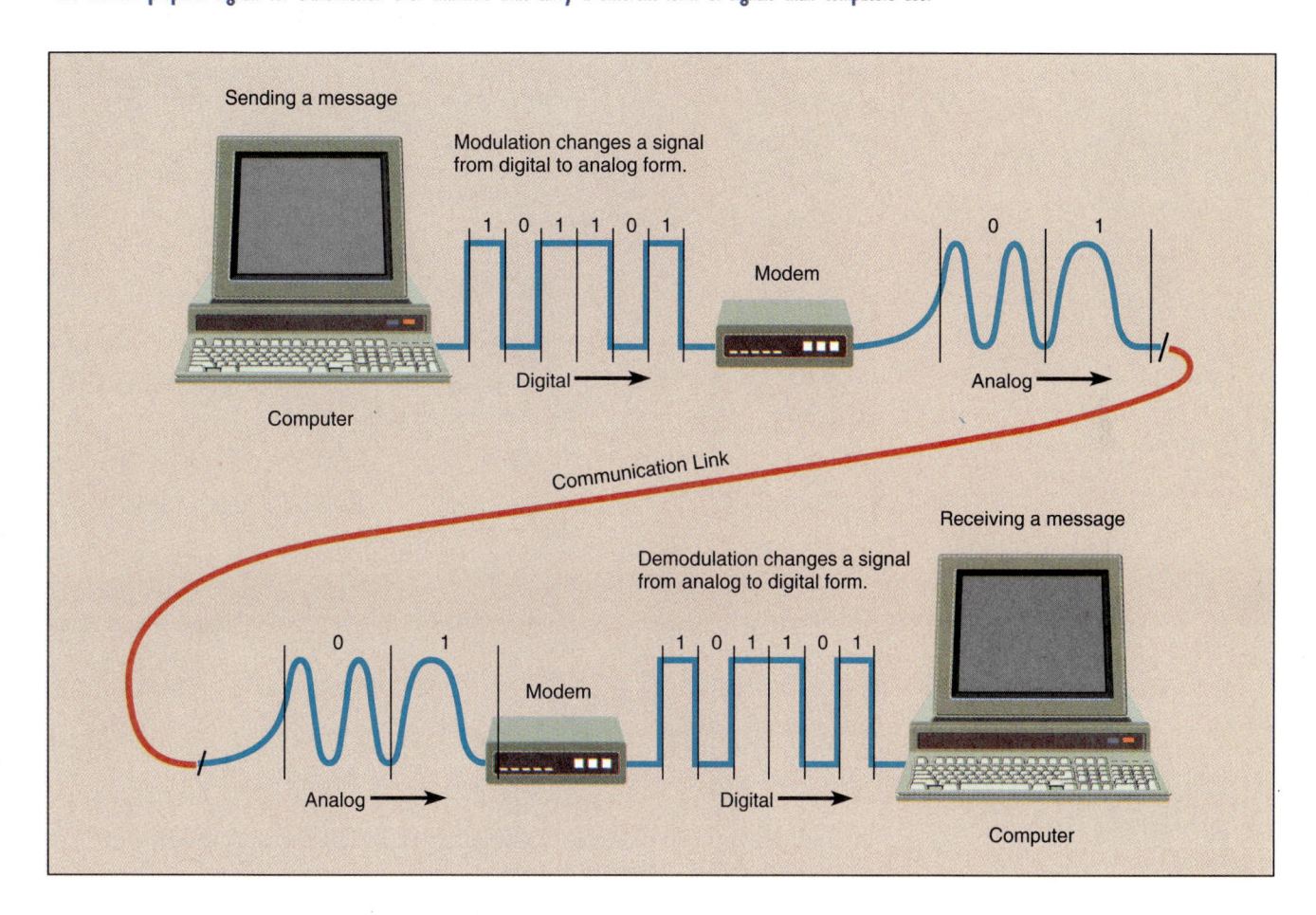

5–10). An internal modem is actually a circuit board installed in a slot inside the computer. An external modem is located outside the computer and is attached to it by cable. Both of these modems are referred to as "direct-connect" because they are plugged into the telephone wall jack via a cable. A notebook computer will most likely have a PCMCIA slot

Figure 5–10 Modems
The modems pictured here are the external modem (left), and the PCMCIA modem card (right).

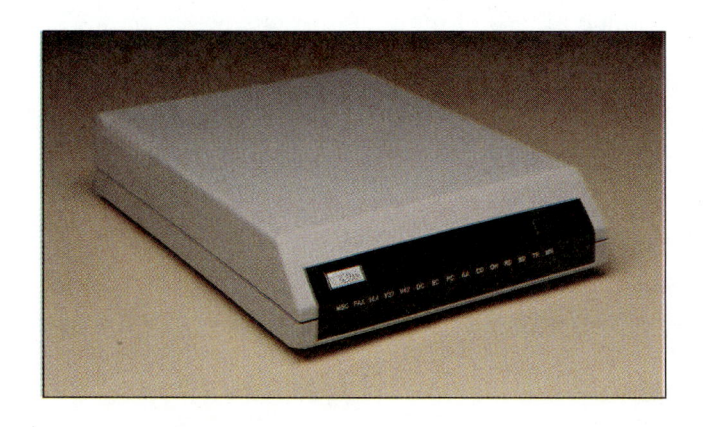

CONCEPT SUMMARY
COMMUNICATION CHANNELS

Type of Channel	Characteristics of Channel	Grade of Channel
Twisted Pairs	• Twisted copper strands • Excellent conductor of electricity • Most widely used media; used for telephone lines • Analog transmission	Voice-grade Data-grade
Coaxial Cable	• Copper and aluminum wires insulated to reduce distortion • High-speed analog transmission	Broad-band
Fiber-optic Cable	• Flexible, narrow tubing • Light impulses are sent along clear flexible tubing • Digital transmission	Broad-band
Microwave	• Similar to radio or television transmission • Transmission must be in a straight line • Used with satellites and ground stations • Analog transmission	Broad-band
Satellites	• Placed in a stationary orbit • Used with microwaves • Extremely fast transmission • Analog transmission	Broad-band

asynchronous transmission A method in which data characters are sent at random intervals and are defined, or separated, by start and stop bits.

synchronous transmission A method in which data bits are sent in a stream at a timed, fixed rate.

into which you can insert a PCMCIA card configured as a modem or a fax-modem (discussed later in this chapter).

Most modems communicate with computers through **asynchronous transmission,** in which data is sent at random intervals and characters are defined, or separated, by start and stop bits. The connection between the two modems always involves **synchronous transmission,** however, which means the transmission occurs by fixed timing, or clock, signals. High-speed modems do support synchronous computer connections, although this is not common in microcomputer environments. Operating speeds for modems range from 300 to tens of thousands of bits per second. The most common modem speed today is 9,600 bps, although 14,400-bps and 28,800-bps modems are quickly becoming the standard for home computer users. Faster modems can also handle slow speeds, however, which is useful for accessing information services that operate at slow speeds.

COMMUNICATION SOFTWARE

A modem requires software in order to work. One important program—terminal-emulation software—"tricks" the computer into acting as an input/output tool for another computer, such as the mainframe or minicomputer at work or at an online information service.

The communication software offers a number of other services, including auto-answer, in which it automatically answers incoming calls, and auto-dial, in which it dials one or more telephone numbers automatically. The modem will also transfer files or messages when the receiving computer answers the telephone. A time delay feature allows you to set a particular time—usually at night, when rates are low—at which the modem calls another computer and transfers files.

When you want to link your computer to another by modem, the communication software requires you to set a number of parameters (or characteristics) so that the communication **protocol** (or rules) by which your computer operates matches that of the computer being accessed and the communication channel being used. The devices can then "agree" on the format of the data being sent or received. (This agreement is called a "handshake.") Protocol includes such things as the speed of transmission, the duplex setting (half or full), and error-detection facilities. (There are a number of standards for sending data, and it is hard to get people to agree on a single standard, so protocol is necessary.)

protocol The description of rules for the formatting of data when transmitting and receiving data over a network.

Modem software usually offers a scripting (or macro) feature in which sets of keystrokes or commands are assigned to one word or keystroke. This can save on telephone bills because less time is spent doing routine jobs. The software also enables data compression so that the same amount of data is transmitted in fewer bits. (A file that has been compressed is called a "packed" file.) Communication software packages include *Crosstalk, White Knight,* and *Timbuktu.*

▶ NETWORKS

The organization that parcels out computer equipment and databases to several locations is said to engage in **distributed processing.** In fact, a number of independent networks may be linked into an even larger network. The networks can be local, regional, national, or even worldwide in scope. They enable an organization to share not only data, but also computer hardware such as expensive printers or a modem link to an information service or public network.

distributed processing A system in which processing can be done at sites other than that of the central computer.

In a network, each point that can send or receive data or both is known as a **node.** A node, or end point, can be anything from a dumb terminal (one that has no independent computing power) to a microcomputer to a full-scale computer system (see Figure 5–11). **Links** are the communication channels that connect the nodes.

node An end point of a network; may be a computer, a printer, a dumb terminal, or some other physical device; a computer processing point that has access to a data network.

link A communication channel that connects nodes.

NETWORK CONFIGURATIONS

Nodes and links can be arranged in several different configurations, or *topologies,* including star, ring, and bus.

Figure 5–11 One Node in a Network
Microcomputers can be integrated into networks that include mainframe systems and workstations at multiple locations.

star network A data communication network in which all nodes radiate from a central computer hub that controls receipt and delivery of all messages.

host computer The central computer in a network.

Figure 5–12 Star Topology
The configuration of nodes individually linked to a hub resembles a star. The popular Ethernet LAN standard is often set up in star topology.

STAR TOPOLOGY

A **star network** has a series of outlying nodes linked by separate connecting lines to the *hub,* or central switching component (see Figure 5–12). The hub, sometimes called the **host computer,** is often a minicomputer or a mainframe. Messages can start at any node. All messages go

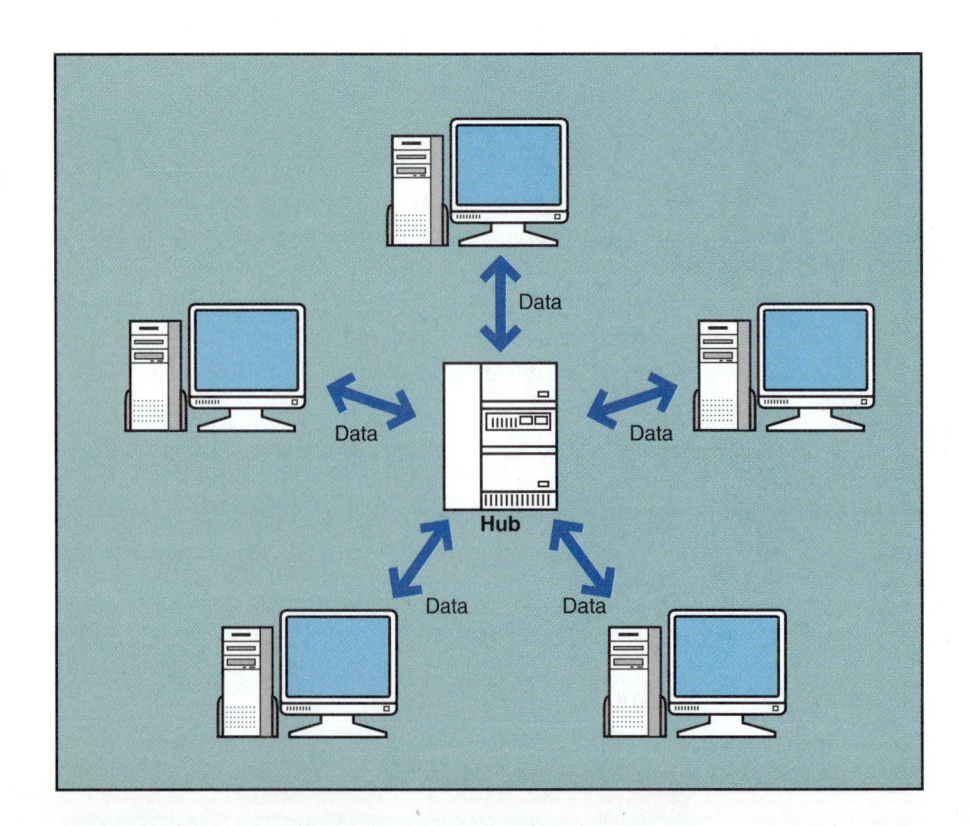

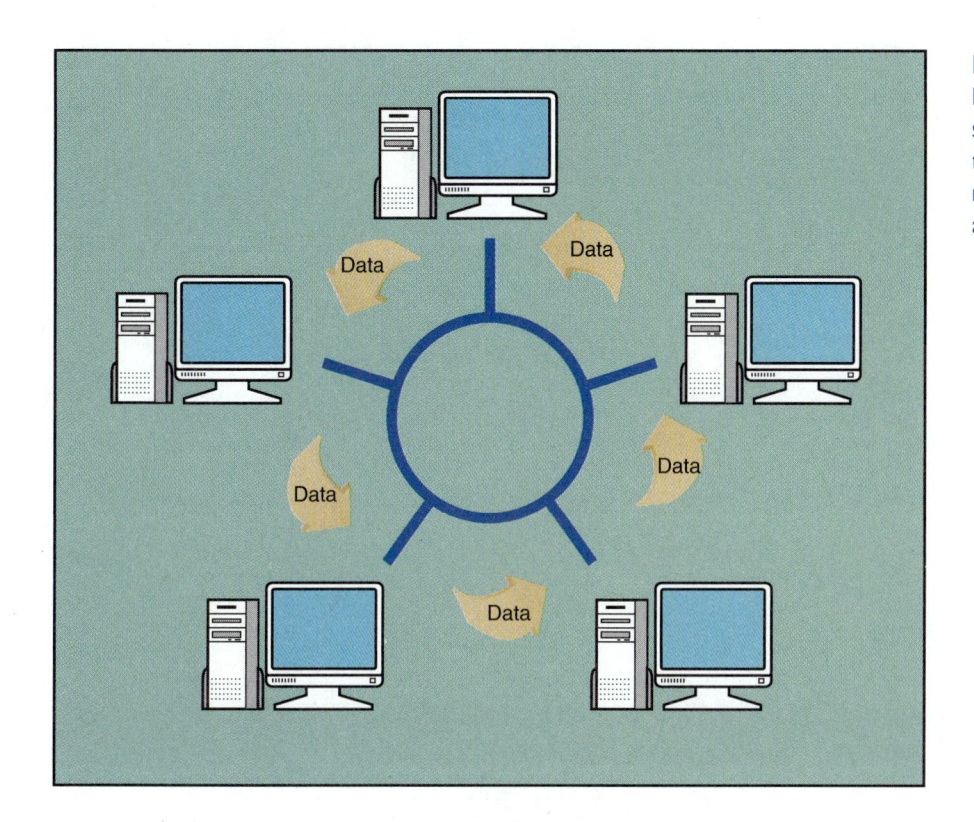

Figure 5–13 Ring Topology
Ring configurations are usually the least expensive approach to setting up a data communications network. The IBM Token Ring local-area network is an example, and peer-to-peer LANs are often set up in ring configurations.

directly to the central computer and are routed to their destinations, similar to the way the telephone system works. Multiple star networks can be linked into a single, large system. For example, one of the nodes of a network can be the hub for another star network. The terminals and secondary networks may be geographically widespread.

The star topology is vulnerable in that when the central computer breaks down, communication among the nodes is completely disrupted. If a single node breaks down, however, this topology makes isolating the problem a manageable task.

RING TOPOLOGY

In a **ring network,** a number of computers are connected to each other along a single, circular path (see Figure 5–13). A message can be originated by any node within the network. The message is then carried around the circular path from one node to the next until it reaches its destination. Traffic moves in one direction only.

Ring topology is often the choice when the computers are geographically close. It represents a comparatively inexpensive way to build a network. Costs—including communication channels, software, and hardware—are minimized because there is no need for a central computer. However, this approach lacks a built-in method for controlling or monitoring overall network operations. In addition, if a link or node fails at any point in the network, the whole network goes down. To prevent this,

ring network A data communication network in which nodes are connected in a continuous circle and in which transmitted messages are passed to all nodes in the network until the destination is reached.

Figure 5–14 Bus Topology
If one node in a bus configuration breaks down, the system can still function effectively. Ethernet, a LAN standard, is sometimes set up in a bus configuration, as are some peer-to-peer LANs.

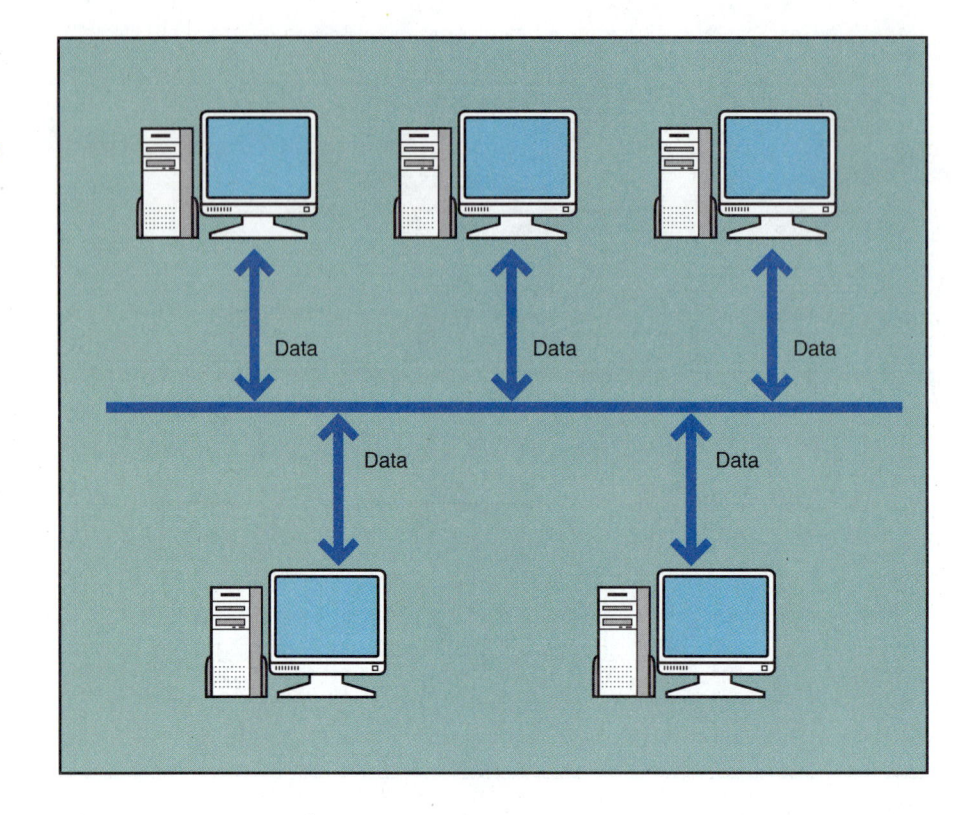

nodes are often linked in a double ring so that the offending point can be bypassed.

Bus Topology

In a **bus network,** each computer plugs into a single bus cable that runs from computer to computer (see Figure 5–14). Each also handles its own communications control. As messages travel along the bus cable, stations monitor the cable and retrieve their own messages. If one node in bus topology breaks down, the system can still function effectively. The bus topology is often preferred when just a few devices are linked.

Wide-Area Networks (WANs)

Networks that cover large geographical areas are called **wide-area networks (WANs)**. WANs generally consist of computers or remote local-area networks (see next subsection) linked through standard telephone lines and microwave transmission. WAN links are generally provided by **common carriers,** which are organizations that have been approved by the Federal Communications Commission (FCC) to offer communications services to the public. The two largest common carriers are American Telephone & Telegraph (AT&T) and Western Union. There are also large public networks, such as Tymnet, Sprintnet, and CompuServe's network.

Although telephone lines do not make the best channel for data communications, a new standard, called Integrated Services Digital Network

bus network A data communication network in which all nodes communicate via a common distribution channel.

wide-area network (WAN) A data communication network designed to serve users over hundreds or thousands of miles; generally implemented by linking computer and LANs over telephone lines.

common carrier An FCC-regulated private company that provides telecommunication facilities for public use.

Figure 5–15 Local-Area Network
LANs permit office workers to share files and facilities. The workstations in this photo are linked to a minicomputer to provide access to massive files and to common peripherals and software resources.

(ISDN), will increase the reliability and flexibility of sending data and video images through existing telephone lines. ISDN expands the bandwidth of conventional telephone lines, and is used widely in Europe.

ISDN will eventually make the telephone system completely digital. This opens the possibility of a worldwide computer network operating by one standard. Already, we are seeing widespread communication through the Internet, a network that links at least 3 million computers around the world, many of them university- and research-related. (See the later subsection "The Internet" and Appendix B.)

LOCAL-AREA NETWORKS (LANs)

Local-area networks (LANs) enable users in an organization to access and exchange information within a single office, building, or other relatively small area (see Figure 5–15). The major advantage of a LAN is that users are able to share files, programs, messages, and expensive devices such as laser printers.

LAN technology has existed for several years, but many companies have not adopted it because of doubts about its cost-effectiveness and reliability. Incompatibility among different systems and devices has also blocked widespread acceptance of LANs. These problems are rapidly being overcome. Accordingly, installation and use of LANs can be expected to increase steadily. Although some experts predict that LANs will lead to the demise of the mainframe, others suggest that demands on the mainframe will increase with linkage to LANs. In fact, most companies will not throw out their investment in large computers; rather, they will change the way they use their mainframes.

local-area network (LAN) A communication-linked group of computers and peripherals located within a single office or building.

LAN Components

Like other networks, LANs have nodes and links. The nodes are the usual components of a computer system: the computers, printers, and storage devices. One or more computers may be specially designated for a particular job, such as communication or network management.

Each computer in a LAN is equipped with a **network interface card (NIC)**, which is a printed circuit board that allows the members of the LAN to communicate. The NIC plugs into an internal slot in the computer and has a cable that connects it to the LAN. It contains the components that allow the computer to send and receive messages on the LAN.

The nodes of the LAN are connected together with cable such as coaxial cable, twisted-pair wire, or fiber-optic cable. A variety of connectors, or plugs, are available that link each type of cable with the appropriate device. The members of a local-area network must normally be positioned within 800 to 1,000 feet of each other, because the strength of the transmission signal decreases as it travels. Thus, short distances enable the signal to be received properly. Multiple LANs and other networks can be joined through bridges connecting similar LANs that do not necessarily have the same protocol, through gateways connecting incompatible networks such as a PC-based LAN to a mainframe-based network, or through routers, which can link only LANs with compatible protocols.

Three common hardware standards in LANs are Ethernet, ARCnet, and Token Ring. These standards employ either the star, ring, or bus network topology discussed in the previous section. There are also *proprietary networks,* that is, networks that are brand-specific and not always compatible with the standards.

The software used to control network operations is referred to as the **network operating system (NOS)**. The NOS controls member access to the network's shared resources. If, for example, two or more members on the network request access to the printer at the same time, the NOS will control the order in which printing occurs. In addition, the NOS normally includes programs that oversee network security and the processing of messages, or electronic mail.

LAN Models

A **client/server LAN** is the most popular LAN model. In this type of LAN, one or more servers (or "back ends") manage the sharing of peripheral devices and the database. The central **server** is a *dedicated* computer—used for a sole purpose—that contains the network operating system and governs operation of the LAN. When multiple servers are implemented, each may have its own function: handling the database, controlling print functions, managing communications such as e-mail, and acting as gateways to incompatible mainframes, minicomputers, or LANs.

Most client/server LANs consist of just a few **clients,** but some handle hundreds. The clients (or "front ends") are the user nodes, or computers, that are connected to the server. At the client computers, the users work

---

network interface card (NIC) An integrated circuit board, or adapter, that is plugged into a slot of a computer on a local-area network and that functions to hook a network cable to the microcomputer; allows the members of the network to communicate with each other.

network operating system (NOS) The computer software that manages a local-area network and handles requests for data and equipment from the members of the LAN.

client/server LAN A local-area network in which the functions of the LAN are designated to specific machines; the clients are the requesting machines, and the servers are the supplying machines.

server A computer dedicated to specific supply functions on a LAN, such as communicating, managing the LAN, and delivering printer power and database information.

client A computer on a LAN that serves as a user node.

Window on Computing

The Future Is Here: Wireless Networks

One of the most widely discussed technologies today is that of wireless networks. This is especially true now that personal digital assistants, or PDAs (usually with pen-based computing), are becoming more reliable and popular. Because of their slow speed and high cost, wireless networks will not replace wired networks; however, they do nicely complement wired networks for added mobility.

Wireless networks do not require PDAs, but people who use wireless communication are often at locations away from their offices and will use equipment such as notebook computers, PDAs, or electronic pagers. In wireless networks, computers communicate via radio waves or infrared links. Wireless communication generally occurs through one-way radio paging, two-way packet radio, or circuit-switched cellular systems.

One-way radio paging transmits brief messages over radio frequencies to an electronic pager. (The pager is available as a PCMCIA device.) The pager is lightweight, and the messages travel rapidly and can be received at frequent intervals. You cannot send messages through the same route, however. Instead, you place a toll-free call to an operator, who transcribes and transmits your messages to the proper recipient. You can place your call through a computer modem.

Two-way packet radio sends messages in packets from a base station to the local recipient or through a regional or national station to a base station near the receiving radio modem. (Packets can be likened to mailing the latest copy of your subscription magazine a page at a time in separate envelopes, each with the necessary addressing. As the pages are received, they are reassembled into the proper order.) The process is slow, but works with any notebook computer. Cost is based on the amount of data you send. The method provides fairly good security, but only e-mail and not faxes can be sent.

Circuit-switched cellular wireless computer communication requires that your cellular telephone be connected to your cellular modem. (Circuit-switched communication is like telephone communication in which one line is linked to another for real-time, dedicated use.) The cell phone sends signals to the nearest cell (radio transmitter/receiver), and then the signals continue on their journey along analog telephone lines. Messages sent by this method are susceptible to interference and can be easily intercepted. In addition, cell modems work only with a few cell phones, and both the equipment and the fees for use are costly.

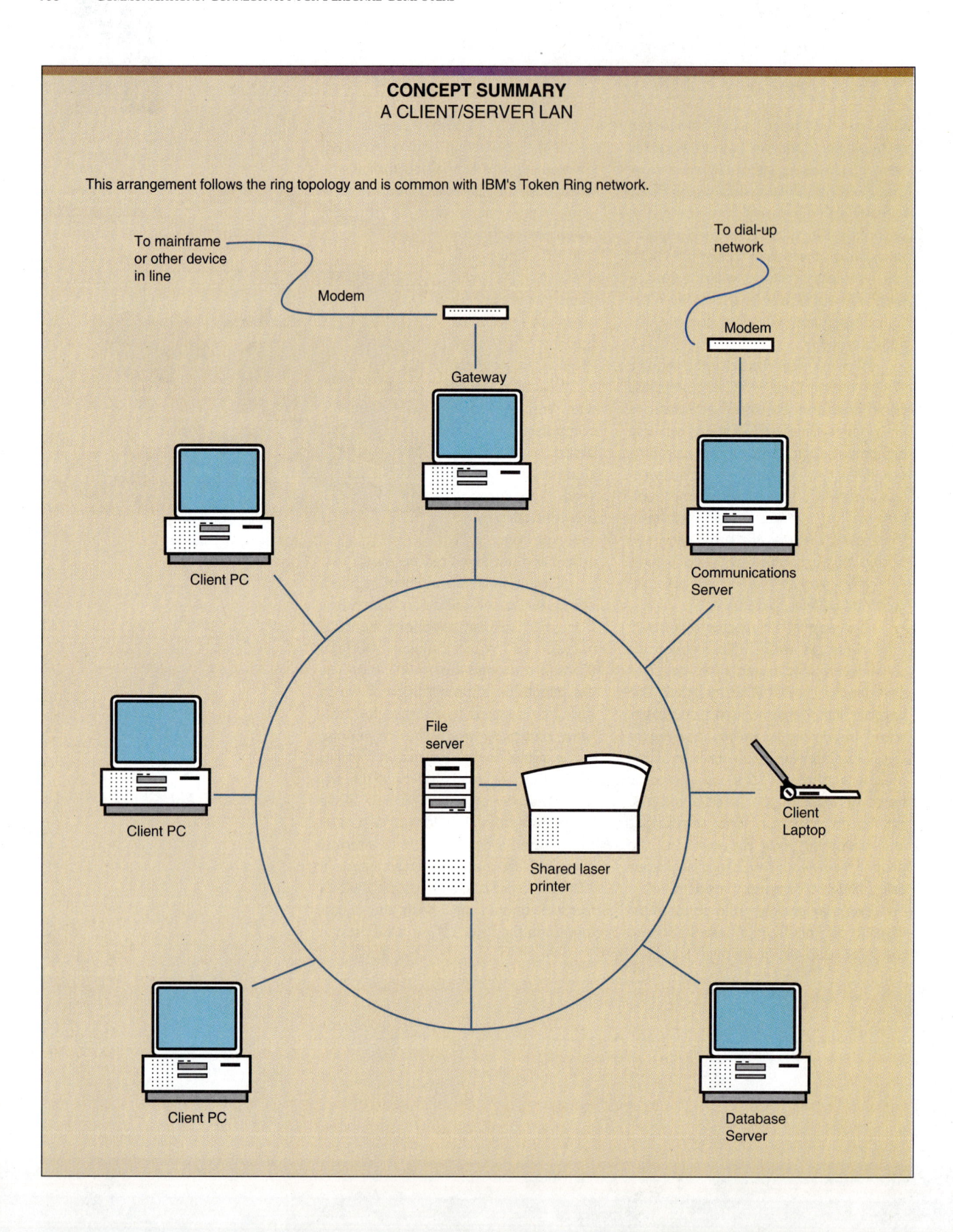

CONCEPT SUMMARY
A CLIENT/SERVER LAN

This arrangement follows the ring topology and is common with IBM's Token Ring network.

To mainframe or other device in line — Modem — Gateway

To dial-up network — Modem — Communications Server

Client PC

Client PC

File server

Shared laser printer

Client Laptop

Client PC

Database Server

on applications such as word processing, payroll, and order processing, and can access the information held in relational databases. Since the database server holds critical data, unauthorized access or system problems can result in disaster. That's why servers need mainframe-like programs that automatically back up data, keep out unauthorized users, and prevent system failures. One popular client/server LAN is NetWare.

Peer-to-peer LANs are gaining in popularity, although they have been common in the past for DOS-based setups, and some experts even predict that they will replace client/server LANs in the near future. This type of LAN can be used in conjunction with client/server LANs. In a peer-to-peer LAN, each computer acts as a server and a client. Thus, each has the same amount of power, and no one computer controls things. Files located on any computer can be made available to other nodes along the line. Each user is responsible for the communication that takes place from his node, and often retains responsibility for securing data on his computer.

Peer-to-peer LANs are inexpensive. They are often installed in small, remote branch offices and connected over dial-up links to a corporate LAN. They work best with a few computers, 10 or so. Peer-to-peer networks cannot, as yet, handle high-volume database work as well as can client/server networks: They often bog down with heavy use. Examples of peer-to-peer network kits include *Simply LANtastic* and *Desk to Desk*.

> **peer-to-peer LAN** A LAN in which each computer has equal power as both client and server.

▶Telecommunication Applications

With a computer and access to telecommunication facilities, the world is your oyster, so to speak. You can call other computer users, go shopping online, and do your banking from your computer. You might even be able to go for days without leaving home, because by commuting to the office through data communication, you can work in your own living room or home office. This section explains just some of the possibilities of using a computer and communication channels.

Electronic Transactions

Computers can handle a variety of electronic transactions, including banking, shopping, and trading stocks. For example, banks have devised a number of computer applications that make it possible to transfer funds via communication between computers. This approach is known as **electronic funds transfer (EFT)**. For example, the Social Security Administration offers an option under which the monthly checks can be deposited automatically into recipients' bank accounts. Similarly, many companies also offer a direct-deposit option for employee paychecks. Depositors can authorize banks to pay certain bills automatically, such as electric or telephone bills, by transferring funds from the accounts of customers to

> **electronic funds transfer (EFT)** An online method that permits the cashless transmission of money electronically between banks and among banks and customers without requiring paper documentation.

Figure 5–16   Fax Machines
Because they permit businesses to send or receive data in a matter of seconds, fax machines are quickly becoming a standard piece of office equipment.

those of the utilities. Some banks are expanding these services by making it possible for customers to enter and authorize EFT transactions from home through personal computers and sometimes through touch-tone telephones.

Just as some customers can access their bank accounts from their home computers, they can also make airline and hotel reservations and go shopping through a computer shopping network. These services may be available via a commercial online information service such as Compu-Serve, as described later in this chapter. Some high school and college courses are available over computer networks, too, so users can work on a degree program at home.

FACSIMILE

facsimile A method of transmitting graphical images over telecommunication lines in which the original document is scanned at the sending end and reproduced at the receiving end. Also called *fax, fax system,* or *facsimile system.*

In the past, **facsimile** (fax) services have played a major role in expanding the transmission of information over communication links. A fax machine is a desktop device that links into a dial-up telephone (see Figure 5–16). The unit can scan and transmit a document or reproduce a document received from another fax unit. To operate a fax, you put the original document in the fax scanner, enter the telephone number of the recipient, and press the start button. As the document is read by the scanner, it is sent electronically over the phone lines to the recipient's fax machine. Within seconds, a facsimile, or look-alike, of the original document emerges from the printer of the recipient's machine.

Variations of the fax machine are designed expressly for microcomputer use. For example, the fax-modem enables you to send documents from a computer to a fax machine rather than to another computer. You can also use a fax-modem to print documents through a fax machine, a handy option if you are on a business trip staying in a hotel. Hundreds of thousands of fax units are in use within business organizations. Both the devices and the transmission are relatively inexpensive.

Electronic Mail

In any business, communication is crucial. Countless messages are exchanged among company employees each day. More and more, businesses are turning to **electronic mail (e-mail)** to speed up the delivery of messages and reduce telephone, paper, and photocopying costs. E-mail involves the transmission of text at high speeds over telecommunication facilities. This can include messages, voice recordings, or images. The "mailbox" that holds your messages is simply a computer file.

> **electronic mail (e-mail)** The process of sending, receiving, storing, and forwarding messages in digital form over telecommunication facilities.

E-mail services can be public or private. Public e-mail services can be accessed through a modem by subscribers of CompuServe or other online information services. Private e-mail services are software packages that are used with a LAN.

Many companies are expanding their e-mail capabilities through the use of electronic calendaring. Under control of this application, managers and other personnel record their travel plans and appointments on computer. When a special event or meeting must be scheduled, the calendars of the affected persons are scanned for acceptable openings. The events can be scheduled for all parties, and e-mail can be used to notify all parties.

Both e-mail and electronic calendaring are often found in applications called *groupware*. Groupware is loosely a technology that enables people to work together on a project, sending messages and commenting on each other's work. Some groupware systems allow people to interact in real time—for example, when two individuals are editing a report, they can see each other's changes as they occur.

Voice Mail

Through **voice mail,** you can leave messages and get a variety of information using nothing but your telephone. You can tap into news services, get traffic reports, conduct surveys, and initiate or receive fax documents and e-mail. The messages are delivered by a computer-generated voice.

> **voice mail** A message system in which a spoken message is converted to digital form and stored in the recipient's voice mailbox until the recipient dials in and retrieves the message in audio form.

A voice-mail system utilizes a computer and the telephone system to record, store, and play back spoken messages. The computer changes the words into digital signals and stores them in the appropriate "mailboxes." When the recipient checks the service for messages, the system delivers the message in audio form. All users of a particular voice-mail service are assigned a unique mailbox number, which allows them to send or receive the voice-mail messages.

Unlike standard telephone answering machines, voice-mail systems allow senders to leave lengthy messages. Receivers can also scan the voice-mail messages more quickly. In addition, a user can send the same message to many different people with just one call.

Figure 5–17 Telecommuting
Commute time can be saved and rents can be reduced by setting up small, satellite offices at locations in residential areas. Work can be coordinated between satellite and central offices via data-communication networks.

telecommuting A plan by which an employee works away from the office and communicate with the office through a computer terminal and telecommunication facilities.

TELECOMMUTING

Perhaps one of the most interesting aspects of telecommunications to contemporary office workers is **telecommuting**—commuting to the office by computer rather than in person. The system offers advantages in cities where office rent is high and mass transit systems or parking facilities are inadequate, and for businesses that do not require frequent face-to-face meetings among employees. Telecommuting provides great flexibility for working parents and employees with disabilities (see Figure 5–17).

Sales representatives and journalists, who are often away from their offices, have successfully employed a kind of telecommuting by taking portable computers and tiny printers with them on assignments. After entering memos, letters, stories, or reports, the employee sends information through a modem and over telephone lines to the office. Once the information has been received at the office, phone messages, edited copy, or other information can be sent back to the original writer. Some companies have even set up satellite offices in which a traveling employee spends one or two days per week, telecommuting the other three days. Telecommuting is suitable for jobs that need to be done with few distractions, such as computer programming, writing, and planning.

Telecommuting does have disadvantages, however. Some employees may not have the discipline to work away from the office. They may fear that "out of sight is out of mind," particularly when promotions and raises are at stake. In addition, managers may worry about the amount of control they have over employees who work away from the office. Some of the wariness about telecommuting can be dispelled by implementing a hybrid plan in which the employee works at home two or three days and comes to the office the remaining days.

Figure 5–18 Videoconference
Electronic meetings are streamlining work and cutting costs for many companies. Instead of traveling to out-of-town meetings, participants can use teleconferencing links such as these.

Increases in telecommuting will affect both cities and business. Businesses may relocate branch offices and even headquarters to states with smaller tax burdens and idyllic rural areas, leaving behind the cities that have depended on them for taxes and rental income. Businesses that provide e-mail, package delivery, and videoconferencing equipment will grow.

TELECONFERENCING

In most large organizations, managers and executives spend a sizable portion of their time in meetings. When these meetings involve travel, expenses for air fare and lodging mount quickly. A number of "conferencing" alternatives are being used to cut down on travel and meeting costs.

A **teleconference** brings participants together in a meeting through the use of telephone voice channels. The simplest form is a **conference call** placed to all participants. A conference call is a public utility service that connects three or more parties for joint conversation. (Many business switchboards also have conference-call capabilities.)

The idea of a conference call can be enlarged through audio conferencing methods. Under this approach, the participants gather in local conference rooms equipped to amplify telephone conversations through speakers. Conferences of this type can be enhanced with slow-scan video methods. Slow-scan video transmits single images from video cameras over telephone lines. This technology has been likened to an "electronic slide show." An audio conference comes closer than a conference call to the environment created when all participants are in a single room.

For a **videoconference,** participants gather in specially equipped facilities (see Figure 5–18). One arrangement calls for one-way video and

teleconference A meeting of parties in multiple locations conducted over telecommunications channels; may involve both electronic and image-producing facilities.

conference call A telephone call that can serve three or more parties for joint conversation.

videoconference A conference that occurs over telecommunication links and that can provide either one-way video and two-way audio or full audio and video through the use of cameras and wall screens.

two-way audio communication. Presentations from one location are covered with video equipment and transmitted to the participating locations. Participants at the receiving sites can respond or ask questions, but only through audio communication. The videoconference is handy in teaching and training situations as well as in presentations that require visual aids. A more sophisticated arrangement involves full, two-way video coverage from all locations.

For a **computer conference,** each participant works at a microcomputer linked to a large computer through a modem and telephone lines. Usually a minicomputer or a mainframe is involved because of the substantial file-handling requirements of this activity. One person typically becomes the facilitator, to keep the group focused on the agenda. Otherwise, computer conferencing is a many-to-many arrangement in which everyone is able to "chat" with everyone else. Messages can be broadcast to everyone or targeted to one or several individuals. Computer conferencing often occurs on information utilities and electronic bulletin boards, described in the next two subsections.

computer conference A conference that occurs by typing messages into computers linked through communication channels.

INFORMATION UTILITIES

One of the benefits of buying a microcomputer is having the opportunity to access a variety of computer networks through which you obtain resources and information and communicate with other computers users. The two most common types of information services are information utilities and electronic bulletin boards.

Information utilities, also called *online information services,* are something like electronic libraries. An information-services organization gathers information required by an identified group of users. It is stored on a computer that can be accessed by modem-equipped computers.

information utility A for-profit business or organization that supplies information and consumer services through telecommunication facilities that are accessible directly by computer.

Users call the information utility, review the information files available, retrieve anything they need, and then sign off. The utility's computer keeps track of all transactions. In most cases, the utilities are profit-making companies that charge membership and usage fees. These include CompuServe, Delphi, GEnie, eWorld, America Online, Prodigy, BRS/After Dark, and Dow Jones News/Retrieval (see Appendix A). In other instances, nonprofit organizations make computer-maintained information available without charge to scientists, students, or others. For example, a number of services make emergency medical information available to health care professionals.

To "log on" to a commercial online service, you must have a computer, a telephone, a modem, and communications software. A special password system ensures that only paid or authorized subscribers gain access. Once connected, you can enjoy a variety of services, such as electronic shopping, travel services, popular newspapers, interactive computer games, and data for research purposes (see Figure 5–19). Electronic mail, bulletin boards, forums for special interests, movie reviews, sports news, and weather are also commonly offered by the commercial services.

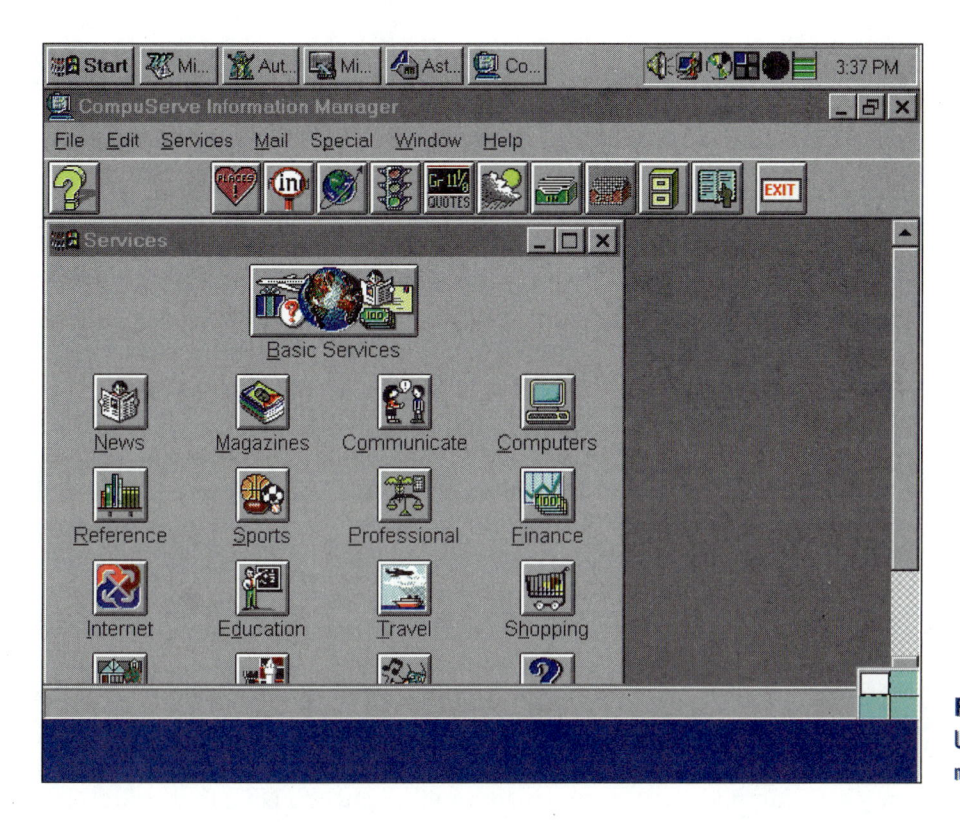

Figure 5-19 CompuServe Menu
Users of CompuServe make selections from menus that offer a wide range of topics.

ELECTRONIC BULLETIN BOARDS

An electronic bulletin board, or **bulletin board system (BBS)**, is a user-run service for posting messages and trading information. Although most are privately run, some are available through information utilities. A privately run bulletin board can be accessed at little or no cost, unless you are calling long distance. Almost anyone who has a telephone, a computer, a modem, and communication software can start a BBS. The manager of a BBS is called a *sysop,* short for "system operator." Some bulletin boards are tied together in large networks, such as FIDONET, the largest such network. Through FIDONET, you can talk with people all over the United States and abroad.

Bulletin boards are often set up for people with special computing interests, such as Apple Macintosh users, *Microsoft Word* users, or *Lotus 1-2-3* users. Many software and hardware companies such as WordPerfect Corp. and Toshiba America offer in-house bulletin boards for customer support. Other bulletin boards are shared by people with a special hobby, such as sports, flying, history, or stamp collecting. Bulletin boards designed for members of associations or professional groups, such as writers, lawyers, nurses, and pilots, usually require special information or codes such as passwords for access. Others are open to almost anybody.

Some bulletin boards make **public-domain software** and **shareware** programs available to anyone who calls. The user simply asks the system

bulletin board system (BBS) A user-run service that permits individuals who have microcomputers to trade messages with others who have similar interests.

public-domain software Programs unprotected by copyright law and available for free, unrestricted public use.

shareware Copyrighted programs that are given away free but with the expectation that satisfied users will voluntarily pay the copyright holder for use of the program.

to transmit the program to his or her computer. Public-domain software is free, but designers of shareware ask that people pay anywhere from $10 to $50 for programs they like and use.

THE INTERNET

The Internet, or "the Net," is more of a concept than a service or commercial venture. Basically, it is a network consisting of tens of thousands of networks, online services, and single-user microcomputers linking users with information. There are roughly 25 million Internet users. (See Appendix B for a guide to the Internet.)

The original concept was devised in 1969 at the U.S. Department of Defense as an experimental project for sharing research between the military and university sources. The project, called ARPANET (Advanced Research Projects Agency Network), was aimed at sustaining communication in case of nuclear war. It consisted of a plan called *dynamic rerouting,* which would automatically reroute traffic to another link if one network link was disrupted by enemy attack. Beginning in 1980, traffic increased on ARPANET because universities were linking up thousands of workstations rather than single, large computers. Shortly thereafter, the National Science Foundation built its own, much faster network, NSFNET, which connected a number of regional networks. By 1990, so much traffic had moved to the more efficient NSFNET that ARPANET shut down.

NSFNET continues to operate the large network, which remains noncommercial and self-governing. By using the standard Internet protocol, other networks, such as CompuServe and Delphi, provide a *gateway* (or connection in which protocol conversion takes place) into the Internet. Although most Internet usage is devoted to communication and research, it makes available a wide array of resources for business and home users, including real-time chatting, weather information, satellite pictures, and games.

The most frequently used functions on the Internet are e-mail, research and file transfer, remote log-in to libraries and other resources, and public discussion forums. A popular activity is the Usenet (or the "net" news), which works a lot like bulletin board services in which users post messages and collect responses. A number of tools help you find what you want on the Internet. Two common ones are Gopher (a menu-based system that works much like a card catalog when you are searching for information) and Telnet (which allows users to log onto a remote computer system).

The Internet has become so popular that when we think of a gateway to the Net, we can in fact imagine a gateway to a vast information superhighway. Students from the United States can talk with students from Sweden. Activists can spread the word about human rights and censorship violations. Hobbyists can exchange information about their collections and crafts. Right now, the Internet seems to be the ultimate goal in

PROFILE

BILL GATES AND MICROSOFT

Many entrepreneurs in the computer industry got started at a very young age. One of the youngest was William H. Gates, who started his first computer-related company while still in high school. He and a school friend, Paul Allen, had been spending a lot of time in the school's computer room. In 1971, Gates wrote a program that analyzed traffic patterns. He and Allen started a company called Traf-O-Data to market the program.

Gates' father wanted him to go to law school, so Gates went off to Harvard. He was thinking about how hard it is to pick a career when Allen showed him a *Popular Electronics* magazine with the Altair 8800 computer on the cover. Within a couple of months, the two flew off to Albuquerque with the first version of BASIC written for the Altair. The program worked, and Gates and Allen formed a company, Micro-soft, to sell it. (The hyphen was later dropped.) Soon, Gates dropped out of Harvard to spend his entire time with the business. In 1978, he and Allen moved the company to Bellevue, Wash.

In 1980, IBM approached Gates to write an operating system for the personal computer it was designing. Gates responded with MS-DOS (Microsoft Disk Operating System), the product that sent Microsoft's profits soaring. Gates retained the rights to MS-DOS, and thus it has been installed on every PC-compatible sold in the world. Shortly after the Apple Macintosh came out with its graphical user interface, Bill Gates saw how easy it was to operate and began working on a GUI for IBM-compatibles. The result was *Windows,* a program that is also sold with IBM-compatibles.

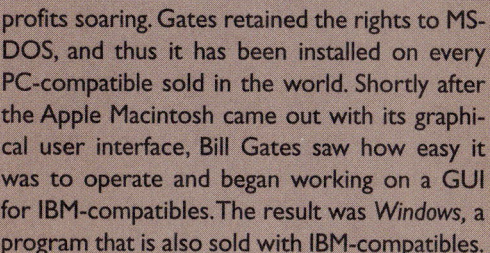

At age 31, Gates undertook a public stock offering for Microsoft. The issue netted him some $350 million in cash. By 1992, he was the richest man in the country, and in 1993 the second richest. Today, Microsoft supplies 80 percent of all the personal-computer-operating-system software in the world and 50 percent of the application software, including *Microsoft Word* for word processing and the spreadsheet *Excel.* Gates is currently active in studying the trends in communications: He would like to have his company supply the standard-operating-system software for accessing the so-called information superhighway.

personal computer communications. We can only imagine what the future will bring.

▶ SUMMARY POINTS

- The same kinds of equipment and communication channels can transmit signals over distances ranging from across the room to around the world. To send and receive messages computers use telecommunication networks. The combination of computer and telecommunication capabilities is known as data communication. A pathway used to carry data or voice transmissions from one location to another is called a communication channel.
- Common communication channels include telegraph lines, twisted pairs, coaxial cable, fiber-optic cable, microwave links, and communication satellites. They are classified by grade, or bandwidth, and by mode of transmission (simplex, half-duplex, and full-duplex).

- Telegraph wires are the least flexible, slowest channel, allowing only simplex or half-duplex transmission. Twisted-pair wires are found in telephone lines. They allow full-duplex transmission.
- Coaxial cable is a high-grade line with a very wide bandwidth used for mainframe cables and television transmissions. Fiber-optic cables consist of hair-fine filaments of glass. They send data in digital signals of pulsed light. They provide high speed, quality, and security to transmissions.
- Microwaves are high-frequency radio signals for high-quality, long-distance communication. A combination of communication satellites and high towers accommodates the curvature of the earth so that the signals are not lost into space. The satellites orbit the earth at the same speed and in the same direction as the earth rotates. Thus, they are fixed targets for microwave signals.
- A modem is the microcomputer's "gateway" to data communications. It is an acronym for "modulator/demodulator," and it performs the basic function of interfacing a computer with a communication channel and converting signals from digital to analog and back again.
- Internal modems reside on printed circuit boards that plug into a microcomputer's expansion bus. External modems are units outside the computer that plug into both the computer and the telephone jack.
- A modem requires communication software to work. The software turns the computer into an input/output device for another computer. The software also offers functions such as auto-dial, auto-answer, and time delay. The modem enables you to set parameters (or characteristics) so that the communication protocol (or rules) used by your computer match those of the computer being accessed and the communication channel being used.
- A computer network is a set of nodes and links. The nodes of a system can be almost any kind of computer or peripheral. The links are the communication channels that connect the nodes. Networks may be local or remote. They allow for distributed processing, in which computer capabilities are placed at the locations where transactions take place and information is used.
- Three common network configurations are star, ring, and bus. A star network links nodes to a central hub. A ring network links computers along a single, circular path, and transmits messages to all nodes in the network until the destination is reached. A bus network is supported by a single, direct, high-speed link to the processor of a central computer.
- Wide-area networks (WANs) link computers and local-area networks over distances through standard telephone lines or microwave transmissions. A local-area network (LAN) is a group of computers and peripherals located within a short range, such as

a single office or building. It enables users to share data, e-mail, and expensive peripherals such as laser printers.
- A network interface card (NIC) is inserted into each member of a LAN to create the physical link between machines. The network operating system (NOS) controls member access to the network's shared resources and manages other LAN functions.
- The two types of LAN are client/server and peer-to-peer. In the client/server LAN, one or more computers act as servers, or devices that govern all or some of the LAN operation, and hold the database. The clients are the units from which users work. In a peer-to-peer network, each computer has the capability of acting as both client and server.
- Common data communication provides organizations and individuals with the capabilities for electronic funds transfer, electronic shopping, school, and travel arrangements. It also includes applications such as electronic mail, facsimile, voice mail, telecommuting, and teleconferencing.
- Two common network information services are online information services and bulletin board systems. Online information services are often for-profit organizations and provide a number of information, researching, and reservation services. Bulletin board systems are user-run services for posting messages and trading information.

▶ Review Questions

1. What is data communication, and how do computers and telecommunications facilitate it?
2. What is a communication channel? How do telephone lines function as channels for data communication? What other channels are available?
3. Explain the terms *modulate* and *demodulate* as applied to personal computing.
4. Describe the functions of modems.
5. Discuss the meaning of *network* as it applies to computer systems.
6. What is a local-area network? Distinguish between a LAN and a wide-area network.
7. Describe the equipment commonly used in a LAN.
8. How does a client/server LAN differ from a peer-to-peer network?
9. Describe at least three ways that telecommunication can be used in corporations.
10. What is an online information service? How do information services differ from bulletin board systems?

▶Activities and Research

1. Before reading Chapter 7 on contemporary concerns, list some guidelines for human behavior over the various types of computer networks.
2. Configure a local-area network for a small branch office with three employees who need to create documents with high-quality output and who need to access the main database at the company's headquarters. Try to specify actual products.
3. Find a number of ways that you—in your own community—could link to the Internet.

CHAPTER 6

POWER APPLICATIONS: TOOLS FOR SPECIAL JOBS

OUTLINE

Learning Objectives
Introduction
Desktop Publishing
    Desktop Publishing Explained
    Typefaces and Fonts
    Style Sheets and Templates
    Functions of DTP Packages
    Print Reproduction
    Concept Summary: Desktop Publishing
Integrated Software and Suites
    Types of Integrated Packages
    Characteristics of Integrated Software
    Concept Summary: Integrated Software
Multimedia Presentations
    Understanding Multimedia

Window on Computing: The Future Is Here: Moving Pictures and Computers
Multimedia Standards
Software for Multimedia Management
The Sky's the Limit
    CAD/CAM
    Expert Systems
    Virtual Reality
    Profile: Edward R. McCracken, 3-D CEO
    Window on Computing: The Future Is Here: This Vehicle Can't Pass Driver's Ed
Summary Points
Review Questions
Activities and Research

LEARNING OBJECTIVES

After reading this chapter, you should be able to:

- Define *desktop publishing*, and explain the role of page composition software.
- Describe features of page composition software.
- Describe integrated software, and list four common types of integration.
- Define *multimedia*, and list its computer requirements.
- Explain how a multimedia application is prepared, and describe uses for multimedia.
- Describe CAD/CAM and detail its uses.
- Tell how expert systems make use of "machine intelligence."
- Define *virtual reality*, and describe some of its practical uses.

INTRODUCTION

The first microcomputers had memory capacities of 16,000 to 32,000 bytes (16K to 32K). Capacities increased slowly to 64K, then to 128K, 256K, 512K, and 640K. Today's memories run into the megabyte range, with the bare minimum now at 4MB. Similarly, hard disks used to cost more than the microcomputers to which they were attached, and they provided relatively little storage space. But prices tumbled in a short time, as storage capacities climbed to 300MB and higher, into the gigabyte range.

As a result of this great increase in capacity, today's microcomputers can handle a variety of jobs once far beyond their capabilities. Desktop publishing, for example, requires large amounts of memory and storage for preparing publications with different typesetting formats, graphics elements, and illustrations. And multimedia applications continue to strain the capacities of many computers. Multimedia combines a variety of multisensory outputs such as text, graphics, sound, and motion, into an integrated whole. Desktop publishing and multimedia, both popular applications, are discussed in this chapter. The chapter also covers integrated software, computer-aided design, expert systems, and virtual reality.

Figure 6-1 Computer Page Makeup
Page makeup capabilities enable daily newspapers to shorten production cycles and to save money on printing composition. Makeup editors work at special terminals such as this one at the Long Beach (California) Press Telegram, a Knight-Ridder newspaper.

Figure 6-2 Desktop Publishing System
Desktop publishing requires graphics and printing capabilities for reproducing a large variety of print styles and graphic images.

▶ DESKTOP PUBLISHING

Desktop publishing (DTP) evolved from electronic publishing methods that have been in use since the late 1970s. At that time, publishers began printing their newspapers and magazines with the aid of large computers (see Figure 6-1). These computers could set type, prepare illustrations, and assemble the type and illustrations into finished pages. Today, similar capabilities are available for microcomputers.

The microcomputer systems employed for desktop publishing require capabilities much like those used to produce newspapers and magazines. First, they need powerful graphics capabilities, usually in the form of a graphics circuit board inserted into a slot inside the computer, and a high-resolution graphics monitor that displays the graphics with precision. Second, they need large amounts of memory and storage to manipulate and hold the very large files that hold the data and graphics. Third, they must be able to generate reproduction-quality outputs, possible only after laser printers and high-quality ink-jet printers became widely available (see Figure 6-2). Besides the hardware, desktop publishing requires another tool—a software application that allows users to prepare page layouts without the aid of skilled graphic artists.

DESKTOP PUBLISHING EXPLAINED

Desktop publishing (DTP) enables you or any organization to produce documents suitable for publication using microcomputer equipment. You no longer need be dependent on a graphic artist and a typesetter to prepare material for printing. After you write the text, you can typeset it and design the final pages, incorporating a number of graphics features commonly seen in newsletters, magazines, books, or brochures. Most packages provide samples so you can study the most effective ways to lay out a page.

The heart of desktop publishing is **page composition software**. This software allows files imported from both word processing software and graphics programs to be placed and manipulated on the same page (see Figure 6-3). Using this software, you design each page of the document, deciding what type styles to use, the number of columns on the page, the amount of space between columns, and the placement of headers and footers. Menus in the page composition software help you select the page design options.

After the design has been created, the page composition software inserts a text file into the page design that was laid out previously. It usually retains formats that you set up with your word processing program, such as tab settings and basic type styles (boldface, italics, and so on). At this point, you can add lines of varying widths and lengths, boxes, symbols, and pictures. You can request the program to hyphenate words at the

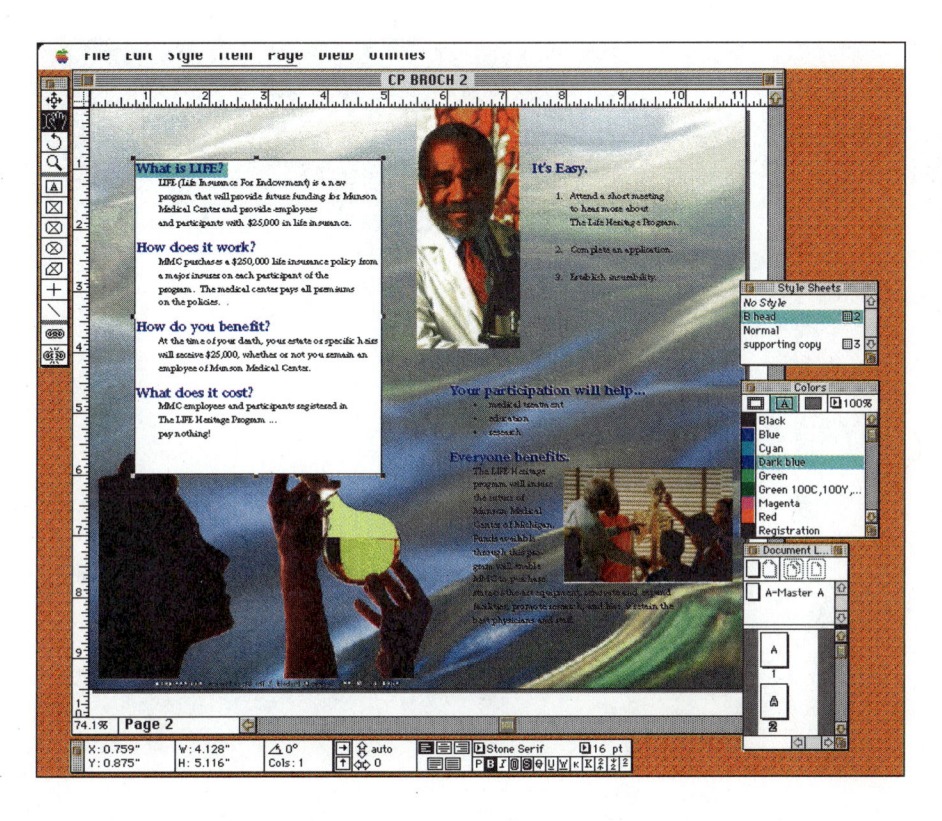

Figure 6–3 Page Composition Software
The style (type size and style, line spacing, indentation, etc.) for the body text or main text in the document, the introduction, and subheads can be selected from menus.

ends of some lines so that characters in the line do not stretch out across the line too much. You can include various elements—or parts making up the page—such as headlines, logos, scanned photographs, captions, and cartoons. You can rotate words for special effects. Figures, tables, and other ancillaries may be numbered automatically—and the numbering changed automatically if you delete one. The software can also generate tables of contents and indexes by gathering together the words and phrases you have marked with special codes. The resulting document can be of typeset or near-typeset quality when output from a laser printer.

Desktop publishing is commonly utilized for creating company newsletters, advertising brochures, proposals, and reports. DTP can result in a significant savings to organizations that would normally send documents out to be typeset. The equipment can be expensive, however, especially a high-quality, color printer capable of reproducing graphics. In addition, many computer users purchase large-screen monitors in order to get the full benefit of the WYSIWYG display so necessary to DTP (see Figure 6–4).

Among the popular page composition packages are *QuarkXPress* from Quark, Inc.; Adobe System's *Pagemaker*, and *Ventura* from Ventura Software. In addition, many popular word processing programs also have page composition capabilities—enough to be called **document-preparation packages**. The following sections discuss common features of both types of software.

desktop publishing (DTP) An activity that uses microcomputer hardware and software tools to set type, lay out complete pages that include text, type, and illustrations, and produce output of near-letter quality, letter quality, or near-typeset quality.

page composition software Software for manipulating text and graphics elements in order to design and produce pages for publication.

document-preparation package Word processing software that includes many elements of page composition software.

Figure 6–4 WYSIWYG in DTP
WYSIWYG features let you see on the computer screen how a document will look when printed on paper.

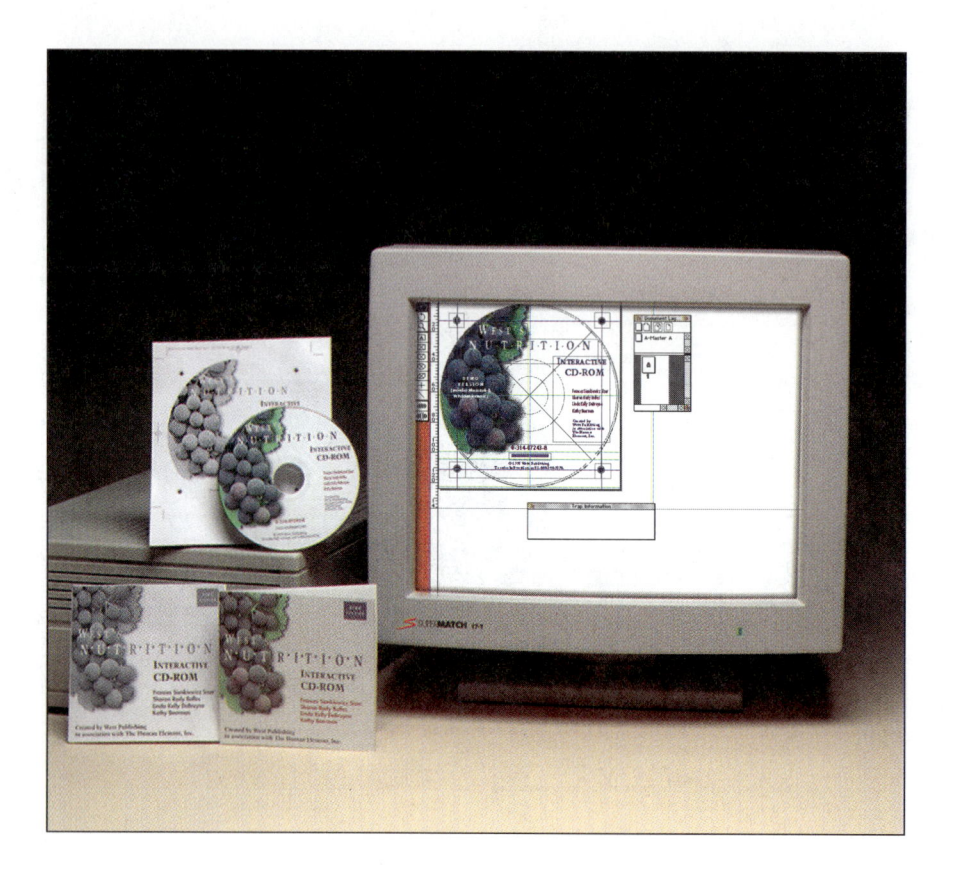

Typefaces and Fonts

Some people use the terms *typeface* and *font*, incorrectly, to mean the same thing. A **typeface** is simply the design for a set of characters. That is, it describes how the type is drawn. Examples include Times, Helvetica, Gothic, and Courier. There are two general categories of typeface: serif and sans serif. Serifs are small decorative marks that look like tiny flags and feet used to embellish characters. Characters without these embellishments are described as *sans serif* (meaning "without serif"). Times (this is Times) is a serif typeface, and Helvetica (this is Helvetica) is a sans serif typeface.

Typefaces also are described in terms of pitch—that is, the number of characters that can fit in an inch. Some typefaces are of fixed pitch, meaning each character gets exactly the same width on a line, and other typefaces are proportional, meaning that the amount of space a character takes up on a line varies with the shape of the characters. `Courier is a fixed-pitch typeface,` and Times is a proportional typeface. `In Courier, a W takes up the same amount of space as a period (.),` but in Times, the period (.) takes up much less space than a W.

A **font** is a specific set of characters that have a number of attributes, including the typeface, but also size, style, and weight. Within the Helvetica typeface, for example, there are many sizes to choose from.

typeface A collection of letters, numbers, and symbols that share a particular appearance; the shape, or design, of print (for example, Times, Helvetica, Courier).

font A set of alphanumeric characters in a particular typeface, size, and style.

Figure 6–5 Scalable Fonts
Fonts in Swfte Int'l's Typecase I can be scaled to any size needed.

Type size is measured in points (a point is about 1/72 of an inch), so

9-point Helvetica looks smaller than 14-point Helvetica.

The style of the print can be changed from plain to *italic,* and the weight can change from plain to **boldface**. Some systems include light and extrabold weights, too.

Thus, Helvetica is the name of a typeface, but 14-point Helvetica bold is the name of a font.

Computers and related devices use two methods to represent fonts. One method is by *bit-mapping*, in which each character is presented as an arrangement of dots. Every font requires a different set of bit-mapped images, and thus they take up a lot of memory. The other method of representing fonts—rapidly becoming popular—is by *vector graphics*, in which the shape or outline of a character is defined geometrically. The advantage of this method is that each font, can be stored in only one default size but displayed in any size.

Fonts described geometrically are called **scalable fonts**, or *outline fonts* (see Figure 6–5). The programs that create the different type sizes by algorithm are called *type managers* or *font managers*. Scalable fonts show off the qualities of high-resolution printers, but do not look very good on low-resolution screens. Therefore, almost all systems use bit-mapped fonts for screen display. In a scalable font, each character is generated as it is needed, and the computations require a powerful microprocessor for

scalable font A font that is defined in shape but not in size and that can be sized to suit the document.

acceptable speed. The font files are smaller, however, and thus need less memory. The PostScript and TrueType systems are scalable fonts.

Some printers include resident fonts, which are internal fonts that come with the printer. Other fonts can be added by inserting ROM cartridges or font cards (printed circuit boards) into the printer. Fonts downloaded into the printer's memory from software are called *soft fonts*. Font managers such as Adobe System's *Type Manager* and Bitstream's *FaceLift* enable you to see on the screen the fonts that are resident in the printer, and also let you use soft fonts included in the package or available in other packages.

page description language A language for defining the layout and contents of a page.

Page composition packages contain a **page description language** that is used to control printers. A page description language details the page layout and the contents of each page to the printer. The printer must support the page description language used by the application. Two common page description languages are Adobe PostScript, associated with Apple Macintosh printers, and Hewlett-Packard PCL (printer control language), found on IBM-compatible machines.

Style Sheets and Templates

style sheet A file that contains formatting instructions but not text; may contain such information as margin sizes, column sizes, tabs, spacing, and fonts.

A **style sheet** allows you to produce a document that is consistent from one page to the next. If you select boldface type for the Chapter 1 title of a document, then all remaining chapter titles should also appear in boldface type. With a style sheet, you can specify the size and style of type and the line spacing, and indicate where headings, subheadings, and footnotes should be placed. Style sheets can be saved for use in future documents. For example, if a company routinely employs a special format for its newsletter, the specifications can be saved in the style sheet file and applied to all editions produced throughout the year.

template A predesigned format for a standard document.

Most page composition packages supply standard style sheets for documents such as business reports, product brochures, and newsletters. These style sheets are sometimes called **templates**. Using these templates, you can simply replace the "dummy" text and images with your own material (see Figure 6–6). Studying the templates, reading books about document preparation, and taking classes can help you learn the principles of effective graphic design.

Functions of DTP Packages

Desktop publishing packages offer a number of features not usually associated with word processing programs. For example, you can scale art to fit a given space, crop pictures, wrap text around pictures in several ways, employ kerning and leading capabilities, and more. The WYSIWYG features of page composition software are more complete and more accessible than those of many word processors. In addition, you usually use a mouse to manipulate the elements of the page—headlines, graphs, text, and pictures.

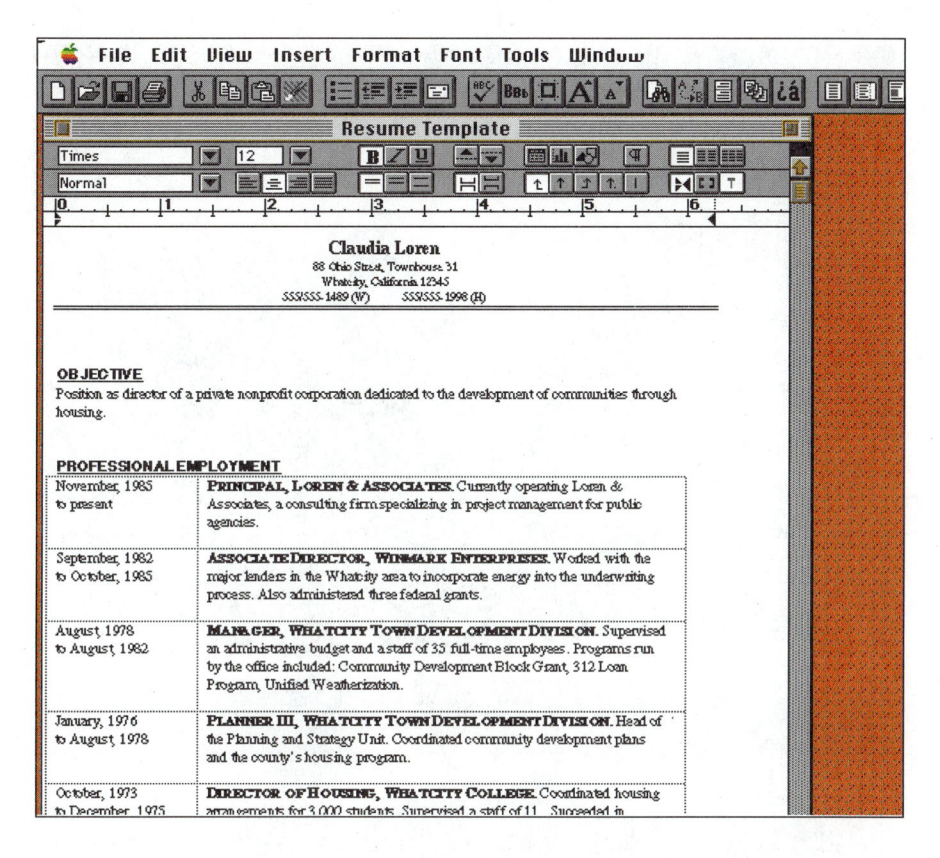

Figure 6–6 Résumé Template
A template for a résumé enables you to simply plug in your own skills and experience, following the style already set up in a style sheet file.

SCALING AND CROPPING

Rarely is a graphic image the perfect size for a page layout. It may be too small or too large or the wrong shape. **Scaling** allows you to increase or decrease the size of an image by percentage without distorting its proportions. Scaling may not solve every problem, however: You may need to change the shape of an image or cut out parts that detract from the primary subject of the picture. The term that describes this activity is **cropping** (see Figure 6–7). Page composition software enables you to do both tasks by computer and retrieve the original image if the results are unsatisfactory.

scaling The process of changing the size of an image yet retaining its proportions.

cropping The process of trimming an image for a better fit on a page or for eliminating unwanted portions.

TEXT WRAP

When you insert text into a page layout, it flows into place at the designated point on each page. This continues until the entire text file is in position, even if it needs to continue from one page to another or fit itself around the spaces marked for pictures. **Text wrap** refers to how text aligns itself around a picture. A *rectangular* wrap means that words are forced into a narrower space to the left or to the right of a rectangular picture that is inserted in a column of text. An *arbitrary* wrap follows the shape of the image (see Figure 6–8). An *irregular* wrap places the text around the image in whatever manner you choose.

text wrap An automatic page composition function in which text flows around an image.

Figure 6–7 Scaling and Cropping
Scaling simply adjusts the size of an image, but cropping cuts out portions of it. A cropped photo may be enlarged to show the significant portions better.
(a) Original photo
(b) Scaling has reduced the size proportionately.
(c) Cropping has removed unwanted parts of the photo and changed its shape.

kerning Adjusting the spaces between characters to create wider or tighter spacing for a more attractive and readable look.

leading The amount of vertical space between lines of type.

KERNING AND LEADING

The appearance of text can be changed through kerning and leading. **Kerning** is sometimes called microspacing. When text is kerned, the distance between each letter is adjusted to make the word look better proportioned. Kerning commonly occurs when text is justified on both the left and right margins. Depending on the software, kerning can be manual or automatic.

Leading refers to the distance between lines (see Figure 6–9). In most word processing programs, leading is preset to single, double, or triple spaces. Some DTP programs offer adjustable leading.

INTERNAL GRAPHICS

Most page composition packages also contain drawing and graphics tools for creating pictures, boxing text, or embellishing titles or headlines. The thickness and texture of lines can be varied, for example. In addition, you

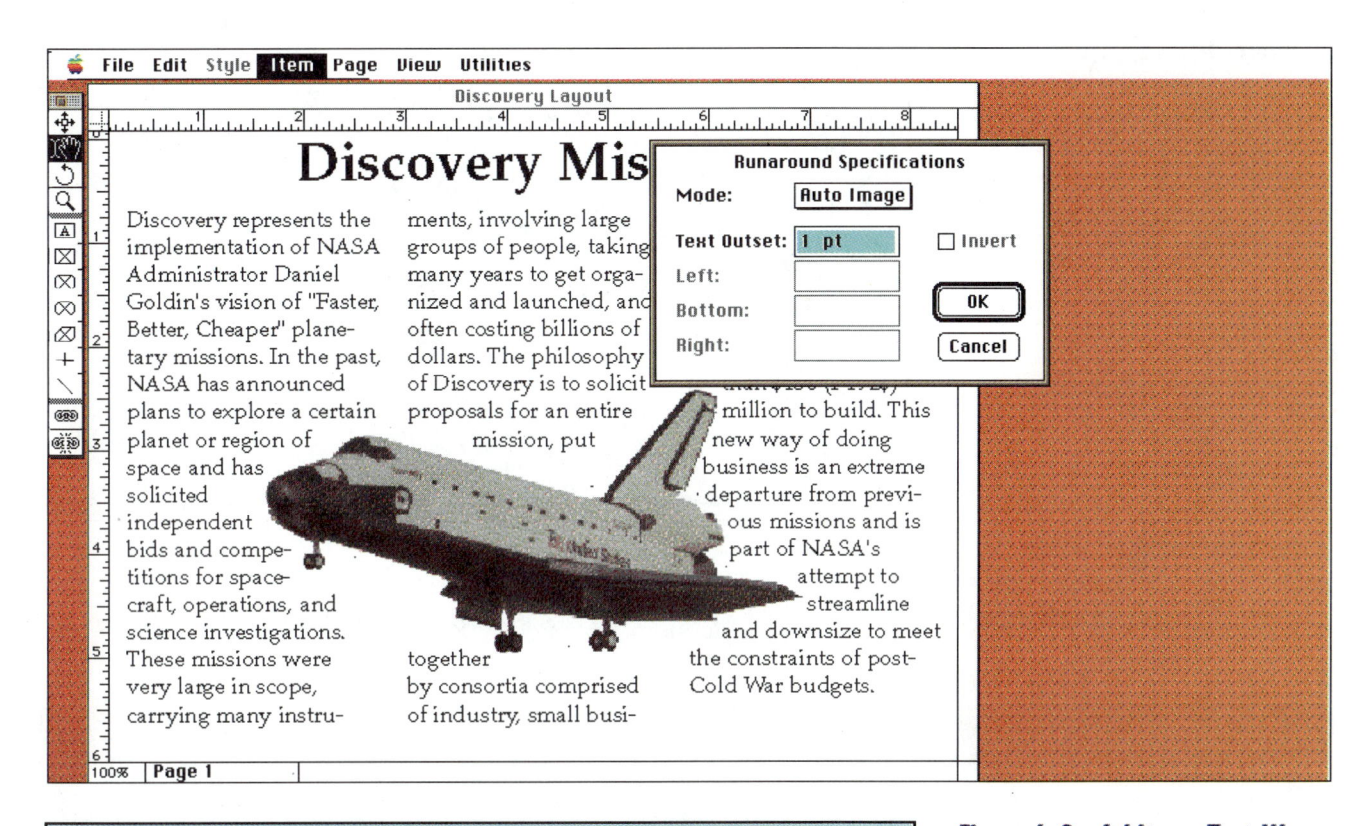

The appearance of text can be changed by kerning and leading. Kerning is sometimes called micro spacing. When text is kerned, the distance between each letter is adjusted to make the word look better proportioned. Depending upon the software, kerning can be manual or automatic.

Leading refers to the distance between lines. In most word-processing programs, leading is preset to single, double, and triple spaces. Some desktop programs offer adjustable leading.

Positive amount of kerning **Kerning**	Kerning set at default **Kerning**	Negative amount of kerning **Kerning**
Double space or adjustable leading set at 14 Leading refers to the distance between lines	Single space or adjustable leading set at default Leading refers to the distance between lines	Triple space or adjustable leading set at 18 Leading refers to the distance between lines

Figure 6–8 Arbitrary Text Wrap
Arbitrary text wrap follows the outline of an image, eliminating the extra space required for boxing the image.

Figure 6–9 Kerning and Leading
Kerning adjusts the space between letters, and leading adjusts the space between lines.

may find a variety of small drawings called *clip art* that you can insert into the documents you build, without worrying about copyrights. Illustrations include art for specific subjects, such as sports, Christmas, 19th century costume, locomotives, animals, food, and tools. Very small

Figure 6–10 Clip Art
Clip art and dingbats can be purchased in special software packages, although many page composition packages also include them.

a **This is draft-quality printing**

b This is near-letter quality printing

c ```
This is letter-quality
type from a typewriter
```

d  This is near-typeset printing

**Figure 6–11  Printer Qualities**
Each of the various qualities of printer outputs (draft quality, near-letter quality, letter quality, and near-typeset quality) has its own purposes.

pieces of clip art (such as stars, check marks, fat pencils, and pen points) that you can use beside headings and subheadings are called *dingbats*. Clip art can be purchased in separate software packages that often include dingbats, too (see Figure 6–10).

## Print Reproduction

The quality of output in a desktop publishing system depends primarily on the printer used. Printers are often characterized by the quality of their output (see Figure 6–11):

- *Draft quality*. Draft-quality (DQ) printers–usually dot-matrix printers–produce a hard copy that is legible and good enough for the first draft or version of a document.
- *Near-letter quality*. Near-letter-quality (NLQ) printers generate an output that approximates the appearance of a typewritten document. Many dot-matrix printers have an NLQ mode that produces print quality suitable for school assignments, letters, and informal communications.
```

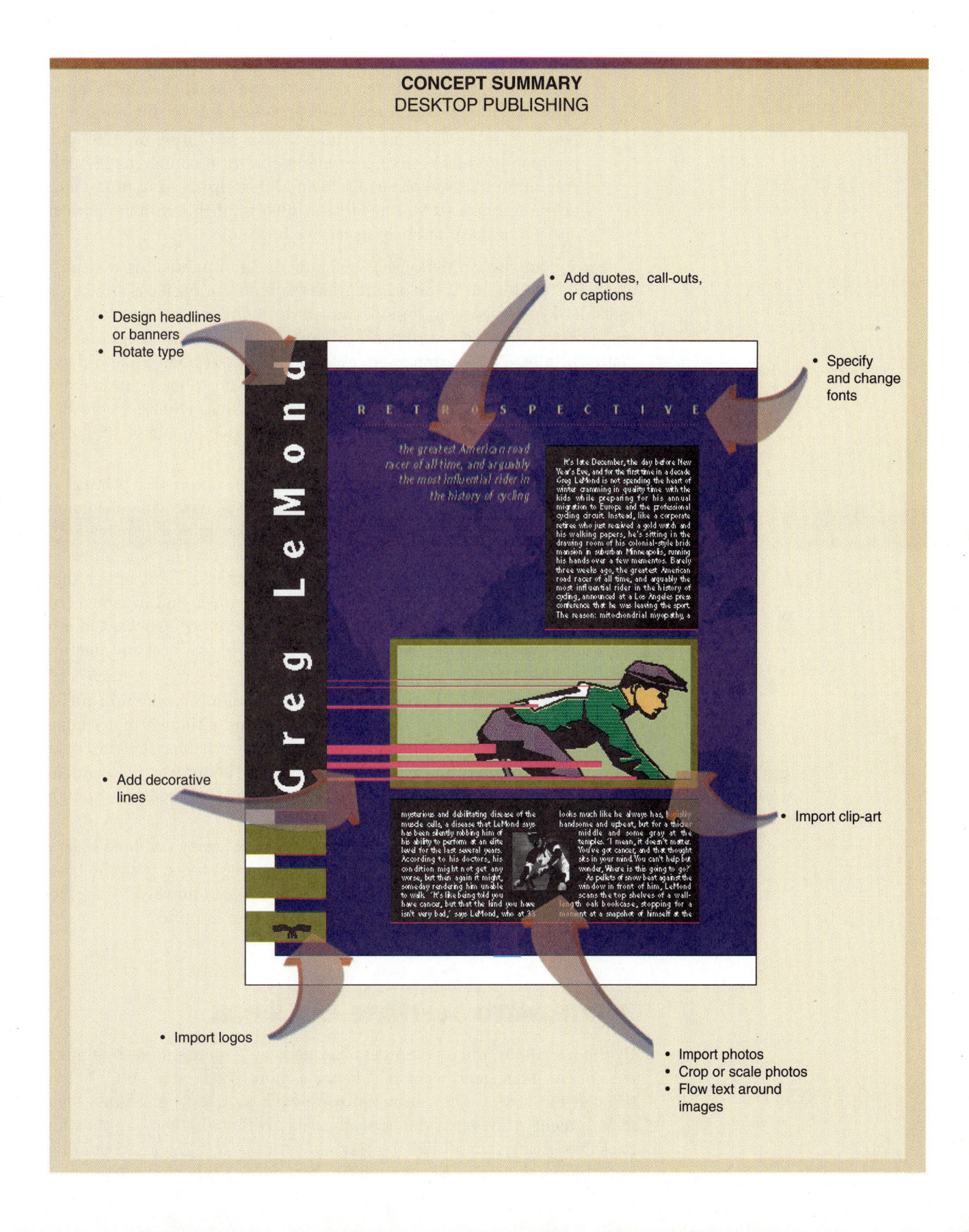

CONCEPT SUMMARY
DESKTOP PUBLISHING

- Design headlines or banners
- Rotate type

- Add quotes, call-outs, or captions

- Specify and change fonts

- Add decorative lines

- Import clip-art

- Import logos

- Import photos
- Crop or scale photos
- Flow text around images

- *Letter quality.* Letter quality (LQ) is suitable for formal communication such as business letters and dissertations. High-quality ink-jet printers and low-end laser printers produce this quality of output.
- *Near-typeset.* Even a laser printer with a resolution of 1,200 dots per inch produces only near-typeset quality. It cannot match high-resolution imagesetters at 1,270 and 2,540 dpi used in professional print shops. (If you need print quality of this caliber, you can enlist a desktop publishing service bureau.)

Most common printers used for home desktop publishing output in black and white, but color printing has been an option for a number of years. The cheapest way to add color is to highlight text and enhance graphics via a multicolor ribbon (red, blue, yellow, and black) on a dot-matrix printer. These printers are able to move the ribbon up and down to select a particular color. The three colors on the ribbon can be combined for printing orange, purple, and green. Thus, with software that supports color printing, you can typically print documents in six colors plus black.

Resolution and color saturation is poor with dot-matrix printers in comparison with the higher-quality output of ink-jet, laser, and even more sophisticated nonimpact printers. Yet even these more expensive solutions may not produce the results you expect. The primary challenges in improving color printing are being able to create brilliant rather than muddy colors, to eliminate blurs and unwanted lines, and to match colors between the monitor and the printer. Manufacturers also want to produce high-quality printers that print quickly and at low cost and that use any kind and weight of paper, including tissue.

The systems currently available for the best color reproduction are too costly for most homes and small businesses. And although many home users can afford some type of black-and-white laser printer, low-end color laser printers are still quite expensive, too. For home use, color ink-jet printers offer the best value, good color rendition, and medium- to high-resolution output.

Desktop publishing is an integration of sorts: It may combine several applications, such as word processing and graphics tools, with the basic DTP package and a good printer. The next section, however, describes packages that are designed solely with integration in mind.

▶Integrated Software and Suites

By the late 1980s, microcomputers had become a standard piece of office equipment. Managers' work had become more productive and efficient through the use of application software such as word processors, data-management programs, and spreadsheets. Although these application packages greatly simplified the tasks of writing, filing, and accounting, one drawback remained: Switching from one application to another required several tedious steps. A company's accountant, for example, might want to use spreadsheet information in a graphics program to illustrate some profit-and-loss figures. With individual software for each application, the accountant would have to save the current file, shut down the current program, load a new program, and open a new file each time applications were switched.

In addition, it was frustrating to find that commands for doing the same type of operation were different from one application to another or that data could not be exchanged readily among the applications. For example, saving a file in one program might involve the F10 function key, while the same operation in another program used the *Control* and *S* keys. Or the data from a data-management program might need to be retyped into an incompatible word processing file.

The frustration of this incompatibility led to a new approach called **integrated software**. Integrated software attempts to maximize both command and data compatibility. Basically, integrated software is two or more usually separate, or **stand-alone**, application programs that work together in the same software package, allowing easy movement of data between the applications.

integrated software Sets of programs that work together, making it possible to mix inputs, processing, and outputs among programs that are ordinarily different and incompatible.

stand-alone Descriptive of a program or system that is self-contained, as opposed to a system or program that is dependent on another.

TYPES OF INTEGRATED PACKAGES

Among the several types of software integration are the popular all-in-one packages and the background utility approach. The all-in-one package is perhaps the type that comes most frequently to mind when the term *integrated software* is heard. The all-in-one package combines several common applications, such as word processing, graphics, spreadsheet analysis, and data management to make a single program (see Figure 6–12). Examples include *Microsoft Office* and *Claris Works*.

An all-in-one package is usually anchored in just one application, such as word processing or spreadsheet analysis, and any other applications support this main application. Thus, the capabilities of the leading application are generally greater than those of the supporting applications. In addition, the functions represented by all components may not be as complete as the functions offered in single-application programs. For example, a word processing module may not be capable of creating multiple columns or generating an index, or an all-in-one package based on a word processor may be weak in the spreadsheet or graphics area. Therefore, a user with highly sophisticated word processing or graphics requirements may find some integrated packages extremely limiting.

The background utility approach basically permits you to load a set of utility software called *desk accessories* into RAM, yet run an application program on top of the utilities (see Figure 6–13). Calculators, calendars, automatic telephone dialers, and notepads are all types of desk accessories. While you are using a word processing program, for example, you can consult the notes you recorded on the notepad desk accessory.

Figure 6-12 Integrated Software
Integrated software makes it possible for a user to access files created under a number of different applications.

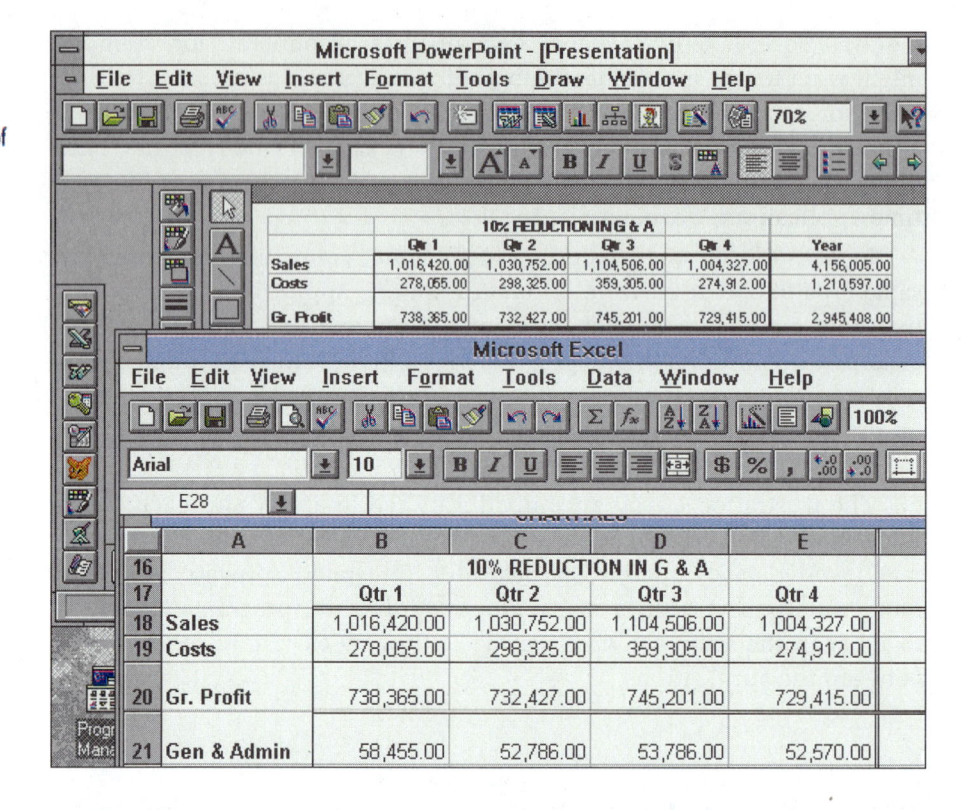

Figure 6-13 Background Utility Approach
Dashboard Accessories program is run with Microsoft Word.

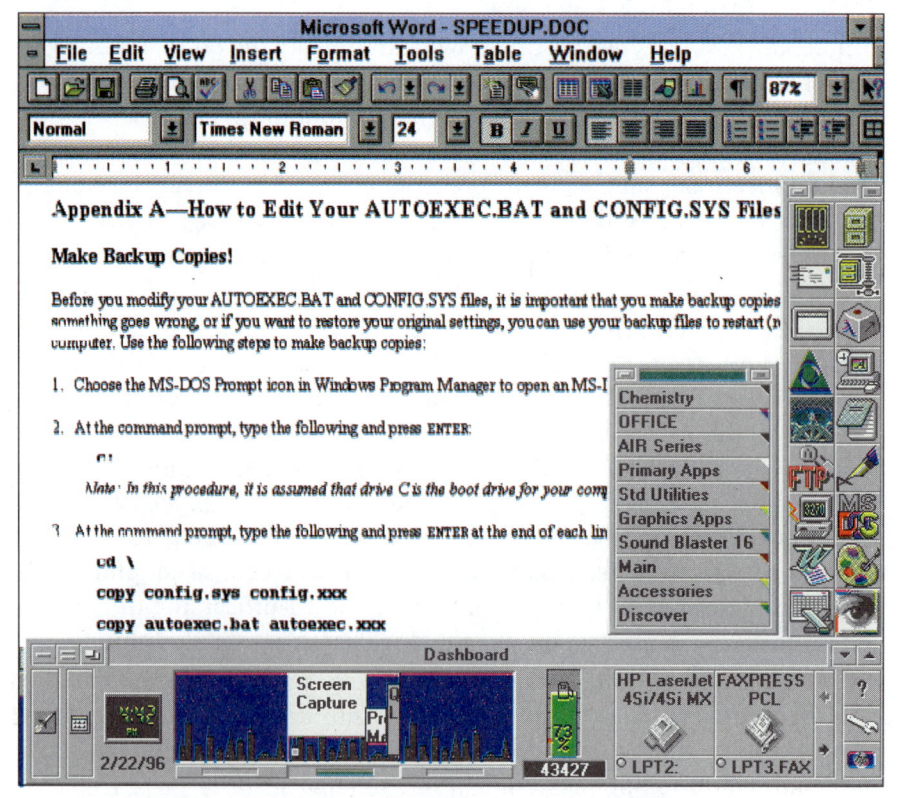

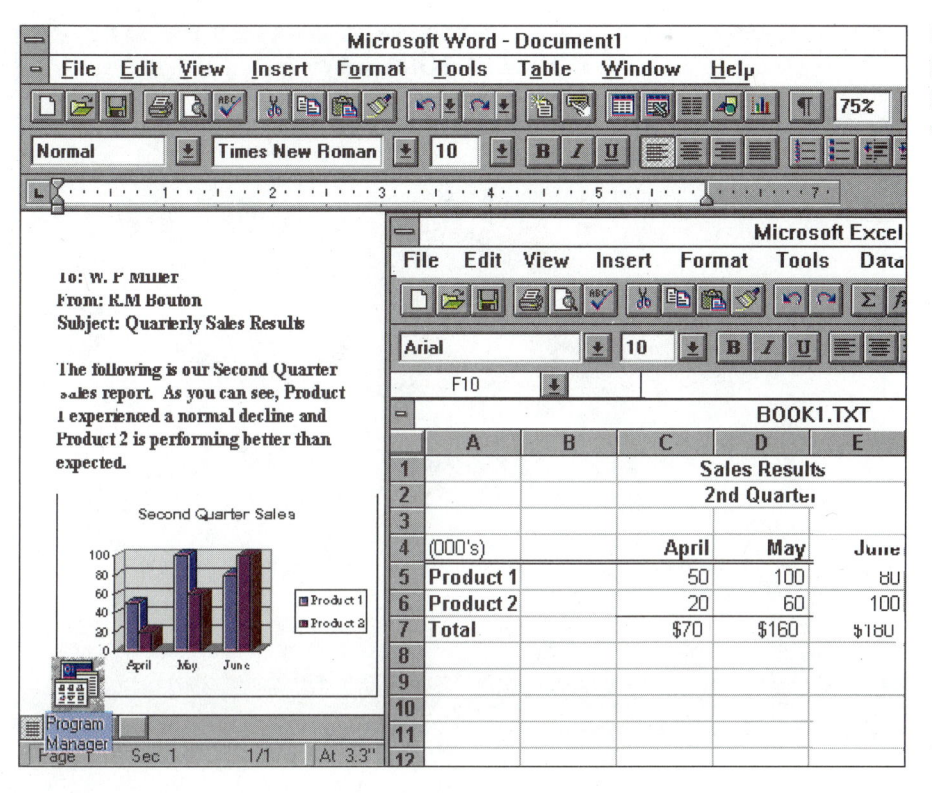

Figure 6–14 Data Movement
Microsoft Office seamlessly integrates a graphic from a spreadsheet (Microsoft Excel) into a word processing document (Microsoft Word).

CHARACTERISTICS OF INTEGRATED SOFTWARE

In a conventional sense, *integration* suggests the blending of two or more parts into a unified whole. Integrated software makes several applications available to a user at one time and makes it easy to move data between applications. Integrated software conforms to these three characteristics:

- The software consists of programs that have traditionally been separate, or "stand-alone."
- The software enables easy movement of data among the separate applications.
- A common group of commands is used for all of the applications in a package.

The individual programs in integrated software are referred to as **modules,** and they appear in their own, separate windows. Common modules are data management, word processing, spreadsheet analysis, graphics, and communication. The data formats in the modules match so that data can be moved easily from one application to another. For example, the mailing list in the data manager can be used by the word processor, or the financial data in a spreadsheet can be turned into a graph by a graphics program, and that graph can be embedded in a report produced on the word processor (see Figure 6–14). This is usually accomplished through a technique known as *the clipboard,* which is basically a fancy

module A part of a whole; a program segment or subsystem, such as that found in an integrated software package.

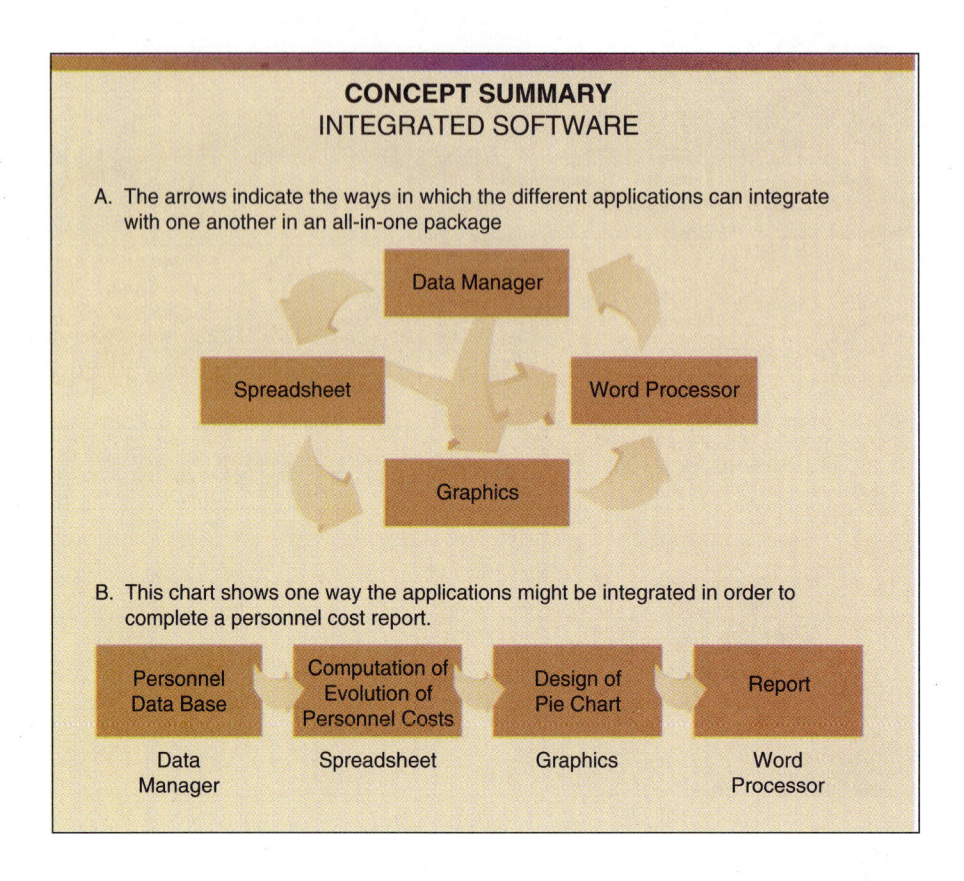

> **CONCEPT SUMMARY**
> **INTEGRATED SOFTWARE**
>
> A. The arrows indicate the ways in which the different applications can integrate with one another in an all-in-one package
>
> ```
>              Data Manager
>
>  Spreadsheet              Word Processor
>
>               Graphics
> ```
>
> B. This chart shows one way the applications might be integrated in order to complete a personnel cost report.
>
> | Personnel Data Base | Computation of Evolution of Personnel Costs | Design of Pie Chart | Report |
> |---|---|---|---|
> | Data Manager | Spreadsheet | Graphics | Word Processor |

name for an allocation of space in memory. Most integrated software, however, does impose some limits on the direction of movement among modules. For example, data can be moved from the graphics module into the word processing module but not from the word processing module into the spreadsheet module.

As you use each module, only one set of commands are needed in order to run the remaining modules in the package. For example, the command that blocks off a section of text in a word processing module is the same as the command that blocks off a section of rows and columns in a spreadsheet. The differences in the programs require certain specialized commands for each, however. For instance, the spreadsheet module may have its own, specialized command for formatting cells into dollar amounts, something the word processor doesn't need to do.

Actually, compatibility among programs is becoming less of a problem than it has been in the past. Software developers are making more of an effort to develop programs capable of working with other stand-alone programs on the market. It is now very easy, for example, to import a *Lotus 1-2-3* worksheet into a *WordPerfect* document. Integration still remains popular, however, because integrated software is "bundled" with most new computers. A new notebook computer may come with the DOS 6.0 operating system, *Microsoft Windows*, and the integrated package *Microsoft Works* already installed on its hard disk drive. This trend enables new computer users to experience five major types of application software without buying five expensive packages. More sophisticated programs can be added as needed.

One outgrowth of this trend is the development of suites. A **suite** is really another name for integrated software. If there is a difference between integrated software and a suite, it is that integrated software is originally planned and developed as a unit, whereas a suite may be a compilation of different, already-existing programs by their manufacturers. Two popular office suites, *Microsoft Office* and *Lotus Office,* for example, include existing programs such as *Word* and *PowerPoint* for *Microsoft Office*, and *Lotus 1-2-3*, *Ami Pro*, and *Lotus Notes* for *Lotus Office*. Suites have been popular because, although expensive, they offer full-fledged versions of productivity software and some utility and planning software at a much reduced rate than all of the packages would cost individually.

suite A set of closely related or interacting programs; integrated sets of programs.

▶Multimedia Presentations

Once upon a time, **multimedia** meant adding sound to motion pictures. For a long time, however, multimedia has played an important role in education theory, drawing on the knowledge that different children learn through different senses. Thus, learning techniques that appealed to sight, sound, touch, and smell were apt to help a greater number of children than one-dimensional techniques that depended on sight alone. The media included film, sound recordings, photographs, drawings, charts, games, and real objects.

multimedia Computer applications that combine text, audio, and graphic components with interactive capabilities; also called hypermedia.

Today, the term *multimedia* is applied to computer systems. It retains the same basic meaning, providing, through computer systems, multiple methods by which people learn and retain information. It is an integration of capabilities rather than of applications. A multimedia computer system not only presents text on a screen, but also provides sound, animation, graphics, photo-quality images, and interactive computer functions with which these elements can be manipulated (see Figure 16–15). The following sections explain how multimedia is used in computer systems.

Understanding Multimedia

Some experts have hinted that multimedia is a solution looking for a problem, implying that most computer applications do not require the extravagance of sound and animation. Yet there are many multimedia packages (called **titles**) available today, primarily in the fields of education, entertainment, and reference, and even the skeptics are beginning to see the potential of multimedia for business.

title The name of a multimedia package.

Multimedia as a multisensory method of improving and speeding understanding of material began to catch on in the mid-1980s when cor-

Figure 6–15 Verbum Interactive
This quarterly CD-ROM magazine features columns in the format at right.

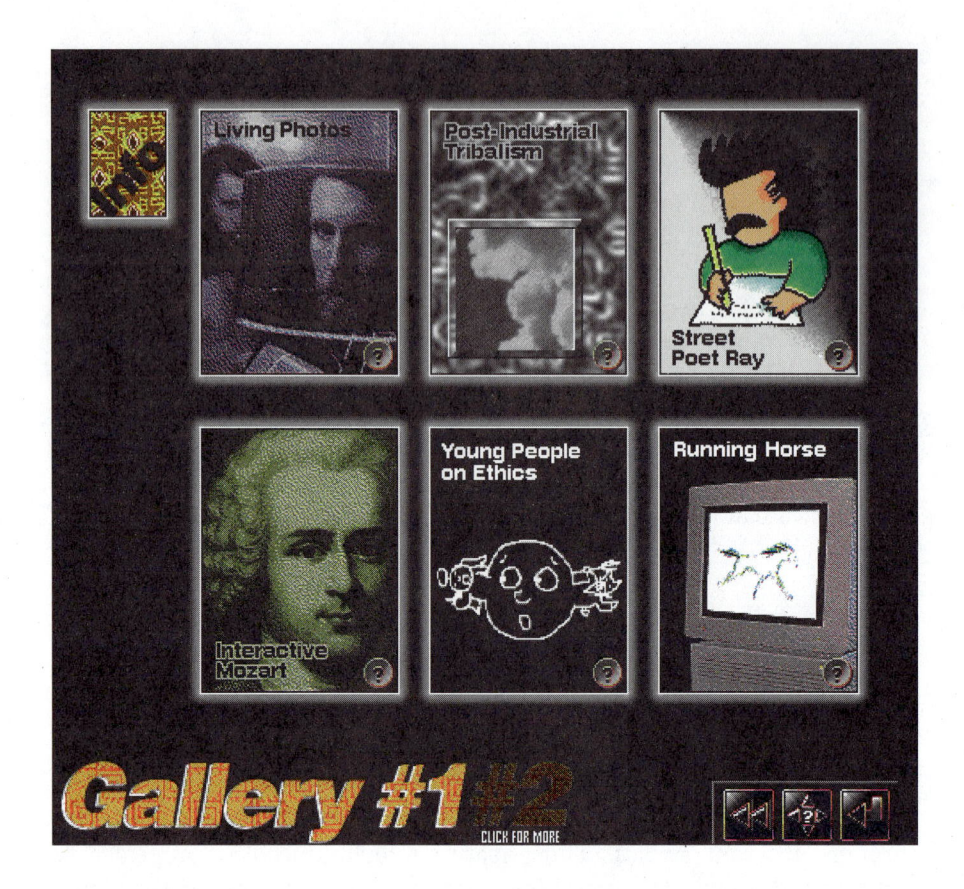

porations used interactive laser videodisks for in-house training. Today's multimedia applications commonly are accessed from CD-ROM disks or through networks (see Figure 6–16). For example, a CD-ROM encyclopedia could include voices, pictures, and music to expand on the text and drawings. The user could ask questions of the encyclopedia to clarify difficult material. A tutorial teaching physiology could include interactive components and animated sequences designed to help medical students understand the design of the human body almost as if they were manipulating a real body. A science museum might offer multimedia productions that show moving models of structures, such as atoms or DNA, that are too small to be placed on exhibit otherwise. Students can make up their own multimedia applications, too. For example, while reading about the Civil War, a student might choose songs and images to combine with oral and written text to present to a class. High school students can learn biology, chemistry, and history through multimedia.

Multimedia plays a double role in business and industry: for training and for promotional activities. Multimedia systems that simulate driving conditions are used to train truck drivers. Some workers learn their complex skills in aircraft maintenance or computer repair through multimedia systems. And businesses use multimedia to make sales presentations that retain a prospective client's attention or to prepare multimedia "catalogs" for customers.

Window on Computing

The Future Is Here: Moving Pictures and Computers

What next? Now you can watch movies on your computer screen. You can play these "movies" with *QuickTime*, the Apple Computer multimedia graphics standard that is found on Macintosh computers as an extension to System 7. *QuickTime* is a low-cost, low-resolution type of video that provides dynamic, time-based data—that is, animation, video clips, and sound—rather than static data, such as words and graphics. With *QuickTime*, you can play, pause, fast-forward, rewind, and advance frame by frame dynamic data, called movies.

The most recent version of *QuickTime*, version 2.0, includes MPEG-1 playback. This feature, when used with an MPEG decompression board, enables the Macintosh to display TV-quality video. MPEG, pronounced *EM-peg*, stands for "Motion Picture Experts Group". MPEG was developed in order to provide full-screen, full-motion video. (*QuickTime's* early releases supported pictures that were only about 2 inches square.) It is basically an International Standards Organization standard for compressing and decompressing images. (The algorithm for compression/decompression is called a *codec*.)

In reality, MPEG is not true-screen video. Rather, it is an expanded quarter-screen video, in which every other pixel has been dropped. As decompression occurs, the picture expands and interpolates to fill the missing spaces. You may see "jaggies," or lines with the stair-step or checkerboard look, because some information is lost.

Other video standards—*QuickTime, Video for Windows, Indeo,* and *Cinepak*—are simpler, but they vary in quality. The first appearance of MPEG was on the *ReelMagic* decompression board released in late 1993 from Sigma Designs, and it has been drawing rave reviews. It is supported in the *Compton's Interactive Encyclopedia, Dragon's Lair,* and *Return to Zork* CD-ROMs.

In order to edit, cut, copy, paste, record, and play dynamic data, you'll need a video editing program. You also will benefit from a video capture card, which accepts analog signals and translates them into digital data; a sound digitizer; and even a camcorder from which you can download your movies into your computer system.

What happens when you insert a movie into document such as a report written on a word processing program is unlike conventional graphics. You paste a still image from the movie into the document. This *poster*, as it is called, retains a pointer to the appropriate movie. By this method, the document's file doesn't become huge, but instead gains only about 10K or so. The document can then access and play the movie as long as the movie file is readily available on a hard disk drive.

A movie could enliven a biology lesson or enhance a training session for new employees. Some word processors, such as *WordPerfect for Macintosh* and *Microsoft Word for the Macintosh*, already support video. Look for other packages to support it in the future.

Figure 6-16 Multimedia Equipment
The most common multimedia components are featured in this photo.

MULTIMEDIA STANDARDS

Because of the amount of material involved in multimedia application, a multimedia system makes extended use of optical-disk technology, which enables the storage of large databases of graphic images, text, and sound. Yet there are really no standards for multimedia at this time, and compatibility among the variety of CD-ROM disks and drives is not guaranteed.

A group of manufacturers including Tandy Corp., NEC Technologies, CompuAdd Computer Corp., and Philips Consumer Electronics Corp. have attempted to bring standards to the multimedia marketplace, forming a marketing organization called Multimedia PC Marketing Council. The standard they have developed is called the Multimedia PC (MPC), and the vendors use an MPC logo on products and upgrade kits designed for multimedia applications. Experts warn, however, that standards set today will become outdated rapidly. Here is some equipment needed for multimedia:

- A computer with a high-end microprocessor
- A double-speed or greater CD-ROM drive
- One 3.5-inch high-density floppy disk drive
- A GUI interface
- High-end graphics hardware and monitor
- 16-Bit sound
- A microphone
- Headphones or speakers
- A mouse

Figure 6–17 QuickTime Movie
Persuasion 2.1 treats QuickTime movies just as it does any other graphics. This movie features a discussion of the benefits of good nutrition.

Also expect high requirements for RAM and hard-disk capacity.

Although you can compile the components for multimedia from various manufacturers, some computer systems are advertised specifically for multimedia. Upgrade kits from a number of companies can bring an IBM PC or compatible system up to the multimedia standards with CD-ROM drives, sound boards, and software. If you own a Macintosh, you may only need to purchase a CD-ROM drive. Apple was actually a multimedia pioneer, with music and video capabilities having been built into its Macintosh computers long ago. New Macintosh computers are outfitted with an operating system extension called *QuickTime* that lets you manipulate moving images called "movies" (see Figure 6–17). *QuickTime* is also available for IBM PCs and compatibles, but the more common standard for PCs is *INVIDEO* (with .AVI files).

Space and speed for full-motion video are the major problems with multimedia. A television shows 30 distinct images per second. Multimedia video images that would approach this speed create storage problems for computers, although there are a number of ways to solve the problem. One way is to reduce the number of colors in the images. In *QuickTime*, the size of the images is reduced to a small area on the screen. In addition, the files are compressed, or packed, so they take up less space on a disk. As technology improves, the storage problem will be reduced, and the animation will be reproduced more clearly and smoothly.

Figure 6–18 A HyperCard Application
By clicking on various parts of this image, you can progress to other topics or more detail on the current topic.

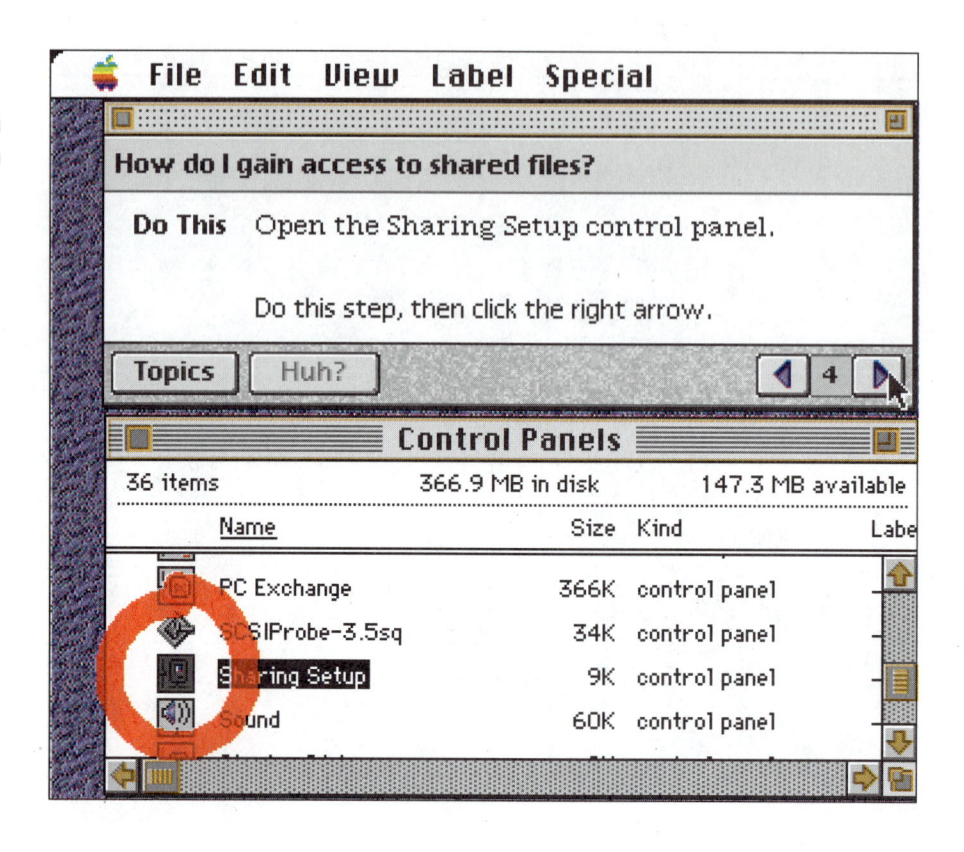

hypertext A method of accessing linked items in a database.

dynamic link A connection between two items that provides interactive access from one to the other.

authoring tool A program that enables you to write hypertext or multimedia applications, usually by combining elements such as text, music, and pictures; also called authoring system.

SOFTWARE FOR MULTIMEDIA MANAGEMENT

Multimedia actually provides a doorway through which you can explore information in any direction, but you need special software to do so. It all began in 1965, when the term **hypertext** was coined to identify a document-retrieval network (or special database system) that included **dynamic links** among the documents. (Dynamic links provide almost instantaneous connections to other pieces of information.) At that time, the information consisted primarily of text, buy today's hypertext-based systems include text, graphics, sound, and video, and are sometimes referred to as *hypermedia* rather than multimedia. In such a system, you can select a word or phrase to reveal related graphics, sounds, and even animation about the particular topic you are studying. An example of today's hypermedia systems is *HyperCard,* by Apple Computer, Inc. (see Figure 6–18).

Although you can buy prepared multimedia packages for *HyperCard*, *HyperCard* provides one **authoring tool**, or authoring system, with which you can create your own multimedia production. Authoring tools enable you to create scripts for automating a presentation by linking together the objects, such as written text, a graph, a drawing, music, and sound effects. They usually support many hardware devices and file formats so that you can build productions with multiple elements. They also provide a framework by which someone else can interact with your production.

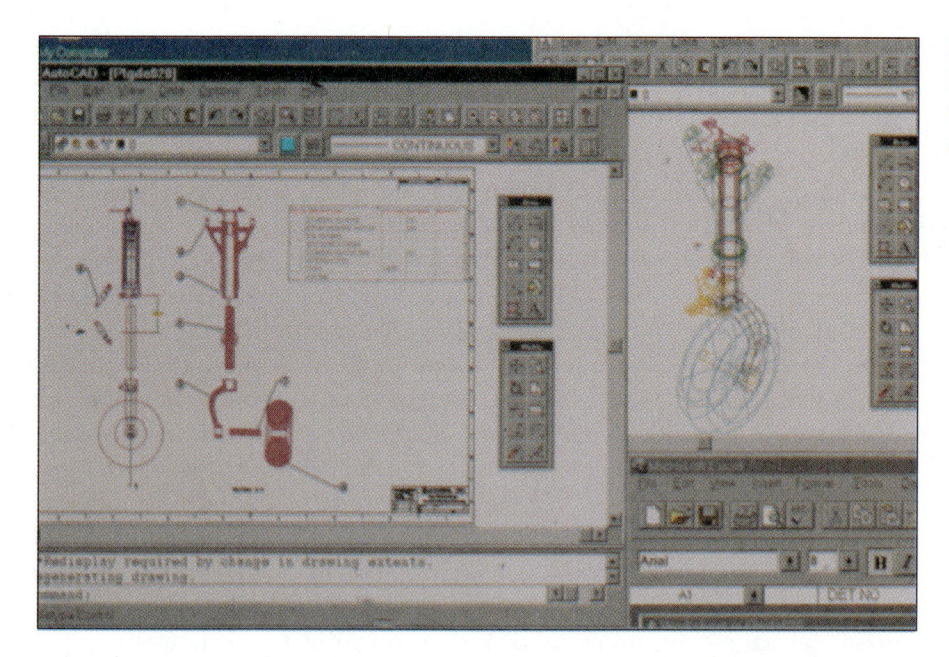

Figure 6-19 CAD Design
Product performance can be previewed through computer-aided design (CAD) software before actual production takes place.

The Sky's the Limit

Is there nothing the computer cannot do? Actually, yes. The computer cannot make life or show emotions or exhibit intuition or enjoy a day at the ball park. It cannot hug your grandchild or predict the future. Yet computers may soon be doing a lot more than we ever anticipated. Already, computer-aided design applications are available for individuals to use with microcomputers. And soon we may be using our home computers with expert systems to help us make decisions, and with virtual reality to experience events that we never could experience otherwise. Onward and upward: The sky's the limit.

CAD/CAM

One of the fastest-growing areas of microcomputer use in industry is **computer-aided design** (**CAD**). CAD allows the engineer to design, draft, and analyze a prospective product via computer graphics (see Figure 6-19). An object may be configured in three dimensions and rotated to display all sides. The object may be drawn in layers, as if there were plastic overlays showing a back, the insides, and a front view. The designer, working with full-color graphics, can easily make changes and test many versions of a product before the first prototype is ever built. A common CAD package is the popular *AutoCad*, which is sold as a basic package with adaptations for particular fields such as architecture and engineering.

CAD can also analyze designs for poor tolerance between parts and for stress points. This can save companies a great deal of money by eliminating defective designs before the money is spent to build a product.

computer-aided design (CAD) The process of designing, drafting, and analyzing a prospective product via special graphics software on a high-end computer; often paired with CAM.

computer-aided manufacturing (CAM) The process, via computer, of designing and testing a manufacturing process and often monitoring the actual making of a product; often paired with CAD.

Boeing even has a three-dimensional design system that includes its own human model who crawls into images on the screen and shows the difficulty a real human might have in reaching an area of a jet that needs a repair.

Computer-aided design is often coupled with **computer-aided manufacturing (CAM)**. The combination is referred to as CAD/CAM. Using CAD/CAM, the engineer can analyze not only the product but also the manufacturing process. Once the rough design of the product has been entered into the computer, the engineer can have the computer system simulate any manufacturing step needed to build the product. For example, if the product must be drilled, the engineer can use a computerized drill that can be guided, either by the engineer or the computer, to simulate the drilling process. This simulation can be helpful in two ways. First, it indicates major problems that may be encountered on the assembly line before it is even set up. Second, the computer records exactly how the tool moved, and stores that information on magnetic media. If that factory uses robots and numerically controlled machinery, those tapes can be used to drive the actual machines in manufacturing the product. In this way, CAD/CAM can take the engineer from idea to final product.

Under traditional CAD/CAM, the prototypes or models of products were produced by hand, even though the parts were designed with a computer. This process often took weeks or even months to complete. Enter a new technology called *desktop manufacturing*. Desktop manufacturing is changing the way three-dimensional prototypes and models are made. The desktop manufacturing systems currently in use or under development employ technologies such as laser sintering, stereolithography, photochemical machining, and laminated-object manufacturing in order to construct a model of a part or product. The model is made of materials such as plastic, laminates, and paper. Mercedes-Benz, for example, created a prototype of an exhaust system for one of its cars via desktop manufacturing.

One desktop manufacturing system currently available employs a computer, a laser, and liquid polymer plastic to create prototypes. The computer system divides the part into pieces, or slices, and then constructs each piece separately using the laser and the plastic. The plastic is shaped and then exposed to the light of the laser so that it will harden. Once all of the pieces are completed, they are glued together to form a whole model. The benefit realized from such systems is tremendous. Tasks that used to take weeks or months can now be accomplished in a few short hours.

Expert Systems

The study of artificial intelligence (AI) seeks to develop techniques whereby computers can help solve problems that appear to require imagination, intuition, or intelligence. In other words, AI is supposed to

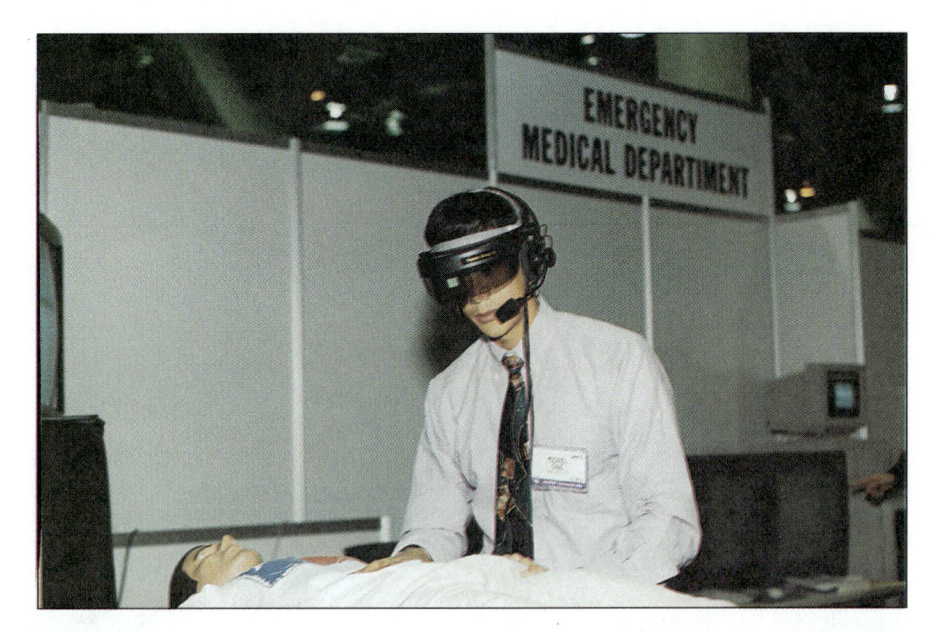

Figure 6–20 Expert System
This person is demonstrating a hands free voice operated medical expert system for emergency room use. This particular system is produced by Knowledge Industries.

resemble human reasoning and action. Because of the disappointments associated with AI research, the term is being used less frequently and such efforts are described instead as "applied intelligence." One of the products of applied intelligence is the **expert system**.

Expert systems cover knowledge in only one field, such as medicine or geology. An expert system is software that evaluates, draws conclusions, and makes recommendations based on a huge database of information (the knowledge base) in the particular field (see Figure 6–20). A medical diagnosis expert system, for example, could make cross-references between the history, symptoms, and test results of a patient and the data in its database, and come up with possible diseases the patient has. This helps the doctor diagnose a puzzling case and set up a plan of treatment. The expert system includes a set of rules for reasoning designed to mimic the decision-making processes of human experts in a narrowly defined field, based on what is known of the human thought processes.

One expert system, is *MYCIN*, which is aimed at diagnosing infectious diseases and recommending appropriate drugs. *Oncocin* advises physicians on the best treatments for cancer patients, and *Caduceus II* holds information about hundreds of diseases and symptoms. *Prospector* is an expert system that helps geologists in locating mineral deposits, and *Dipmeter Advisor* helps oil companies find good locations for drilling. *Taxadvisor*, developed by R. Michaelsen at the University of Illinois, helps users with estate planning by determining ways in which they can minimize income and death taxes and also by making investment and insurance recommendations. The *ACE* system, developed by Bell Laboratories, identifies trouble spots in telephone networks and recommends appropriate repairs and preventive maintenance. *STEAMER* is a

expert system A form of applied intelligence software designed to imitate the decision-making processes of experts in a specific field.

Figure 6–21   Virtual-Reality Equipment
In order to participate in virtual reality, you usually need special equipment such as goggles and gloves.

virtual reality A computer arrangement, including hardware and software, that enables a person to experience and manipulate a three-dimensional world that exists only in projected images; includes simulated touch as one more sense in the multisensory world of multimedia.

system for training inexperienced workers to operate complex ship engines. The Internal Revenue Service will soon have an expert system for detecting suspicious deductions and errors on tax returns. American Express employs an expert system to authorize questionable charges. Expert systems can help users find the information they want among the thousands of databases and resources available on a computer network. You can even buy an expert system shell such as *VP-EXPERT* with which to develop your own expert system.

Thus, expert systems are used in many fields: law, medicine, engineering, business, geology, financial analysis, and tax analysis, among others. They perform such functions as recommending strategies, diagnosing problems (such as illnesses), analyzing structures, and training personnel. Expert systems can cut costs, boost quality, and improve productivity, and they have the potential of functioning better than any single human expert in making judgments within their own areas of expertise.

VIRTUAL REALITY

The ultimate in multimedia technology is **virtual reality**, in which three-dimensional images are delivered through specially wired goggles and gloves, creating the illusion of being inside a scene and moving through it. Inside the goggles, two slightly different views of the scene are projected on tiny liquid-crystal screens. Because neither eye perceives from exactly the same perspective, a three-dimensional effect is produced. Moving your head changes the view, just as in real life. A special joystick or a data glove loaded with sensors and optical fibers enables you to "manipulate" the virtual objects (see Figure 6–21).

Figure 6–22 Virtual-Reality
(a) The R-360 videogame, controlled by a joystick, simulates a jet fighter as it rotates and spins 360 degrees.
(b) Final adjustments are made on a data suit. Just as a data glove enables the user to interact in a virtual world with his hand gestures, the body suit lets the wearer use the entire body to interact with a program or another person wearing another data suit.
(c) At Magic Edge, a pilot flies a non-moving flight simulator to practice for a motion based model.
(d) Air traffic controllers in the next decade may be using virtual-reality equipment to guide planes.

The core of a virtual-reality system is a database that contains data about the focus of the system—for example, a brain scan, specifications for a plane's instrument panel, or the description of a specific room, such as a kitchen or bathroom. When the user dons the equipment and starts the system, the computer renders a virtual-reality environment, or "world", based on the information in the database. The user can then interact with the world, touching and manipulating objects to see what happens next (see Figure 6–22).

Virtual reality delivers multisensory information, particularly sound and touch, and it is interactive. These characteristics make it ideal for training or learning experiences. In fact, a virtual-reality system is a glorified expert system. Virtual reality has been used by pilots-in-training to

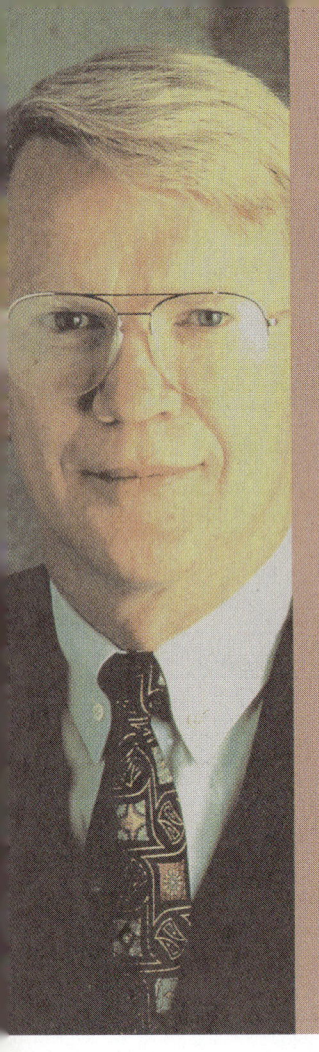

Profile

Edward R. McCracken:
Silicon Graphics' Chairman and CEO

Ordinary personal computers are not powerful enough to help produce a *Jurassic Park* movie or fabricate scenes in which Forrest Gump meets President John F. Kennedy and John Lennon or precisely locate once-inoperable brain tumors. Instead, the computers employed for such applications are powerful, three-dimensional graphics workstations. With these systems, scientists, engineers and creative professionals create intricate, textured three-dimensional images which can be viewed and manipulated from all angles.

Silicon Graphics Inc., the company that creates these unique products, is headed by Edward R. McCracken, a 50-something engineer who has worked in Silicon Valley for more than 26 years.

Raised on a midwestern farm in Iowa and educated as an electrical engineer, McCracken started his career at Hewlett-Packard and moved to Silicon Graphics as its President and Chief Executive Officer in 1984. He manages Silicon Graphics' finances conservatively, yet pushes the company to create products in short 12- to 18-month cycles, forbidding employees from planning products more than two years in advance. He encourages a casual working atmosphere, one where innovative and creative employees thrive and the company is able to quickly adjust to changing market conditions. Under McCracken's leadership, Silicon Graphics has grown its visual computing leadership to an over $2.2 billion business.

learn how to fly and land airplanes. Catepillar Inc. is testing virtual-reality models of its earth movers to improve performance and visibility of the real equipment. Chrysler Corp. hopes that a system it is developing in conjunction with IBM will cut months off the car design process by allowing engineers to spot problems before expensive prototypes are built. The Army is working on an advanced network for battlefield simulations. In medicine, virtual-reality tools can be used to create 3-D images that help surgeons plan procedures or even assist in surgeries from remote locations. In industry and sports, virtual reality could help improve performance and analyze repetitive-stress injuries. A homeowner could "walk through" a virtual model of the plans for a new kitchen and family room.

Virtual reality can be used to test the convenience and location of instruments in a jet, appliances in a kitchen, and buttons on a factory control panel before the products are ever built. It could be employed to teach new surgical techniques to surgeons. In psychotherapy, it could assist a patient in altering his or her perspective of a problem. Since students comprehend images much faster than they do columns of numbers, virtual-reality programs can help them study concepts of algebra, geometry, and physics. Literature could come alive, and history be experienced.

Window on Computing

The Future Is Here: This Vehicle Hasn't Passed Driver's Ed

If you want a demonstration of a neural network on the job, you should see Alvinn at work. Alvinn (Autonomous Land Vehicle in a Neural Network) is a modified, self-driving Chevy van that depends on neural networks for accurate navigation. (A neural network is computer programming that simulates the behavior of neurons in the human nervous system.)

Alvinn is outfitted with cameras programmed to recognize shapes such as trees and other cars. Other cameras detect colors, for differentiating the yellow lines from the black pavement, for example. Inside the vehicle, a network of four workstations processes the data and tells small motors to turn the steering wheel, step on the brake, work the gearshift, or accelerate the vehicle. Alvinn's neural network learns to drive along different types of roads, such as dirt lanes and four-lane highways, by using its cameras to "watch" a human do the same job for five minutes. One caveat, Alvinn: Watch out for snow! You could mistake it for white lines along the side of the road.

Some projects costing millions in research money resulted in vehicles capable of only 10 miles per hour and able to stay on the road for only a mile or so. Alvinn has already set a record of more than 55 mph over a 21-mile stretch of road. Of course, the Pentagon is highly interested in driverless jeeps that could roam throughout a battle area, detecting land mines and spying on the enemy, without endangering the lives of troops. The technology could be used for newspaper delivery, too. Now, let's be practical: How about a self-driving lawn mover or golf cart?

As the discussions of software applications have shown, computers have the potential to influence the ways we learn and interact. Word processors, databases, and spreadsheet software have already changed the way corporations and institutions study and conduct their business. Graphics and CAD/CAM programs have helped business and industry design products and procedures and communicate with employees and clients. Desktop publishing has brought previously specialized tasks within the capabilities of children. Finally, multimedia, expert systems, and virtual reality are providing new tools with which to teach students, train employees, and make decisions. Nothing can quite replace actual experience, but technology can certainly make the process a little easier.

▶Summary Points

- Microcomputer software developers are now presenting a flurry of "power" applications previously unachievable because of the shortfalls in memory, storage capabilities, and computing power for microcomputers.
- One of these applications is desktop publishing, which uses page composition software to prepare for publication materials imported primarily from word processing and graphics files. Page composition software enables the user to create a page layout into which graphics and text are placed.
- Features of page composition software include WYSIWYG capabilities, multiple columns, automatic figure numbering, generation of tables of contents and indexes, scaling and cropping of graphic images, automatic text wrap, style sheets, templates, fonts, kerning, and leading.
- A piece of equipment that has made desktop publishing attractive for business use and professional in quality is the laser printer. Color printing is also becoming more popular and feasible, although good color resolution and matching is generally associated with the most expensive printers.
- Integrated software is the combination of two or more application programs (usually stand-alone applications), permitting easy movement of data among the applications and using a group of common commands across all applications. Typically, one program in the set is stronger than the others, while the others support the main program. The individual applications in an integrated package are called modules. Collections of existing software that already work well together have been compiled into office "suites."
- Multimedia computer applications present text, sound, animation and video motion, graphics, and photo-quality images with inter-

active computer functions with which the user manipulates the elements. In essence, multimedia is multisensory.
- Most multimedia titles can be grouped into one of three categories: education, entertainment, or reference. Multimedia is often used for training workers and instructing students.
- Multimedia requires the use of a CD-ROM disk and disk drive, which enables the storage of large databases of graphic images, text, and sound. Generally, a powerful computer with a great deal of memory and a high-capacity hard disk drive is required, as well as a mouse, a sound card, and headphones or speakers.
- The computerization of multimedia is sometimes referred to as hypermedia. To navigate through a hypermedia application, you would use a hypertext application such as *HyperCard*. *HyperCard* also provides an authoring tool for creating a multimedia production.
- Computer-aided design and computer-aided manufacturing (CAD/CAM) enable engineers to control the design of a product from idea to manufacturing. The CAD part is for designing and testing the product; the CAM part sets up and controls the manufacturing process. Desktop manufacturing systems even produce prototypes (models) by computer operations.
- Expert systems evaluate, draw conclusions, and recommend actions based on a knowledge base and a set of rules designed to imitate the reasoning of experts in a given field.
- The ultimate multimedia technology is virtual reality, in which three-dimensional images are delivered and manipulated through special goggles, gloves, or joysticks. A virtual-reality system provides the added dimension of touch, albeit through simulation. Virtual reality is valuable in certain types of training instruction and in education applications.

►Review Questions

1. What is desktop publishing? What is page composition software? How does the second contribute to the success of the first?
2. What can page composition software provide that helps a user create a good-looking document? What do you think the user contributes to the creation of a good-looking document?
3. What is the role of laser and ink-jet printers in desktop publishing?
4. Define *integration* as it is used in conjunction with software.
5. What are the common characteristics of integrated software packages?
6. What is an all-in-one package? What is the advantage of using such a package? What is the disadvantage? How does the term *suite* fit this type of software?

7. How does multimedia differ from the other types of computer applications previously discussed? What are some requirements for a multimedia system?
8. Of what purpose is the authoring tool in multimedia?
9. How is computer graphics important to all three types of software (desktop publishing, integrated software, and multimedia)?
10. What computer options are available to engineers for designing and producing a product?
11. What is an expert system? Give some examples.
12. How is virtual reality like multimedia? How is it like an expert system? Of what uses are multimedia and virtual reality beyond entertainment?

▶Activities and Research

1. Compare the features of a low-end desktop publishing package with those of a high-end word processing program.
2. How could multimedia and virtual reality influence a person's perception of events, unlike normal television and movie images?

CHAPTER 7

CONTEMPORARY CONCERNS

Learning Objectives
Introduction
Criminal Conduct and Ethics: Responsibility for Computer Actions
    Computer Crime
    Hacking
    Piracy
    Security Measures for Organizations
    Concept Summary: Security Problems
Privacy
    Privacy Issues
    Profile: Protector of Civil Rights on the Final Frontier: the Electronic Frontier Foundation
    Legislation
Window on Computing: The Data Vendors
Concept Summary: Abuse of Data
Ergonomics
    Computer Related Health Problems
    Ergonomic Design
    Safety Issues
    Window on Computing: The Future Is Here: You Bet Your Life
Summary Points
Review Questions
Activities and Research

LEARNING OBJECTIVES

After reading this chapter, you should be able to:

- List and discuss several issues of computer use related to personal responsibility for computer actions.
- Define *computer crime*, and describe its four categories.
- Describe and discuss legal factors involved in privacy and piracy.
- Discuss some methods of computer security and crime prevention.
- Define *ergonomics*, and relate workstation design to ergonomics and safety issues.

INTRODUCTION

The invention of computers made work a lot easier for many people, but it also presented problems of its own. Computers became one more area for creative criminals to explore. Computers made more trouble for people through their sometimes-gargantuan errors. Computers made it possible for almost anyone to root around in data that we once thought private—or at least restricted. And now there is a good chance that working with computers all day long may not be good for your health.

Despite these problems, computers have allowed for people with some types of disabilities to communicate with their family and friends. They have provided a conduit through which people exchange information and ideas and by which students learn both by rote and by creative thinking. They have enabled industries to employ machines and robots for dangerous work. Thus, many people can benefit from the invention of computers. This chapter presents a few of the issues and challenges inherent in using computers.

Criminal Conduct and Ethics: Responsibility for Computer Actions

When you were in school, were you ever tempted to copy someone's homework for the next day's class or sneak a look at someone else's answers during an exam? Have you ever been tempted to take something from a store without paying for it? At work, did you ever want to claim credit for someone else's suggestion or peek at files that held confidential information about other employees? Did you ever try to place the blame for a mistake on a co-worker? Most of us have fleeting thoughts of engaging in these types of behavior, but we don't actually carry out the actions. What we do in these situations depends on our code of ethics. Ethics are the morals on which we base our behavior. They are standards by which we tell the difference between right and wrong and act accordingly.

Ethics apply to our behavior around computers, too. Perhaps an acquaintance has bragged about getting into a university's database and changing his grades or accessing a bank's computer and changing his credit rating. Maybe a friend wanted to copy some of your software to avoid paying for her own. You might even know someone who has used a computer and modem to get into the computer files at a hospital, school, or business just to see if it was possible. If you have strong personal morals, you probably would refrain from these activities. Your conscience would tell you to follow a code of **computer ethics** based on your other beliefs of right and wrong. Computer ethics are the standards by which we judge the correct uses of computers.

Unfortunately, an act may seem less serious when it occurs at a computer rather than in front of humans. This is because people see a computer as an impersonal machine. The pain felt by a victim of thieves is not so obvious when the theft occurs by hitting a few keys rather than by mugging someone on the street. In addition, finding the computer thief—or even detecting the crime—is sometimes very difficult (see Figure 7–1).

Attempts to govern computer activity present problems, too. Some computer experts believe that limiting access to any type of computer activity constitutes a violation of the right to free speech and access to information. The content of messages sent over computer networks must, as well, be protected from prying eyes and censorship. Bulletin board systems, especially, can be open to misuse by both law enforcement and users. For example, civil libertarians fear actions like those of the Secret Service who attempted to shut down dozens of computer bulletin boards in order to stop a group of youthful computer enthusiasts suspected of trafficking in stolen credit-card numbers, telephone access codes, and other such information. The invasions of privacy that occurred could have set disturbing precedents for future prosecutions. Nevertheless, on bulletin boards, it is easy to voice libelous opinions, post access codes to company computers, describe methods of building weapons, or insert programs called viruses that could destroy other users' software and data files—all unsavory activities.

---

computer ethics Standards of moral conduct in computer use; a way in which the "spirit" of some laws are applied to computer-related activities.

Figure 7–1 Networking
Electronic funds transfer made possible with a home computer and telephone poses a threat to billions of dollars in databases. Detection of crimes committed through computer networks is difficult.

In order to safeguard the potential of free and open inquiry and yet to limit criminal activities such as those just mentioned, lawmakers have been trying to reach a balance between protection and repression in privacy legislation. Civil libertarians will be active in finding ways to protect rights in cyberspace—that universe occupied by audio and video signals traveling across state and national borders at nearly the speed of light. In addition, computer users must assume responsibility for their own actions, for any standards will be meaningless if people cannot or will not govern their own behavior.

This section describes the types of computer activities that are considered crimes and some of the methods implemented to secure computer systems from criminal activities.

COMPUTER CRIME

Computer-related crime is more of a problem than most people realize. Americans are losing billions of dollars every year to high-tech thieves whose activities often go undetected and unpunished. Estimates of losses range from at least $2 billion to more than $40 billion per year. No one really knows how much is being stolen, but the total appears to be rising rapidly.

Computer crime is defined as a criminal act that poses a greater threat to a computer user than to a nonuser, or a criminal act that is accomplished through the use of a computer. In keeping with this definition, the term *computer crime* covers two types of activities: (1) using a computer to commit crime, and (2) damaging hardware, software, or data. Perpetrators may change computer input or programs in order to get money, data, or even merchandise. They may steal computer time or software from an employer or a school. Sometimes, the criminals damage the actual hardware or software. The basic categories of computer crime are outlined next.

computer crime A criminal act that poses a threat to those who use computers or that is accomplished through the use of a computer.

Sabotage and Viruses

Sabotage occurs with the "weapons" of flooding, fire, sledgehammers, electromagnets, and any other means by which damage can be inflicted on computer hardware, programs, and data. This type of sabotage is more common in organizations than it is toward individuals and their microcomputers.

Although sabotage can be inflicted through physical means, it also happens when someone introduces a **virus** into the system. Viruses can affect the systems of both organizations and individuals. A virus is a set of software code that makes something happen to a computer system without its owner knowing it. It works by replicating itself and attaching itself to other programs. Viruses can infect systems through networks, although the majority of virus infections occur via floppy disks. Once a virus is in a system, it may attempt to erase or change the data on the hard disk. Although viruses are very difficult to guard against, there are programs that can detect and counteract them (see Figure 7–2).

To compound the difficulties, a new generation of highly destructive "stealth" viruses appear to be spreading into some systems. They are called stealth viruses because their authors have designed them to avoid detection by antivirus software, much as a Stealth bomber tries to avoid radar. They are also difficult to remove once found.

Theft of Services

Theft of services includes utilizing a government's or a company's computer for personal gain. For example, a politician may conduct campaign

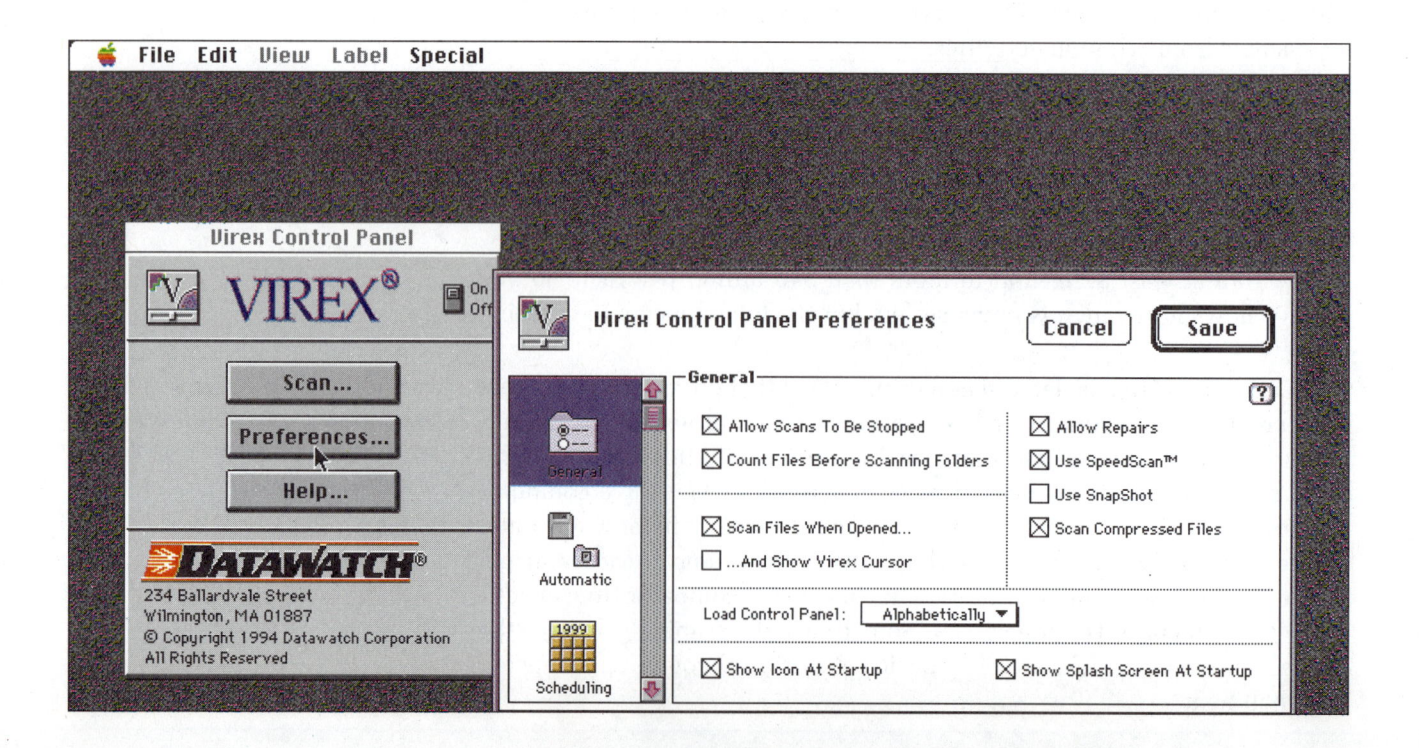

virus A form of sabotage in which a computer program wreaks havoc on a system by destroying data, causing malfunctions, or harassing a user.

Figure 7–2 Antivirus Software
Virex is a program for microcomputers that can detect and delete some of the well-known viruses.

mailings via a city's computer, or a professor may sell university data to outside businesses. An organization's computers may be employed to conduct freelance services after working hours. Wiretapping is another technique by which to gain unauthorized access to a computer system. By "piggybacking" onto a legitimate user's line whenever the line is not being used by the authorized party, a person can gain free access to the user's privileges with a commercial online information service or to a corporate mainframe.

THEFT OF PROPERTY

Theft of property occurs when a person steals merchandise from a company whose orders are processed by computer. These crimes are usually committed by internal personnel who have knowledge of the operations. Through record manipulation, dummy accounts can be created that direct a product order to be shipped to an accomplice outside the organization. Two other common property crimes are the theft of computer equipment itself and software **piracy** (see sections later in this chapter).

piracy Unauthorized copying, distribution, or use of software.

FINANCIAL CRIMES

Financial crimes are committed when a person uses a computer for illegal monetary gain. The criminal may make out multiple checks to the same person or reroute checks to false addresses. In round-off fraud, the thief collects fractions of cents in customers' bank accounts that are created when the current interest rates are applied. These fractions are then stored in an account created by the thief. The thief is assuming that fractions of cents collected from thousands of accounts on a regular basis will someday yield a substantial amount of money.

Most computer crimes are *white-collar crimes*, that is, they are committed by professional people or office employees who have easy access to computer systems and data. For example, an angry programmer may "get even" with his company by leaving a few lines of code that destroy company data months after he has been fired. A data-entry clerk may stumble on a way to siphon off a few cents from the interest on all the savings accounts in a bank. An accountant may copy a company's expensive spreadsheet and database software for private use.

A growing concern is that computer systems will become targets for terrorists because of the crucial roles that computers play in conducting a nation's business and military affairs (see Figure 7–3). The awareness that a criminal in one country could tap the computers in another country and through them switch goods or funds to a third country is raising questions of international law as well as of security. In fact, the ease with which computers can transfer data across national borders is creating a security dilemma of a dimension all its own.

Several factors may explain the rash of computer crimes: lax security in data-processing areas; the intrinsic flexibility of computers; the spread of microcomputers and their simplified operating instructions; the teach-

Figure 7–3 Securing Data
Data communication security is of special concern for organizations that exchange data. V One's SmartGate ensures private communications for both private and public networks. Their use of mutual authentication and encryption provides a protective environment over an open network.

hacking The activity of computer enthusiasts who feel challenged to break computer security measures without authorization.

ing of computer skills to students at an early age; and the ease with which a lot of sensitive data can be accessed.

HACKING

Hacking is the activity of computer enthusiasts who are challenged to explore every potential of a computer. Although it originally had a positive connotation, describing hard-working and persistent programmers, it now commonly describes unsavory and sometimes-illegal activity. (The term *cracker* refers to a hacker bent on malicious activity, as opposed to the hacker merely obsessed by curiosity.) Such activity includes breaking computer security measures designed to prevent unauthorized access to a particular computer system. Hackers do this for a number of reasons, including gaining access to confidential data, getting illegal computer time, finding out about different types of operating systems, using services such as long-distance calling or online information services without charge, or simply taking up a challenge. Regardless of the reason, this type of hacking is the same as committing a crime.

Not only trained experts but skilled amateurs have been able to crack computer systems. A student in Los Angeles did a quarter of a million dollars in damage to a leasing corporation by raiding its computer system, causing the system to collapse. In New York, four 13-year-olds electronically broke into several corporate computers in Canada, destroying some files at one company.

A primary purpose of criminal hacking is, of course, to get an access code, and access codes are at the heart of a major problem for businesses: telephone toll fraud. The culprits use telephone credit-card and account numbers to make long-distance calls—even to foreign countries, including drug-exporting countries. They may tap into 800-number accounts, tying up a company's 800 lines and sticking the company with bogus calls. Hackers often gain access to a company's long-distance telephone account via auto-dialers, which are computer programs that repeatedly do the dialing and punch in possible access codes until access is established. (In the United States, you can legally redial only up to 15 times.) Companies that employ the PBX systems are particularly vulnerable if they take advantage of the direct inward system access (DISA), which allows traveling employees to call the home office and by entering a code, make long-distance calls on the company's account.

Access codes are not always attained through electronic wizardry. Many are acquired from telephone company employees, in company dumpsters, over the airwaves (from cellular phone use), and at public telephones. Those who, through binoculars, video cameras, or simply good eyesight, spy on people making telephone credit-card calls at public phones are called "shoulder surfers." Although hackers do use these access codes, the big-league "telecrooks" are organized crime and drug dealers. Some even set up storefronts as locations for "customers" to "buy" long-distance phone calls.

Needless to say, hacking activity that involves the unauthorized use of other computers and computer services is illegal. Some states have enacted laws against hacking. And at the federal level, there is the Computer Fraud and Abuse Act of 1986, which provides protection against computer abuse in a few areas. For example, an individual is prohibited from knowingly accessing a computer without authorization to obtain information that is protected by the Right to Financial Privacy Act of 1978 or information contained in the file of a consumer reporting agency. An individual is also prohibited from knowingly accessing a government computer or the computer of any federally insured financial institution, and viewing, using, modifying, destroying, or disclosing information stored in the computer, or interfering with the regular use of the computer. Offenders may be imprisoned for up to 20 years and fined up to $100,000.

More recently, concern has focused on abuses during the actual transmission of data. This led to the drafting of the Electronic Communications Privacy Act of 1986, which prohibits the interception of data communications (for example, electronic mail) by a third party—the government, the police, and/or an individual—without proper authorization, such as a search warrant. The act also makes it illegal for a provider of electronic

Figure 7–4 Copyright Notice
Copyright protection applies to most commercial software packages. Notices of copyright protection are displayed when the covered systems are loaded into computer memory, as shown in this photo.

communications services to divulge knowingly the contents of a communication, except to the intended parties. This law does not protect e-mail transmitted within one company, however.

Piracy

Software piracy is the illegal copying of copyrighted software. It includes making copies of copyrighted software for resale to a friend or other person and copying software that belongs to a friend or a business for personal use.

Software is protected by the U.S. Copyright Act of 1978 and the Software Copyright Act of 1980. The creator of an original work possesses a copyright from the moment the work is fixed in some tangible medium, such as hard copy or disk storage. Since March 1, 1989, when the United States became a member of the International Berne Copyright Convention, most formal requirements of registration and identification have become optional. Because of the legal advantages and the relatively minor cost, however, authors should register their works with the Copyright Office and place a copyright notice on all copies of their works. A copyright notice is the sign ©, the word *copyright*, or the abbreviation *copr.* along with the name of the copyright owner and the year of the work's first publication (see Figure 7–4.)

Two of the most important rights granted exclusively to authors under copyright law are the right to reproduce their work and the right to create a derivative work. Except for minor exceptions, only the holder of a copyright has the right to authorize copying of the protected material. The two most notable exceptions permit (a) the buyer of a work to make one archival copy for backup purposes and (b) the fair use of selected portions of copyrighted material in an extremely limited manner for educational purposes. Only the copyright holder has the right to develop derivative works, such as translations, based on the original copyrighted material.

Most current legal cases about copyrights involve illegal bulletin board uses, corporate misuses, and the sale of pirated software. With estimates of losses being in the $10 billion range each year worldwide, these cases are being heavily prosecuted. In fact, according to copyright law, a company can be held liable for piracy even if the copying is done without a manager's knowledge. In contrast, individuals who copy software for personal use will probably not be caught, but they knowingly violate a law: Copying copyrighted software is illegal. By conscience, however, most people do not make illegal copies of their software. In addition, most computer users realize that if they use pirated software, they run the risk of getting a virus, complements of the pirate.

When you buy software, you actually don't own it; you merely have a license to use it. In addition, by law, the use of the software is restricted to one computer at a time and one user at a time. This is important if you are employing a network such as a local-area network in your business. But the restriction can be overcome by obtaining a site license that permits multiple users of the program on the network.

Some software manufacturers do not rely solely on the copyright law to safeguard their products. They protect their software with codes that making copying disks hard or that destroy some data when a disk is copied. This practice decreased in 1983, when the major software companies decided to "unlock" their disks because the copy-protection codes prevented users from making an archival copy, which is legal, and also prevented the use of the software with hard disks. Thus, many software companies—especially those that deal in entertainment software—employ a form of off-disk copy protection that may require typing a special number, word, or code found on a special card that cannot be photocopied or on a randomly selected page in the user's manual that comes with the software.

Software that falls outside of copyright protection is termed **public-domain software** and is therefore available for unrestricted use. This normally occurs when the author decides not to protect the copyright interest and publishes the software with that stipulation. Software developed with public or grant funds may also be contractually transferred into the public domain. Such software is frequently found via electronic bulletin

public-domain software Programs unprotected by copyright law and available for free, unrestricted public use.

shareware Copyrighted programs that are given away free, but with the expectation that satisfied users will voluntarily pay the copyright holder for use of the program.

board systems, in magazines, or through user groups. **Shareware** is copyrighted material and is not considered in the public domain, although it is obtainable without charge. The ethics of shareware demand that anyone who uses a shareware program pay a registration fee, often $25. The philosophy behind shareware is that users are in the best position to judge the value of a program and that authors, if they know their fees depend on it, will produce a high-quality product.

So far, we have discussed copyright as it pertains to entire programs. What do copyright laws have to say about using portions of a work? In most cases, you must have the permission of the author to use portions of a work; however, the law grants you "fair use" of a work without such permission. Most generally, this exception gives you the right to quote excerpts in a review or criticism to make a point or in a scholarly work to support or illustrate a point. In addition, some authors give permission to use material in exchange for acknowledgment of the source in your work. For example, *CorelDRAW!* includes 18,000 pieces of clip art on a CD-ROM. You cannot resell the clip art, but you can use it in newsletters or other publications as long as you say who produced the clip art. Some people feel that if you change an image such as clip art or a photograph, then you can claim it as your own. In fact, manipulating a copyrighted image makes it a derivative work, and derivative works are also protected by copyright law.

SECURITY MEASURES FOR ORGANIZATIONS

Most security problems are accidents: errors, omissions, fires, and so on. With careful planning and proper training, companies and individuals can avoid these problems. They can back up their data and keep updated copies of important data at a secure location other than the location of the computer. (Some experts like to present the topic of backup as "restoration," in order to stress that, rather than a chore, backing up data is an important individual or company priority.) To increase physical security, companies can put computer equipment in rooms that are controlled for humidity, heat, and leaks. They can install equipment that prevents their systems from being damaged by lightning or power glitches.

password A special word, code, or symbol, designed for security purposes, that must be entered into a computer system before a user can gain access to the system's resources.

The problem of computer crime, however, is hard to control completely. Organizations frequently use **password** systems to ward off unauthorized users, and lock up removable hard disks or hard disk drives overnight. Listed in Figure 7–5 are some ways that organizations deal with theft, privacy, and piracy. Some of these methods can be adapted for small businesses.

In order to stop crime, some large organizations have combined several security measures, so that access to a computer is granted only after users pass several tests. Most of these methods require special equipment

Figure 7–5 Common Security Measures
Most companies implement a variety of security measures. The challenge is in maintaining, updating, and testing the effectiveness of the measures.

In order to deal with security problems, companies may do some of the following procedures:

- Define ethical behavior for all employees, and set standards for hiring and training

- Deal with misuse immediately

- In a password system, change the passwords a few times per year

- Watch for careless behavior, such as taping passwords to drawers or throwing out important printouts without shredding them

- Use physical means of identification such as ID tags and electronic keys or cards

- Lock the computer room, if necessary

- Scramble sensitive data

- Use dial-back measures to control telephone access. Dial-back requires the user to telephone the computer, give a password, and then hang up. If the user and password check out, the computer calls the user back and allows access. The user must also call from an authorized location

- Restrict employees from using their own software on company machines as one method of protection against viruses

that may be too expensive for small businesses, however. They include the following:

- Something known, such as passwords
- Something given, such as fingerprints, nose prints, or even a scan of the retina
- Something done, such as writing signatures
- Something owned, such as magnetic cards or electronic keys (see Figure 7–6).

The amount of security needed for any system is dependent on four factors: the value of the hardware; the value of the software; the cost of replacing the hardware, software, or data; and the cost of the security controls (see Figure 7–7).

Many security measures can still be overcome by a smart technician or a good buddy. In the end, an employer must depend on the ethical behavior of his or her colleagues and employees. Defining and instilling standards for ethical behavior in all employees is a major deterrent to

Figure 7–6 Security Devices
Access control is an important aspect of physical security for information systems. Devices such as data keys and identification cards help protect stored data by limiting access to the data.

Figure 7–7 Securing Computer Facilities
Data at some organizations is so valuable that little expense is spared in protection measures. Access to computer installations may be restricted by lock or entry equipment that requires special badges.

problems with security. A company must, however, exercise a great deal of care at the outset in the selection and screening of employees, especially those who will have access to computers, terminals, and computer-stored data. When an incident does occur, it must be clear that such behavior will not be tolerated and the employee will be discharged.

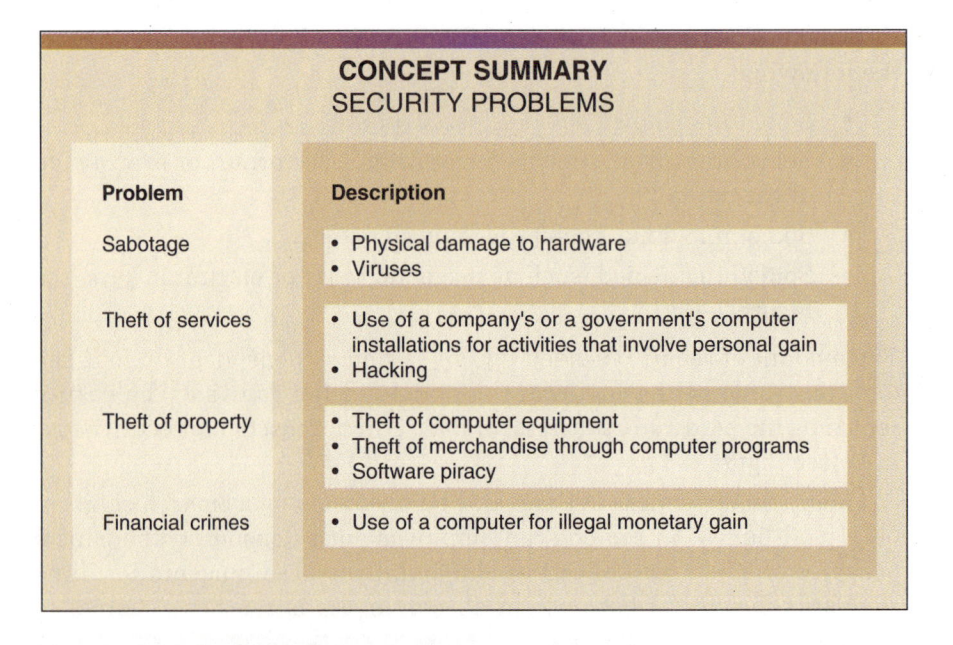

CONCEPT SUMMARY
SECURITY PROBLEMS

Problem	Description
Sabotage	• Physical damage to hardware • Viruses
Theft of services	• Use of a company's or a government's computer installations for activities that involve personal gain • Hacking
Theft of property	• Theft of computer equipment • Theft of merchandise through computer programs • Software piracy
Financial crimes	• Use of a computer for illegal monetary gain

▶ PRIVACY

A California woman could not rent an apartment because her name was in a computer database of renters who had caused trouble with previous landlords. A woman in Illinois failed to get an appointment with the doctor of her choice because the doctor she called checked a service, called Physicians' Alert, that lists patients who have filed civil suits against doctors, and sure enough the woman's name was there. A man in New York who could not get a job after trying for months finally got a notice for dishonorable discharge from the army—although he had never been in the army. That was when he realized that a former college roommate was using his name and Social Security number and had accumulated jail records and bad credit ratings that were appearing in his files.

Computers are the main means by which businesses and governments collect and store information about people. Thus, many people face problems like these when their names get into databases, often without their knowledge. Their **privacy** is invaded. Privacy is simply the right to be left alone. It involves the right of people to decide what, when, and how personal data is shared with others. It includes the right to have personal information protected from abuse. Computers, however, make it so easy to get information that privacy is often neglected. When all of this data was kept on paper files, it was harder to obtain, and outdated paper files were often destroyed to make room for new ones. Computer storage, however, has made it much easier to keep large amounts of data for long periods of time.

privacy The right of individuals to choose when and whether data about themselves is made public.

PRIVACY ISSUES

If you are an average U.S. citizen, data about you appears in 39 federal, state, and local government databases and in 40 private files (see Figure 7–8). Computers have made the collection and storage of this data easier, and have made its exchange quick, easy, and cheap. In fact, data collection and storage by computer is so simple that organizations collect far too much data—including data that they do not really need.

The federal government is the largest collector of data. The government's databases hold information about anyone who has served in the armed forces, had a physical or mental disability, had a driver's license suspended, committed a crime, received Social Security benefits, owned a boat, traveled to foreign countries, or completed an income tax return.

The schools you attend and the companies you work for are finding it easier to use computers for storing files, too. These files are probably the most complete records kept about you. Information entered into the files may include school grades, standardized test scores, behavior evaluations, work records, results of psychological and physical exams, stays in hospitals and clinics, transfers, personal references, and disciplinary actions. Other organizations collect data, too—banks, credit agencies,

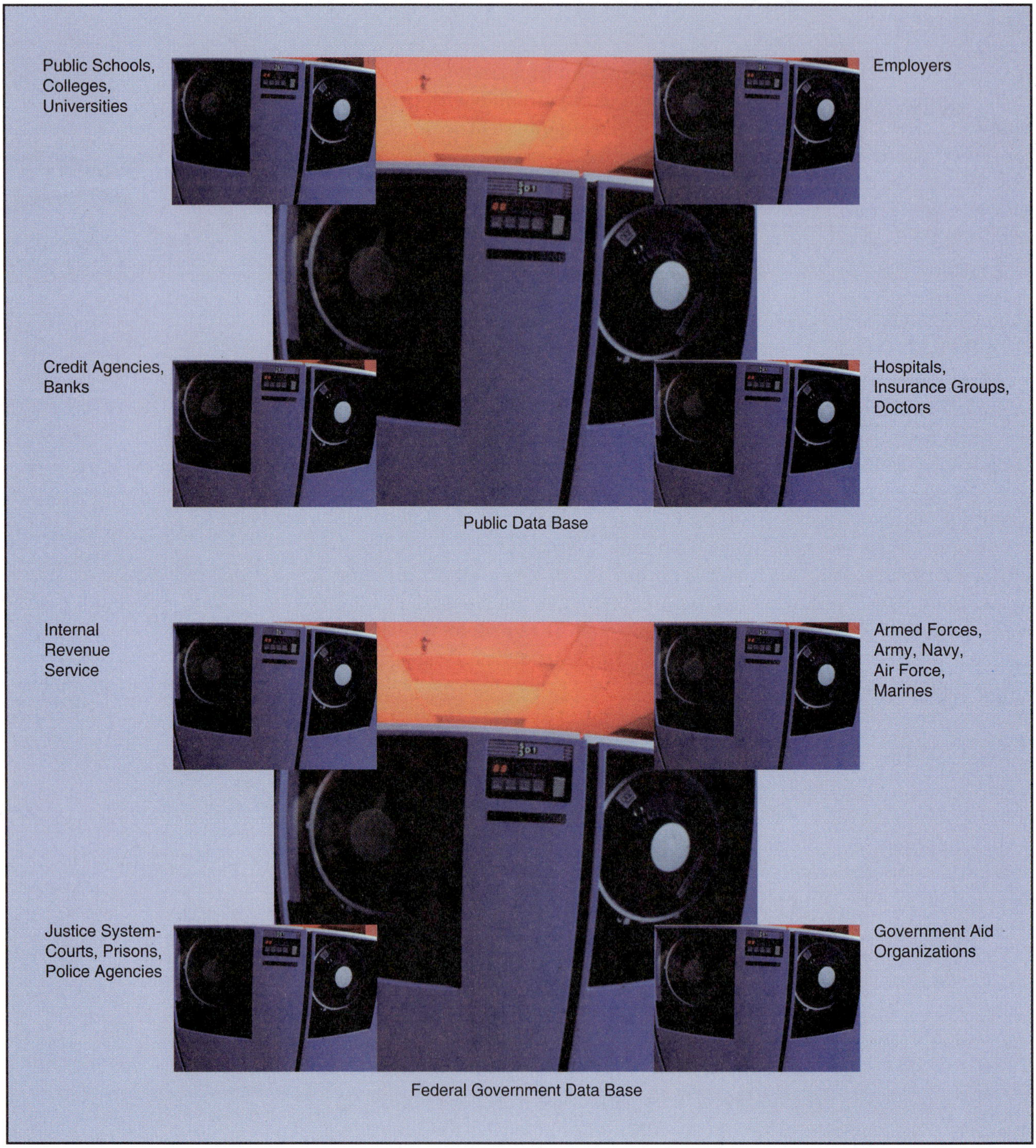

230 • Contemporary Concerns

[Figure shows databases labeled: Public Schools, Colleges, Universities; Employers; Credit Agencies, Banks; Hospitals, Insurance Groups, Doctors — all connecting to Public Data Base. Internal Revenue Service; Armed Forces, Army, Navy, Air Force, Marines; Justice System—Courts, Prisons, Police Agencies; Government Aid Organizations — all connecting to Federal Government Data Base.]

Figure 7–8 Databases
Data about an individual is kept in so many databases that you can see how John Q. Public could be completely unaware of what data is recorded about him.

insurance groups, and hospitals. So you can see that it would be hard for you to keep track of who has data about you.

Concern about the unauthorized use of data was highlighted by a fracas over *Lotus MarketPlace*. This product was a database on CD-ROM that

PROFILE

PROTECTOR OF CIVIL RIGHTS ON THE FINAL FRONTIER: THE ELECTRONIC FRONTIER FOUNDATION

Armed with a solid financial backing from prestigious members of the computing industry and a sincere dedication to protect all citizens' constitutional rights as applied to computing, John Perry Barlow and Mitch Kapor (yes, the Mitch Kapor of Lotus 1-2-3 fame) initiated the creation of the Electronic Frontier Foundation. EFF was founded in 1990 to assure privacy rights freedom of expression in digital media, with emphasis on applying the principles of the Constitution and the Bill of Rights to computer-based communication.

Such early cases as that of Craig Neidorf, who published an internal BellSouth document (which the telephone company falsely valued at many thousands of dollars) in his electronic magazine, inspired the original founders to organize their efforts to quell a new form of Future Shock—the social crisis created as America entered the Information Age with no laws for the protection and conveyance of information itself. Charged with interstate transport of stolen property and facing a possible sentence of 60 years in jail and $122,000 in fines, Neidorf was released when it was discovered that the same document was published by the telephone company itself in a book readily available for a $14 fee.

The Foundation views itself as guardian, advocate and innovator serving the public interest in the Information Age. Utilizing a combination of technical, legal, and public policy expertise, they remain true to their vision by defending civil liberties in the courts, participating in online forums, and publishing their well-read newsletter—the EFFector. They are dedicated to civilizing the electronic frontier, making it both useful and beneficial to all while maintaining the free and open flow of information and communication.

The Electronic Frontier Foundation can be contacted at 1550 Bryant Street, Suite 725, San Francisco, CA, 94103; 415-436-9333 (voice), 415-436-9993 (fax); ask@eff.org (Internet) and http://www.eff.org on the World Wide Web.

---

provided detailed demographic data on households and businesses in the United States. Lotus canceled the product just before its release, after a deluge of protests from people who feared it would violate their privacy. The problem was not that the data was available—most of the data was already maintained on minicomputers and mainframes. Rather, the worry focused on the fact that the data could be accessed and used easily and cheaply.

The major concerns about the issue of privacy can be summarized as follows:

- Too much personal information about individuals is collected and stored in computer files. This information is too easy to access and share and too difficult to challenge and change.
- Organizations are often making decisions based solely on the contents of these files.

- Much of the personal data collected about individuals may not be relevant to the intended purposes.
- The accuracy, completeness, and currency of the data may be unacceptably low.
- The stored data may not be secure.

Despite the problems associated with data collection, organizations do need data. Using computers to store data can save time and money, alert managers to risks, and help in making decisions by providing the most current information. Businesses need data for choosing employees and spending money. Schools need it in order to check student progress and improve teaching methods. Hospitals need it to be able to treat patients properly and get paid for their services. Companies need data for developing new products and evaluating the effectiveness of advertising. The government benefits from data by finding abusers of government services, which in turn benefits taxpayers. Consumers want their credit-card purchases approved quickly and want to be able to cash checks anywhere. In fact, most people voluntarily provide personal information whenever they fill out forms for healthcare providers, credit-card applications, and club memberships.

LEGISLATION

The question is how to deal with an organization's need for information and still protect each person's privacy. Several laws have been passed that deal with this question (see Figure 7–9). For example, the Fair Credit Reporting Act of 1970 protects people against false information about their credit histories. Sometimes files contain errors that prevent people from getting credit cards or taking out a loan for a new home. The law lets people see their credit histories so that they can challenge and correct errors.

The most sweeping federal legislation is the Privacy Act of 1974. This act gives people the right to see information kept about them by federal agencies and the right to correct wrong information. Under this law, the government cannot keep records about a person's religious or political beliefs. A big part of the Privacy Act limits how a government agency can use data: A government agency must tell a person if it wants to use personal information for a different reason than originally planned. It must also safeguard the contents of files and databases. There is a loophole, however. If an agency wanted data for "routine use," little notice is needed. The loophole allows government agencies to cross-check the files of different agencies. These cross-checks, sometimes called *computer matching,* let the government find people who do not pay off student loans or keep up their child support payments. The government can also find people who get unlawful government funding or who pay too little in income taxes.

Legislation	Provision
Fair Credit Reporting Act (1970)	Gives individuals the right to access and correct credit data about themselves. Credit agencies may share information with anyone with a legitimate business need (and legitimate is not defined).
Freedom of Information Act (1970)	Allows individuals to have access to data about themselves that was collected by federal agencies. (A law suit may be necessary to get the data, however).
Privacy Act (1974)	Restricts federal government in the way it shares or uses information about individuals. The law allows many exceptions.
Family Education Rights and Privacy Act (1978)	Regulates access to computer-stored records of grades and behavior evaluations in public and private schools.
Right to Financial Privacy Act (1978)	Limits federal government access to customer records of financial institutions.
Computer Fraud and Abuse Act (1986)	Provides for the prosecution of unauthorized access to government and financial institution computers. It is limited in scope.
Electronic Communications Privacy Act (1986)	Protects the confidentiality of communications without proper authorization such as a search warrant.
Video Privacy Protection Act (1988)	Prevents retailers from disclosing a person's video rental records without his or her consent or a court order.
Computer Matching and Privacy Protection Act (1988)	Prevents the government from comparing certain records in order to find a match. (There are exceptions).

Figure 7-9 Privacy Legislation
This chart identifies the main privacy laws and their provisions. Many have loopholes, exceptions, and other drawbacks.

Many state laws are patterned after the Privacy Act of 1974. These laws are generally similar to one another, varying mostly in how each state defines a particular term or violation. Some state laws address the unlawful access to databases in even more detail than federal laws. For example, South Dakota prohibits the disclosure of passwords. In Hawaii, all unauthorized computer use is considered a felony. Idaho laws, on the other hand, make a distinction between accessing information (a misdemeanor) and altering information (a felony).

Much still remains to be done about guarding data. There are many loopholes and variables in existing privacy laws. Both states and the federal government need to pass effective legislation and prosecute offenders effectively. One such effort was the Computer Matching and Privacy Protection Act of 1988, which sets up procedures for the computer matching of federal data. Even with current legislation, relatively few cases of information and privacy violation have been litigated. Since one problem of privacy violation is that data is transferred and disclosed without the knowledge or consent of the subjects, people are not likely to know how data about them is used and may not realize they have a claim to take to

Window on Computing

The Data Vendors

If you own a business and want to hire a receptionist and a couple of production workers, what can you ask the people who apply for the jobs? The information you can legally require varies from state to state, but may include the following: convictions for crime, performance at previous jobs, moving violations and accidents, worker's compensation claims, and medical history. You cannot ask an applicant about the following: marital status, age, citizenship, race, religion, lifestyle, children, or arrest record, with no convictions.

Many employers today want as much information as they can get about prospective employees, however, because they are facing rising costs from theft and other crimes committed by workers. Often, previous employers are afraid of libel suits and refrain from giving negative references. Polygraphs in the workplace are illegal, too, and questioning applicants can be a legal mine field if employers ask the wrong questions. Thus, when employers can't get the information they want from the applicant or from the previous place of employment, they may turn to data vendors such as Equifa and Apscreen. Through these vendors, they can get credit files, school records, driving violations, insurance claims, purchasing habits, and assorted other information they believe would help them decide who to hire. Once upon a time, all the records were on paper, and after a period of years many files were destroyed to make room for more. Today, disk storage makes it possible to keep records much longer, meaning that employers can learn about events that happened long ago. Figures show that the additional information has reduced theft and turnover, too, by weeding out potentially problematic employees. Obtaining data is so popular that the data-vending industry has grown to $1 billion per year.

The largest data vendors generally have built reputations for thoroughness and accuracy. Most do remind customers that their data should be just one aspect of the preemployment investigation. Getting data from such a source may be expensive, however, running anywhere from $100 to thousands of dollars for each applicant. Thus, some employers resort to cut-rate dealers in data. These dealers compile data from courthouses, motor vehicle departments, credit bureaus, and other sources. The problem is that some of the data from the cut-rate dealers cannot be used legally when hiring someone. Dilemmas, dilemmas.

CONCEPT SUMMARY
SECURITY PROBLEMS

Problem	Description
Sabotage	• Physical damage to hardware • Viruses
Theft of services	• Use of a company's or a government's computer installations for activities that involve personal gain • Hacking
Theft of property	• Theft of computer equipment • Theft of merchandise through computer programs • Software piracy
Financial crimes	• Use of a computer for illegal monetary gain

court. Furthermore, privacy litigation is somewhat contradictory in concept: By taking claims to court, litigants may expose private aspects of their lives to a far greater extent than the initial intrusion.

▶ ERGONOMICS

To most people, **ergonomics** is a relatively new science, but the idea of changing the work environment to suit the worker has been around since the 1940s. The term *ergonomics* is derived from a Greek word meaning "work." Ergonomics first became an established science during World War II, when, after fliers were crashing planes because the instrument panels and controls were too difficult to master, ergonomists redesigned the controls, making them easier to use. Following the war, the specialists continued streamlining aircraft controls. Gradually the same principles used in aircraft design were applied to other areas.

Currently, ergonomics is being applied to a vast array of products. The brake light now mounted in the rear window of all new cars is the culmination of a battle between ergonomists and designers. Designers find the placement of the light aesthetically offensive; ergonomists feel it catches the eye of other drivers better than traditional brake lights, thereby improving the safety of new cars.

Ergonomists are very much needed in the computer industry, and the number of full-time ergonomists in the United States has been increasing steadily (see Figure 7–10). The first Apple II microcomputer, the machine for which the term *user friendly* was coined, was famous for its "unfriendly" keyboard. The machine had the *Reset* control key located next to the *Return* key, so when pressing *Return* users often accidentally pushed the *Reset* key at the same time, causing an immediate loss of all data in memory. The problem was corrected on subsequent machines.

ergonomics The study of the physical relationships between people and their work environment, with the purpose of designing computer hardware and software that will improve user productivity and comfort.

Figure 7-10 Ergonomics
An ergonomist helps design workstations that can help improve worker health and productivity.

Since this early Apple mistake, ergonomists have spent a great deal of time designing keyboards that really are user friendly. Some of the improvements include standardizing symbols and layout, sculpting keys for each touch, and making keyboards detachable. There are many other computer features that were designed with ergonomic principles in mind, such as the Apple mouse and the Hewlett-Packard touch screen. This section describes some of the physical problems related to computer use and some practical solutions that can resolve the problems.

Computer Related Health Problems

The primary concern of ergonomists working in the computer industry today is the worker in the automated office who spends the entire day in front of a video display terminal (VDT), or monitor (see Figure 7–11). Studies have shown that absenteeism and a high annual turnover rate are related to the stress resulting from extensive computer use. In addition to creating stress, working at terminals for prolonged periods of time may cause physical problems. With back problems making up 25 percent of worker's compensation claims by office executives, and repetitive-motion injuries (repetitive-strain injuries, or RSIs) on the rise, it pays to examine environmental conditions and machine design in the office. The four major problem areas computer users face are eyestrain, aches and pains, excessive fatigue, and stress.

Eye Fatigue

The typical distance between the eye and printed material for ordinary desk work is from 14 to 16 inches, but people using computers usually have a viewing distance of about 25 inches. Some workers must continu-

Figure 7–11 The VDT User
A person who sits at a video display terminal all day may develop physical problems from resting his hands incorrectly while using a keyboard and from staring at the screen without blinking.

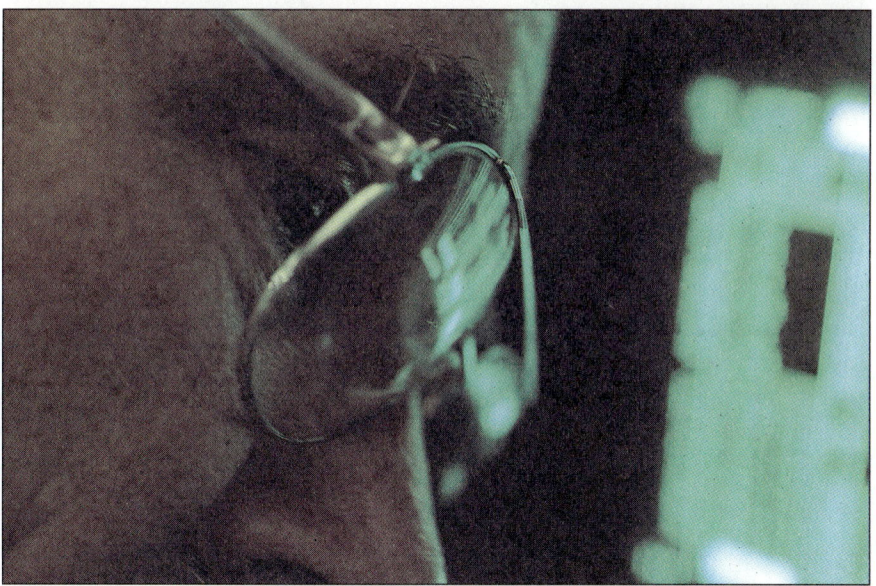

Figure 7–12 Video Display Glare
Video displays can lead to eyestrain if they are used continually over long hours. Improper lighting and poor-quality monitors also contribute to eyestrain.

ally refocus from paper to monitor, and others spend long periods of time looking only at the screen. The constant flicker as some screens refresh (or redraw data) adds to eye irritation. The size of characters that appear on the screen as well as the screen contrast also contribute to eyestrain. Then there is screen glare from nearby fluorescent lights and windows (see Figure 7–12). Some recent research has shown that workers in the 20s and 30s using computers need reading glasses long before they would under normal circumstances. The long-term effects of these eye changes is under investigation, but—though eye fatigue is annoying—there is no evidence to indicate permanent damage.

Aches and Pains

Lower-back pains are common among computer users because of the rigid posture associated with staring at the screen for long periods of time. The position most workers take is even more fixed than that of typists, because typing requires more body movement. Because of poor posture and work habits, some people end up with repetitive-strain injuries (also known as cumulative trauma disorders) that may manifest themselves as carpal tunnel syndrome (a nerve compression injury), tendonitis (irritation of the tendons), or other assorted wrist, neck, shoulder, and elbow problems. Even using excessive force during keystrokes can contribute to such disorders. Carpal tunnel problems can result from keeping the elbows elevated, bending the wrists, resting the wrists on the edge of the desk top, and striking the keys hard. When the wrist is bent, for example, finger motion generates friction—and therefore injury—because the ligaments passing through the carpal tunnel rub against one another.

Excessive Fatigue

Many employees who use computers have a generalized feeling of depression and tiredness. Eyestrain and poor posture contribute to the problem. Yet, for many employees, the ever-present computer screen is a constant reminder to continue working rather than stretch or take a break.

Stress

Stress is something all workers face, but employees who use computers find the tireless nature of the computer a constant challenge. Stress results from the real or imagined need to keep up with co-workers and please bosses who can easily monitor computer output. It can also be a consequence of difficult-to-use software and hardware that malfunctions frequently.

Ergonomic Design

Ergonomists suggest a number of solutions to alleviate problems with computer use in the office and at home. Some involve the actual physical design and arrangement of equipment and furniture, and lighting (see Figure 7–13). Generally, a desk designed for pen or pencil writing is too high for comfort when you are typing on a computer keyboard or even looking at the monitor. Thus, the keyboard is often placed on a surface a few inches lower than desk height (which is normally about 30 inches) (see Figure 7–14). Your forearms should be neither raised nor lowered in order to reach the keyboard. If the elbows are held at a 90° angle and the arms and hands are parallel to the floor, the keyboard should be about where the thumb joints are. At the least, the wrists should be straight. For most typing purposes, your hands should "float" above the keyboard rather than resting on it. (Some keyboards, however, are designed so you

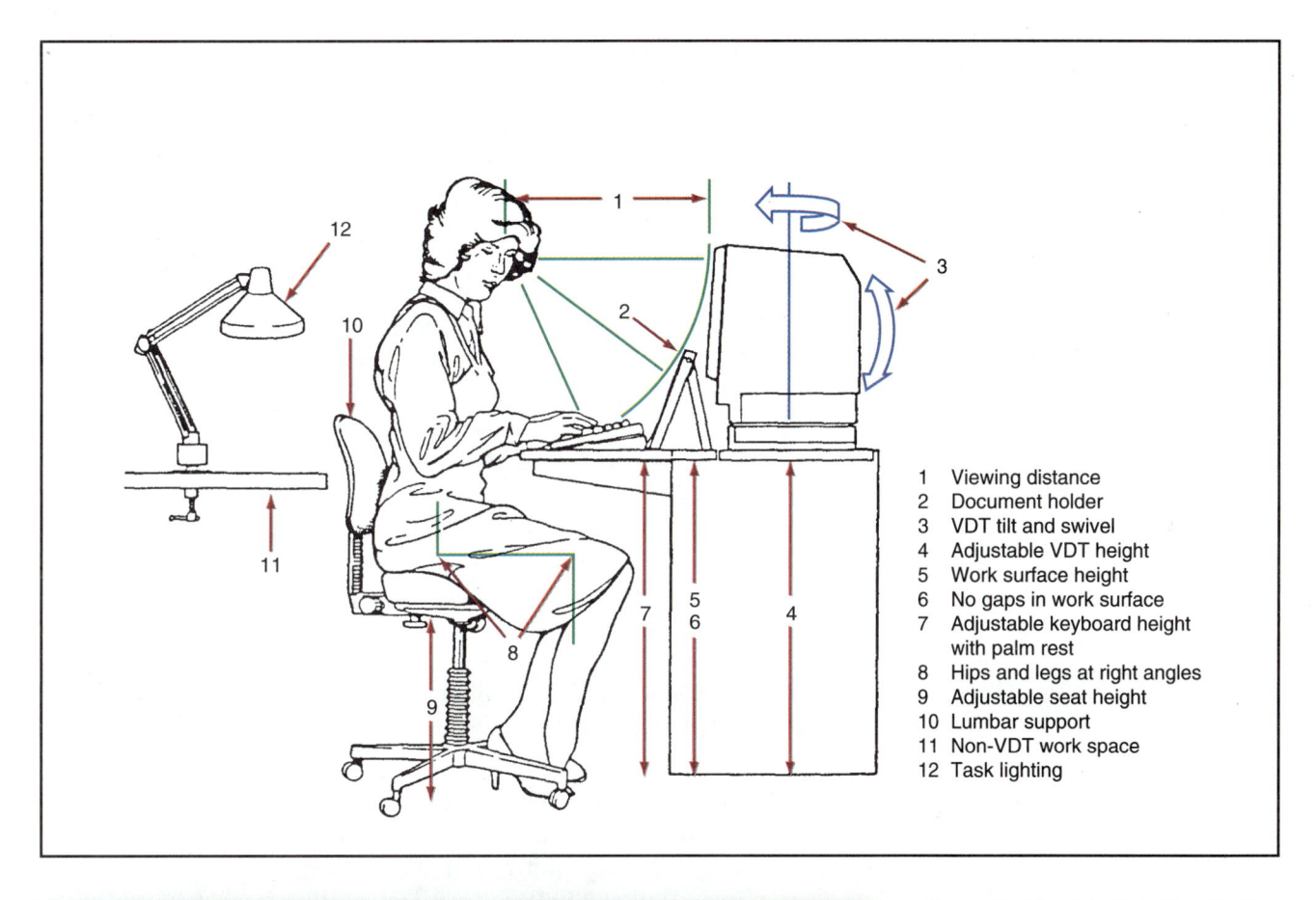

1. Viewing distance
2. Document holder
3. VDT tilt and swivel
4. Adjustable VDT height
5. Work surface height
6. No gaps in work surface
7. Adjustable keyboard height with palm rest
8. Hips and legs at right angles
9. Adjustable seat height
10. Lumbar support
11. Non-VDT work space
12. Task lighting

Figure 7–13 Workstation Design
An efficient workstation provides comfortable support for the body and the ability to view all work areas and materials. Some key features of workstation design are noted in this illustration.

Figure 7–14 Keyboard Location
Specially designed, adjustable keyboard trays are part of a good working environment. In addition, special keyboards will help you hold your hands and arms in an ergonomically correct position.

can rest your palms comfortably on them during lulls in typing). A few manufacturers, including Apple, offer keyboards that are vertically split in half and pivot outward to adjust to the user's posture. The mouse should be at the same height as the keyboard. When sliding the mouse around on the desktop, you should use your entire arm rather than anchoring your arm on the desktop and simply pivoting at the wrist.

Manufacturers of office furniture, taking suggestion from ergonomists, have begun designing chairs to help combat lower-back pain. Some of the features incorporated into a well-designed chair include controls that allow users to adjust, at the touch of a lever, the height of the seat from the floor and the height and angle of the back. A chair should also cushion and support the curve of the lower back. Some workers use backless kneeling chairs, which redistribute weight from the lower back and backside to the knees.

Reducing glare is another objective of ergonomics. Screen filters that reduce glare act to increase contrast, thereby creating less eyestrain. An antiglare filter should not interfere with the clarity of the screen display, however. Many new VDT screens are being manufactured with matte finishes to reduce glare. The screens may also come with tilt and swivel options so you can position them to avoid glare. In addition, screen resolution is being improved so the contrast of characters is sharper. (The resolution should be the same as the resolution on a printed page.) High refresh rates on monitors can also reduce eyestrain. Hard-to-read green-on-black screens are being replaced by those with black characters on white or near-white backgrounds.

Office lighting can help reduce glare from a screen, too. The best lighting is indirect and natural. If you are setting up your system near a window, be sure that you will not have to be looking toward the window to see your screen display. Similarly, sunlight coming from directly behind you can create glare on the screen display. Position your setup so the window is beside you, or else use blinds or curtains to soften the incoming light. If natural lighting is unavailable, the next best option is incandescent lighting, particularly Chromalox bulbs, which almost replicate natural daylight. If a small, focused lamp is used, however, it should not aim direct light on the screen, nor should it shine directly into your eyes. Rather, it should shine sideways on papers and not produce glare on the computer screen. Using a document holder can help eliminate some glare from papers you are reading in conjunction with your computer work.

Despite all this talk about designing an ergonomically correct office, some of the best ways to relieve stress and strains due to computing cost nothing. Primarily, ergonomists recommend that you get up frequently and walk around for a few minutes (ideally, a short stretch every half-hour, but a minimum of 15 minutes every 2 hours). This practice helps alleviate excessive fatigue and stress. In addition, correct posture can eliminate many of the problems often attributed to furniture or computer design. Once you are sitting and looking at the screen, you should train yourself to blink often in order to rest your eyes. This occurs naturally when you are reading a newspaper or book, but somehow stops when you begin reading a computer screen.

Safety Issues

If you are spending a great deal of time in front of a computer monitor, will the emissions from the monitor harm you? Recently, scientists have been seeking answers to questions about the possible health effects of long-term exposure to extremely low-frequency (ELF, from 1 Hz to 1,000 Hz) and very low-frequency (VLF, from 1,000 Hz to 400,000 Hz) electromagnetic fields. For example, they are studying the relationship between VDTs and miscarriages, which as yet is inconclusive. The issue encompasses electrical wiring, televisions, hair dryers, and other household appliances as well as computer monitors. Even wireless communications are being examined. The general consensus at this time is that the electrical and magnetic fields produced by computer monitors do not pose a great health risk. However, you should be aware that the emissions are stronger at the back and sides of the machines. (Try to stay at least 5 feet away from the back and sides of your neighbor's monitor as well.)

European countries such as Sweden and Germany have already passed legislation to protect workers' health. For example, in Sweden, the government has recommended that VDT workers spend no more than 4 hours a day at a terminal. Some European countries are regulating VDT construction and usage as a precaution against the danger of emissions from the VDTs, even though any dangers associated with VDT emissions have not been substantiated by research.

Some U.S. cities and states are considering passing laws that would reduce many of the problems VDT operators face. They are attempting to control the design of VDTs and keyboards, and they also want to require rest periods for VDT workers. In 1990, the city of San Francisco led the way by passing the first legislation to mandate ergonomics guidelines for VDT operators. Undoubtedly, similar laws will one day exist around the country.

Corporations will benefit from the legislation in the long term through increased worker health and productivity. In the meantime, you can protect yourself by buying a low-radiation monitor that adheres to the Swedish National Board for Measurement and Testing MPR II guidelines. (A more recent standard developed by TCO, Sweden's office workers union, is even more stringent on limits and requires that measurements be taken closer to the monitor than required by MPR II standards.) You can avoid the emissions of an old monitor by staying an arm's length away from the front of the monitor, because electromagnetic fields decay within that distance. In addition, using an active-matrix LCD instead of a CRT-based video display eliminates the emissions problem.

Another emission that concerns computer users is ozone gas, which can be a mild to severe irritant. This gas, which is given off in detectable levels by almost all laser printers and photocopier machines, is an unstable molecule that is produced only when the printer is printing and that quickly breaks down to oxygen.

Window on Computing

The Future Is Here: You Bet Your Life

You might not want to play this you-bet-your-life game: It occurs in the intensive care unit (ICU) of a few major hospitals throughout the world. The ICU is already scary enough, both for the patient and for the family. The patient seems nearly helpless, being hooked up to mechanical and electronic machines for monitoring life functions and for life support. And now, a few hospitals want to hedge bets on whether the patient lives or dies: They are using a computer program called APACHE III, from APACHE Medica Systems, Inc., that evaluates the patient's chances for survival.

APACHE stands for "acute physiology, age and chronic health evaluation." To use it, a doctor responds to 27 questions in the program, describing the patient's medical history, the severity of illness or injury upon arrival at the hospital, the treatment, lab results, and vital signs. Then the program compares this information with a database of over 17,000 patients treated in the past and issues daily scores that estimate the patient's likelihood of dying, the length of hospital stay, and the amount of medication and other intervention needed in the specific case. The output is a single number from 0 to 100, with 100 being the best chance of survival. Of course, the program's results are not the only factor a physician considers before charting a course of action.

APACHE is an example of case-based reasoning, which draws inferences from thousands of actual experiences. To make its evaluation, it searches a vast store of knowledge—the patient database—that a single doctor could not possibly have. Although the program sounds morbid, its use can lead to faster intervention when the program indicates improvement in a patient's condition. It can also help reduce overtreatment of terminally ill patients. Critics worry that insurance companies will be clamoring for information provided by the program in order to set rules and limits of insurance coverage based on APACHE's scores. A computer can only crunch numbers, however; thus, critical medical decisions will still be made by patients, their families, and their physicians.

In laser printers, the primary source of ozone is the corona wire, which produces an electrical discharge that makes the toner powder adhere temporarily to the print drum just before the paper passes over the drum. Laser printers that use corona wires have special filters that control the level of ozone emissions. If your laser printer has a corona wire (you can find out from the service provider), the ozone emission control system should be checked and the ozone filter replaced every 50,000 pages. Consult your owner's manual for specifics. You can also take a few precautionary measures at home to control exposure. Place your printer in a well-ventilated place. Keep the area dust free to avoid dirty filters, and be sure the printer's exhaust fan blows *away* from you.

This chapter has given you some idea of the problems associated with computer use. Yet, regardless of the problems, you can see how computers can help you learn, conduct business, achieve competency at work, and keep up with new technologies. Although you may not learn how to write a computer program or how to repair a disk drive, you can learn to employ computers in meeting challenges of the future and enriching your life.

►Summary Points

- Computer ethics concerns the standard of moral conduct for computer use. Although lapses in ethics are largely the result of human nature, any legal standards or company policies will be meaningless if people cannot or will not govern their own behavior.
- In a broad view, computer crime can be defined as any criminal act that poses a threat to computer users or is accomplished through the use of a computer.
- Four types of computer crime are sabotage, which involves damage to a computer system or software and includes viruses; theft of services, in which a government's or company's computer is used for personal gain; theft of property, in which merchandise, computers, or software are stolen; and financial crimes, in which a computer is used for illegal monetary gain.
- Today the term *hacker* designates those who try to gain unauthorized access into a particular computer system. One objective of hackers is to use services such as telephone and online information services without payment.
- Piracy is the illegal copying, use, or distribution of software. Software is protected by U.S. copyright law, which gives authors control over duplication and derivative use of their works.
- Exceptions to copyright law are public-domain software, which falls outside of copyright protection and is available for unrestricted use, and shareware, which is copyrighted material available to the public in exchange for a voluntary donation to the copyright holder.

- Companies secure their systems by creating backups of their data, using password systems, and locking up their data or their data-processing areas. They may require a number of inputs, such as fingerprints, nose prints, signatures, magnetic cards, and electronic keys, before users are granted access to their computers. A cost/benefit analysis can determine how much security is warranted in a particular company's circumstances.
- Many government agencies and private organizations keep records about people. The major privacy concerns about this proliferation of data involve the collection of too much personal information in computer files, accuracy and currency of the information, use of the information, and the security of the information.
- A number of federal laws have been enacted to deal with privacy invasions, including the Privacy Act of 1974. States have patterned their privacy legislation after this comprehensive law.
- Ergonomics is the study of relationships between people and their environment, with the goal of improving the productivity, comfort, and safety of workers. Typical problems in the ergonomics of computer workstations involve eye fatigue, aches and pains, excessive fatigue, and stress.
- Properly designed furniture and computer equipment, as well as correct lighting, can improve the ergonomics of a workstation. Practices such as getting up frequently to walk around, correcting your posture, and blinking while reading material on the computer screen does decrease discomfort while working at a computer.
- Emissions from monitors and laser printers raise the question of the safety of this equipment, but following commonsense guidelines while using such equipment decreases exposure greatly.

▶ Review Questions

1. What are computer ethics? How do ethics fit in with an organization's policies and regulations about computer use?
2. What is computer crime? List four common types of computer crime.
3. Who are the people who commit computer crime?
4. Why is hacking an important issue? What is hacking?
5. How do some companies attempt to protect copyrights of software? What benefits do authors derive from copyrighting their work?
6. List four security measures, from the text and from the figures, that companies small and large can implement to help protect their data and computer installations.

7. What major concerns do people have about the issue of privacy as it pertains to computers?
8. Name two specific ways that government has tried to deal with the issue of privacy. What are some problems with implementing privacy laws that are too restrictive?
9. How can computers and other office equipment increase the discomfort of workers who operate the machines? What is the term for the study of this relationship between people and machines?
10. Describe a few simple practices that can improve the comfort of a person using a computer.

►Activities and Research

1. What does employee loyalty have to do with computer ethics? Discuss some ways in which a corporation can protect itself against employee-committed computer crime.
2. What are some problems that a company faces when asked to comply with laws concerning people with disabilities? How could adaptations for such employees actually benefit a company?
3. Find out what you should do about software you no longer want or old disks of software for which you have obtained updates.
4. Research a topic for another issue that interests you, such as telecommuting, robots and other automation in factories, degree of access to fiber-optic cable lines, or transactions such as home shopping through computers.
5. Find out how your state protects your privacy or your company's computer installations from unwanted intrusions.

Appendix A

Consumers' Guide to Computing

Outline

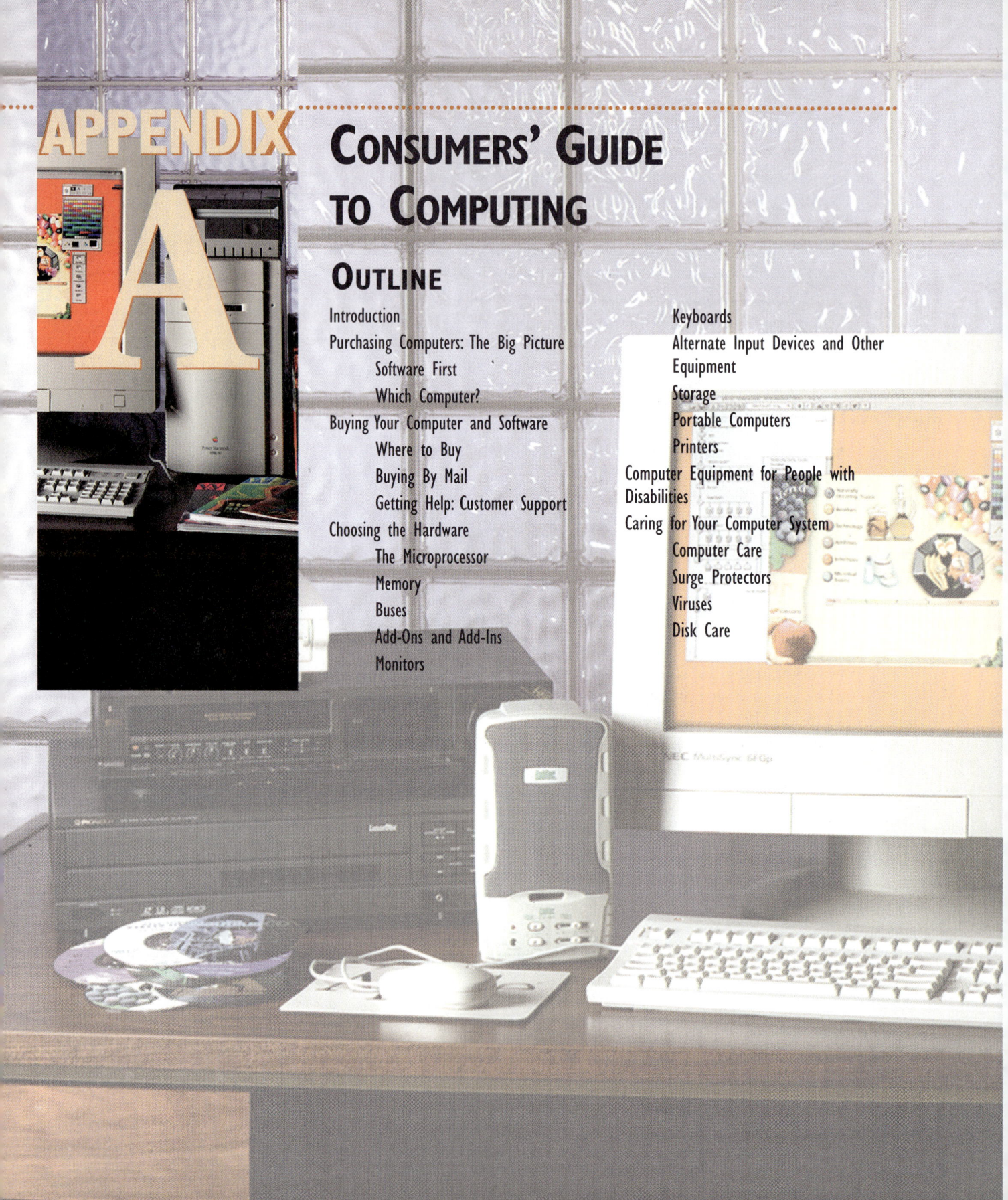

Introduction
Purchasing Computers: The Big Picture
    Software First
    Which Computer?
Buying Your Computer and Software
    Where to Buy
    Buying By Mail
    Getting Help: Customer Support
Choosing the Hardware
    The Microprocessor
    Memory
    Buses
    Add-Ons and Add-Ins
    Monitors

Keyboards
    Alternate Input Devices and Other Equipment
    Storage
    Portable Computers
    Printers
Computer Equipment for People with Disabilities
Caring for Your Computer System
    Computer Care
    Surge Protectors
    Viruses
    Disk Care

Introduction

For a number of reasons, buying a microcomputer and software can be difficult and time-consuming. As with stereo components and other appliances, there are many models of microcomputers. Choosing just one can seem impossible. Even the price range is wide—from a few hundred dollars to well over $10,000 for a high-end machine (that is, one that has great capabilities). Add to that choice the hundreds of peripheral devices, add-ons, and worthwhile software packages from which to select and the task seems indeed complex and confusing.

A computer represents a major investment for most people, so care must be taken not to make expensive mistakes. Spend time learning about the different systems on the market and analyzing what you want to do with a computer before making a decision. Otherwise, your computer purchase may end up in the closet gathering dust. The sections that follow provide some guidelines for choosing software and hardware.

►Purchasing Computers: The Big Picture

If you are buying a computer for yourself or your small business, one decision has probably already been made for you. Most likely you will be buying a microcomputer, of which there is a wide variety of options.

Experts often recommend that you choose the software and then match the hardware to the demands of that software, because the software determines how much memory you require, what kind of operating system is necessary, and whether you need high-quality graphics capabilities. Although this is a good policy, there may be other factors involved in the final decision. For example, you may need to buy a computer that is compatible with one you use at work, or you may require several software packages to accomplish the jobs you want to do. In addition, most of the new computers sold today have more than enough capabilities and memory for normal home use, such as school work, financial planning, letter writing, games, and hobby databases. Furthermore, some special uses, such as desktop publishing and multimedia, and some popular software, such as *Microsoft Windows* and *Windows* applications, work better with large amounts of memory and additional capabilities. Consider the following guidelines before choosing your new system.

1. Have a good idea of what you want to do with your computer, and try to project future needs.
2. Know the basic functions and names of both hardware and software.
3. Be sure that all equipment and software is compatible within the system.
4. Be sure you get the latest versions of items bundled with your purchase. This is important because earlier versions of some products do not work with the latest versions of other products.
5. Set price limits, but don't be overly price conscious. By identifying your intended uses, you already will have defined some price limits. Be sure you understand exactly what is included for the price. You may need additional cash outlays for printing or sound capabilities.
6. Find out about warranties, service, help, and return policies.

There is always some question about whether to buy now or wait for further reductions in price or new technologies. Today, hardware and software are already so powerful that they can meet most home computer users' needs for 5 years or more. And if you have considered future needs in your initial purchase, then you should be able to add features to your system for quite some time. Waiting for more favorable prices or new technologies can have penalties: By postponing your purchase, you are losing the values and services of a microcomputer now.

Software First

The primary question to ask yourself is what you want to do with your computer. Once you know this, you can pick software that fits your needs. To choose the best software package for you, you should educate yourself by talking with a knowledgeable friend, joining a users' group, or reading software reviews in computer magazines. You can test several programs of the type you are considering, and try more than one type of computer.

During testing, use sample data that are representative of the jobs you will be doing. Also, be sure the software will handle the amount of data you will be entering. Know about how much room you need for the software and about how much data you will be using at once—10 pages or 200 pages of text, a day's figures or a month's figures of financial data, text or complex drawings. Both software needs and data needs determine how much memory, speed, and storage to get.

Be sure the software can grow as your needs and abilities expand. A good program will let you run the program using only the basic commands needed to accomplish the application, and then allow you to learn more sophisticated commands as you need them.

Make sure that the screen display is organized clearly and logically and that the help screens are truly helpful. Evaluate your comfort level with the command style, often called the "look and feel," of the program. Check the clarity of documentation, such as user's manuals and tutorials, and look for on-screen help that you can call up as needed. Answer the following questions: How easy is the program to use? How much time do you want to spend learning how to use a program? Will you be learning many different programs, or just one or two? Do you want a menu-driven program, or do you want to learn all of the commands with no menus available? Do you want menus, with the option of using key commands? Would you feel more comfortable with a GUI?

Because much of the software you buy will be upgraded as time goes by, you may want to purchase a computer that has more capabilities than the minimum a particular software package requires. Some software is sluggish when run at minimum speed with limited memory. Having more than adequate capabilities for now will also make it easier to add to your software library later.

Which Computer?

Once you know some of the brand names of computers, you may wonder what the difference is among them. There are some very basic platforms of computers commonly found today in homes. A platform defines the standard around which a system can be developed. For example, some common platforms are Apple Macintosh computers with System 7.x, IBM-compatible PCs with *Microsoft Windows,* and IBM-compatible PCs with OS/2. Individual platforms can be specified in further detail according to the microprocessor used, the computer model name, and so on. Common Apple computers include the Performa (a mass-market computer), the Quadra, and the most recent and most powerful Apple, the Power Mac. IBM computers include the Value Point, the Aptiva, and the PS/2. IBM-compatibles are made by a myriad of companies, including Compaq, Dell, Gateway 2000, Acer, Hewlett-Packard, and Toshiba.

Some software is available for only one platform. Other packages have versions for different platforms. If the software you need requires a specific platform, then a major decision has already been resolved. Otherwise, consider a platform's ease of use, popularity, and cost.

From the beginning, Apple Macintosh computers were noted for their ease of use. This was evidenced mainly in the graphical user interface, or GUI (see Chapter 4). A GUI requires more memory, however, and may run more slowly than command-line user interfaces. In addition, some people find that using the mouse and the menus is cumbersome and slow. They often prefer the speed of key commands. On the other hand, the Macintosh GUI ensures that Macintosh programs have a consistent look and feel: Once you have learned how to operate one program, it is easy to learn the basic conventions of another. GUIs available for IBM platforms include *Microsoft Windows* and the user-friendly GUI interface in IBM's sophisticated operating system, OS/2. Experts predict that all operating systems will include GUI features in the future.

A Macintosh computer system is easy to set up, and software and hardware compatibility is less of a problem than it is with DOS-compatible machines. The sound and graphics are already built into the Macintosh computers, too. DOS-based machines are usually less expensive than the Macintoshes, however, even after you have bought the extra equipment you may need. Although you can buy an entire computer system as a package in either platform, it is also possible to buy components from different manufacturers. Especially for the PC, there seems to be a plethora of options for monitors, storage, and other equipment if you are planning on buying pieces from two or more manufacturers. This is often where the confusion begins about what to buy. It may be better to purchase your first computer as a package, with the exception perhaps of the modem and peripherals such as a printer and a scanner, until you know more about computers and have used one for a while. (A warning: Installing a new device yourself may void the warranty on your original computer or even on the new piece of equipment. Check the fine print every time you buy a new product.)

Always be sure that the components and software you buy are compatible with one another. Remember that Macintosh computers are *not* compatible with the IBM lines. They have different microprocessors and different file formats. Thus, without special software it is difficult to share data between the two types of computers. The recent joint venture among Apple, Motorola, and IBM has resulted in the production of the Power

PC, which can run software on both Macintosh computers and *Windows*-equipped IBM-compatibles. This system could provide the solution to people who have a wide variety of computing needs.

Buying Checklist

I will use my computer for the following:
- _____ Word processing
- _____ Personal finances
- _____ Business graphics
- _____ School work
- _____ Publications
- _____ Multimedia
- _____ Other (specify): _____

- _____ Office and business work at home
- _____ Record keeping (hobbies, research, etc.)
- _____ Drawing and design
- _____ Online information retrieval
- _____ Game playing
- _____ Expert systems

These factors are important to me:
- _____ Ease of use and short learning curve
- _____ Approximate number of programs
- _____ Must-have software (specify): _____
- _____ Macintosh System-7 compatibility
- _____ DOS compatibility
- _____ OS/2 compatibility
- _____ Portable model
- _____ Phone support from retailer
- _____ Online support
- _____ Users' groups
- _____ Warranties

- _____ Clarity of instruction
- _____ Accommodation of large files
- _____ Power PC
- _____ Unix compatibility
- _____ Cost (specify amount): _____
- _____ Desktop model
- _____ Phone support from manufacturer
- _____ Classes
- _____ Expandability of system
- _____ Return and refund policies

I need the following basic components and features:
- _____ 32-bit processor
- _____ 16-bit bus
- _____ Local bus
- _____ 8MB memory
- _____ Memory-management capability
- _____ 14-inch screen
- _____ Horizontal screen
- _____ Large screen
- _____ 640 by 480 resolution
- _____ Nonflickering (look for a noninterlaced monitor with a high refresh rate, 70 Hz or more)
- _____ High-quality display (no fuzziness, bleeding, or poor contrast)
- _____ Display controls for brightness, contrast, and focus
- _____ Glare shielding
- _____ Detached keyboard
- _____ Wrist pad
- _____ 80MB to 200MB hard disk drive
- _____ Tape backup system
- _____ Virus protection

- _____ Processor clock speed (specify): _____
- _____ 32-bit bus
- _____ 5 to 8 expansion slots
- _____ More than 8MB
- _____ 256K external RAM cache
- _____ 15-inch screen
- _____ Vertical screen
- _____ 256 colors at high resolution
- _____ 1,024 by 768 resolution
- _____ Screen saver
- _____ Tilt and swivel
- _____ Adjustable keyboard
- _____ High-density floppy disk drive
- _____ Hard disk of over 200MB
- _____ CD-ROM drive
- _____ Surge protection

Other components for my system include:
- _____ Math coprocessor
- _____ Sound
- _____ Mouse
- _____ Speakers or headphones
- _____ Other (specify): _____
- _____ Dot-matrix printer
- _____ Laser printer
- _____ Adaptations for special needs (specify): _____

- _____ Graphics coprocessor
- _____ Modem or fax-modem
- _____ Scanner
- _____ Microphone
- _____ Ink-jet printer
- _____ Special printer needs (specify): _____

▶Buying Your Computer and Software

Once you have decided on the software you want and have determined its hardware requirements, you are ready to make the purchase. Should you go to a computer store? order by mail? The following sections offer some suggestions about purchasing your system.

Where to Buy

As a home computer buyer, you probably will purchase your computer and peripheral equipment from a retailer or a mail-order house. Retailers include department stores, office supply stores, computer stores, and computer chain stores. In addition, some national computer chains, such as CompUSA, have built large superstores that stock a wide variety of devices and software. The sales personnel at some department stores and outlets may lack the knowledge or sensitivity you need in making your choices, so be sure you feel comfortable with the salespeople. Computer stores are often staffed with knowledgeable people and in most cases have an in-house service department. You also get a hands-on prepurchase trial there. Buying through a local store makes it easier to return the computer to have additional hardware installed, too. Prices at such stores, however, are usually higher than at the other types of stores mentioned. And the salespeople may know about only the models they sell.

Some computers are sold exclusively through mail order, and since mail-order prices can also be very good, you may want to consider this option. If you are not buying through the manufacturer, be sure the reseller is authorized to pass on the manufacturer's warranty.

Each computer product you buy, whether through a store or a mail-order house, should be covered by a warranty. This includes a specified amount of time during which you can return the product for refund—usually a 30-day, money-back guarantee. Warranties should be firm and in writing. Usually valid for 1 to 5 years, they provide for the replacement of faulty parts or the entire unit, excepting obvious user abuse, any time within this time period. Ask the dealer if the system maker's warranty covers the entire computer, including the hard disk drive. Also be aware of any action that might invalidate the warranty, such as installing a component yourself or using a product such as an inferior laser printer toner cartridge.

Buying by Mail

Buying computers by mail may mean lower prices; but just as often, it is the convenience that attracts a mail-order shopper. Reputable companies offer high-quality machines, good service, telephone inquiries, and meaningful warranties. Many mail-order computer companies emphasize value, not price. They offer convenience and service, especially for communities that may not have a computer store. You should be able to call a mail-order company, place an order, receive it overnight or in a few days, try out the product for 15 to 30 days, and, if not satisfied, return it cash back, without hassle. Technical help will probably be available by phone, and repair services timely and efficient. Warranties will likely be for no less than a year. The products sold by reputable mail-order companies typically contain exactly the chips, the memory, the drives, and so on that the system's designers intended the system to have and advertised to have.

Ordering computer equipment by mail has the disadvantages that orders can get fouled up and equipment you receive might be faulty. Most companies, however, help you fix the problems over the telephone or will send replacements quickly. When you buy from a mail-order house, you should know exactly what you want and feel comfortable with the knowledge you have about computers.

Most of the rules for mail-ordering computer equipment are the same as for ordering clothes, gifts, furniture, or any other products by mail. Research whether the company you are dealing with is reputable, either by reading reviews or talking to knowledgeable friends. You might also check with the Better Business Bureau in the dealer's area. You can even ask the vendor for a list of customers in your area that you can contact to find out about the vendor's performance. Any magazines that carry the vendor's advertisements can also tell you whether any complaints have been registered. Several computer magazines have also carried articles rating mail-order vendors and brand-name resellers. You can locate these articles through library services such as the *Reader's Guide to Periodical Literature* and computer search services. Also, know exactly how you are planning to use the equipment so that the equipment you order will be powerful enough to run the software you will be using and produce the output you need.

Guidelines to Buying Mail-Order Computer Equipment

1. Be sure the dealer you telephone is authorized to give you the manufacturer's warranty.
2. Clarify everything about your order (full name of the person taking the order, order number, firm price, make, size, exact components, whether the parts are new or reconditioned, and so on), and have the salesperson repeat your order. Verify that your order is in stock, and ask for a delivery date.
3. Follow your phone call with a letter that lists all details and policies to which you have agreed.
4. Keep all the information about your order in a special folder, even the advertisement that prompted your order. Include the date you placed your order.
5. Always pay by credit card, because your credit-card company can back you up if there is some dispute and if you have followed the credit-card company's guidelines for making a claim against the vendor. The credit-card company may also be able to give you added warranty protection.
6. When the package arrives, check the condition of the cartons. Do not sign for a package that looks as if it has been mishandled—that is, one that is badly crushed or torn. Otherwise, open the package immediately and verify the shipment.
7. Keep the original packing materials in case you must return the products for repair or refunds.
8. Try the equipment to be sure it works correctly before sending in the warranty cards.
9. Watch out for extra fees, such as additional shipping or handling charges, restocking fees (for returned merchandise), or accessory costs, that may not have been added to the price of the product.
10. Be aware that many mail-order companies require you to call for a return authorization number before you return any products.
11. Be wary of restrictions on sales ("All sales final," "Refunds for credit only," or "Returns subject to approval"), and watch out for disclaimers in advertisements that say compatibility is not guaranteed.
12. Be sure you understand a company's policy regarding substitutions and replacements.

Getting Help: Customer Support

When you first open the packing boxes holding your new hardware or software, you will find user's manuals that tell you how to install and operate the product. Even well-written documentation may not be adequate for describing a very complex activity, however. When you are stumped, you should be able to call the location where you bought the product to receive help. If you can travel to the dealer's location, you can ask the dealer to demonstrate how to do a particular job. Otherwise, you will have to rely on a telephone call.

Most companies provide an 800 number to call, often called a "hot line." The company person you reach should be well enough informed to provide advice and troubleshooting tips. Increasingly, companies are offering free support only for the first 30 to 90 days after you place the initial call, thereafter charging for technical help via 900 phone numbers. Many companies have fax-back or MCI mail help, too.

Some companies offer online electronic bulletin boards staffed by technicians. You can leave a message on the bulletin board and a technician will respond. You can also download software updates that correct bugs or simplify a procedure. Bulletin boards, and often the 800 numbers, are available 24 hours a day, which is convenient if you work late into the night or if you are in a different time zone than the company. Online information utilities such as GEnie and CompuServe may offer manufacturers' forums through which products and problems are discussed.

If you require more help than a phone call can provide—for example, if you need to learn how to use a complex software package—consider attending classes, workshops, and seminars offered in your community. Call the local schools, scout troops, YMCA, community colleges, vocational schools, colleges, and universities to find out if these organizations have any upcoming sessions that are open to the public.

Most newsstands and bookstores carry a wide variety of magazines that cover computer uses, equipment, software, games, and online access. In many localities, you'll find users' groups, that is, informal groups of owners of a particular microcomputer or program who exchange information about their systems. (Users' groups also form around applications and related topics, such as real estate, medicine, desktop publishing, and education.) The value of users' groups comes from the accumulation of knowledge and experience ready to be shared by members. Finding a local group is not always easy. Dealers and manufacturers may have information on such groups.

►Choosing the Hardware

Increasingly, office supply stores and other large retail outlets offer complete computer systems that will serve basic computing needs for many families. The prices are good, and much of the decision making about equipment has been done for you. These systems often are not powerful enough for complex graphics tasks and desktop publishing, however. To purchase a system that suits more than basic computing needs, you will probably want to buy a more powerful computer. This may involve purchasing the components separately. The following sections describe some of the features to look for in the individual components of a computer system.

THE MICROPROCESSOR

An ad says a particular manufacturer offers a 66 MHz 486DX2 system, a description that is meaningless unless you know that the numbers refer to the type of microprocessor (or processor) the system contains. Microprocessors are identified in three primary ways: the model number or name, the bandwidth (or bit architecture), and the clock speed. Intel, which supplies microprocessors for IBM and Tandy, is well known for its various 80486 (often shortened to "486") and Pentium microprocessors. Apple Macintosh computers use 68030 or 68040 microprocessor manufactured by the Motorola Corp. Motorola also produces the Power PC 601 processor used in Apple Power Mac computers.

CPU power also depends on the bit architecture and the clock speed of the microprocessor. *Bit architecture* (or internal design) determines how much data the computer can handle at once. The most common architecture today is the 32-bit design, in which the CPU can handle 32 bits, or 4 bytes, of data at once. The more data a CPU can handle, the faster the computer operates. The bit architecture is sometimes called the *bandwidth* or the *word size*. Most of today's microprocessors are 32-bit processors.

Clock speed is the speed at which the CPU executes an instruction. It is described in terms of a megahertz rating. Mega means *million* and hertz means *number of cycles,* or *pulses, per second*. A megahertz, abbreviated MHz, is equal to 1 million cycles, or ticks, per second. The CPU requires a fixed number of these ticks to execute each instruction. Every computer has an internal clock that regulates this speed and synchronizes the various components of the computer. The faster the clock—that is, the higher the CPU's megahertz rating—the faster the computer. Microprocessor clock speeds range from 25 to well over 100 MHz, although the most common are 50, 60, 66, and 90 MHz.

Programs written for use with high-end microprocessors will not run on less powerful microprocessors, although programs written for the lower-end microprocessors are compatible with the high-end microprocessors. Your best bet is to try out your main application on each of the configuration combinations you are considering.

MEMORY

Every computer comes with a certain amount of RAM, but RAM chips can be added to increase the amount of memory. It is best to fill up the motherboard with chips before adding a separate memory expansion board, because the chips on the board can access the CPU directly without going through the expansion bus. Remember that the stated minimum amounts of memory may be barely adequate to run a particular software package. More is better. Many computers come with a standard 4MB of memory, but most experts recommend 8MB. You may want to compare the cost of buying more than enough memory at the outset with the cost of adding memory later. Also look at the amount of memory in the RAM cache. The recommended amount is 256K.

A discussion of additional memory can become quite complicated when focused on IBM computers and compatibles. This is due to the way DOS was designed. Back in the early days of personal computing, engineers believed that 1MB or RAM was all that would ever be needed by microcomputer users. Of that 1MG of RAM, the first 640K of memory, called *conventional memory,* was available to users. The remaining 384K, called *upper memory,* was for special system functions. Soon, users were wanting to create complex graphics and large spreadsheets, and there wasn't enough memory for that. So the engineers had to figure out how to trick the computer into creating more memory. They came up with a number of options over the years, including *expanded memory* and *extended memory.*

You may need additional memory and a special operating system or memory-management program to "tweak," or fine-tune, your system to use all available memory for running software. Your computer store or user group can help you with this problem. The new *Windows 95,* being independent of DOS, bypasses this problem. Other operating systems for IBM-compatible computers—Windows NT and OS/2—also circumvent the problem. With Macintosh computers, which are based on a different operating system, you have never had to worry about this block to memory size.

Buses

A *bus* is a collection of wires through which data is sent from one part of the computer to another. The bus commonly referred to in computer advertisements is the *expansion bus,* which lets all of the various computer components, such as expansion boards (or adapter cards), and external devices, such as printers, communicate with CPU. Your computer will come with the bus built in. You really don't need to know much about the bus except to be sure that the devices you purchase are compatible with the bus your computer has. One thing to watch for, however, is the number of expansion slots the bus provides. Having only three slots can cripple the expansion of your system. Five to eight is better.

In computer advertisements, you may see references to the *local bus.* The local bus actually refers to the bus on which the CPU sits. The advantage of having the local bus option is that video chips or other items can be inserted directly into the motherboard for faster processing. As yet, there is no standard for the local bus, but the Video Electronics Standards Association (VESA) has announced its standard for IBM and compatibles called *VESA Local Bus (VL-Bus)*. This design concept has been used on the Macintosh, where it is called the *processor direct slot*.

Add-Ons and Add-Ins

Items that you add to the computer's inner circuitry or to a program are often called *add-ins* and *add-ons*. These products can be hardware or software capabilities that increase the power of your computer. The main software packages you use determine the add-ins and add-ons you need.

Although some people use the terms to mean the same thing, the technical usage applies to different products. *Add-in* applies to chips you install on a board that is already located inside the computer. Memory chips and coprocessor chips are add-ins installed on the motherboard, for example. (Coprocessor chips take over some of the computing, such as mathematical calculations or graphics calculations, from the main processor.) The term *add-on* describes a circuit board, cartridge, or program that is installed to increase the capabilities of a computer or software. *Add-in* rarely is used in referring to these items.

A number of circuit boards, or *expansion cards* as they are also called, can be added to a computer. The primary ones add memory, sound, video, speed, or modems to your computer. You can also use boards for attaching scanners, mice, fax capabilities, disk drives, and light pens to your system. The boards are inserted into slots on the expansion bus, and since there is only a limited number of slots, you must plan your configuration carefully. Today's computers have so many capabilities built in that you may not need additional boards.

Monitors

Some microcomputers, notably portables, have built-in video displays. For most systems, however, you will have to purchase a monitor. Your ability to see the displays on your monitor and to minimize related eyestrain can be important factors in determining your productivity and the quality of results delivered by your microcomputer. Factors to consider include the following:

- The clarity and dimensions of the screen display
- The focus, contrast, and brightness of the displayed image
- The color values of the display

Monitors offer varying levels of image resolution, or *clarity*. The resolution is determined by the number of image points, or *pixels* (picture elements), on its screen. The greater number of pixels, the better the resolution. Common resolutions are 640 by 480 and 1,024 by 768. In a monitor described as 640 by 480, the pixels are arranged in 480 lines of 640 pixels each.

The maximum resolution and the color that you see on a screen is determined by the monitor, but special software is needed for governing the use of pixels and colors. This software, in the form of logic circuitry, is stored in chips often plugged into the local bus or placed on a video board (also called *video adapter card, video display card,* or *graphics card*). The video board and the monitor work together, and thus the monitor must have the required number of pixels to support the resolution that a particular board offers. Most new systems support the current graphics capability, so you may not need to worry about video circuitry unless you are upgrading a system or purchasing components built by different manufacturers. You will simply look for video boards with high graphics capability, enough memory to support 256 colors at high resolution (at least 1 MB), and a high refresh rate—that is, the rate at which images are redrawn. Video boards that support higher refresh rates—of 70 Hz and over—will help reduce or eliminate annoying flicker. Judge your own reaction to flicker, for it affects people differently.

You might read all you can about monitors, but the best way to judge a monitor for its quality, clarity, and glare is simply to look at it. Be sure to look at graphic displays, as well as character displays. Eliminate any prospective monitors that show fuzzy lettering, bleeding colors, or poor contrast. Pay attention to the clarity and accuracy of the colors. On a clear screen, such as an empty word processor screen, look for evenness of tone without a noticeable dark spot. Check to see whether straight lines bow in or out at the center of the screen and whether the images are as sharp and clear at the edges as they are at the center of the screen.

Make sure there is a way to control the brightness, contrast, and focus the display, which will permit you to adjust the display to suit the lighting conditions of the room in which you are working. Glare can be a stubborn nuisance, too. Most new monitors are designed to reduce glare, either by the shape of the screen or by some type of antiglare property. Snap-on glare covers are available for most monitors as well. Tilt-and-swivel display stands can provide a better viewing angle for the elimination of glare and to minimize muscle tension in the neck.

Most monitors are 14-inch displays or smaller, but large-screen models are available that show displays of 15, 16, 17, 20, or 21 inches. (The dimensions are measured as with television screens—in inches diagonally across the screen from one corner to the opposite corner.) A GUI such as *Windows* works best with at least a 15-inch screen. If you will be doing desktop publishing or graphic work, you may want to investigate the large screens. Unfortunately, large-screen monitors are expensive and heavy, weighing up to 50 pounds.

Keyboards

Keyboards for microcomputers are available in one of two forms. They can be built in to the computer case or detached from it. Laptop and notebook computers have keyboards designed in the computer case. Some older Apple products also have the keyboard in the same unit as the computer. Detached keyboards on desktop models may be either connected to the computer by a cord or operated remotely by batteries. Battery-operated keyboards are linked with the CPU through infrared or radio-frequency transmitters. Keyboards that are part of the machine's enclosure cannot be adjusted, and typing for long periods of time on these can be tiresome. Detachable keyboards usually adjust to two or more angles.

The only way you can chose a keyboard that suits your typing style is to try out a number of keyboards and decide for yourself. The feel of the keys and the "thipping" sound varies from keyboard to keyboard, but the standard touch-sensitive keys on most computers are faster and quieter than typewriter keys. You may want a wrist pad to support your wrists while typing. You might also consider one of the new, ergonomically correct keyboards in unusual shapes and angles designed to decrease the occurrence of repetitive-strain injuries.

Most desktop computers have numeric keypads built into their keyboards. These conform to the standard layout of calculator keypads, with the characters 0 through 9, a decimal point, arithmetic functions, a *Clear* key, and an *Enter* key.

ALTERNATE INPUT DEVICES AND OTHER EQUIPMENT

Keyboard entry may be too slow or awkward for some jobs. You can buy a number of different input tools that enable you to bypass the keyboard for entering commands or using graphics software (see Chapter 2). Among the most common are the mouse and its variation, the trackball. Before buying one of these devices, test the ones you like by sitting down at the computer and trying them. (You cannot administer a true test while standing.)

Depending on the complexity of the tasks you need to perform, you might require specific equipment such as the following:

- Graphics tables
- Joystick
- Light pen
- Touch screen
- Scanner
- Microphone
- Voice synthesizer
- Voice recognition unit
- External modem or fax modem
- Speakers or headphones

These devices are application specific. If your applications lend themselves to use of these units, read magazine articles and product literature to familiarize yourself with the available options. A users' group can also help you determine your needs for such equipment. (Remember that multimedia applications require equipment that may not come with your computer.)

STORAGE

The storage devices that come with most computer systems are the hard disk drive and the floppy disk drive. The general rule of thumb for hard disk drives is to buy the largest capacity you can afford. Disk capacities of 270MB, 540MB, and up to 1.37GB are common.

Just because you will be using a hard disk drive doesn't mean you don't need a floppy disk drive. Since most software comes on floppy disks, you will need the floppy disk drive in order to transfer the software to your hard disk drive. Most likely this drive will handle 3.5-inch floppy disks, which are encased in hard plastic. A small spring-activated shutter covers the read/write notch where the disk drive accesses the disk. Most drives today handle double-sided, high-density disks (*high density* refers to the amount of data that can be packed onto the disk). You probably will not need a drive that handles the old 5.25-inch floppy disks.

Other drives you may want to consider are the following:

- High-capacity tape cassette or cartridge system for backing up the contents of your hard disk
- CD-ROM drive for use with multimedia applications

PORTABLE COMPUTERS

Laptop and notebook computers used to be a novelty. Up until now, they have lagged behind the technology of desktop models, being used primarily for the special needs for computing-on-the-run of salespeople or students. They were not serious contenders as replacements for desktop PCs; in fact, most of their data had to be downloaded onto PCs for serious computing to take place. Thus, the small size of laptops was not enough to win over serious PC users.

Today, notebook computers are powerful enough to be your only personal computer. The notebooks, weighing in at under 8 pounds, are more powerful machines than earlier laptops and at a reduced price, too. The high-capacity hard disk and the amount of memory are what turned the portable computer from a specialized device into a computer for general use. Most notebooks use the same microprocessors as found in popular desktop models. With 4MB to 5MB of RAM and an 80MB hard disk drive, notebook computers can comfortably handle most applications.

A significant difference between notebooks and desktop models is the display. A regular desktop model uses a television-like screen that is almost as deep as it is wide. The notebook uses a flat-panel technology, often liquid-crystal display (LCD), which looks like the display on a digital watch. Flat-panel screens are less bulky and require less power than monitors. The image is not as sharp as images on high-quality desktop monitors, but flat-panel displays are improving and are already available in color. Most screens display VGA-resolution images.

The keyboards on notebook computers approximate the keyboards on desktop models. The spacing between the keys and the size of the keys are generally the same, but the location of function keys may vary among the different brands. Some models include a trackball. For reasons of space, numeric keypads are not included, but they can be purchased as external devices to plug into the computer.

Battery life on notebook computers is still a problem. Although most laptops employ several power conservation technologies, battery life is usually 7 to 8 hours. Recharge time can run into a couple of hours, too. You can also plug notebook computers into the wall outlet for use.

Printers

Your choice of printers includes a range of devices that deliver wide variations in speed, quality, and price. The printer you purchase should conform to the work you will be doing. If you will be doing a lot of writing that requires rough drafts, a dot-matrix printer may be all you need. Dot-matrix printers also print the outputs of graphics programs, but with low- to middle-quality results. For higher quality output, consider an ink-jet printer. If your work requires high-quality output for both graphics and text, you'll need a laser printer. Once you have decided what type of printer you need, you can begin to shop for quality and price. Always obtain some output from each printer you are considering, and compare it with samples of the output you need to produce. You will pay more for faster speeds and higher print quality.

Most printers use standard-size sheet paper, although some have a wide carriage for larger, fan-fold paper. In addition, many printers are adapted for heavy-stock paper, envelopes, postcards, and labels. Printers that accept paper by the sheet are friction-fed, and normally have paper trays that hold from 50 to 250 sheets at a time. Ink-jet and laser printers are sheet-fed printers. Dot-matrix printers, on the other hand, are usually tractor-fed machines, with teeth or pins on wheels attached to both sides of the printer that catch into holes along both sides of continuous paper folded accordion-style into a fan-fold stack and then draw the paper into the printer. When printing is finished, you tear the sheets apart along the perforated cuts. You can usually adapt a tractor-fed printer to accept single sheets of paper by attaching a sheet feeder, basically a molded plastic bin that allows for automatic feeding and stacking of individual sheets of paper.

Remember that each type of printer has extra costs in the form of consumables such as special paper, ribbons, and toner.

►Computer Equipment for People with Disabilities

Computers have opened an entirely new world for people with special needs. Such equipment ranges from special software to special adjustments for individuals with limited motor control. In fact, entire computer systems have been designed to enable even those who are most physically limited to communicate using a puff of air or an eye twitch or a chin movement.

For those with motor control difficulties, there are special keyboards with large keys. And miniature keyboards are available for people who have the use of only one hand or who must wield a typing stick to press the keys. Other innovations enable even the most seriously disabled to work at a computer. The user employs a simple tool or switch to enter a selection from a menu into the computer. The switches have been designed to work with any muscle the individual can control. Joysticks with fire buttons are the most common of these switches. Lever switches activate with head motion, and leaf switches are used with the elbow, under the chin, or in the mouth. Brow-wrinkle switches are attached to the forehead with a sweatband. For those who can breathe only and not move, sip-and-puff straws enable them to activate the switch via blowing and inhaling.

There are two ways selections can be displayed for use with these various types of switches. One is an alphanumeric scanner on the screen that continuously highlights a set of letters and numbers, one after another. By activating the switch for the appropriate highlighted letter, the user can build up words, write programs, and run software. The other type of system simply displays the keyboard or menus on the screen and works with a point-and-shoot device. Usually, this device acts as a mouse and is mounted on the head. Once the selection is pointed at, the user enters the selection by activating a switch or puffing a breath. The switch or the puff straw is usually attached to the headset. This type of data entry is time consuming, but it works. Most of these systems can be used with word-prediction software to eliminate some of the time-consuming selections. Word-prediction software anticipates what word the user is entering by printing a list of possibilities, whereupon the user can either enter additional letters to narrow the possibilities or pick one word from the list.

The ultimate in technology for people with disabilities is the Eyegaze Computer System from LC Technologies of Fairfax, VA. This system substitutes light for touch. It operates by detecting the retinal reflection produced when light strikes the eyeball. This phenomenon is called "bright eye." The user just focuses his gaze on the monitor. A low-power infrared light mounted below the monitor screen illuminates the eye. The beam is reflected off the cornea, then picked up by the image-processing software on the monitor that continually computes where on the screen the gaze is aimed. A selection is made by a longer duration of the gaze, actually only a fraction of a second. As the user becomes more proficient with the system, the duration time of the gaze can be reduced to speed up the process. The monitor can display a virtual keyboard or menus for controlling the environment or communicating with people.

Other systems rely on spoken commands. Two of the companies associated with voice recognition are Dragon System, Inc., and Kurzweil Applied Intelligence, Inc. Generally, a voice recognition system with a large vocabulary must be "trained" to recognize the speaker's voice. The speaker must enunciate clearly and pause between words. Voice-recognition systems enable a person with a disability not only to use a computer, but also to control the environment by actually telling the computer to do certain things, such as turn off the lights or turn on the oven.

Blind people can work on computers that use braille or speech synthesizers. They can also buy braille printers, braille displays (on which they feel the output in the patterns made by the braille dots), and braille keyboards. They do not have to rely on braille devices, but instead can purchase speech synthesizers for use with optical-recognition software. These systems—used either with microcomputers or as stand-alone configurations—scan printed material and produce output as synthesized speech. The actual speech synthesizer is an add-on board. It turns letters into *phonemes*, the smallest units of speech, and outputs the speech through a speaker located outside the computer.

►Caring for Your Computer System

The key to keeping computers and disks in good working order is to use common sense when handling them. Care should begin as soon as you purchase the computer. When you select the system, it is advisable to include surge protectors, virus protection, and screen savers, as discussed in the subsections that follow. When transporting your system home (or anywhere else, for that matter), be sure never to leave it in a hot car for an extended period of time. Before touching your new equipment (and before every use thereafter), make sure your hands are clean. After unpacking the equipment, save the original packaging in case you want to transport your system again. Select a clean room with humidity that is neither too high nor too low for your system. Set the computer on a sturdy desk or table away from direct sunlight, heating units, and air conditioners. Then follow the hints for continual care that are discussed next.

Computer Care

When connecting or unplugging the equipment, always hold the cable by the connector at one end rather than by the cord. *Always* use a grounded outlet, and *never* attach an adapter plug to bypass the three-pronged grounding. Do not force a connector into a socket. The cables should be firmly connected at the sockets. If you cannot get the pieces to join easily, call the dealer or a technician for help. If a cable becomes frayed or otherwise damaged, disconnect it. Any time you add or remove a piece of equipment, always unplug the machines from the electrical receptacles.

Always follow the manufacturer's instructions for starting up and turning off your system. There is usually a short ritual of steps, to be taken in a given order, that will protect your hard disk drive and other components. Generally, it is advisable to turn the computer on and off as few times as possible during a day: Once on and once off is the rule, unless you are going to be away from the computer for more than 4 hours. This is because moving parts suffer wear and because nonmoving parts are affected by the power surge and temperature changes of start-up. Turn the computer off at night.

While the computer is turned on, avoid moving it or jolting it or the table on which it sits. Be especially cautious if you have a hard disk drive system. If you should accidentally bump a processor unit with an internal hard drive or even an external hard disk drive, the disk could contact the read/write heads and crack or break. During hard disk operation, the head does not touch the disk. If a head crash occurs, however, then the head has scratched or burned the disk and you will need to replace both the head and the disk. Head crash can happen when dust gets in the system or if you jolt the computer during operation. Most hard disks have an automatic head "parking" feature that locks the head in a safe position so the disk will not be damaged when you transport the system.

Do not block the vents on any piece of equipment. Before touching the computer, be sure to ground yourself, to discharge static electricity. Touch a metal object, for example, or stand on an antistatic mat at the computer. Static electricity can damage the tiny circuits in the computer. You can buy mats for under the keyboard and other components that help prevent damage from static electricity.

When you are finished with the computer, cover the equipment with a static-free dust covers. Dust and dirt carry electric charges that can break the flow of current through the microcomputer. An accumulation of dust can also create a buildup of heat that might cause chips to fail. Debris lodged in a floppy disk drive can increase the number of input and output errors you experience.

Food, liquids, eraser crumbs, paper clips, and other such materials should be kept away from the equipment. Food crumbs, eraser crumbs, and small items such as miniature paper clips can lodge between and under the keys, causing them to malfunction. Sticky materials such as soft drinks and fruit juices can jam the keys on the keyboard, or, worse, cause the electronic parts to fail. If a thin, clear liquid is accidentally spilled on the keyboard, turn off the system, turn the keyboard upside down to let the liquid drain out, and let it dry for at least 24 hours. This may avoid repair costs. If the liquid is sticky, however, you should take the keyboard to your dealer for repair. (You can buy lightweight, flexible, transparent keyboard covers through which you can type, although these may shift annoyingly if you are a speedy typist.)

Treat other equipment, such as printers, with the same care as you do your computer. Read the directions that come with each peripheral to see if any unusual care rules should be followed. For example, the instructions that come with laser printers may recommend that you remove the toner cartridge before moving the printer. External disk drives may come with special antistatic wrappers to cover the cable connector that plugs into the computer. The cover should be placed on the cable end whenever the disk drive is disconnected from the computer.

If you are leaving your computer and monitor on for extended periods of time during which you are not using it, turn down the brightness control on the monitor. Otherwise, the image on the screen could "burn in" and permanently damage the screen. There are *screen-saver* programs available that remove or vary the image on the screen when the computer is on but idle. *Screen blankets* black out or dim the screen, and *screen animators* display images that continually move around the screen so that no one image is in a particular location long enough to burn into the screen. Some screen savers must be activated by a user command, and others activate automatically after a particular image has been displayed for a specified time.

Before cleaning equipment, be sure to disconnect the power cord. Most user's manuals recommend cleaning equipment casings with a soft, damp (but not wet) cloth. Add a drop of liquid detergent to the cloth to remove stubborn stains or dirt. Do not use household cleansers, ammonia, powders, or solvents such as cleaning fluid, any of which can mar the finish on the casings. On new monitors, a small amount of household glass cleaner can be sprayed on a soft cloth, to wipe the screen. (Be sure to check the manuals for how to clean the monitors of computers that are older than 5 years or so.) Do not spray the cleaner directly onto the screen, however, because the liquid may drip into the interior of the machine and cause electrical damage. You should also clean the mouse on a routine basis. Most user's manuals will tell you how to disassemble and clean a mouse. The insides of printers can usually be cleaned to remove paper dust and bits of paper. Use a soft brush, a lint-free cloth, or a small can of compressed air. Some manufacturers may recommend a miniature vacuum cleaner rather than compressed air, however, because compressed air tends to blow dust and dirt even further into a machine's components. These vacuums can work on your keyboard, too. Your dealer or mail-order house may also stock special cleaning kits.

Even though you take the greatest care, there may be times when equipment or software does not work. The problem may be simple to find. First, check that the machine is properly plugged in and that the connections to printers and disk drives are secure. Second, read the manual. It may give troubleshooting tips for some types of problems. And third, try to run the software in another machine. If it does not work in a second or third machine, the problem may be with the software rather than the hardware. If these simple checks do not solve the problem, it is time to call an expert.

SURGE PROTECTORS

You may wonder what effect there is on your computer when it is already on and the room lights flicker. Such a slight drop in power is called a *sag;* a prolonged sag is called a *brownout.* When a sudden drop is followed by a sudden increase in power that lasts just fractions of a second, a *spike* has occurred. An increase in power that lasts somewhat longer is called a *surge.*

No community is exempt from occasional surges or drops in power, or even complete power failures. Your computer could flick off, in which case you would lose any unsaved data. In addition, the hard disk drive could be damaged. All computers come with some surge protection built into the power supply unit, but it is a good idea to buy a separate device called a *surge protector* or *surge suppressor.* This device prevents sudden and powerful electrical variations from harming your system by collecting and diffusing the excess voltage before it can reach your computer. It usually has six or more sockets into which you plug your computer, printer, and other peripherals. Surge protectors generally cost anywhere from $10 to a few hundred dollars.

Most computers can withstand prolonged voltage dips of about 20 percent. But for even greater protection, you can buy a UPS, or uninterruptible power supply. A UPS is a power supply with a battery that, in the event of a complete power outage, maintains power, keeping the computer running for the few minutes it would take you to save data that is in RAM and to shut down the system according to the manufacturer's directions. One type of UPS is the standby power system (SPS), which monitors the power and activates as soon as it detects a problem. By this method, however, there will be a few milliseconds during the switch when the computer is not receiving any power. An online UPS system avoids this power lapse by providing continual power even when the power line is functioning properly. Either type of UPS may cost more than a home user is willing to spend, however, and offers more protection than is usually needed.

Warning: A surge protector or UPS will *not* protect your computer from lightning. Be sure to disconnect your computer from the electrical outlets (and from the telephone outlet if you use a modem) if a lightning storm is expected or when you are leaving for a trip.

VIRUSES

There has been at least one instance of commercial software being infected by a virus. Aldus Corp. unwittingly made thousands of copies of a graphics software package named *Freehand* that was contaminated with the so-called "Peace" virus. On March 2, 1988, a universal message of peace was displayed on the screens of several thousand Macintosh computers when they were turned on. The viral program then deleted itself.

Some of the recent viruses are not as innocuous as the Peace virus. Two brothers in a computer store in Lahore, Pakistan, sold cut-rate software that they had infected with a virus. When the software disk was inserted into a computer, the virus would copy itself into the computer's memory, where it would later be copied onto other disks placed into the machine. It would then scramble the contents of these disks. The brothers said they created the virus to punish purchasers of bootlegged software.

So what is a virus? It is a program that can, without a person's knowledge, change the way a computer operates or change the programs or data files stored on the computer. The virus copies itself onto another program by adding itself to the program or by overwriting some of the codes in the program. Its primary task is replication. Examples include: Stoned, which displays the message "Your PC is stoned—LEGALIZE MARIJUANA" while at the same time destroying the information that makes it possible to access files on your disk; Cascade, in which all characters on the screen collapse to the bottom of the display; Joshi, which is a *bomb* (any computer virus that is triggered by a date, a time, or an event); and Jerusalem-B, a bomb that erases programs you try to run on any Friday the 13th and writes black boxes to your screen.

A virus ridges piggyback on another program. A variation of the virus is the *worm,* a self-contained program that works its way through computer systems. In early March 1988, a computer science graduate student released a worm that ultimately jammed 6,000 computers around the United States. Within 24 hours, it had spread to approximately 100,000 computers. The worm was passed through the Internet, which back then tied together a large number of university and government computer systems. The worm wound itself through the computers, using up valuable computer time and memory space. Fortunately, this was a "benign" worm that did not destroy data. However, countless hundreds of hours of computer personnel time was spent cleaning up the systems.

Another variation of the virus is the Trojan Horse, which is a useful program that hides a destructive program. When triggered, it causes damage, such as erasing a hard disk. It does not replicate like a virus, however.

The most successful virus exhibits no obvious signs, but you may suspect a virus if any of the following problems occur:

- Changes in program length
- Slow operation
- Unexplained disk activities
- Unexplained reductions in memory or disk space
- Unusual screen activity or error messages

- Changes in times or dates
- Failure of a program to execute

Some of these problems may be due to factors other than viruses, however.

Viruses and their variations are difficult to avoid, because many microcomputer users employ a variety of disks and networking systems. For example, electronic bulletin boards may contain infected public-domain software that users download into their microcomputers. It is easy for the authors to insert viruses into these programs that can infect any computer used to download them. It is estimated that only about 7 percent of viruses enter a system through a modem, however. Instead, most users get viruses by sharing floppy disks that contain legitimate programs or demo programs or even, in some cases, just data.

To compound the difficulties, a new generation of highly destructive "stealth" viruses appears to be spreading into some systems. They have received this name because they are designed to avoid detection by antivirus software, such as a Stealth bomber avoids radar. They are also difficult to remove once found. They demonstrate that virus writers are becoming more skilled at hiding their work from detection.

About 180 companies in the United States alone are in the business of marketing computer security products and services to prevent these problems. Products include antivirus programs designed to detect and ward off viruses and password generators that automatically create new passwords to keep ahead of hackers trying to break into a system via stolen security codes.

Antivirus programs can scan new software to block incoming viruses or can seek out established viruses. They identify viruses by searching a

---

How to Protect Your System from Viruses

1. Back up data files frequently.
2. Use recommended antivirus software to scan files and programs regularly for viruses.
3. Rescan if you have used a repair program after discovering a virus: The first virus may have hidden another virus.
4. Check all floppy disks for a virus after "disinfecting" your system.
5. Be careful who you allow to use your computer.
6. Use only your own disks.
7. If there is a chance that someone else will be using your computer without your knowing it, consider purchasing a password protection program.
8. Don't buy software whose shrink wrap looks like it has been changed or tampered with.
9. If possible, scan any new software with your antivirus program *before* installing it.
10. Access networks, bulletin boards, and databases with caution.
11. If you download a program from a BBS, test it from a floppy disk if you can. If you must use the hard disk, put all other program files in their own subdirectory to isolate them. Any virus then may affect only the current directory or subdirectory.
12. Never install untested software of any kind in the root directory. If a program does not list the author's name, address, and telephone number, do not run it.
13. Do not copy programs from friends or business associates. This is one of the most common ways that viruses are passed between microcomputers. Even computer technicians can pick up a virus from one customer and pass it along to another on a disk.
14. Do not buy or use bootlegged software.
15. Watch your system for signs of trouble, such as unusually slow loading or processing times or unusual error messages.

system for program-code patterns unique to each computer virus. They can identify where the virus resides—in memory or in a file or in the special start-up area of a disk known as the boot sector, for example—and then can destroy the virus. Most antivirus programs have a terminate-and-stay resident module that stays in RAM and constantly monitors your system for viruses. Other antivirus programs simply inform you when an unauthorized program is being copied into your computer's main memory. A number of antivirus programs help you delete or repair infected files. One problem with antivirus software, however, is that it may not be updated frequently enough to deal with new strains of viruses.

Most computer professionals believe that the best protection for the average user is common sense. See the box about virus protection for some points they make. Following these rules will go a long way toward preventing most viral infections.

Disk Care

Floppy disks need to be handled gently. Keep all disks away from magnets and magnetic fields that can erase or scramble the data stored on them. Magnetic items include external disk drives, monitors, printers, telephones, radios, and even paper clips that have been stored in magnetic containers. Heat can also damage disks, so store them away from sunny windows. Because automobiles can get very hot when the sun is shining, even on a cool day, avoid leaving disks in the car. Use felt-tip pens to write on labels that are already attached to the disks, and press lightly when writing. Pressing hard or using ball-point pens can leave little dents on a disk's recording surface that can ruin the data. Keep the disks away from dirt, ashes, food, and liquids. Even smoke particles can affect the way the disk and drive interact. Store all disks away from heat or cold and upright in boxes designed for holding disks, to prevent warping. *Never* store a disk in a disk drive.

The 3.5-inch disks have hard plastic cases that make it difficult to damage the disks. Thin, metal slides, or shutters, protect the areas where the disk drive accesses the actual disk. The drive moves the metal slide before reading the disk. Do not flick these shutters back and forth, because dust and fingerprints could damage the exposed disk.

A 5.25-inch disk requires extra precautions, because its jacket is flexible and parts of the disk inside are exposed. For example, the jacket has an oval notch that allows the disk drive to read the recording area of the disk. There is also a small hole that helps the drive find the data and programs on the disk. Never fold or bend a flexible disk. If you do, the disk drive may not be able to get the data stored on the disk or record new data on it. Never touch any exposed recording areas of a disk, because dirt and oil from your fingers can attract dust and ruin data. Keep the disks in their paper envelopes when not in use. The envelopes protect the disks from dirt and dust that can damage the data on the disks. Do not bind them together with rubber bands or paper clips; this could bend or crease some of the disks.

Before inserting a 5.25-inch disk into a drive, take it out of its paper envelope. The vinyl jacket should never be removed, however, unless you plan to throw the disk away. Either size disk should be held at the label end, so that the exposed read/write notch on a 5.25-inch disk or the shutter end of the 3.5-inch disk goes into the disk drive first. Never force a disk into the drive; slide it in gently until it clicks into place.

APPENDIX B

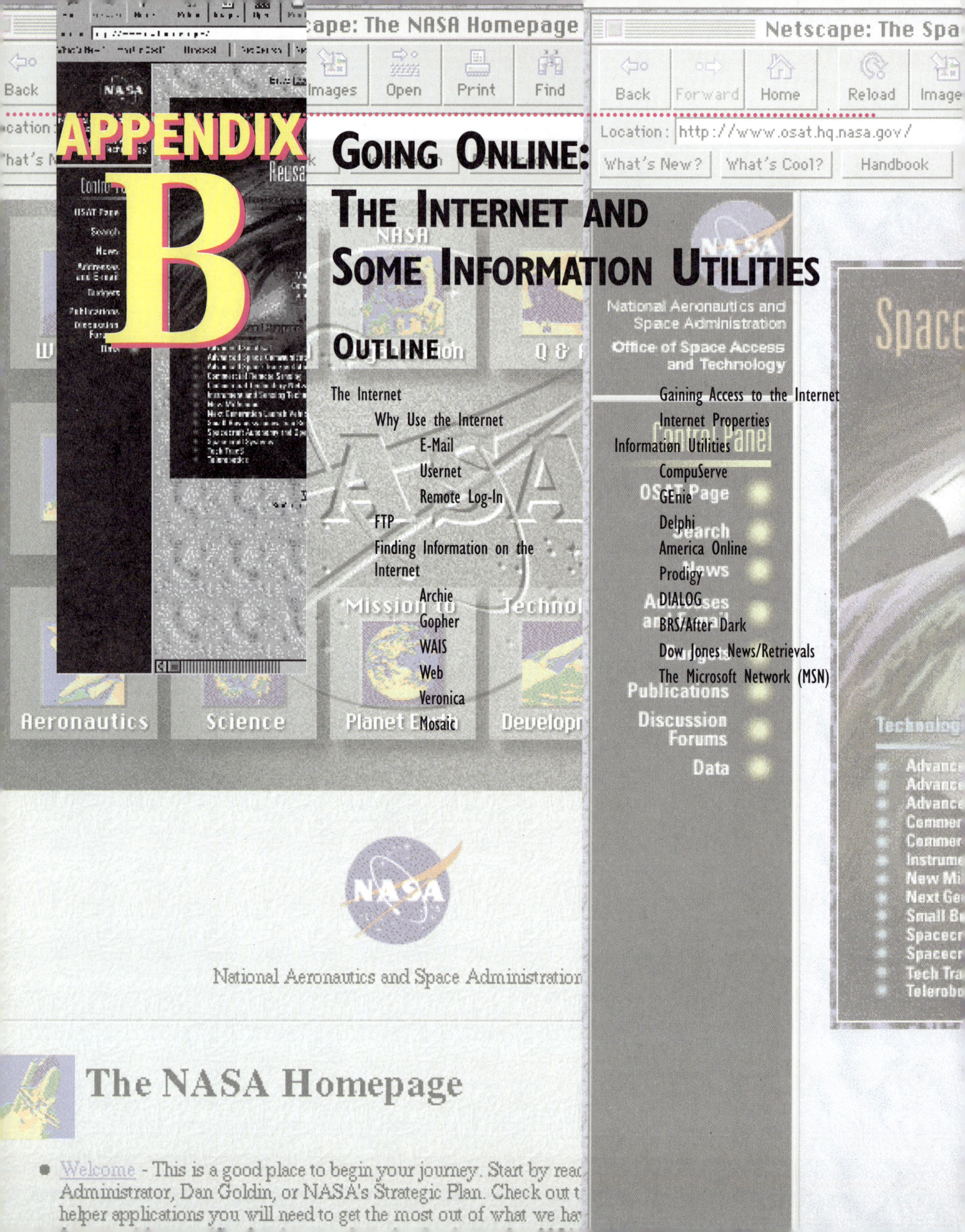

Going Online: The Internet and Some Information Utilities

Outline

The Internet
   Why Use the Internet
      E-Mail
      Usenet
      Remote Log-In
   FTP
   Finding Information on the Internet
      Archie
      Gopher
      WAIS
      Web
      Veronica
      Mosaic

Gaining Access to the Internet
Internet Properties
Information Utilities
   CompuServe
   GEnie
   Delphi
   America Online
   Prodigy
   DIALOG
   BRS/After Dark
   Dow Jones News/Retrievals
   The Microsoft Network (MSN)

The NASA Homepage

- Welcome - This is a good place to begin your journey. Start by read Administrator, Dan Goldin, or NASA's Strategic Plan. Check out t helper applications you will need to get the most out of what we ha

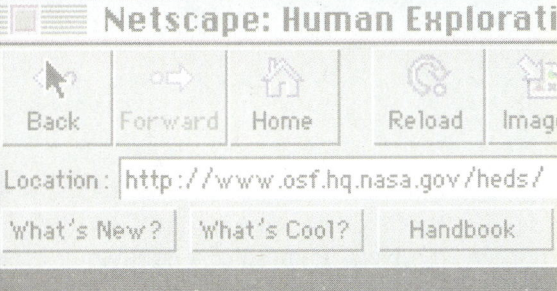

INTRODUCTION

You may have heard of people who sit for hours in front of a computer playing games, writing programs, and experimenting. You may think those people lose a sense of reality. Yet these computer hobbyists may have been using their computers to keep in touch with a greater variety of people and events than you would ever have imagined. This contact with "the real world" occurs through telecommunications, not over the back-fence. Not only are there a variety of commercial information services and the Internet to tap into, but there are also many private electronic bulletin boards that anyone can access, as long as they have the correct equipment and software.

►The Internet

As introduced in Chapter 5, the Internet, or "the Net," is more of a concept than a service or commercial venture. Loosely, it is a network consisting of tens of thousands of networks, online services, and single-user microcomputers that links users with information. There are roughly 25 million users utilizing the service for communications, research and entertainment for both business and home.

Why Use the Internet?

The Internet is a cooperative, user-supported system; there is no control center or corporation. Accessing the Internet puts you in touch with millions of people and thousands of institutions around the world. The most popular functions on the Net are e-mail, news, remote log-in to libraries and other resources, and public discussion forums. The Internet also offers options for real-time chatting (Internet Relay Chat), weather information, satellite pictures, and games. Some of these functions are described next.

E-Mail

The Net's e-mail services let you exchange messages with other people, the difference from your usual e-mail being in the network's scope: As long as you know the address of the recipient, you can communicate with millions of people all over the world. An easy way to get involved with e-mail is to join a mailing list, through which you receive mail on a specific topic. There are many mailing lists on a wide variety of topics. The most well-known one is Listserv, an application found on BITNET. BITNET (Because It's Time Network) is an academic network linking educational institutions. It uses a different protocol than Internet but can send e-mail through an Internet gateway.

Usenet

A popular activity is the Net news exchange, or Usenet, which works a lot like bulletin board services in which users post messages and collect responses. The public messages are classified into various news groups, of which there are hundreds, ranging from technical subjects to social and recreational topics to regional interests. Hobbies and jokes also are popular topics. There are more than 7,000 Usenet news groups, including "alt.internet.services," which contains the Internet Services Frequently Asked Questions (FAQ) list and Scott Yanoff's "Special Internet Connections List" of the hundreds of services available on Internet.

Remote Log-In

Both e-mail and Usenet are available throughout the Net. You must go through a system connected directly to the Internet proper, however, if you want to use remote log-in and anonymous FTP (see next subsection). Remote log-in lets you log in (access or connect) to one Internet system from another remote Internet system. It is also known as *Telnet,* which is the name of both the application and the protocol, or command, that provides this function. Remote log-in lets you browse through databases and card catalogs.

FTP

Anonymous FTP (file transfer protocol) is similar to remote log-in. It enables an organization to set up an anonymous account and place in it files and archival information that the organization is willing to distribute freely. FTP is both the name of the program and the name of the command used to transfer files. Through FTP, you can access government documents, such as supreme court decisions, works with expired copyrights, works that are in the public domain or are specifically written for the Internet community, library card catalogs, and games and other software. There are directories that list services available through anonymous FTP. Not all files listed in the directories are accessible to every user, but there is more than enough information to keep one person busy.

Finding Information on the Internet

A number of tools help you find what you want on the Internet, but they are not always easy to use. As time passes, more GUIs and menu-driven tools will be available for accessing the Internet. Several of these tools are described here.

Archie

Archie is a search tool developed by McGill University. To find the FTP archives, you type text-strings for words that might be found in file names or file descriptions that hold topics of interest. You access Archie either by logging on to the computer running the Archie application or via e-mail.

Gopher

Gopher is a menu-based system that works much like a card catalog when you are searching for information. It lets you search using the cursor and the *Return* key. It was developed at the University of Minnesota (home of Golden Gophers) to enable campus network users to access information without special training. If you locate something of interest on the menu, the Gopher gets it by using FTP or by starting a Telnet session so that you don't have to go through the mechanics of finding the resource's address and accessing it yourself.

WAIS

WAIS (Wide Area Information Servers) is both the program and the protocol for full-text word searches on more than 400 databases. You select the database sources and enter the word or words to be used for the search, then WAIS does the searching.

Web

World-Wide Web (or WWW) relies on hypertext links, in which documents are linked by association. In other words, you can select a word or topic in the original document to activate a link to another, related source. WWW documents can include graphics, sound, and video. The Web was developed at CERN, a European high-energy physics laboratory in Geneva, and made available to the public in 1991.

Veronica

Veronica (Very Easy Rodent-Oriented Net-wide Index to Computerized Archives) is a search tool employed within gophers. This tool makes it easier to search for resources available to gophers.

Mosaic

Mosaic is the current "killer app" and most popular interface on the Internet today. Developed by NCSA (the National Center for Supercomputing Applications), it is considered a Web browser and allows point-and-click navigation of the World Wide Web. Several software companies have refined and enhanced Mosaic and now offer it for commercial use. Among those are Quarterdeck Corporation and Spyglass Inc.

Netscape's Navigator

The most popular of all the Web browsers finds its roots in Mosaic as well. Totally revamped and enhanced to include integrated e-mail, security and multimedia capabilities, Netscape's Navigator has been chosen for integration into and use with several commercial online services. It is estimated that two-thirds of all browsers in use today are Netscape's Navigator. Microsoft's Internet Explorer is its closest competitor.

Yahoo

One of the first in its class Yahoo, a Web search directory, was developed by two Stanford doctoral students. It's well-organized, hierarchical subject guide is cross-referenced and updated regularly. Search results are also listed by category making it easy to determine their relevancy to your search terms. Other search engines and directories include Alta Vista, Excite, Lycos, and InfoSeek.

Gaining Access to the Internet

Most computers attached to the Internet employ the Unix operating system. Since you are probably using another operating system, you will need to go through an intermediary connection. To get on the Net, you need a computer, a modem, an online Internet account (from Delphi or one of the hundreds of service providers), a word processing program that uses ASCII, DOS, or text format, and telecommunications software to access the intermediary connection.

The Internet can be tapped in a variety of ways. Students at university and colleges usually have "free" Internet accounts. Even if you are not a student or an employee, you can, for a monthly fee, sometimes utilize a university's access. Your place of employment may also have a feed to the Internet. Most frequently, however, you will need to access an intermediary connection. For example, some commercial providers, such as CompuServe and America Online (see later), sell access to the Internet. Delphi (also see later) and The Well (Whole Earth 'Lectronic Link) offer full access to the Internet. Some bulletin board services may allow access to the net's e-mail service, through which you can also get Archie. In addition, you can link through MCI Mail, or Fidonet. You could also have a direct connection—TCP/IP, or Transmission Control Protocol/Internet Protocol—installed professionally on your computer.

Several software packages are available that facilitate your trip through the Internet. Among them are VersaTerm-Link from Synergy Software and TCP/Connect II from InterCon Systems Corp., both for the Macintosh, and Internet Chameleon from NetManage and O'Reilly's and Spry's Internet in a Box.

Internet Etiquette

The Internet is probably the most open network in the world. Approximately 2 million computers are linked to it. More are being added every day, with services such as America Online now offering e-mail gateways. The added traffic has created a problem of Internet etiquette, for veteran users have already established sets of customs and manners for using the Net. Among the most common breeches of etiquette is asking questions that are already answered in the FAQ files. Thus, it is recommended that new Internet users read the information in the FAQ files before posting questions. In addition, "newbies" can grasp the gist of interesting-sounding news groups by reading the contributions for a couple of weeks before adding their own opinions. While on the Internet, do not "crack" into bank computers or other private information accounts. Keep messages to a reasonable size, and keep comments relevant to a group's topic and current "thread" of discussion. Read the "read-me" files found in special mailing lists and newsgroups.

For further information, you can browse through the many books available about the Internet. Several magazines are devoted to various aspects of online activity, and you can always ask someone in a users' group to help you get started. To find a dial-up provider near you and get more information about the Internet, call InterNIC Information Services at (619) 455-4600. Also check the Internet services provided through online information utilities such as those described next.

▶ Information Utilities

Increasingly, part of the reason for purchasing a microcomputer is to access online information services and bulletin boards. To utilize such a service, you need a modem, access to a telephone line that can be linked to your system, and a software package that supports telecommunication operations.

Online information services are profit-making enterprises, and exist by charging users for services. Most charge an annual or monthly membership fee. On joining, the user gets an operations manual, a directory of services, and a password that permits access to the system. Most information utilities can be assessed through local or 800 telephone numbers, but some may require long-distance phone calls for which there is a charge. In addition to the membership fees, there are usually hourly "connect" fees that begin around $4 and can go as high as $300. Rates often vary with the time of the day you are connected and the type of information you wish to access. Some services also charge a separate fee per search. Some telephone companies charge for modem use, too, which adds to the cost. The value of online information services lies in the time saved, because online database references are faster and more convenient than traditional library research.

A subscription to a service can provide news, movie reviews, sports news, weather reports, and lots of other information. Most services offer forums for special interests, often called SIGs for "special-interest groups." Some of the most popular activities on online services today involve interactivity—game-playing, real-time conferences, and messaging.

For each online subscription, you get a password and/or an identification number, to help prevent someone else from stealing service on your subscription while you pay for it. Once you connect to the service's computer (commonly referred to as the *host computer*), you can browse through the files and download—or transfer to your computer—anything you want to study at more length. (Some items cannot be downloaded.)

A few of the many commercial services are discussed briefly next. Current magazines frequently describe the most recent upgrades to the services and where to get further information. Check the yellow pages of a city telephone book or an 800-number directory for company telephone numbers. Ask a friend or a users' group to help you get started.

CompuServe

CompuServe is one of the largest information services available to individual and family users, with over 2,000 different forums, departments, and services. It is always changing and adding to its resources. The service offers many computer games and allows you to shop at home by browsing through an electronic catalog. It provides e-mail services (including e-mail exchange to the Internet), the Associated Press wire service, *U.S. News and World Report,* a few daily newspapers, and forums for special-interest and professional groups. It also supplies weather information, travel services for airline and hotel reservations, market information through D&B Dun's Market Identifiers and Disclosure 11 Reports, brokerage services, multiplayer games, lifestyle information (about health issues, religion, hobbies, automobiles, and so on), and educational resources such as *Grolier's Academic American Encyclopedia,* U.S. government information, Peterson's college database, dissertation abstracts, and the Science and Math Education Forum.

CompuServe's IQuest, for which there are extra charges, provides a gateway to over 900 additional databases, many of which are drawn from online services such as DIALOG and BRS.

GEnie

GEnie (General Electric Network for Information Exchange) offers hundreds of products and services. GEnie is organized into a menu structure, which includes a main menu via which you access submenus. It is well known for its bulletin boards and real-time forums, called RoundTables, which include personal computing for a number of brands of microcomputers; programmers; professional services for fields such as law, medicine, writing, photography, and education; computer products; and special interests such as genealogy, aviation, history, trains, and electronics. GEnie also offers a variety of financial services, such as the Dow Jones News/Retrieval, an electronic investment advisor called VESTOR, and stock and securities quotations. It has a wide variety of games you can play with other GEnie subscribers or download to play by yourself. In addition, it offers an e-mail gateway to the Internet.

One unusual service that GEnie provides is a Genealogy KnowledgeBase that helps you find materials or organizations that will aid your own genealogy research. In addition, you can use GEnie e-mail, CB simulator functions, and a very complete and exotic home shopping service.

Delphi

Delphi, like CompuServe, was a pioneer in telecommunications. It is known for its user-friendly atmosphere and seems more like a BBS than a formal online service. Navigation through it is clear and simple. For a fee, Delphi offers full Internet access—Telnet, Gopher, WAIS, Usenet, and others—and provides online help for Internet use.

Delphi offers computer-specific hints and software, games, and information services such as news wires, business information, and travel information. You have access to shopping, electronic mail, and real-time conferencing—that is, conferences in which you talk with other users and receive immediate responses. Online conferencing occurs in groups such as the Clubhouse, the Forum, special groups for users of particular computers, and the Science Fiction group for readers, writers, and fans of science fiction. There is also a professional translation service for translating text to and from Spanish, French, German, Italian, Portuguese, and other languages. A Just Kids area provides activities such as Baby-sitter's Club and Online Sesame Street. One unique feature that Delphi gives members in good standing is a chance to act as a sysop (system operator) for a bulletin board system, under its auspices, called a Custom Forum.

Delphi has a shareware program called D-lite that enables you to capture and copy e-mail so you can read and answer your messages offline and save on connect charges.

Recently, News Corporation, Delphi's parent company and MCI Communications Corporation announced a joint venture to launch a new Internet-based online service for consumers and businesses. The yet-to-be-named service will combine MCI Mail, Delphi Internet Services, and Kesmai Corp.'s online games, among others.

AMERICA ONLINE

America Online (AOL) is well known for its easy-to-use graphical screens. It enables you to access bulletin boards for special interests, very complete and up-to-date software libraries with both public-domain and shareware programs, games, and forums for real-time chatting. Its libraries are extensive, including *Compton's Encyclopedia,* and its forum leaders monitor discussion to be sure participants stick to the subject. One of its most innovative features is Center Stage, a mass-audience conference in which the audience can ask questions of the moderator and "whisper" to other participants. It also offers a new, high-resolution graphics interactive game from TSR, Inc., called *Neverwinter Nights.* To play the game requires the installation and registration of additional software. Much of AOL's news is drawn from *USA Today,* and it has the usual financial and market information. You can also access information from the *Chicago Tribune,* HomePC, and Cable News Network, as well as participate in forums hosted by magazines such as *Time* and *Bicycling.* It offers some shopping and reference services, and provides access to the World Wide Web, Gopher, FTP, and Usenet newsgroups on the Internet.

Prodigy

A relatively new competitor in the information service market is Prodigy, a joint venture between Sears and IBM. It is geared toward individuals and families, and is the largest online service. Prodigy is a menu-driven, very user-friendly service that allows subscribers to shop at home, perform banking tasks, make airline reservations, and access a wide variety of news and entertainment information sources. Sports buffs can access ESPNET, a sports information service made available through an alliance with the cable TV sports network ESPN.

The bulletin boards, called "clubs," are monitored carefully for subject matter and gossip. There are no software libraries. Prodigy does, however, offer a wide variety of shopping services, through which you can buy just about any product you wish. It also serves as an advertising medium for about 200 companies. These companies pay for advertising on the system according to how many times an advertisement is accessed by subscribers and also by the number of products sold to subscribers. The advertising is controversial, however, because parents may not want their families to be subject to the constant sales pitches.

Prodigy is the largest dial-up access provider to the World Wide Web and was the first major online service with a link to the Internet.

DIALOG

DIALOG, part of Knight-Ridder's Business Information Services Division, contains more than 425 databases, for which it represents itself as the "World's Largest Online Knowledgebank." Its comprehensive Information Retrieval Service includes coverage of virtually every area of study, including art, music, humanities, business, aerospace, biology, chemistry, physics, and zoology. DIALOG offers full-text news wire services, such as Associated Press, UPI, and Knight-Ridder Financial News. It also contains the text of other publications, such as journals, as well as the text of patents, books, and trademarks, and it lists information about more than 12 million companies, using sources such as Dun & Bradstreet and Standard & Poor. DIALOG also offers the KNOWLEDGE INDEX, which presents over 90 popular DIALOG databases at reduced rates after 6 P.M. on weekdays and during most of the weekend. The number of available databases is limited, but each provides easy access that requires no special training.

BRS/After Dark

A low-cost database service that operates during evening and weekend hours is BRS/After Dark. (BRS stands for "Bibliographic Retrieval Services.") This service, a subset of BRS/Search system, which is also an information service, provides nearly 100 databases. The system is called "after dark" because it is available during off-hours—6 P.M. through 6 A.M.

(your time zone) Monday through Thursday and 6 P.M. Friday through 6 A.M. Monday.

Dow Jones News/Retrieval

The Dow Jones News/Retrieval Service is designed with business information in mind, and its primary users are business professionals and individuals interested in business. There are various user levels, with varying membership fees. The system employs a menu approach.

Information is provided on every company listed on the New York and American stock exchanges, as well as some on selected companies whose stock is traded over the counter. You can get historical stock market quotes and current information that is only 15 minutes behind the action on the exchange floors. The service also gives corporate earnings estimates and price/volume data. With a Dow Jones News/Retrieval subscription, you additionally can get UPI summaries of local and national news, news stories from various financial newspapers and magazines, such as the *Wall Street Journal,* and access to the *Grolier's Academic American Encyclopedia.* The service offers an archive of publications, too, including the *Wall Street Journal,* the *Washington Post,* and *Forbes,* among many others. It has movie reviews and weather information, and allows you to shop from home. The service also offers three software packages with which you can record and manipulate information from the News/Retrieval databases.

Dow Jones offers, by request, a free copy of TextSearch Plus, a Windows-based software program that makes searching for publications in the News/Retrieval text library much easier. The program allows office storage of search strategies so searches can be rerun without rekeying. It is also studying ways to reduce and simplify its rates.

The Microsoft Network (MSN)

An industry first, Microsoft's client software for its online service, MSN, shipped as an integrated part of its latest operating system, Windows 95. The client software is included free, but you still have to sign up and pay a fee for the service. It utilizes the same interface as Windows 95, so finding files and performing keyword searches in MSN is just like finding files on your computer.

MSN's content areas, for now, include Business and Finance; Home and Family; Computers and Software; Sports, Health, and Fitness; Education and Reference; Science and Technology, and Arts and Entertainment. MSN also provides e-mail, bulletin boards, chat rooms and file download libraries. Hardware and software support is plentiful and Microsoft's own is the definitive support source. Other information resources include C-Span, U.S. News & World Report, The New York Times, and Microsoft's Bookshelf CD-ROM reference library and Encarta Encyclopedia.

MSN also includes an interactive web browser, the Internet Explorer, for near transparent Internet connectivity. Other Internet capabilities include FTP, Gopher, IRC, and Telnet. Although instant connection (using a shortcut in the operating system) is a plus, a drawback is the inability to tell which windows being displayed on your computer are from MSN and which are not. In other words, if you are not careful you could accumulate expensive connect time without even knowing it.

APPENDIX C

Bombs and Disasters: What to Do When Your Computer Doesn't Cooperate

Outline

Introduction
Software Problems
Problems with Files
Disks

Mouse or Keyboard
Monitor
Printers
Calling Tech Support

INTRODUCTION

No matter how user-friendly a particular computer or a piece of software is, eventually something will go wrong. Is there a Mac user alive who hasn't had to deal with the dreaded bomb? Or a PC user who realized he's accidentally deleted a file?

Some people have more problems with their computers than others; this may be due to an inferior machine, poorly written software, or an odd mixture of components. No matter how often or seldom problems occur, however, dealing with them is frustrating. Yes, the little, bright button says OK, and no, it's not okay, but you have to get past the disaster screen. Naturally, problems seem to crop up when that report is due or when the repair shop is closed. The key is not to let panic set in. This appendix presents some of the more common problems and some possible solutions—some of which seem obvious and common-sense, but which may be elusive when something actually goes wrong.

Before continuing, here are two warnings that can save either your computer or you:

- Always turn off the computer and unplug it before wiping it off, installing a hardware device, or moving it.
- Never open the monitor even if the computer and monitor are turned off. The monitor retains voltage and can deliver quite a shock if you touch its insides. You can be seriously injured.

That said, a third important habit is always to make backup copies of your files and programs. And never say "never." The report or lesson plans you were sure you'd never use again will most certainly have to be retyped from hard copy next year when you need handouts for that program or class you agree to present to another group.

These three practices can prevent many problems, but there are a number of other steps you can take to avoid disaster, or to start troubleshooting when disaster does strike.

- Check for loose or improper hardware connections. Be sure that clamps on connectors are actually clamped into place and that the screws on connectors are firmly screwed in. Be sure that connectors are inserted into the proper receptacles.
- It is also possible that an outlet or power strip is dead. Unplug the outlet connector, and try a lamp or some other appliance to be sure the outlet is working. Unplug the computer and its equipment from the power strip, and try a lamp in the power strip, too.

- If you have just installed a new program or a new device such as a CD-ROM drive and you have problems, remove the new component and then reinstall it. Be sure you have installed the driver software for the device. Then be sure that you have restarted the computer after installation. Without restarting, the driver won't have been activated.

- Whenever you add or change a component to the computer—whether it be hardware or software—you may need to reboot the system so that the new item will be activated. Your directions for installation should tell you to do this, but after a phone call or other interruption, it's easy to forget what you need to do. Rebooting does not hurt your computer, even if you must do it many times.

- Know that an application may need more than the minimum stated requirements for all aspects of it to work smoothly and quickly.

- Check any selections you may have made to customize your computer or program. An incorrect choice may cause a compatibility problem and prevent your system from operating at optimal performance.

- Some recurring problems happen because you may have purchased incompatible components for your machine or are using out of date system software or driver software.

The sections that follow describe further problems and corrective actions, according to topic. Some solutions are specific to IBM PCs and compatibles or to Macintosh computers, but most apply to both platforms.

▶ Software Problems

Software is very likely to be the culprit when a problem occurs. For example, Windows has frequently been the cause of conflicts, crashes, or other errors. If you are running DOS, however, the specific application is more likely to have caused the problem. One way you can find out if software is the problem is to try the software in another machine. If it does not work, most likely the problem is in the software. You'll need to contact the company by phone, online service, or bulletin board in order to find out what the problem is and perhaps get a "patch" that corrects a flaw in programming.

A common problem lies in the amount of memory required to run a program. Frequently, minimum requirements for memory are just that—minimum. To smoothly and quickly install and run all parts of a program, you'll probably need 1MB to 2MB or more RAM than required. (The manual or software box usually states a recommended amount of memory if optimum performance depends on more than the minimum required.)

Modern computers let you load several programs at once. When you try to open a program, a message may announce that not enough memory is available for the last program you try to load. Quit all programs that are already open, and then open only the program you want to use.

A common practice when using games or memory-intensive graphics programs is to use a boot disk to start your computer. The boot disk contains only the minimum instructions needed to operate your computer, and thus, more memory is free for your application. Sometimes the manuals for such software tell you how to create the boot disk, because the company is already aware that its program can cause problems when used with the entire operating system. Once you've made the boot disk, you simply turn off the machine, insert the disk into the floppy disk drive, and restart the computer. Using only the minimum system software, however, can cause some applications to run slowly or incorrectly.

Having too many items in memory can cause the computer to "freeze" because there may not even be enough memory left for the computer to signal a problem. This often occurs when you have created a large file without saving it for a long period of time. A file that has been saved can release some of its data in RAM to make room for more, but the computer tries to retain all the unsaved data it can until it is bloated, and it "bombs." You'll generally need to restart your computer when this happens, but first try to save the file by using the *Save* key command that comes with your application—usually the *Ctrl* or *Command* key with the *S* key. If this doesn't work, you have most likely lost all material not previously saved. (On the Macintosh, you will see a little bomb on the screen, but if this happens often, reinstall the System using the disks that came with your Mac. If you still get the bomb, call your Apple dealer or tech support.)

Reboot your IBM PC computer by pressing *Ctrl, Alt,* and *Delete* keys simultaneously. On the Mac, try pressing *Command, Option, Esc* to quit the program. A message may appear asking if you want to "Force program to quit? Unsaved changes will be lost." Click on the Force Quit button. If your Mac responds to the mouse and keyboard, try saving any unsaved work and then restart.

If the key commands routine doesn't work to reboot your computer, you'll need to press the reset switch or turn off the power and restart the machine. Just be sure to wait 10 seconds or more before restarting your computer. (Find the reset switch *before* you need to use it.)

The following instructions provide an alternative way to restart your Macintosh:

1. Choose Restart from the Special Menu or from the dialog box on the screen, if you can.
2. Hold down the *Command* and *Control* keys while you press the Power On Key.
3. If nothing happens, press the reset switch, marked with a triangle.
4. If this fails, turn off the computer using the power switch. Wait at least 10 seconds and then turn it on again.

On IBM computers, software instructions may crash into each other in memory, especially when Windows is being run. When this happens, you may see an "Application Error" message. Before doing anything, be sure to write down any information in the message. Then hold down the *Ctrl* key and press *Esc*. If you are lucky, the action will result in the Windows' Task List. At this time try to open the application you were using. You may be able to retrieve your work. Unfortunately, you probably will have lost all of your work. If the *Ctrl-Esc* key combination does not work, you will have to reboot your system. If similar problems happen often, you may need to reinstall Windows or remove some of the options.

Likewise, faults in system software can cause problems when you first start up the computer. For example, on Macintosh machines, you may not be able to get past the Welcome to Macintosh message. When this occurs, the Finder is probably corrupted. (That means that data has become jumbled, rarely through a fault of your own.) Restart your Macintosh with the disk containing System and Finder. Then drag a fresh copy of Finder from the floppy to the System Folder on the hard drive. Select *Restart* from the Special menu.

Thus, many problems result in error messages that appear on the screen. Write down what you were doing when the message appeared, and write down the message and its number if there is one. Then restart your computer. Most software problems are temporary and restarting usually corrects the problem. If the problem recurs however, make sure that all programs, desk accessories, and system extensions you're using are compatible with the system software. If you consistently get error messages when running software, try running a diagnostic utility such as Norton Utilities, these will check for corrupted directories. A user's group or your computer dealer may be able to help you if the problem is occurring with other machines.

When the computer won't start at all (on the Macintosh, a "sad Macintosh" icon appears), there is a problem with the system software or the computer hardware. Try starting up with a different startup disk. If the problem occurs again, then consult your dealer or service provider.

As a Macintosh user, you can determine whether parts of your software are causing the problem, by restarting the machine while holding down the *Shift* key. This temporarily turns off all system extensions. If your computer now works okay, then remove all extensions from the Extension Folder (which is inside the System Folder) and put them back into the Extension folder one at a time. Restart after you add each one. This procedure should uncover the offending extension.

As an IBM PC or compatible user, you may need to check whether there are too many "terminate-and-stay-resident" programs and device drivers loaded into conventional memory. If DOS software runs slowly in Windows, your hard drive may be older and thus, slow. Replace it with a newer IDE drive with access time of 12ms or less.

▶Problems with Files

On early computers, the great fear was that you would forget to save a program, accidentally delete a file, or give a program the same name as another (meaning that the new file replaced the old). There were no error messages announcing your mistake, and thus your work was lost. On today's computers, you almost always receive messages warning you of impending doom.

On an IBM-PC or compatible computer, you can usually retrieve a file that you accidentally deleted. If you are running DOS 5.0 or later, you can "undelete" a file by entering UNDELETE (filename) at the C:\prompt. You need to supply the full path and name of the file you accidentally deleted. If you are not sure what the filename is, enter UNDELETE *.* DOS will put a list of file names on the screen, and ask if you want to recover the file. Press Y. You can also undelete files by entering UNDELETE/ALL. DOS then supplies random first letters for the files, but you can rename them later.

Accidentally deleting files on Macs is not the problem that it can be on PCs. On the Macintosh, you are always asked if you want to save a file if you accidentally hit the close box or press *Command* and *W* keys together, which is the key command for *Close*. Even if you happen to drag a file to the Trash can—for example, if you drag a folder to the Trash not realizing that the file is in it–the file remains there until you select *Empty Trash* from the Special menu. In System 7, the files remain in the Trash even if you restart the computer. (In System 6, the Finder may automatically empty the trash before you realize what has happened.)

In a DOS program, a message says "Access Denied" when the application refuses to let you save the file. Very likely, the problem is that you have tried to enter a file name that already exists. Use a different file name and save again. In Windows, a message tells you that another file exists and asks if you want to replace the first file with the new one. If the answer is no, you'll need to rename the new file.

On Macs, you cannot delete a file that is opened. You see the message "The item *History Report* could not be deleted, because it contains items that are in use. Do you want to continue?" Click on Stop to stop the action, or click on Continue to let the computer take over until you can save the file and close it.

(If you can't save files on a floppy disk, that disk may be locked. Make sure the tab on the back of the disk is in unlock position, so that the square hole is closed.)

On Macs, retrieving files is usually no problem: You simply point and click at the filename or file icon. On IBM machines without Windows, you'll need to type the filename to retrieve it. All of a sudden, you see the message "Bad command or filename." Simply try typing the item again; you probably misspelled the filename.

➤ Disks

If you see a message that the floppy disk is unreadable, you may simply need to initialize it. On the other hand, when you insert a disk, you may get a message that amounts to the following: "This disk is damaged. Do you want to initialize it?" Do not move forward with the initialization. Instead cancel the action, eject the disk, and insert it again. Sometimes a minor misalignment in a drive causes a problem that disappears the next time you insert the disk. If you continue to get the message, however, either the disk or the drive is likely to have been damaged at some point.

Today, most people are using 3.5-inch floppy disks and disk drives with their computers. On these drives, there are no doors to open so that you can pull the diskette out. Instead, you generally press the *Ctrl* and *E* keys together (*Command* and *E* keys on the Macintosh) to eject a disk. What do you do if a disk will not eject? In case of failure, you can eject the disk "manually," as follows. Disk drives for the 3.5-inch disks have a tiny hole near the drive's opening. Carefully insert the end of a large straightened paper clip into this hole, and push gently until the disk is ejected. If the disk still does not eject, you will have to take the drive to be repaired.

(Before going the paper-clip route on Macintosh, try ejecting the disk by holding down the *Command* and *Shift* keys and pressing the number 1 key to eject a disk from the internal disk drive. If this doesn't work, turn off the computer. If the disk isn't automatically ejected at this point, hold down the button on your pointing device while you turn on the computer again. Only if failure occurs at this point, should you use the straightened paper clip.)

With the proliferation of CD-ROM drives, you may eventually encounter problems with CD-ROM disks, too. A common one is putting the disk into the drive upside down—that is, with the label face down. Open the drive and turn the disk right side up so that you can read the label. (Most CD-ROM drives have the little hole for the paper clip routine in case the drive tray does not eject.)

➤ Mouse or Keyboard

You'll rarely have problems with mice or keyboards. If either device does not respond, check the cables to see if they are firmly in place. A keyboard that does not respond may need to be replaced. If the pointer does not move—or jerks around wildly—when you move the mouse, you may need to clean the mouse rather than replacing it. See the instructions that came with the mouse to take it apart and remove the dirty buildup.

One other problem is commonly associated with keyboards or mice, and that is spills. People who drink coffee, tea, or water while computing run the risk of splashing or spilling liquid on the keyboard. If this happens, shut down your system and turn the keyboard upside down until the liquid drains out. Let the keyboard dry for 24 hours, and usually you can use it as if nothing happened. If the liquid was sticky, however, you may have to replace the keyboard.

➤ Monitor

You have turned on your system but the monitor is completely dark. Some monitor brightness and contrast controls can totally black out the monitor when they are turned way down. Check to see that these controls have not been accidentally moved. If nothing happens, make sure that the monitor is actually turned on.

Occasionally, the screen image flickers or is distorted. If this happens, be sure the cables are securely connected. If loose cables do not seem to be the problem, check to see if a nearby device such as a fluorescent light, radio, microwave oven, another monitor, or even the computer is causing interference. Move the device away from the monitor to see if the screen condition improves. If flicker or distortion continues, consult your technician.

As we noted earlier, monitors carry a great deal of electricity. Suppose you adjust the brightness or contrast controls on the monitor or touch the unit to move it and you feel a current clear to your funny bone. This means that your monitor is leaking electricity, a symptom of careless design and workmanship. A monitor with this condition is likely to be a danger to you and a fire hazard for your house. Get rid of it and buy a new, highly rated monitor.

➤ Printers

Is there any device that is trouble free? Certainly not printers, where all sorts of nasty things can happen to paper.

Actually, paper is the most common cause of printer problems. If the printer doesn't seem to be working, check it to see if the paper is feeding correctly or if it needs refilled. If a page prints off center, tears, skews, or crumples, check a number of items:

- The paper tray may be too full, causing paper to feed incorrectly.
- The brackets holding the paper in place are incorrectly positioned.
- The paper wasn't "fanned" before it was put into the tray.

Never put paper with staples through a printer. Don't use letterhead paper that has been printed using low-temperature dyes or thermography in a laser printer or in an ink jet printer that uses heat, because the "ink" can peel away or melt inside the printer and cause damage.

Now that we have dealt with paper, let's look at the printer itself. If the printer does not respond to a print command, turn the printer off and back on again. Be sure that you have chosen the correct printer from the software. If an out of memory message appears, you may be printing too many fonts and complex images in a document. Split the print job into two or more sections.

Occasionally, you may need to *stop* a print job because you realize you've left out some material or made some mistakes. On the Macintosh, you can usually stop print by pressing the *Command* and *period* (.) keys. If several documents are in the print queue, select the Mac icon in the upper-right corner of the desktop. Select Print Monitor. When the list of files waiting to be printed appears on the screen, select the one you want to cancel and click on the Cancel Printing button.

To stop printing from Windows PCs, hold down *Ctrl* and press *Esc*. If Print Manager is listed in the menu of active programs that appears, double-click on it to activate it. If not, double-click on Program Manager, and select the Main program group; now double-click on the Print Manager icon. When Print Manager loads, a list of files waiting to be printed will appear on the screen. Select the document you want to cancel, then click on the Delete button. This removes the file from the print queue, and you can now switch back to the application by holding down *Ctrl* and *Esc* again and double-clicking on the application name. Make your changes, and start the print job again.

►Calling Tech Support

When you see an error message on the screen, before taking any action write down the message and its ID number. Make a note of exactly what you were doing when the problem occurred. This information can be helpful if you need to call a company's technical support line in order to solve a problem.

Tech support lines are busy and it may take you a while to get through. To shorten your own time with tech support, you should be prepared to talk only about the problem at hand and have some basic information ready before you even call. In fact, it helps to be at your computer when you place the call.

Here are some common bits of information tech support will want to know when you call:

1. What version of software, model of computer or device, microprocessor, registration number, and other descriptions identify your system?
2. What are the brand names and description of accessories such as extra cards, CD-ROM drives, disk compression programs, memory managers, extensions, or other programs and hardware you are running. (In Windows, you can enter MSD to run Microsoft Diagnostics to find out some of these things.
3. How much memory do you have?
   On PCs, you can tell by watching the last number that appears

during the machine's memory check when you turn on the computer. On DOS 4.0 or higher, type MEM at the C:\ prompt.

On Macintosh machines, look in the Get Info file.

4. How much free disk space do you have?

Type DIR at the C:\ prompt.

On Macintosh machines, the amount of disk space is located in a bar at the top of an icon window.

5. Have you defragmented your hard disk drive recently? (If you have not done this in a month or so, it is likely that many of the files on the disk have become noncontiguous and that condition can cause problems that should be resolved before you call technical support.)

6. Have you checked your system for viruses?

It always helps to have collected this information ahead of time, so that you will not be scrambling at the last minute to locate registration numbers, serial numbers, amount of memory, and so on. If your computer has crashed, you may not even be able to get this information when you need to call technical support.

Some parting advice: Write down any user hints about your specific software or hardware on file cards, and arrange the cards in some semblance of order: by program, device, type of error, and so on. Check the columns, bug boxes, and even letters to the editor in computer magazines and look through bulletin board systems for items pertaining to your system. (Why use file cards instead of an online file? When your computer misbehaves, you most likely will not be able to access an online file.) If a problem arises, you'll have a mini technical support "line" that you can consult before calling the technicians.

GLOSSARY

access To get data from or to retrieve data; the ability to get information by computer or to use a computer or program.

alert box An outlined area that appears on the screen to give information or a warning or to report an error message during use of an application program; often needs no response other than acknowledgment (clicking on the OK button, for example).

algorithm A sequence of steps needed to solve a problem.

analog transmission The sending of data in which the signal is in the form of a wave.

antivirus program A program that helps you thwart viruses that might invade your system.

application software A set of instructions that controls the execution of a user job, such as writing a document, working on a spreadsheet, playing a game, or using a typing tutor program; also called *application program* or, simply, *application*.

arithmetic/logic unit (ALU) The portion of a computer processor that carries out computations and the comparison functions that make up logical operations of a computer.

assembly language A low-level—that is, machine-oriented—programming language that uses abbreviations to code instructions rather than 1's and 0's or complete words.

asynchronous transmission A method in which data characters are sent at random intervals and are defined, or separated, by start and stop bits.

authoring tool A program that enables you to write hypertext or multimedia applications, usually by combining elements such as text, music, and pictures; also called *authoring system*.

back up To make a copy to prevent data loss in case the original material is lost or damaged.

bandwidth A rating of communication channel capacity; expressed in bits per second and also known as *grade*.

binary digit See *bit*.

binary number system The number system that uses the digits 0 and 1; often called base 2 as opposed to base 10, which is the decimal system with which we are familiar.

bit Short for "binary digit"; an individual 1 or 0 value used in computer coding.

block A selected section of a document.

block operation A feature by which a section of a file can be selected for copying, moving, or deleting.

boot To load the first piece of software (usually the operating system) that starts a computer; a cold boot occurs when you turn on the computer from the "off" position; a warm boot occurs when you reset a computer that is already turned on.

bug A program error.

bulletin board system (BBS) A user-run service that permits individuals who have microcomputers to trade messages with others who have similar interests; usually informal and offered at little or no cost except for telephone bills. Also known as *electronic bulletin board*.

bus A set of wires, real or "printed," through which data are sent from one part of the computer to another.

bus network A data communication network in which all nodes communicate via a common distribution channel.

byte A series of bits, usually eight, used to encode a letter, number, or special character and operated on as a unit.

cache memory A type of high-speed RAM usually built onto the microprocessor, used to help speed the execution of a program. Also known as a *high-speed buffer* or *RAM cache*.

CAD See *computer-aided design*.

CD-ROM Pronounced *see-dee-ROM*; stands for "compact disc read-only memory." A form of optical disk from which data can be read but not altered or recorded.

cell The unique location in an electronic spreadsheet where a row and a column intersect; can hold a label, a value, or a formula.

central processing unit (CPU) The portion of the computer system that controls execution of program instructions and the processing of data items.

channel See *communication channel*.

character A single letter, number, special graphics symbol, or symbol such as ?, #, &, -, /, *, or space; requires one byte of storage.

chief programmer team (CPT) A method of organization used in managing software development projects under which a chief programmer supervises programming and testing.

chip Solid-state circuitry on a tiny piece of silicon or gallium material; may contain millions of electronic components.

circuit board See *printed circuit board*.

clicking Pressing and immediately releasing a button on the mouse.

client A computer on a LAN that serves as a user node.

client/server LAN A local-area network in which the functions of the LAN are designated to specific machines; the clients are the requesting machines, and the servers are the supplying machines.

clip art Ready-to-use illustrations and symbols for enhancing text output; usually created by professional artists for nonartists to use.

clock A timing device that generates the basic fixed-rate pulses by which the operations of a computer are synchronized.

clock speed The speed at which a microprocessor executes instructions or at which an expansion bus operates; the number of electronic pulses a microprocessor can produce each second; expressed in megahertz (MHz).

clone A computer that functions exactly like another, better-known product; can refer to software or other hardware, too.

coaxial cable A high-capacity transmission link that consists of a single wire, insulated and bound as protection from electromagnetic interference.

code Short for the lines of instructions written in a programming language, which is a set of vocabulary and syntax, or grammatical rules, for writing a computer program.

command A message from you to the computer that tells it what to do. A command may be given by choosing an option from a menu or pressing a key or key combination; it may also be given via input equipment such as a mouse or trackball.

command-line user interface A user interface that requires the user to type commands in a special code in order to tell a computer what to do next.

common carrier An FCC-regulated private company that provides telecommunication facilities for public use.

communication channel A medium, or pathway, for carrying data or voice transmissions from one place to another.

communication satellite An earth-orbiting vehicle equipped and positioned to relay microwave signals from earth stations, or towers.

compatible Descriptive of software and hardware that can be used together without any bad effects, even though they have been produced by different manufacturers; also applied to computers that can act as IBM computers do but are not IBM computers.

compiler A language translator that accepts an entire program or module (the source code) written by a programmer and generates machine-language instructions (the object code).

computer An electronic device used to accept, process, store, access, and display information without human intervention.

computer-aided design (CAD) The process of designing, drafting, and analyzing a prospective product via special graphics software on a high-end computer; often paired with CAM.

computer-aided manufacturing (CAM) Process, via computer, of designing and testing a manufacturing process and often monitoring the actual making of a product; often paired with CAD.

computer ethics Standards of moral conduct in computer use; a way in which the "spirit" of some laws are applied to computer-related activities.

computer conference A conference that occurs by typing messages into computers linked through communication channels.

computer crime A criminal act that poses a threat to those who use computers or that is accomplished through the use of a computer.

computer programming language See *programming language*.

conference call A telephone call that can serve three or more parties for joint conversation.

configuration The specifications for, or items needed to use, a piece of software or hardware.

connectivity The capability of a computer system to use information gained by linking computers and information resources.

context-sensitive help On-screen help that is relevant to the action currently being accessed or completed.

controller The component that regulates the operation of a peripheral device; controls the transfer of data from the computer to a peripheral device.

control structure A method used to direct the flow of logic in a computer program.

control unit The part of the microprocessor that controls operations of the CPU and coordinates the functions of other devices within a computer system.

coordinates In a spreadsheet program, the column letter and row number that identify a particular cell. For example, the coordinates D5 name the cell in column D and row 5. Can be used in formulas or in another cell to transfer a value to that cell.

coprocessor A processing chip that assists the CPU in doing certain types of operations; for example, a math coprocessor does complex math operations.

CPU See *central processing unit*.

cropping The process of trimming an image for a better fit on a page or for eliminating unwanted portions.

cursor A symbol, such as a solid rectangle, an underline bar, or a vertical bar, that shows the current location on a computer screen and indicates the point at which the next input will appear.

data Facts; the raw material of information.

database A collection of facts that are stored in a well-organized way so that many people can access the same information for different purposes.

data communication The process of enabling digital devices such as computers to communicate with each other.

data-management software An application program used to organize, access, and control information arranged in fields, records, and files.

debug To find and correct errors in a program.

decision step A program logic pattern in which the computer makes a choice based on an evaluation between two or more paths that can be taken; also called *selection*.

default setting A built-in value, such as a format setting for single-spaced lines, that a program applies unless instructed otherwise by the user.

density The compactness of data on a disk or tape.

desktop model The style of computer system that consists of several separate components and that resides on a desktop; generally not easily or conveniently transported.

desktop publishing (DTP) An activity that uses microcomputer hardware and software tools to set type, lay out complete pages that include text, type, and illustrations, and produce output of near-letter quality, letter quality, or near-typeset quality.

dialog box An outlined area that appears on the screen to request user input. For example, you may format a character's font through a dialog box.

digital computer A computer that uses electronic (not mechanical) parts and that handles discrete, or individually distinct data.

direct-access storage Storage from which data can be obtained in any order; an example is a disk.

disk A round plate made of metal or some type of plastic used as a direct-access form of storage; the two basic types are magnetic and optical.

disk drive The mechanical device that holds and processes magnetic or other disk media.

distributed processing A system in which processing can be done at sites other than that of the central computer.

documentation Written material that tells about a program or piece of equipment; in programming, it includes definitions, explanations, charts, and changes to the program.

document-preparation package Word processing software that includes many elements of page composition software.

dot-matrix printer A printer that forms character images as a series of points, using an impact mechanism that strikes an ink ribbon against the paper. The pins are arranged in a matrix of rows and columns, and only the pins needed for forming a particular character are selected.

download To transfer a program or data from a remote, or host, computer to one's own computer or from a computer to a peripheral device.

downsizing Moving applications to microcomputers from larger computers.

draw program A program used for creating and manipulating objects such as lines, curves, ovals, circles, rectangles; appropriate for creating images to scale.

driver The program that controls a device.

DTP See desktop publishing.

dynamic link A connection between two items that provides interactive access from one to the other.

electronic bulletin board See *bulletin board system*.

electronic mail (e-mail) The process of sending, receiving, storing, and forwarding messages in digital form over telecommunication facilities.

electronic funds transfer (EFT) An on-line method that permits the cashless transmission of money electronically between banks and among banks and customers without requiring paper documentation.

emulation A program's or device's imitating another program or device.

erasable optical disk An optical disk technology that can be written to, read from, and erased.

ergonomics The study of the physical relationships between people and their work environment, with the purpose of designing computer hardware and software that will improve user productivity and comfort.

expansion board A board that holds chips and circuit paths and that can be inserted into a slot on the motherboard of a computer for the purpose of adding some feature to the computer such as more memory or greater graphics capability. Also called *circuit board* and *interface board*.

expansion slot See *slot*.

expert system A form of applied intelligence software designed to imitate the decision-making processes of experts in a specific field.

facsimile A method of transmitting graphical images over telecommunication lines in which the original document is scanned or digitized at the sending end and reproduced at the receiving end. Also called *fax, fax system*, or *facsimile system*.

feedback A check within a system that helps determine whether goals are being met; the return of information about the effectiveness of a system.

fiber-optic cable A communication channel that consists of hair-thin strands of glass that carry data as pulses of light.

field An item consisting of one or more characters that are related logically.

file A group of related records stored together; a specific unit of data stored on a disk or tape.

file name A name given to a file for purposes of storage and retrieval.

file server See *server*.

flat-panel display A flat screen that shows images much like the display on a digital watch; used on portable computers.

floppy disk The name given to the mylar, flexible, disk-shaped storage medium coated with a magnetizable substance; rotates within a plastic jacket; also called *diskette*.

floppy disk drive The mechanical device that rotates and reads the floppy disk.

flowchart A picture in which symbols stand for the flow of operations, data, and equipment of a program or system.

font A set of alphanumeric characters in a particular typeface, size, and style.

forecast A plan that helps you predict what will happen to some numbers when other numbers change. An electronic spreadsheet lets you try out quickly a lot of numbers in a forecast so that you can see what action is needed to achieve the results you want (for example, increased earnings or a better grade in a class).

formula A mathematical expression, or equation; in a spreadsheet, a formula uses the values of one or more

other cells to derive new figures, such as totals.
fourth-generation language (4GL) A high-level technique that makes it possible to assemble a series of query commands as an operational program, enabling end-users to develop some programs directly; associated most often with databases.
full-duplex transmission Transmission in which data travel along a line in both directions at once.

generation A stage; in computer technology, a stage usually much improved over an earlier stage.
gigabyte (GB) Approximately 1 billion bytes (or characters); 230 bytes.
grammar checker A program that enables you to find syntax errors in a text document.
graphical user interface (GUI) A user interface that employs graphics (icons, menus, pointers, buttons, and windows) to simplify the user's interaction with the computer; usually includes a mouse for input; enables you to avoid using complex and arcane typed commands.
graphics tablet An electronic pad on which a user draws images with a puck or stylus. Sensors under the pad identify the locations and transmit image-creating data to the computer. Also called *digitizing tablet*.

hacking The activity of computer enthusiasts who feel challenged to break computer security measures without authorization.
half-duplex transmission Transmission in which data can travel along a line in either direction, but in only one direction at a time.
hard copy Output that is printed on material such as paper.
hard disk A rigid, disk-shaped storage medium, usually made of metal and coated with a magnetizable substance, encased in a hard disk drive; sometimes refers to the entire drive.
hard disk drive The machine that rotates and reads the hard disk.
hardware The physical components of a computer system (for example, keyboards, printers, monitors).
high-level language A language based on macro commands that cause a computer to execute a full sequence of instructions from a single entry; geared more toward the user than the machine.
host computer The central computer in a network.
hypertext A method of accessing linked items in a database.

IBM-compatible All computers that are compatible with IBM PCs, meaning they can run the same software as an IBM PC.
icon A picture or graphic symbol used to represent such things as an application, a software function, a document, a folder, or a disk; one of several devices designed to make computers easy to use.
impact printer A printer that forms impressions by striking a ribbon against a sheet of paper with a print mechanism.
information Data that have been organized and processed so they are meaningful.
information system A system in which data are the inputs and information is the output.
information utility A for-profit business or organization that supplies information and consumer services through telecommunication facilities that are accessible directly by computer.
ink-jet printer A nonimpact printer that forms impressions with fine sprays of ink onto paper.
input Whatever goes into the computer, such as instructions, commands, or data; also used in verb form.
input device A piece of equipment used to enter data into a computer system.
install To put a program onto a hard disk.
instruction set Rudimentary instructions built into the microprocessor for performing arithmetic, comparison, and storage and retrieval operations.
integrated circuit (IC) A complete electronic circuit on a tiny silicon chip.
integrated software Sets of programs that work together, making it possible to mix inputs, processing, and outputs among programs that are ordinarily different and incompatible.
interpreter A high-level language translator that evaluates and translates a program one statement at a time, enabling the programmer to work interactively while programming.

K See *kilobyte*.
kerning Adjusting the spaces between characters to create wider or tighter spacing for a more attractive and readable look.
keyboard An input device similar to a typewriter keyboard that permits the typing of alphanumeric characters as well as commands entered through special function keys.
kilobyte (KB) 1,024 (210) bytes, often rounded to 1,000.

label A word or other information in a cell that describes the contents of another cell, a group of cells, or an entire spreadsheet. A label cannot be used in calculation.
LAN See local-area network.
language-translator program A program (often classified as a system program) that changes into machine language a computer code made up of words and symbols.
laptop A portable microcomputer that weighs less than 12 pounds and can be fit into a briefcase. Laptop computers operate on batteries, making them usable in travel and remote situations.
laser printer A printer that generates images through use of a laser beam that passes over the surface of a xerographic drum.
leading The amount of vertical space between lines of type.
light pen A device that enables a user to enter images into a computer by moving a point of light across a display screen.

link A communication channel that connects nodes.
load To read information such as a program or data into computer memory.
local-area network (LAN) A communication-linked group of computers and peripherals located within a single office or building.
loop A program logic that causes a series of instructions to be executed repeatedly as long as specified conditions remain constant.

machine cycle The time period in which the CPU gets, interprets, and executes one computer instruction.
machine language The only language that a computer can run directly. It codes the computer's electrical states in combinations of 1's and 0's.
macro A keyboard command of only one or two keystrokes that activates an assigned sequence of instructions or string of text.
magnetic disk A circular storage medium on which data items are recorded magnetically for direct- (random-) access reading and writing.
magnetic tape A storage medium on which information is represented by magnetic spots on continuous ribbons of oxide-coated acetate.
mail merge The process of printing form letters automatically, using, for example, both a word-processing file containing the letter and a database file containing the names and addresses.
mainframe A large computer that can handle very large amounts of data very quickly and support many users, programs, and peripheral devices in the same time frame; so named because in the past the main processing unit of this computer consisted of a series of circuit boards mounted within a frame structure.
megabyte (MB) Represents 1,048,546 bytes, or approximately 1 million bytes (or characters.)
megahertz (MHz) A unit of electrical frequency equal to 1 million cycles per second; measures a CPU's clock speed.
memory Internal physical storage that consists of chips and holds instructions and data needed for processing, sometimes referred to as *main memory, primary storage,* or *internal storage.*
menu A set of available functions or information displayed on the screen; may be in the form of a list or a bar or a set of icons.
menu-driven program An interface design under which access to functions and services is controlled through lists from which options are selected.
MHz See *megahertz.*
microcomputer A small computer (desk-size or less) that uses a single microchip as its processor; also called *personal computer* or *home computer.*
microprocessor A programmable processing unit on a single microchip.
microprocessor The CPU of a microcomputer; contained on a single silicon chip.

microwave link A communication channel that transmits and receives signals through use of high-power, short-wavelength radio signals carried through the atmosphere in straight lines.
MIDI interface MIDI stands for "musical instrument digital interface." The interface enables you to connect MIDI instruments, such as synthesizers, to your computer and to input and output music; often used with multimedia applications.
minicomputer A computer that is smaller in capacity and price than a mainframe but that delivers full-system capabilities. The minicomputer got its name by comparison with the large-scale computers that dominated the market when it was introduced in the mid-1960s.
modem Acronym for modulator/demodulator; a device that prepares digital computer signals for analog transmission over telephone lines and then prepares the analog signals for reentry into a computer.
module A part of a whole; a program segment or subsystem, such as that found in an integrated software package.
monitor A video display device or screen used for showing output; usually of cathoderay technology.
motherboard The main circuit board of a microcomputer.
mouse A gesture-based input device that can be rolled on a solid, flat surface to direct the movement of the cursor on a screen.
multimedia Computer applications that combine text, audio, and graphic components with interactive capabilities; also called *hypermedia.*
multitasking Running two or more programs on a computer at once.

nanosecond A billionth of a second.
network A communication system linking two or more computers and their peripherals.
network interface card (NIC) An integrated circuit board, or adapter, that is plugged into a slot of a computer on a local-area network and that functions to hook a network cable to the microcomputer; allows the members of the network to communicate with each other.
network operating system (NOS) The computer software that manages a local-area network and handles requests for data and equipment from the members of the LAN.
node At end point of a network; may be a computer, a printer, a dumb terminal, or some other physical device; a computer processing point that has access to a data network.
nondestructive read/destructive write Description of RAM operations in which stored items can be read repeatedly without being erased, but are destroyed when new items are written over them.
nonimpact printer A printer that forms impressions without requiring the physical striking of print characters against ribbon and paper by a print mechanism.
notebook A portable microcomputer that weighs less than 8 pounds and can be fit into a briefcase.
notepad computer A small, portable computer with a

flat display screen that can detect and interpret the movements of a stylus with which you write on the screen.

object-oriented programming (OOP) A programming technique in which program modules are usable with different objects, or elements, rather than having to be recorded for each different use.

online Connected directly to a computer.

open To activate a document or application.

operating system The set of system programs that a computer uses to manage its own operations.

optical disk A storage medium that relies on the use of laser beams for storing and retrieving data.

output Anything that comes out of a computer in a form that is useful to people; also used in verb form.

output device A device that presents information from a computer in human-readable form.

package A software program for retail sale that has been prewritten by professional programmers.

page composition software Software for manipulating text and graphics elements in order to design and produce pages for publication.

page description language A language for defining the layout and contents of a page.

paint program A program for creating and manipulating pixels in order to create images; appropriate for free-hand drawing.

palmtop A pocket microcomputer that weighs less than 1 pound and has limited functions.

password A special word, code, or symbol, designed for security purposes, that must entered into a computer system before a user can gain access to the system's resources.

peer-to-peer LAN A LAN in which each computer has equal power as both client and server.

pen-based interface A user interface in which the primary input is handwriting and the operating system contains pattern recognition software to interpret the input.

peripherals External devices such as keyboards and printers that are attached to the computer.

piracy Unauthorized copying, distribution, or use of software.

pixel Short for "picture element." An individual point of light on a display screen that can be lit or unlit; can be made of different shades of gray or different colors.

plotter A device that delivers outputs in the form of drawn images.

port An interface on a computer where a printer or some other device can be plugged in.

presentation graphics High-quality, professional-looking graphics that present numerical information in an easy-to-understand format, such as a pie chart or bar graph.

printed circuit board A board that holds chips and circuit paths and that can be inserted into a slot on the main board, or motherboard, of a computer for the purpose of adding some feature to the computer, such as more memory or greater graphics capability; sometimes called *expansion card*.

printer A machine that prints characters or other images on paper.

print formatting The function of an application program in which the appearance of the text is set up for printing.

printout A document generated on a printer linked to a computer. Also known as *hard copy*.

privacy The right of individuals to choose when and whether data about themselves are made public.

process To transform data into useful information by classifying, sorting, calculating, or summarizing.

program A set of instructions that, when executed causes a computer to do particular tasks; also called *software*.

programming The writing of a computer program.

programming language A code in which a computer program is written

programmer The person who writes computer software.

prompt A symbol, message, or cue that indicates that the operating system or a program is ready for input.

proper program A program in which each module has only one entry point and one exit point.

protocol The description of rules for the formatting of data when transmitting and receiving data over a network.

public-domain software Programs unprotected by copyright law and available for free, unrestricted public use.

query To ask for, or request, specific information from a database.

random-access memory (RAM) The array of microchips used to build the storage area within a computer's CPU. Data items and program segments can be recorded and retrieved on RAM devices.

read-only memory (ROM) The form of memory that holds items that can be read, but not erased or altered by normal input methods.

read To access (for example, to detect what is written in random-access memory, in read-only memory, or on a disk or tape).

real memory Actual RAM memory, as opposed to virtual memory.

real-time Describes the ability of a computer to respond immediately and provide output fast enough to control the outcome of an event.

record A collection of related fields.

refresh Re-energize; recharge; the refresh rate for a monitor is expressed in hertz.

register The special high-speed storage area on a microprocessor that receives data, holds them, and transfers them immediately during processing.

relational database A database, arranged in tables, that enables the user to open and use data from several files at one time for cross-referencing and linking information in the files.

resolution The sharpness or clarity of displayed images

or characters.

right-sizing A term that describes using the correct equipment for a purpose and often includes moving applications to microcomputers from larger computers.

ring network A data communication network in which nodes are connected in a continuous circle and in which transmitted messages are passed to all nodes in the network until the destination is reached.

ROM See *read-only memory*.

scalable font A font that is defined in shape but not in size and that can be sized to suit the document.

scaling The process of changing the size of an image yet retaining its proportions.

scanner A device for direct input that senses information by the reflection of light on a document and transmits the data in digital form to a computer.

screen saver A program designed either to blank out the screen or to set up an animated sequence in order to prevent ghosting or burn-in when the computer and monitor are on but not in use.

scroll To move text or images on and off the screen in order to see all of the material in a file.

search A function that finds a designated string of characters in a document.

semiconductor A substance, such as silicon or gallium, whose conductivity is poor or improved, depending on the addition of another material or energy such as light.

sequential-access storage Storage from which data items must be read one after another, in a fixed sequence from the beginning to the end; an example is magnetic tape.

server A computer dedicated to specific supply functions on a LAN, such as communicating, managing the LAN, and delivering printer power and database information.

shareware Copyrighted programs that are given away free, but with the expectation that satisfied users will voluntarily pay the copyright holder for use of the program.

shell An operating environment layer that separates the operating system from the user and typically involves a menu-driven or a graphical user interface.

silicon A material found in quartz and sand that conducts or does not conduct electricity, depending upon the material or chemical added to it.

simple sequence A program logic pattern in which statements are executed one after another in the order in which they are stored.

simplex transmission Transmission in which data travel along a line in one direction only.

slot An opening and connector inside a computer that allows for the installation of a circuit board for additional memory or some other capability that enhances the performance of the computer.

soft copy A temporary display, such as monitor output, of machine output.

software package A prewritten program that can be purchased for use with a particular computer to do a specific job; usually includes the program, on disks, and a user's manual.

source-data automation Techniques for automating and speeding the input process by gathering data directly from documents or special instruments when and where an event takes place.

spelling checker A software program or module, usually found in word processing programs, that checks words in a document against words in a dictionary file, to detect misspellings.

spreadsheet An application program that takes the place of paper ledger sheets to store, manipulate, and analyze numeric data.

stand-alone Descriptive of a program or system that is self-contained, as opposed to a system or program that is dependent on another.

star network A data communication network in which all modes radiate from a central computer hub that controls receipt and delivery of all messages.

stepwise refinement The process of repeatedly refining steps in a top-down design.

storage Retention of programs or data on media such as floppy disks or hard disks that are external to the computer's processor or memory.

stored-program concept The idea that programs can be stored in a computer's memory and can be switched electronically rather than by resetting switches and rewiring the computer.

structured programming A top-down, modular approach to program design that emphasizes division of a program into logical sections to improve programmer productivity and program clarity.

style sheet A file that contains formatting instructions for text, but does not contain text; may include margin settings, line spacing, paragraph indentation, and the like.

suite A set of closely related or interacting programs; integrated sets of programs.

supercomputer The most expensive, largest computer; can process over 1 billion instructions per second.

synchronous transmission A method in which data bits are sent in a stream at a timed, fixed rate.

synergism A situation in which the combined efforts of all parts of an information system achieve a greater effect than the sum of the individual components.

syntax The grammatical rules of a programming language.

system A group of related elements that work toward a common goal.

system analyst A computer professional responsible for analyzing an organization's objectives and operations for ways to improve operations that may include implementing computer technologies.

system program Software, such as the operating system and utility programs, that manages computer resources at the machine level rather than at the user level; programs that coordinate the operation of computer circuitry and assist in the development and execution of applications.

system software Programs that manage the computer circuitry at a low level and control the execution of user application programs.

system unit The part of a microcomputer that contains the CPU and memory.

tape drive A storage device that holds and processes magnetic tape media.

task switching The capability of an operating system that enables you to have two programs loaded at the same time so that you can work back and forth between them.

telecommunication The transfer of data from one point to another over distances, using telephone lines, microwaves, and/or satellites.

telecommuting A plan by which an employee works away from the office and communicates with the office through a computer terminal and telecommunication facilities.

teleconference A meeting of parties in multiple locations conducted over telecommunications channels; may involve both electronic and image-producing facilities.

template In a spreadsheet program, a set of predefined formulas and formats ready for user entries; also, a pre-designed format for a standard document.

text wrap An automatic page composition function in which text flows around an image.

title The name of a multimedia package.

top-down design A programming design technique in which a solution is defined from the general to the specific in terms of functions and subfunctions to be performed.

touch screen A monitor screen that makes it possible for users to select programs and functions by touching designated places on the screen.

trackball A gesture-based input device in which a ball resting on top of a base is rolled to direct the cursor or other pointer on the screen.

transistor A device that controls electric current flow without using a vacuum tube.

twisted-pair cable A communication channel that consists of pairs of wires twisted together and bound into a cable; commonly used for telephone transmission.

typeface A collection of letters, numbers, and symbols that share a particular appearance; the shape, or design, of print (for example, Times, Helvetica, Courier).

user A person who uses computer software or has contact with computer systems.

user friendly A descriptive term for hardware and software features that promote ease of use and lessen frustration for computer users.

user interface The method by which a user communicates with a computer.

users' group An informal group of people with a particular microcomputer, software package, or computer interest who meet to exchange information about hardware, software, and support.

utility program A program that performs a specific task, usually relating to managing system resources such as files and disks.

vacuum tubes A glass bulb (resembling a light bulb) from which almost all air has been removed and through which electricity can pass.

value A number that is entered into a cell.

videoconference A conference that occurs over telecommunication links and that can provide either one-way video and two-way audio or full audio and video through the use of cameras and wall screens.

virtual memory A technique in which portions of programs and data are swapped back and forth between storage and memory, giving the illusion that memory is unlimited.

virtual reality A computer arrangement, including hardware and software, that enables a person to experience and manipulate a three-dimensional world that exists only in projected images; includes simulated touch as one more sense in the multisensory world of multimedia.

virus A form of sabotage in which a computer program wreaks havoc on a system by destroying data, causing malfunctions, or harassing a user.

voice mail A message system in which a spoken message is converted to digital form and stored in the recipient's mailbox until the recipient dials in and retrieves the message in audio form.

voice synthesizer An output device that uses stored patterns of sound to assemble words for output that imitates the human voice.

"what-if" analysis A planning activity during which numerous values are changed in a spreadsheet in order to project consequences of possible future conditions; sometimes referred to as a *scenario*.

wide-area network (WAN) A data communication network designed to serve users over hundreds or thousands of miles; generally implemented by linking computers and LANs over telephone lines.

window A frame that displays all of or a portion of a file, message, or menu on the screen.

word A group of bits considered as an unit that a computer can handle at once.

word processing A computer application designed for the preparation of text; involves writing, editing, formatting, and printing.

word wrap A feature in word processing that starts a new line automatically when the current line is filled.

workstation A term for a powerful microcomputer used primarily for engineering and design purposes.

WORM Stands for "write once, read many." An optical disk that can be recorded only once but read from many times.

WYSIWYG Pronounced *wizzywig*, and stands for "what you see is what you get"; identifies a program's capability to display text on the screen as it will appear when printed on paper.

INDEX

Abacus, 13
Access codes, hacking and, 223
ACE, 207
Ada, 129
Add-ins, 257
Add-ons, 257
Adobe PostScript, 188
Adobe System, 185, 188
Aiken, Howard, 18
Alert box, 77–78, 80
Algorithm, 137
Allen, Paul, 177
All-in-one package, 195
Altair 8800, 24
Alvinn (Autonomous Land Vehicle in a Neural Network), 211
American Express, 208
American Standard Code for Information Interchange (ASCII), 42–43
American Telephone & Telegraph (AT&T), 164
America Online, 280
Ami Pro, 82, 199
Analog transmission, 152
Antivirus software, 220, 268–269
APACHE III, 242
APACHE Medica Systems, Inc., 242
Apple Computer Inc., 255
 history of, 25
  multimedia presentations and, 203
  WYSIWYG and, 78
Apple II, 73
Application software. *See also* Software
 defined, 4
Applied intelligence, 207
Approach, 94
Apscreen, 234
Aptiva, 250
Arbitrary wrap, 189, 191
Archie, 275
ARCnet, 166
ARPANET, 176

Artificial intelligence, 206–207
Assembly language, 125
Asynchronous transmission, 160
Atanasoff, John, 19
Atanasoff-Berry Computer (ABC), 18–19
Attribute match, 84
Authoring tool, 204
AutoCad, 205

Babbage, Charles, 15–16
Background utility approach, 195, 196
Back up, 68
Bandwidth, 155, 255
Bar graphs, 100
Barlow, John Perry, 231
BASIC, 128
Bays, 65
Bell Laboratories, 124, 207
Berry, Clifford, 19
Binary number system, 40
 instructions and, 50
 memory addresses and, 46
Binary representation, 40–42
Bit, 40
Bit architecture, 255
Bit cells, 45
Bit-mapping, fonts and, 187
Bitstream, 188
Block, 83
Block operation, 83
Boole, George, 18
Boot, 110
Bootstrap loader, 110
Boxes
 alert, 77–78
 dialog, 77
Brigham, Tom, 33
Browsing, 97
BRS/After Dark, 281–282
Bug, 137
Bulletin boards
 free speech and, 218
 misuse of, 218
Bulletin board system (BBS), 175–176

Bus, 52
Bus networks, 164
Buses
 defined, 256
 expansion, 256
 local, 256
 purchasing a computer and, 256–257
Business
 computers in, 29–30
 multimedia use and, 200
Bus networks, 164
Byron, Augusta Ada, 17
Byte, 41
Bytes, units of, 42

C, 131–133
Cache memory, 47
Caduceus II, 207
Carpal tunnel syndrome, 238
Catepillar Inc., 210
CD-ROM, 66–68
 multimedia presentations and, 200
Cell, 90
 active, 90
 locations of, 91
Central processing unit (CPU), 43–45
 arithmetic/logic unit, 45
 control unit, 44–45
 defined, 6
 machine cycle, 50
Chief programmer team (CPT), 144–145
Chip, 23
Chrysler Corp., 210
Cinepak, 201
Circuit boards, 52
Clarity, 257
Client, 166
Client/server LAN, 166, 169
Clip art, 191–192
Clipboard, 197–198
Clock, 52
Clock speed, 255
Coaxial cables, 155

COBOL, 22, 133–134
Code, 125
Command-line user interfaces, 116–117
Commodore Business Machines, 25
Common carrier, 164
Communication channels, 153–161
  coaxial cables, 155
  communication satellite, 156–158
  defined, 153
  fiber-optic cables, 155–156
  microwave link, 156, 157
  modems and, 157–161
  telegraph lines, 154
  twisted pairs, 154–155
Communication satellite, 156–158
Communication software, 160–161
Compatible, 74
Compiler, 125
CompuAdd Computer Corp., 202
CompuServe, 164, 176, 279
Computer-aided design, 205–206
Computer-aided manufacturing, 206
  desktop manufacturing, 206
Computer-assisted instruction (CAL), 28
Computer-based training (CBT), 29
Computer codes, 42–43
Computer conference, 174
Computer crime, 219–222
  civil rights vs. criminal behavior, 218–219
  defined, 219
  detection of, 218, 219
  financial crimes, 221–222
  hacking, 222–224
  laws against, 223
  piracy, 224–226
  sabotage, 220
  security measures for organizations, 226–228
  telephone toll fraud, 223
  theft of property, 221
  theft of services, 220–221
  viruses, 220
  white-collar crimes, 221
Computer ethics, defined, 218
Computer Fraud and Abuse Act, 223, 233
Computer matching, 232
Computer Matching and Privacy Protection Act, 233
Computers. *See also* Microcomputers
  care of, 263–266
  classifications of, 7–9
  connecting, 52–53
  criminal conduct and ethics for, 218–228
  defined, 1
  "father" of, 15–16
  first generation, 21
  fourth generation, 23–27
  history of, 13–27
  how it works, 48–52
  in information system, 6–13
  input hardware, 53–60
  mainframe, 8
  minicomputers, 8–9
  notepad, 58
  output methods, 60–65
  for people with disabilities, 262–263
  processing speeds, 6–7
  reliability of, 7
  second generation, 22–23
  storage in, 7
  super, 8
  third generation, 23
Computers, purchasing, 248–270
  add-ons and add-ins, 257
  alternate input devices and other equipment, 259–260
  buses, 256–257
  buying checklist, 251
  choosing the computer, 249–251
  customer support, 254
  guidelines for, 248
  keyboards, 258–259
  mail-order purchases, 252–253
  memory, 255–256
  microprocessor, 255
  monitors, 257–258
  portable computers, 260–261
  printers, 261
  software, 249
  storage, 260
  warranties, 252
  where to buy, 252
Computer software. *See* Software
Computing-Tabulating-Recording Company (CTR), 17
Conference call, 173
Configuration, defined, 2
Connectivity, 12
Context-sensitive help, 79
Controller, 53
Control signal, 60
Control structures, 139–141
Control unit, 44–45
Conventional memory, 256
Copyright
  derivative work, 226
  software and, 224–225
Copyright Act of 1978, 224
CorelDRAW!, 226
Countess of Lovelace. *See* Byron, Augusta Ada
Crick, Reg, 16
Crime. *See also* Computer crime
  computers and, 218–228
  white-collar, 221
Cropping, 189, 190
Crosstalk, 161
Cumulative trauma disorders, 238
Cursor, 55
  defined, 82
  movements, 82
  position of, 82–83
Customer support for computers, 254
Cut-and-paste, 83–84

Data
  defined, 2
  path of, through information system, 4–6
  in a system, 5
Database management system, 94
Databases
  defined, 94
  federal government and, 229, 230
  privacy issues and, 229–232
  relational, 96
  resumes and, 98
  uses of, 232
Data communication, defined, 153
Data-management software, 94–97
  data organization, 94–96
  defined, 94
  field, 94–95
  file, 95
  querying and reporting, 97
  record, 95
  relational database, 96
Data manager, 94
Data representation, 40–43
Data vendors, 234
dBASE, 94
Debug, 137–139
Decision step, 140

Default settings, 85
Deletions, 83
Delphi, 176, 279–280
Demodulation, 157, 159
Design software, 104
Desk accessories, 195
Desk to Desk, 169
Desktop manufacturing, 206
Desktop publishing, 184–194
  basic steps in, 184–185
  clip art, 191–192
  computer capabilities required for, 184
  defined, 184, 185
  dingbats, 192
  document–preparation package, 185
  functions of packages, 188–192
  internal graphics, 190–192
  kerning and leading, 190, 191
  page composition software, 184, 185
  print reproduction, 192–194
  scaling and cropping, 189, 190
  style sheets and templates, 188
  text wrap, 189
  typefaces and fonts for, 186–188
  uses of, 185
  WYSIWYG in, 185, 186
Diagnostic routines, 110
DIALOG, 281
Dialog box, 77, 80
Difference Engine, 15–16
Digital audiotape (DAT), 68
Digital computer, 40
Dingbats, 192
Dipmeter Advisor, 207
Direct-access storage, 66
Direct input, 58–60
  scanners, 59–60
  sensor input, 60
  speech recognition, 60
Disabilities, computer equipment for people with, 262–263
Disk drive, 65
Disks
  care of, 269–270
  troubleshooting for, 290
Display outputs, 60–62
  flat-panel display, 61
  gas plasma display, 61
  liquid-crystal display, 61
Distributed processing, 161
Document-preparation package, 185

DOS based computers, advantage/disadvantages of, 250
Dot-matrix printers, 62–63, 261
Dow Jones News/Retrieval, 282
Draft quality printers, 192
Drag-and-drop, 84
Dragon Systems, Inc., 28, 263
Draw programs, 100–104
  defined, 99
Driver, 53
Drum plotters, 64
Dynamic data exchange, 114
Dynamic link, 204

Echelon Corporation, 11
Eckert, J. Presper, 18–19
Editing, word processing and, 82–83
Education, microcomputers
EDVAC (Electronic Discrete Variable Automatic Computer), 20
Electroluminescent display, 61
Electronic bulletin boards, 175–176
Electronic Communications Privacy Act, 223, 233
Electronic Frontier Foundation, 93, 231
Electronic funds transfer (EFT), 169–170
Electronic mail, 171
Electronic thesaurus, 84
E-mail, Internet, 274
ENIAC (Electronic Numerical Integrator And Calculator), 18–19
Equifa, 234
Erasable optical disk, 68
Ergonomics, 235–243
  computer design and, 238–240
  computer related health problems, 236–238
  defined, 235
  eye fatigue, 236–237
  keyboards and, 238–239
  mouse and, 240
  office furniture, 239–240
  office lighting, 240
  ozone gas and, 241, 243
  safety issues, 241–243
  uses of, 235–236
  video display glare, 237, 240
  video display terminals and, 241

Ethernet, 166
Ethics
  computer, 218
  defined, 218
  security and, 227
E-time, 50
Excel, 89
Excessive fatigue, ergonomics and, 238
Expanded memory, 256
Expansion board, 52
Expansion bus, 256
Expansion cards, 257
Expert systems, 206–208
  applications of, 207–208
  medicine and, 207
Exploding pie charts, 100
Extended Binary Coded Decimal Interchange Code, 42–43
Extended memory, 256
Extremely low-frequency, long-term exposure to, 241
Eye fatigue, 236–237
Eyegaze Computer System, 262–263

FaceLift, 188
Facsimile, 170–171
Fairchild Semiconductor, 23
Fair Credit Reporting Act, 232, 233
Family Education Rights and Privacy Act, 233
Feedback, defined, 6
Fiber-optic cables, 155–156
FIDONET, 175
Field, 94–95
File name, 75
Files, 75–76, 95
  defined, 75
  exporting, 76
  icon and, 75
  importing, 76
  opening, 75
  troubleshooting for, 289
Financial crimes, 221–222
First generation computers, 21
Flatbed plotter, 64
Flat-panel screens, 261
Floating-point numbers, 91
Floppy disk, 66
Floppy disk drive, 66
  purchasing, 260
Fonts, 186–188
  bit-mapping, 187

defined, 186
  outline, 187–188
  scalable, 187–188
  softs, 188
  vector graphics, 187
Forecast, 92
Formats, printing, 85, 87
Formula, 90–91
Fortran, 127–128
FORTRAN, 22
Fourth-generation computers, 23–27
Fourth-generation languages, 135
Freedom of Information Act, 233
FTP, 275
Full-duplex transmission, 154

Garbage in, garbage out (GIGO), 7
Gas plasma display, 61
Gates, Bill, 177
General Electric, 21
Generation, 20
GEnie, 279
Gesture-based interfaces, 119
Gigabyte, 42
Global search and replace, 84
Gopher, 176, 275
Grammar checkers, 85
Graphical user interfaces, 117–118
  ease of use and, 250
Graphics card, 258
Graphics software, 97–104
  bar graphs, 100
  line graphs, 100
  paint and draw programs, 100–104
  pictographs, 100
  pie charts, 100
  presentation graphics programs, 99–100
  slide shows, 100
  uses of, 99
Graphics tablet, 56–57
Graphs, spreadsheets and, 93
Groupware, 171

Hacking, 222–224
  access codes and, 223
  defined, 222
Half-duplex transmission, 154
Handshake, 161
Hard copy, 62
Hard disk, 65–66
Hard disk drive, 66
  purchasing, 260

Hardware
  compatibility and, 74
  defined, 2
  input, 53–60
Hardware, purchasing
  add-ons and add-ins, 257
  alternate input devices and other equipment, 259–260
  buses, 256–257
  keyboards, 258–259
  memory, 255–256
  microprocessor, 255
  monitors, 257–258
  portable computers, 260–261
  printers, 261
  storage, 260
Health, computer-related problems, 236–237
Help, 79
  context-sensitive, 79
Hewlett-Packard PCL, 188
High-level languages, 125–135
  Ada, 129
  BASIC, 128
  C, 131–133
  COBOL, 133–134
  Fortran, 127–128
  Pascal, 128–131
  RPG, 135
Hollerith, Herman, 16–17
Holloway, Barrie, 16
Hopper, Grace Murray, 54
Host computer, 162
Howard, Ron, 33
HyperCard, 204
Hypermedia, 204
Hypertext, 204

IBM (International Business Machines Corporation), 17, 21, 73, 123
  history of, 25
IBM computers,
  files, troubleshooting for, 289
  memory and, 256
  multimedia presentations and, 203
  page description language, 188
  printers, troubleshooting for, 292
  software, troubleshooting for, 288
  WYSIWYG and, 78
Icons, 75, 118
Illustration software, 104
Impact printer, 62
Indeo, 201

Industry, multimedia use and, 200
Information, defined, 2
Information system
  components of, 2–4
  computers in, 6–13
  defined, 2
  path of data through, 4–6
Information utilities, 174, 278
Ink-jet printers, 63, 261
  color, 194
Input/output instructions, 111
Input, defined, 5
Input devices, purchasing, 258–260
Input hardware, 53–60
  direct input, 58–60
  graphic tablet, 56–57
  interactive input, 54–58
  keyboard, 55–56
  light pen, 56–57
  mouse, 56–57
  notepad computer, 58
  scanners, 59–60
  sensor input, 60
  speech recognition, 60
  touch screen, 56–57
  trackball, 56–57
  virtual reality, 58
Insertions, 83
Install, 74
Instruction set, 48, 50
  reduced instruction set computer, 51
Integrated circuit (IC), 23
Integrated Services Digital Network, 164–165
Integrated software, 194–199
  all-in-one package, 195
  background utility approach, 195, 196
  characteristics of, 197–199
  clipboard, 197–198
  module, 197
  suite, 199
  types of, 195
Intel, microprocessor, 255
Intel chip, 24
Interface boards, 52
Internal Revenue Service, 208
International Berne Copyright Convention, 224
Internet
  America Online, 280
  Archie, 275
  BRS/After Dark, 281–282

CompuServe, 279
Delphi, 279–280
DIALOG, 281
Dow Jones News/Retrieval, 282
e-mail, 274
  etiquette, 277–278
  finding information on, 275–276
FTP, 275
gaining access to, 277
GEnie, 279
Gopher, 275
history of, 176
information utilities, 277–278
Microsoft Network, 282–283
Mosaic, 276
Netscape's Navigator, 276
Prodigy, 281
reasons to use, 274
remote log-in, 274–275
Telnet, 275
Usenet, 274
Veronica, 276
WAIS, 276
Web, 276
Yahoo, 276
Interpreter, 125
INVIDEO, 203
Irregular wrap, 189
I-time, 50

Jacquard loom, 15–16

Kapor, Mitch, 93, 231
Kerning, 190, 191
Keyboards, 55–56
  ergonomics and, 238–239
  purchasing, 258–259
  troubleshooting for, 290–291
Kilobyte, 42
Kurzweil, Ray, 65
Kurzweil Applied Intelligence, Inc., 263
Kurzweil Reading Machine, 65

Label, 90
Language-translator program, 125
Laptop computers, 9, 11
  purchasing, 260–261
Large-scale integration (LSI), 23
Laser printers, 63–64, 261
  color, 194
  ozone gas emission, 241–243
LC Technologies, 262
Leading, 190, 191
Letter quality printers, 192, 194

Lighting, office, 240
Light pen, 56–57
Line graphs, 100
Link, 161
Liquid-crystal display, 61, 260–261
Load, 74
Local-area networks (LANs), 165–169
  client/server, 166, 169
  components of, 166
  peer-to-peer, 169
Local bus, 256
Loop, 140
Lotus 1-2-3, 89, 93, 199
Lotus MarketPlace, 230–231
Lotus Notes, 199
Lotus Office, 199
Lower-back pain, 238
Low-radiation monitor, 241

Machine cycle, 50
Machine language, 125
Macintosh computers, 177
  ease of use, 250
  microprocessor, 255
  multimedia presentations and, 203
  page description language, 188
  Power Mac, 122
  WYSIWYG and, 78
Macintosh computers, troubleshooting
  alternative way to start, 287
  disks, 290
  files, 289
  printers, 292
  software, 288
Macro, 78
MacWrite, 82
Magic Edge, 209
Magnetic core memory, 22
Magnetic disks, 65–67
Magnetic tape, 68
Mail merge, 88
Mail-order computer equipment, 252–253
Mainframe, 8
Manufacturing
  computer-aided, 206
  desktop manufacturing, 206
Massively parallel processing, operating systems, 115
Mauchly, John, 18–19, 125
McCracken, Edward R., 210

Medicine
  APACHE III, 242
  computers in, 30–32
  expert systems and, 207
Megabyte, 42
Megahertz (MHz), 52, 255
Memory, 45–48
  cache, 47
  capacity of, 183
  conventional, 256
  defined, 6, 45
  expanded, 256
  extended, 256
  magnetic core, 22
  measurement of, 47
  purchasing a computer and, 255–256
  random-access memory, 46–47
  read-only, 47–48
  real, 114
  upper, 256
  virtual, 113–114
Memory protection, 113
Menu-driven programs, 117
Menus, 118
  pull-down, 76
Michaelsen, R., 207
Microcomputers. *See also* Computers
  arts and entertainment, 32–34
  in business and industry, 29–30
  capacity of, 183
  defined, 1
  education and, 28–29
  in the home, 27–28
  in science and medicine, 30–32
  types of, 9–10
  uses of, 1
Microprocessor, 43–45
  arithmetic/logic unit, 45
  bit architecture of, 255
  clock speed of, 255
  control unit, 44–45
  defined, 9
  purchasing, 255
Microsoft Corp., 119, 123
Microsoft Network (MSN), 282–283
Microsoft Office, 199
Microsoft Windows, 250
Microsoft Word, 77, 82, 201
Microwave link, 156, 157
Minicomputer, 8–9
Mitchell, Jim, 102
Modem

defined, 157
communication software, 160–161
transmission by, 157, 159
types of, 157, 159
Modulation, 157, 159
Module, 139, 197
Monitor, 60–62
Monitors
care of, 265
health-related problems, 236–238
health risk and long-term exposure to, 241
pixel, 61
purchasing, 257–258
quality of, 61
resolution of, 61, 257
troubleshooting for, 291
video display glare, 237, 240
Morphing, 33
Mosaic, 276
Motherboard, 43–44
Motorola Corp., 255
Mouse, 56–57
ergonomics and, 240
troubleshooting for, 290–291
MPEG (Motion Picture Experts Group), 201
MS-DOS, 119, 177
Multimedia, 28
Multimedia PC, 202
Multimedia PC Marketing Council, 202
Multimedia presentations, 199–204
amount of material for, 202–203
authoring tool, 204
CD-ROM and, 200
computer systems for, 203
defined, 199
dynamic link, 204
equipment needed for, 202
history of, 199–200
hypertext, 204
role of, 200
software for, 204
storage and, 203
titles, 199
uses of, 200
Multitasking, 113–114
MYCIN, 207

Napier's Bones, 13–14
Natural languages, 135
Near-letter quality printers, 192

Near-typeset printers, 192, 194
NEC Technologies, 202
Neidorf, Craig, 231
Netscape's Navigator, 276
NetWare, 169
Network interface card (NIC), 166
Network operating system (NOS), 166
Networks, 161–169
bus network, 164
defined, 12
host computer, 162
link, 161
local-area networks (LANs), 165–169
node, 161
proprietary, 166
ring network, 163–164
star network, 162–163
wide-area network, 164–165
wireless, 167
Neural network, 211
Neuron Chip, 11
Node, 161
Nonimpact printer, 63–64
Notebook computers, 9, 11
personal computer memory card, 49
purchasing, 260–261
Notepad computer, 58
pen-based interface, 119
NSFNET, 176

Object code, 125
Object linking and embedding, 114
Object-oriented programming, 135–136
encapsulation, 135–136
inheritance, 136
polymorphism, 136
Oncocin, 207
Online information services, 174
Open, 75
Operating systems, 110–124 *See also* System programs
capabilities of, 111–114
command-line user interfaces, 116–117
data and instruction exchange, 114
graphical user interfaces, 117–118
massively parallel processing, 115
menu-driven programs, 117

Microsoft Windows, 119–121
MS-DOS, 119
multitasking, 113–114
OS/2, 123
PC DOS, 119
pen-based interfaces, 119
recent trends in, 112
shell, 116
System 7, 122
task switching, 112–113
types of, 110–111
Unix, 124
utility program, 111
Optical disk, 66–68, 202
CD-ROM, 66–68
erasable optical disk, 68
WORM, 66–68
OS/2, 123
Outline fonts, 187
Output, defined, 6
Output methods, 60–65
display outputs, 60–62
draft-quality, 62
near-letter quality, 62
printers for document outputs, 62–64
voice output, 64–65
Ozone gas, 241–243

Package, 13
Page composition software, 184, 185
Page description language, 188
Pagemaker, 185
Paint programs, 100–104
defined, 99
tools for, 101
Palmtop, 9, 11
Paradox, 94
Pascal, 128–131
Pascal, Blaise, 14
Pascaline, 14
Password, 226
PC DOS, 119
Peer-to-peer LAN, 169
Pen-based interface, 119
Performa, 250
Peripherals, defined, 2
Personal computer memory, 49
Personal Computer Memory Card International Association, 49
Personal computers, 9. *See also* Microcomputers
Philips Consumer Electronics Corp., 202

Pictographs, 100
Pie charts, 100
Piracy, 221
Pixels, 61, 257
Planar board, 43
Plotters, 62, 64
Pointing devices, 118
Port, 53
Poster, 201
Power Mac, 122
PowerPoint, 199
Presentation graphics programs, 99–100
  defined, 99
  uses of, 99
Printed-circuit board, 53
Printers, 62–64
  care of, 265
  color, 194
  dot-matrix, 62–63
  draft-quality, 192
  impact, 62–63
  ink-jet, 63
  laser, 63–64
  letter quality, 192, 194
  near-letter quality, 192
  near-typeset, 192, 194
  nonimpact, 63–64
  page, 63
  page description language, 188
  plotters, 64
  purchasing, 261
  quality of, 192–194
  troubleshooting for, 291–292
Print formatting, 85–88
Printout, 62
Print preview, 78, 79
Privacy, 229–235
  defined, 229
  legislation and, 232–235
  number of databases on individual, 229–230
  summary of issues of, 231–232
Privacy Act, 232–233
Processing, defined, 6
Processor direct slot, 257
Prodigy, 281
Programming languages, 126–136
  advantages of, 126–127
  fourth-generation languages, 135
  high-level languages, 126–135
  object-oriented programming, 135–136
  Structured Query Language, 135
Programs. *See also* Software

programs
  defined, 4
Program testing, 142
Prompt, 116
Proper program, 140
Property, theft of, 221
Proprietary networks, 166
Prospector, 207
Protocol, 161
PS/2, 250
Public-domain software, 175, 225–226
Puck, 56
Pull-down menu, 76

Quadra, 250
Quark, Inc., 185
QuarkXPress, 185
Quattro Pro, 89
Query, 97
QuickTime, 122, 201, 203

Radio Shack, 24
Radio Shack TRS-80, 73
Range, 90
Read-only memory, 47–48
Real memory, 114
Real-time, 22
Record, 95
Rectangular wrap, 189
Reduced instruction set computer (RISC), 51
ReelMagic, 201
Register, 45
Relational database, 96
Remington Rand, 21
Remote log-in, 274–275
Repetitive-strain injuries, 238
Report generator, 97
Report Program Generator (RPG), 135
Resolution, 61
Resumes, 98
Ribbons, 76
Right-sizing, 10–13
  defined, 12
Right to Financial Privacy Act, 223, 233
Ring network, 163–164
Roach, John, 24
ROM basic input/output system, 47
R-360 videogame, 209

Sabotage, 220
Sachs, Jonathan, 93

Sans serif, 186
Scalable font, 187–188
Scaling, 189
Scanners, 59–60
  full-page, 59
  sheet-feed, 59
Science, computers in, 30–31
Screen readers, 65
Screen-saver programs, 265
Scroll, 75, 80
Search, 84
  attribute match, 84
  global search and replace, 84
  whole-word match, 84
  wild-card match, 84
Second generation computers, 22–23
Security
  common measures for, 227
  ethics and, 227
  for organizations, 226–228
Sensor input, 60
Sequent Computer Systems Inc., 115
Sequential-access storage, 68
Serif, 186
Server, 166
Shannon, Claude, 18
Shareware, 175, 225–226
Sigma Designs, 201
Silicon, 23
Silicon Graphics Inc., 210
Simple sequence, 140
Simplex transmission, 154
Simply LANtastic, 169
Slide rule, 14
Slide shows, 100
Slot, 52
Smythe, Doug, 33
Soft copy, 61–62
Soft fonts, 188
Software
  antivirus, 220
  application, 4
  choosing and purchasing computer, 249
  communication, 160–161
  compatibility and, 74
  copyright and, 224–225
  data-management, 94–97
  design, 104
  documentation and help, 79
  files, 75–76
  graphics, 97–104
  history of, 27, 73
  illustration, 104

installation, 74
integrated, 194–199
loading, 74
macro capability, 78
menus, 76
package, 13
piracy, 221, 224–226
public-domain software, 225–226
shareware, 225–226
site license, 225
spreadsheets, 89–93
stand-alone, 195
system, 4
troubleshooting for, 286–288
undo, 78
windows, 77–78
word processing, 81–89
WYSIWYG, 78
Software Copyright Act of 1980, 224
Software development, 125–145
  chief programmer team, 144–145
  control structures, 139–141
  documentation, 140, 142
  programming languages, 126
  program testing, 142
  stages of program development, 136–139
  structures programming techniques, 139–145
  system software and language translation, 125–126
  top-down design, 139–140
Software package, defined, 74
SoftWindows, 122
Source code, 125
Source-data automation, 30, 59
Speech recognition, 60
Spelling checker, 84–86
Spreadsheets, 89–93
  cell, 90
  explanation of, 89–92
  formatting options of, 92–93
  formula, 90–91
  general features of, 92–93
  graphs, 93
  label, 90
  template, 92
  value, 90
  "what-if?" analysis, 89, 91–92
Sprintnet, 164
Stand-alone, 195
Standby power system (SPS), 266
Star network, 162–163
STEAMER, 207–208

Stepwise refinement, 139
Storage, 65–68
  CD-ROM, 66–68
  defined, 7, 65
  direct-access, 66
  magnetic disks, 65–67
  magnetic tape, 68
  multimedia presentations and, 203
  optical, 66–69
  purchasing a computer and, 260
  sequential-access storage, 68
Storage media, 65
Stored-program concept, 20
Stress, ergonomics and, 238
String, 84
Structured programming, 139–145
  chief programmer team, 144–145
  control structures, 139–141
  documentation, 140, 142
  program testing, 142
  top-down design, 139–140
Structured Query Language (SQL), 97, 135
Style sheet, 87, 188
Stylus, 56
Suite, 199
Supercomputers, 8
Surge protectors, 266
Synchronous transmission, 160
Synergism, 7
Syntax, 137
Sysop, 175
System 7, 122
System, defined, 4
System analyst, 137
System board, 43
System software, 125–126
  defined, 4
System unit, 43–53
  defined, 43
  memory, 45–48
  microprocessor, 43–45
  motherboard, 43–44

Tabulating machine, 16–17
Tandy Corp., 202
Tape drive, 68
Taxadvisor, 207
Telecommunication applications, 169–176
  electronic bulletin boards, 175–176
  electronic mail, 171
  electronic transactions, 169–170

facsimile, 170–171
information utilities, 174
internet, 176
telecommuting, 172–173
teleconferencing, 173–174
voice mail, 171
Telecommunications, 172–173
  defined, 152
  history of, 152–153
  See also Communication channels
Teleconferencing, 173–174
Telegraph lines, 154
Telephone toll fraud, 223
Telnet, 176, 275
Template, 92, 188, 189
Tendonitis, 238
Terabyte, 42
Texas Instruments, 23
Text wrap, 189
  arbitrary, 189, 191
  irregular, 189
  rectangular, 189
Thesaurus, 84
Third generation computers, 23
Timbuktu, 161
Title, defined, 199
Token Ring, 166
Toner, 63
Toolbars, 76
Toolkits, 76
Top-down design, 139–140
Touch screen, 56–57
Trackball, 56–57
Transistor, 22
Troubleshooting
  calling tech support, 292–293
  disks, 290
  general suggestions, 285–286
  monitor, 291
  mouse or keyboard, 290–291
  printers, 291–292
  problems with files, 289
  software problems, 286–288
TRS-80, 24
Twisted-pair cable, 154
Twisted pairs, 154–155
Tymnet, 164
Typeface, 186–188. *See also* Desktop publishing
  defined, 186
  pitch of, 186
  san serif, 186
  serif, 186
  style sheet, 188

Type Manager, 188

U. S. Census Bureau, 21
U. S. Navy, 22
Undo, 78
Uninterruptible power supply, 266
UNIVAC I, 21
Unix, 124
Upper memory, 256
Usenet, 274
User, defined, 2
User interfaces, 114–119
   command-line user interfaces, 116–117
   gesture-based interfaces, 119
   graphical user interfaces, 117–118
   menu-driven programs, 117
   pen-based interfaces, 119
Users' groups, 254
Utility program, 111

Vacuum tube, 19, 21
   problems of, 21
Value, 90
Value Point, 250
Ventura, 185
Ventura Software, 185
Veronica, 276
Very-large-scale integration, 25
Very low-frequency, long-term exposure to, 241
VESA Local Bus, 257
Video adapter card, 258
Videoconference, 173–174

Video display card, 258
Video display terminal
   health-related problems, 236–238
   health risk and long-term exposure to, 241
   video display glare, 237, 240
Video for Windows, 201
Video Privacy Protection Act, 233
Virtual memory, 113–114
Virtual reality, 58, 208–210
   defined, 208
   uses of, 209–210
Viruses, 220, 266–269
   antivirus programs, 220, 268–269
   defined, 267
   nature of, 267
   protection from, 268
   signs of, 267–268
   stealth, 268
VisiCalc, 73
Voice mail, 171
Voice output, 64–65
Voice recognition system, 28, 263
Voice synthesizer, 65
von Neumann, John, 20
VP-EXPERT, 208

WAIS, 276
Watson, Thomas J. Sr., 17
Web, 276
Western Union, 164
"What-if?" analysis, 89, 91–92
Whirlwind I, 22
White-collar crime, 221
White Knight, 161

Whole-word match, 84
Wide-area network (WAN), 164–165
Wild-card match, 84
WIMP, 118
Windows, 77–78, 118–121, 177, 250
   advantages/disadvantages of, 121
WingZ, 89
Wireless networks, 167
Word, defined, 42
WordPerfect, 82, 201
Word processing, 81–89
   cursor position and automatic word wrap, 82–83
   default settings, 85
   defined, 81
   entering and editing text, 82–84
   insertions and deletions, 83–84
   mail merge, 88
   other features, 88–89
   print formatting, 85–88
   purpose of, 81
   search functions, 84
   style sheet, 87
   uses of, 81–82
   writing aids, 84–85
Word size, 255
Word wrap, defined, 83
Worksheet, 92
Workstation, 9
WORM, 66–68, 267
WYSIWYG, 78, 79, 185, 186
   defined, 78
Yahoo, 276

PHOTO CREDITS

1 © The Photographers Library, Uniphoto; **3** top © Frank Siteman MCMLXXVV, Uniphoto; **3** center © Mary Kate Denny, Uniphoto; **3** bottom © Chuck Savage, Uniphoto; **4** left, courtesy of Apple Computer, right, courtesy of Hewlett Packard; **5** left, © Christopher R. Harfis, Uniphoto; right, courtesy of Symbol Technology; **8** © Cray Research; **9** © DEC Corporation; **10** top © Michael W. Davidson, Photo Researchers, left courtesy of Apple Computers, Inc., center © Michael Newman, Photo Edit, right, courtesy of Sun Microsystems; **11** © Mark Richards, Photo Edit; **12** left, © Christopher R. Harfis, Uniphoto, center, © Michael W. Davidson, Photo Researchers, top right courtesy of Apple Computers, Inc., bottom right courtesy of Hewlett Packard; **13** © Art Tilley, Uniphoto; **14** © top Crown copyright, Science Museum London; **14** left courtesy of IBM; **14** right courtesy of IBM; **15** left The Science Museum/Science & Society Picture Library, London; **15** top right courtesy of IBM; **15** bottom right courtesy of IBM; **16** top left courtesy of IBM; **16** bottom left courtesy of IBM; **16** bottom right courtesy of IBM; **17** The Science Museum/Science & Society Picture Library, London; **18** © Iowa State University Photo Service; **19** courtesy of Unisys Corporation; **20** The Institute for Advanced Study; **21** courtesy of Unisys; **22** courtesy of IBM; **24** bottom left and right courtesy of Radio Shack, a division of Tandy Corporation; **25** top left, top right, bottom left courtesy of Apple Computer, Inc.; **25** bottom right Commodore Business Machines; **26** top and bottom courtesy of IBM; **28** courtesy of Mark Michael; **29** courtesy of Broderbund Software, Inc.; **30** courtesy of Symbol Technologies, Inc.; **31** top courtesy of 3M; **31** bottom courtesy of National Center for Supercomputing Applications, Champagne, IL; **32** top Electronics Cadaver Credit; **32** bottom © 1995 New Line Cinema; **33** courtesy of Gryphon Software; **38** © Michael W. Davidson, Photo Researchers; **39** © Tony Freeman, Photo Edit; **44** courtesy of Apple Computer, Inc. and Intel; **45** © Michael W. Davidson, Photo Researchers; **47** courtesy International Business Machines, Inc.; **49** courtesy of Hewlett-Packard Company; **51** courtesy of Motorola; **52** (left and right) © Tony Freeman, Photo Edit; **53** © West Publishing Company; **54** courtesy of United States Navy; **57** (top left) © Clark Dunbar, Uniphoto, (top right) courtesy of Logitech; (center) courtesy of Comshare, (bottom left) © David S. Lavine, Uniphoto, bottom right © Wacom Technology Corporation; **58** (top) © West Publishing Company, (bottom) © Peter Menzel; **59** © West Publishing Company; **61** courtesy of Sun Microcomputers; **62** courtesy of Hewlett-Packard Company; **63** courtesy of Epson, Inc.; **64** courtesy of Hewlett-Packard Company; **66** © courtesy of Seagate; **67** (bottom left) © courtesy of Pinnacle Corporation, (bottom right) © courtesy of 3M; **72** © David Young Wolff, Photo Edit; **74** © West Publishing Company; **81** © Bachmann, Uniphoto; **93** courtesy of Mitch Kapor; **98** courtesy of Microtech; **102** © the Kobal Collection; **108** © Fotostudio and Fachlabor-Digitale Bilder; **109** © The Computer Museum, Historic Collection; **110** © West Publishing Company; **115** courtesy of Sequent Computer Systems Inc.; **116** © West Publishing Company; **123** © Mark Kauffman, Sygma; **128** © The Computer Museum, Historic Collection; **144** © John Henly, Jon Feingersh, Llewellyn, Uniphoto; **150** Michael Newman, Photo Edit; **151** © Joel Feingersh, Uniphoto; **152** © photo by Benedict Kruse; **154** twiste pairs cables; **155** coaxial cable; **155** © Joseph Palmieri, Uniphoto; **157** left, © Bob Daemmrich, Uniphoto; **157** right, © Chris Cross, Uniphoto; **159** © West Publishing Company; **159** right, courtesy of Hewlett Packard; **162** © Doug Milner, Uniphoto; **165** © Bonnie Kamin, Photo Edit; **167** Elena Rooraid, Photo Edit; **170** © Michael Newman, Photo Edit; **172** © Mark Richards, Photo Edit; **173** Charles Gupton, Uniphoto; **177** © Bettman Archive; **182** © Peter Menzel; **183** courtesy of Hewlett Packard; **185** lower left, courtesy of Sun Microcomputers; **190** © Peter Menzel; **202** © West Publishing Company; **203** © West Publishing Company; **207** courtesy of Knowledge Industries; **208** © Peter Menzel; **209** upper left, © Peter Menzel; **209** upper right, © Peter Menzel; **209** lower left, © Peter Menzel; **209** lower right, © Peter Menzel; **210** courtesy of Silicon Graphics; **211** © Stock Market; **216** © Llewellyn, Uniphoto; **217** © Jeff Greenberg, Uniphoto; **219** courtesy of Bank of Boston; **222** courtesy of V One; **225** © West Publishing Company; **228** upper right courtesy of Security Dynamics; **228** middle left, courtesy of Gemplus; **231** courtesy of John Perry Barlow; **234** © Jeff Feinger; **236** © courtesy of TRW; **237** upper, © Llewellyn, Uniphoto; **237** © Berle Chemey, Uniphoto; **239** © Al Cook, Uniphoto; **242** © Richard Hutchings, Photo Edit.